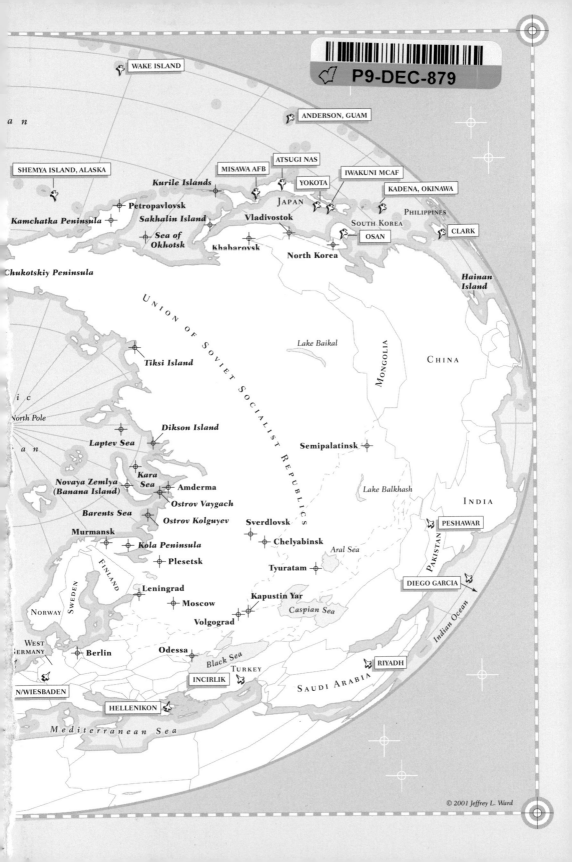

ALSO BY WILLIAM E. BURROWS

BY ANY MEANS NECESSARY

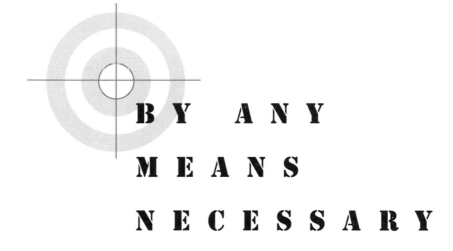

BY ANY
MEANS
NECESSARY

America's Secret Air War in the Cold War

WILLIAM E. BURROWS

Farrar, Straus and Giroux
New York

Farrar, Straus and Giroux
19 Union Square West, New York 10003

Copyright © 2001 by William E. Burrows
All rights reserved
Distributed in Canada by Douglas & McIntyre Ltd.
Printed in the United States of America
First edition, 2001

Owing to limitations of space, all acknowledgments for permission to reprint previously
published material can be found on page 399.

Library of Congress Cataloging-in-Publication Data
Burrows, William E., 1937–
    By any means necessary : America's secret air war in the Cold War / William E.
Burrows.— 1st ed.
        p. cm.
    Includes bibliographical references (p.   ) and index.
    ISBN 0-374-11747-0 (alk. paper)
    1. United States—Foreign relations—Soviet Union.   2. Soviet Union—Foreign
relations—United States.   3. United States—Foreign relations—1945–1989.
4. United States—Foreign relations—Communist countries.   5. Cold War.
6. Air warfare—History.   7. Espionage, American—Communist countries—History.
8. Intelligence officers—United States—Biography.   9. Air pilots, Military—United
States—Biography.   10. Aerial reconnaissance, American—History.   I. Title.

E183.8.S65 .B89 2001
327.1273'047'09045—dc21

                                                                    2001023622

Designed by Debbie Glasserman

To Joelle, our two doctors, and closing the circle

*And to the memory of my friend Mert Davies,
a giant among men in all ways, and one of
the great heroes of this story for moving the
game to a safer place*

The cold war had the distinction of not costing any lives.

Dr. Edward Teller
The New York Times
May 14, 1999

We are engaged in a war. Just as strongly as if we were actually fighting. In wars people make sacrifices. . . . I know his life wasn't wasted. Today's war with Russia is every bit as hot and every bit as important as any we have ever fought to keep ourselves free.

1st Lt. Joseph B. Maddalena,
to the parents of Capt. Dean B. Phillips,
who was shot down and killed ten days
earlier on a reconnaissance mission near
the USSR
July 10, 1960

By its very nature, the bureaucracy is insular and protective. Lies beget lies. Lies empower people. At its worst, government is about deception and power is about abuse. While there are valid operational needs to have and keep secrets, the reality is that by abusing secrecy restrictions, one can cover up incompetence and protect careers.

Carlos C. Campbell
former Navy intelligence officer

 Contents

Preface

THIS IS THE story of one part of the most immense and intensive intelligence collection effort in American history. It is probably impossible for any individual to grasp in meaningful detail the full extent of Western intelligence operations during the cold war. Not counting outright espionage—the cloak-and-dagger stuff professionals call HUMINT—military intelligence collection extended from the depths of the oceans to a place that is a tenth of the way to the Moon.

U.S. Army airplanes, which for the most part were smaller and had a shorter range than their Air Force and Navy counterparts, routinely made reconnaissance forays over the "fence" that separated Eastern and Western Europe. The operations were flown in direct support of NATO ground forces and were justified by the Army's need for up-close intelligence for any possible up-close ground combat. Similarly, to take one more example, Navy submarines on intelligence missions prowled the seven seas to monitor friend and foe alike. They still do. It generally escaped public attention, but two U.S. Navy Los Angeles–class attack submarines were in the neighborhood when Russia's Northern Fleet held exercises in the Barents Sea in August 2000. They therefore closely monitored the destruction of the nuclear attack submarine *Kursk*, which took 118 sailors to their deaths.

I have chosen to focus mainly on long-range airborne reconnaissance operations flown against the Communist bloc, and particularly against the Soviet Union, roughly from 1950 to 1970. There were four basic reasons for concentrating on that period.

The early 1950s was a time when I first became aware that a larger world existed far from where I lived. I followed military aviation throughout high school, during the Korean War, and remember to this day the occasional short articles that told of one or another of our planes allegedly losing its way because of foul weather or navigation problems and being attacked by enemy aircraft. Of course I had no way of knowing what was really going on. This project offered an opportunity to find out, and also to revisit my lost youth.

Those were also the formative years of modern aerial reconnaissance. The machines that flew out of that incubator in turn developed into aircraft and ultimately spacecraft with which I became somewhat more familiar and which represent extraordinary technology (the SR-71 and the digitized KH-11 satellite being only two of many examples). So this was a chance to trace the fast-developing technology back almost to its origin.

In addition, the events described here occurred at a supremely important—and dangerous—time. The missions were designed and flown during a period when two intensely hostile ideological camps were developing and stockpiling weapons that could have annihilated each other and the rest of the world. The men, machines, and missions described here not only existed within that formative cat's cradle of danger, violence, and potential unspeakable catastrophe, but they fundamentally helped shape it. The paradox of "overhead" reconnaissance, which amalgamates the airborne and spaceborne varieties, is that it provides both targets for unparalleled death and destruction, and knowledge—finished intelligence—that reduces dangerous surprises and therefore encourages peace.

Finally, I wanted to write a story about people, not a catalogue of airplanes and missions, and the operations undertaken during those two decades were particularly rich with people. It was axiomatic during my formative professional years, when I reported for newspapers, that ultimately we wrote about people for people, because they are invariably more interesting than machinery. Even an unreconstructed air and space junkie knows that, ultimately, it is people who conceive and build the planes, fly and die in them, and grieve for loved ones who don't return. Every woman I interviewed who was widowed, orphaned, or who lost a brother or a father in a shootdown responded with relief and enthusiasm when I explained that I was not simply stringing together war stories but trying to portray human beings in danger, under stress, and suffering anguish. Similarly, men who flew the missions responded to questions about their reactions to facing the possibility of imminent death with real interest because it got them to plumb their own emotions. Robb Hoover, for example, used the French word *frisson* to describe what he felt when he looked out the window high over the Arctic and saw the largest air-to-air missile in the world, up close, under the wing of a menacing Soviet fighter. It means shudder, but one equates it with sudden, reflexive terror, with hair standing up on the back of the neck.

The essential elements of this story—the operations—only make sense when they are depicted within the larger framework of the cold war itself. It is the obligation of older hands to describe the imperative circumstances of their time as they relate to the central story. It was unsettling but instructive for me to learn that the war in Vietnam might almost have been the Spanish-American War as far as most of my students are concerned. So too the cold war, now more than a decade gone, and quickly receding in a society that prides itself on looking forward, not back. But people of a certain age remember duck-and-cover drills in their classrooms, the ubiquitous yellow-and-black fallout shelter signs with triangular radiation symbols on them, and food and water stored in olive green containers in the shelters.

That is why I have gone to some length to describe how communism was perceived in the United States in my lifetime. It was taken to be what toxicologists would call an especially active and dangerous culture. It was a culture that many of the protagonists in this book would argue had to be watched constantly, by any means necessary.

BY ANY MEANS NECESSARY

DEATH OF A FERRET

THE SCENE ON the other side of the Plexiglas, far beyond the steady, rhythmic drone of the engines and the reach of the machine guns, was sublime. It could have been a classic Chinese scroll, a Song dynasty painting, come to life. Capt. John E. Roche, belted securely in the copilot's seat, took in a vast landmass shrouded in early morning fog. He couldn't make out the coastline, but he could clearly see several mountain peaks towering above the thick mist. Roche guessed that they were seventy to a hundred miles away. The mountains and the mist had an ethereal quality. But they were not Chinese. They were Siberian.

Roche, aircraft commander Capt. Stanley K. O'Kelley, and the others in this particular plane's crew had been told two days earlier, on the morning of July 27, that they were to take off the following night on a nine-hour mission. It was relatively short notice because they would be replacing another crew whose aircraft had developed mechanical problems. Planes and their crews always stayed together. Most planes had idiosyncrasies that took getting used to. So did most crews.

The day—July 27, 1953—figured importantly in history and decisively in the fate of John Roche, Stan O'Kelley, and the other sixteen men who were now flying a United States military aircraft toward Soviet airspace. It was the day the armistice was signed that ended the Korean War.

It was understandable that the cease-fire was celebrated by long, boisterous parties at U.S. military bases throughout East Asia, including at Yokota Air Force Base outside of Tokyo, where O'Kelley and his crew were stationed. Booze was officially prohibited at the celebrations, but the only people who took that order seriously were the officers who issued it, and maybe they didn't, either. The parties at Yokota were thrown on the night of the 28th, as O'Kelley and his crew got ready to fly, and would cause a number of ground personnel to sleep later than usual the following morning because of a number of afflictions. Stan O'Kelley went to one of them, but he was a good aircraft commander who had a mission to fly in a matter of hours, so he left early and got some sleep.

In South Korea itself, however, the mood in the Air Force's crack fighter units—notably the Sabrejet-wielding Fourth and Fifty-first Fighter Wings—was somewhat different. The fighter fraternity was an intensely competitive, self-defined elite that traced its bloodline back to the legendary Eddie Rickenbacker's Hat in the Ring Squadron and Manfred von Richthofen, imperial Germany's fabled Red Baron, and his Flying Circus. Like their ghostly predecessors, the brotherhood kept score by kills. Five victories in the air conferred the status of ace on a man; ten made him a venerated double ace: a tiger. Capt. Joseph McConnell, Jr., won the Korean "ace race" with sixteen kills.

The armistice meant the fighter pilots would have to stop attacking enemy planes to run up their scores. But Capt. Ralph S. Parr, who flew a yellow-banded F-86F Sabrejet in the renowned Fourth Fighter Wing, needed only one more kill to join the pantheon of double aces. His fighter carried six machine guns in its nose that could chew an opponent to shreds. Parr and three other pilots in the wing were flying escort near the Yalu River on the afternoon of the 27th, just before the armistice took effect, when they spotted a twin-engine Soviet Ilyushin Il-12 transport, which he later reported had red stars on its wings, heading east. After making two identification passes, Parr pounced on the unarmed propeller-driven aircraft, guns blazing in long bursts. It blew up in midair. Parr's was the last kill of the Korean War.

In a heated exchange of diplomatic notes that started almost immediately, the Department of State chose to ignore the fact that the Il-12 was an airliner, not a combat aircraft, and instead insisted that it had been shot down over North Korea and was therefore fair game. The Soviet Foreign Ministry was just as adamant that it had been attacked over Manchuria, not North Korea, and was therefore technically out of bounds (though American fighter pilots, unable to suppress boyish exuberance, had routinely poached in the "priviledged sanctuary" that harbored MiGs north of the Yalu throughout the war). More to the point, the infuriated Russians maintained that the Il-12 was on a regularly scheduled civilian flight to Vladivostok and that the fifteen passengers (reportedly including advisers heading back to their country) and six crewmen on board had therefore been murdered well inside China in a "pirate-like attack." Evidence indicated that the Il-12 was in fact taking the most direct route from Lu-Shun in China to Vladivostok, which cuts across the extreme northeastern tip of North Korea. And that's where Parr bagged it. But the boundaries are so close that most of its wreckage apparently came down in China, and that's how the Russians, who were notoriously thin-skinned, made their case. They were undoubtedly in a vengeful mood.

The next day, the 28th, O'Kelley, Roche, and their navigators, 1st Lts. Edmund J. Czyz, Lloyd C. Wiggins, the radar navigator, and James G. Keith, the nose navigator, had gone to the mission planning room. This mission would require three navigators because their plane's precise location at any given moment would be supremely important. Czyz, the chief navigator, used standard celestial navigation and dead reckoning. Wiggins would keep track of where they were with radar. And Keith, sitting in the glassed-in nose, would watch for landmarks. If Czyz and Wiggins couldn't agree on exactly where they were, Jim Keith had the tie-breaking vote.

Maj. John Norton, an operations officer, had handed O'Kelley a file containing precise instructions for the mission itself. It laid out the course of the flight on an aerial navigation chart in a series of coordinates and bearings, each of them at a specific altitude. Once the nature of the mission was absorbed, Roche left the room, followed a short time later by O'Kelley. The navigators stayed behind to plot details on their own charts.

At about 10:45 that night, with everyone dressed in flight gear, O'Kelley's crew had sat on wooden folding chairs in a Quonset hut that served as a briefing room for a final explanation of what was supposed to happen. "We were to fly out from Yokota," Roche would later recall in a written deposition, "climb on course to Wajima Homer (a radio station check point on a small island off the Japanese coast north of Nagoya), then on a course of approximately 315 degrees, climbing to an altitude of approximately 18,500 feet. Upon reaching a position of 133 degrees east longitude and forty degrees north latitude, we were to climb to an altitude of 25,000." They were instructed to follow that course until they reached a control point over the Sea of Japan at 5:30 a.m. on the 29th. It would be forty minutes after sunrise on a beautiful morning. From there, O'Kelley or Roche would make a series of right turns at precisely calculated intervals, which would keep them on a track off the coast of North Korea and then Siberia.

That, at any rate, is what John Roche said for the record after the incident that ended the flight. And most of it was true. But because the nature of his work required a special security clearance, and no doubt because he was coached by Air Force Security Service personnel, Roche understood that certain facts had to be left out of the story. Those facts had to do with the real reason they were flying to Siberia, not the "official" one, and so Roche's account would have to be "sanitized" (which is the intelligence world's fastidious way of saying censored).

After the navigation briefing O'Kelley and the others had gone to a routine meeting with Capt. James H. Keeffe, the unit's weather officer. He had told them there would be thunderheads and some rain as they headed out of Japanese airspace, but that there would be clear skies and only ground fog the rest of the way out and back. The fog would not be a problem. Whatever Keeffe's military specialty, he savored the excitement of combat missions and had hitched rides on more than a dozen of them. He had planned to go on this one, too, but since it was his wife Sandy's birthday, he decided to stay behind and celebrate the occasion with dinner and dancing, maybe at one of the lingering armistice parties. The decision to honor his wife instead of his ego probably saved his life.

Keeffe's presentation had been followed by one from a captain named Gorman, an intelligence officer, who explained what they were supposed to do that night. Then Gorman had gotten down to worst-case scenarios. O'Kelley and the others had heard this part so many times they had it memorized. If they had to crash-land or bail out and were captured, Gorman had told them, lamely, they should demand to be taken to the American ambassador in Moscow. "Keep insisting on seeing him or talking to him," he had advised. The nature of their work made the suggestion seem like black humor. The cover story, Gorman had explained yet again, was that they were on a routine training mission in a B-29-type aircraft and that there were more than the usual number of crewmen on board because some were trying to increase their monthly flying time. Finally, as usual, he had warned them to keep strict radio silence starting at one hundred miles outbound from Yokota. Except for short, coded position reports every half hour indicating they were all right, which would be sent to a National Security Agency listening post, relayed from there to Far East Air Force Headquarters, and then sent to operations, they were to stay off the air until they reached that point coming home.

In the event they did go down in Siberia and bailed out or survived a crash landing, every man in the crew carried a silk scarf, known in the fraternity as a "blood chit," that said in Russian its bearer was a member of the U.S. Air Force and a substantial reward would be paid for his safe return. But everyone in the fraternity knew that a substantial penalty, say execution on the spot, would be paid to any Russian who was caught protecting an American airman. There was no delusion on that one.

The secrecy was pervasive because O'Kelley's and his crew's mission was to collect detailed information on the radars that protected Vladivostok and its environs from air attack. The way to do that was to provoke the Russians into turning the things on so their vital signs could be monitored and recorded. It was like trying to get a bull to charge by coming close and waving a cape at it.

O'Kelley and his crew came from Forbes Air Force Base, out-side of Topeka, Kansas, and were on temporary duty—TDY in mil-itary jargon—in Japan. They were members of the Strategic Air Command's 343d Strategic Reconnaissance Squadron, which was, itself, one of three squadrons in the Fifty-fifth Strategic Re-connaissance Wing. While in Japan, the 343d operated un-der the jurisdiction of the Ninety-first Strategic Reconnaissance Squadron. The 343d was an electronics intelligence unit, or ELINT unit in the shorthand of the military intelligence commu-nity. Its assignment was to collect detailed information on enemy radars so they could be jammed, tricked, flanked, or destroyed to protect attacking U.S. bombers if war came. Navy patrol planes did the same thing against both land radars and those on Soviet and other nations' ships. One of them, in fact, had the distinction of becoming the first U.S. aircraft on such a mission to be shot down when it was attacked by Soviet fighters on April 8, 1950, off the Latvian coast. All ten crewmen disappeared.

Radar antennas send out pulsating high-frequency radio sig-nals at the speed of light. When part of the signal hits a target—in this case, an airplane—it is reflected back to the antenna and a receiver. The target aircraft's distance from the radar is calculated by measuring the time it takes the signal to reach the airplane and return. Following the "blips" on a radar screen tells its operator how many planes there are and which way they are headed. In 1953 the Soviet Union, like the United States and other nations, used three basic kinds of radar: early warning, search, and fire control or gun-laying. Early warning radars, similar to those at airports, usually had very large dishes that constantly swept the sky for hundreds of miles to spot planes that were far away. They could therefore give early warning of an attack. With the intrud-ers located, search radars that worked with fighter-interceptor squadrons or missile batteries would be turned on to pinpoint the targets and guide the defending planes or missiles to them. Fi-nally, fire control radars used narrow signal beams to lock onto the targets and send precise data on the enemy's speed, range, and direction to the interceptors or missiles. Gun-laying radars, a species of the fire control type, provided the same service for antiaircraft batteries.

Since the Russians thought their survival rested squarely on these radars, and since they knew that the receivers and antennas themselves were very high-priority targets for NATO bombers, they built many more of them than were needed, used overlapping coverage, and changed their signal frequencies, pulse repetition rates, and other operating modes regularly. One notorious example, a so-called V-beam fire control radar known as the P-20 by its users and code-named Token by NATO, operated on five different frequencies (the V stood for the Roman numeral five). One sweep would reveal a target's distance, direction, height, and probable route. Thirteen months before O'Kelley's and Roche's fateful flight, six of the impressively complicated devices were first spotted by reconnaissance crews working the Black Sea coast.

The game was an unending battle of wits between the radar designers, the flyers who were supposed to steal their radars' secrets, and the people who used the secrets to develop the machines that were supposed to jam the radars on war day so the bombers could get to their targets and incinerate them.

Outfits like the 343d Strategic Reconnaissance Squadron were supposed to locate all three kinds of radars, pinpoint their positions, and record their vital signs. Since search and fire control radars were turned on only when the early warning radars picked up a potential threat, it was often necessary to appear threatening—to "tickle" or "exercise" them—by feinting an attack. But the Russians, Chinese, North Koreans, and others understood the nature of the situation and they therefore tried not to turn on their search and fire control radars; not to be baited into giving away their systems' capability. That raised the ante. It forced American and British reconnaissance crews to make ever more realistic and more dangerous simulated attacks. They often did that by flying in as close as they could—an in-your-face straight dash at the radar—and sometimes by using several planes in some sort of formation or even by penetrating enemy territory itself.

It was dangerous work because radar and fighters were inseparable partners. Radar was useless unless it was used to direct fighters and, later, surface-to-air missiles to the attackers. And fighters needed radar to find the attackers. The fighters, in particular, were a constant threat to the reconnaissance crews because their pilots' job was to protect their frontier from intrusion through deadly force if necessary. So the business of getting the radar turned on and taking its measure was given an appropriate name, ferreting, after the nocturnal predators that invade the holes of prairie dogs and other varmints on the American plains and flush them out. By the early summer of 1953, Air Force and Navy ferrets routinely flew around the entire Communist periphery, and chiefly along the Soviet Arctic coast and up and down the entire length of eastern Siberia, from the Bering Strait to the huge naval installation at Vladivostok. The ferrets flew day and night throughout the year on missions that typically lasted ten hours. There were as many as three ferret flights a week against Vladivostok alone, according to Keeffe and others. Some would be monotonous "milk runs" along the coast. Others would be hair-raising sprints right at the radars and then fast retreats back out to sea before the fighters found them.

Forty percent of the time, Jim Keeffe explained, Russian fighters wouldn't even bother to take off. Most often, the MiG or Sukhoi pilots would scramble and then make nonfiring passes to show the American intruders in the most vivid way that their fate rested in the hands that gripped the sticks where the firing buttons were. Snapshots of MiGs "tucked in"—flying in formation so close that their pilots were clearly visible—circulated in the reconnaissance squadrons. Asked at a debriefing how a ferret crew could tell the MiG's intentions at that range, one wag with a dry sense of humor said, straight-faced, "By the expression on the pilot's face." But when the reconnaissance planes got too close to Soviet or Chinese airspace, the fighters would come up like angry hornets and the situation turned very tense.

In order to protect all the secrets in this twilight war and not provoke attacks by their embarrassed quarry, the ferret's world was kept under an exceptionally tight security blanket. To be sure, photoreconnaissance was also classified, but its existence had been widely known since aviators started pointing their clunky cameras out of biplanes in World War I. But ferreting radar was a newer and far more arcane operation and it was rigorously concealed. Ferret crews were strictly forbidden to talk about what they did with any outsider, including their comrades in arms in other units, or with their own families. The "need to know" principle—share information *only* with those who need to know it— was drummed in from the day they took their oaths. Spies, they were warned repeatedly, were everywhere. The secrecy was so obsessive that when O'Kelley and his crewmen left for an operation that kept them away for a week or more, his wife Margaret and the other wives were forbidden to reduce the number of bottles of milk they ordered for fear of betraying their husbands' absence to spying milkmen. Yet the women had no clear idea what their husbands were doing. Other airmen who were not members of the inner sanctum never questioned the rigid rules because they, too, were part of a culture that lived with secrets and took their protection for granted. The brotherhood's loved ones accepted the pervasive secrecy on the theory that the government knew best. At least they accepted it in the beginning.

The machine with which the radar at Vladivostok was to be ferreted that night was called an RB-50G. It was a propeller-driven, souped-up version of the famous B-29 Superfortress that had carried the air war across the Pacific to Japan and dropped atomic bombs on Hiroshima and Nagasaki. Boeing, which made the B-29, did what any automobile manufacturer would have done. It took a successful product and modified it to extend its life. The basic B-29 airframe was given four more powerful Pratt & Whitney engines and a larger vertical tail so it could maneuver at higher altitude and was renamed the B-50. Everything else was basically the same. B-29s had been practically invincible in the closing months of World War II, when they saturation-bombed the home islands and used their highly concentrated firepower in tight formations to keep what was left of Japan's Zeros and other propeller-driven predators at bay. But eight years later, they and their B-50 successors faced far more dangerous enemies: jet-propelled MiG-15s and MiG-17s that could fly twice as fast as the Zeros, reach a higher altitude, and strike without warning.

The MiGs had turned the B-29s and B-50s from venerable Superfortresses to vulnerable cows. They were lumbering relics that were supposed to fill the breach until they could be replaced by faster, swept-wing jets.

This particular RB-50G—R for reconnaissance, G for the seventh or electronic intelligence version—was one of fifteen B-50 bombers that had been converted specifically to ferret radar and eavesdrop on radio communication. It originally carried the Air Force serial number 47-145, but it had been changed to 9653 in the belief—unwarranted as it would turn out—that it was going to be rotated from Yokota back to Forbes on September 6. Like many other Superfortresses, it also had a name bestowed by its crew, though not one the Air Force would have wanted to see on page one of the morning paper or in a movie newsreel. It was called *Little Red Ass*, a name bestowed by 1st Lt. Albert S. Bentley, Jr., a crew member. The term was Air Force slang for "I don't want to be here." And red, a color easily seen from the air in case it crash-landed, was also the color of 9653's large tail. (Its entire underside was painted black to reduce reflection during night missions, so it was also called a "black-belly" B-50, which had suitably sinister implications.)

Bentley had asked the Walt Disney Studio to design appropriate nose art for the plane. But the cartoonists who created *Cinderella, Pinocchio*, and *Fantasia* no doubt decided that portraying that particular part of gross anatomy ran counter to their studio's carefully maintained aura of wholesomeness. Prudence therefore took precedence over patriotism. The Disney people artfully begged off by saying that the request had to come from the Air Force in Washington rather than a unit in the field. That, of course, was not going to happen. Undaunted, Bentley and his pals had flight caps made that showed a red ass begrudgingly kicking up its heels on an unwilling red donkey. And in honor of their skipper, each hat also carried the name of its owner with an honorific O' before his name: "O'Roche."

The RB-50G had a ninety-nine-foot-long cylindrical fuselage with wide-view Plexiglas windows in the nose and two of thirteen .50-caliber machine guns as a stinger in its tail. The greenhouse nose gave its pilot and copilot an exceptionally good view. Unlike other B-50s, however, this RB-50G and its fourteen sisters did not have one radar dome, but five, and several specialized antennas. Besides O'Kelley, who was the pilot and aircraft commander, and Roche, the copilot, *Little Red Ass* ordinarily carried fourteen other crewmen. These included Czyz, Wiggins, and Keith, the navigators; M. Sgt. Francis L. Brown, the flight engineer, who sat right behind O'Kelley and Roche; a central fire control specialist, S. Sgt. Donald W. Gabree, who remotely operated five electrically controlled machine guns; a tail gunner; and two waist gunners (one of whom, A1c. Roland E. Goulet, was also the radioman). Except for the absence of a bombardier, who was unnecessary because ferrets carried no bombs, that was roughly the standard crew of a Superfort.

The remaining six crewmen made the RB-50G anything but standard. In technical manuals and other official publications, they were variously called Electronic Warfare Officers, Electronic Counter Measures Officers, or simply Operators. But they called themselves ravens, or sometimes crows, after a World War II ferret mission code-named Operation Raven. Don Gardner, a veteran raven, dryly put the name down to the fact that "crows and ravens steal things." The word, after all, is the root of "ravenous." But these ravens were after kernels of information, not corn. They were the ones who actually ferreted the opposition's radar. Everyone else's job was to get them and their heavy electronic equipment to the target and bring them back with intercepted signals. Those signals—the enemy radars' signatures—were continuously updated, refined, and analyzed for Air Force and Navy target folders. Five ravens sat side by side, like old-time telephone operators at switchboards, in the plane's extensively modified forward bomb bay. The sixth sat in a pressurized compartment toward the rear. (The rear bomb bay itself was turned into an auxiliary fuel tank that held 1,125 gallons of gasoline to increase the plane's range.) Each raven used a different combination of electronic hardware to search for, capture, and analyze radar on frequencies that went from relatively low to very high.

First in line was raven 1, the "big raven": 1st Lt. Warren J. Sanderson. Next came raven 2, Maj. Francisco J. Tejeda; raven 3, 1st Lt. Robert E. Stalnaker; raven 4, Capt. John C. Ward; and raven 5, ordinarily, but not this night, Lieutenant Bentley. Raven 6, 1st Lt. Frank E. Beyer, Jr., was the lone raven in the pressurized rear compartment. Beyer had been a college track star, a model-airplane builder since childhood (he built and flew them in his spare time at Yokota), a gifted amateur cartoonist, and, like most of the others, was a pilot in his own right. Frank Tejeda, thirty-six, came from central Los Angeles and was the son of Mexican immigrants. He had flown photoreconnaissance missions at the end of World War II and then, like many other recce types, had put in fifteen months flying supplies to Berliners during the airlift in 1948 and 1949. Like the other ravens, he had learned his new trade during three months of intensive training at Keesler Air Force Base in Biloxi, Mississippi.

The ravens worked in a cramped, windowless compartment filled with racks of black boxes that were bolted and stacked on worktables in front of them. The area, a claustrophobe's nightmare, was dimly lighted and usually out of communication with the rest of the plane. Lt. John Marks, a raven in another crew, said that the RB-50G's propellers would sometimes pick up ice and fling it against the fuselage where he and the others were sitting, making a bloodcurdling crack like a gunshot. Bentley would remark years later that "we were probably the poorest paid spies in existence."

Each Electronic Counter Measures station on an RB-50G had a contour seat, shaped to accommodate a parachute, in front of a carefully arranged bank of sensors that did for the flying ferret what ears and nose do for its earthbound namesake. Six separate boxes, for example, were bolted onto the cramped worktable in front of Sanderson, who sat just behind the navigator and therefore was closest to the nose. Two of the devices, called APR-9s, soaked up a radar's vital signs—frequency, pulse repetition frequency, pulse width, scan type and rate, and other important signatures—in the high-frequency range of 1,000 to 10,750 megacycles. The high-pitched transmissions came over both audibly through the raven's headphones and visually as lines on a screen that appeared and disappeared and climbed and dived in split seconds like a mountain range in violent spasm. Another was a direction finder called an APA-17B. Plugged into an APR-4A search receiver, it would show exactly what direction the radio or radar signal was coming from. Combining that information and the distance the signal traveled with the position of the plane at the instant the signal was intercepted pinpointed the location of the radar. It was similar to the radio compass direction finders that are standard equipment on most planes, civilian and military, which point to radio stations that are broadcasting. Still other receivers intercepted radio signals, provided pictures of the radar signals, and recorded both. Boxes were everywhere. Each of the six stations had specific hardware that did specific things and they did not vary from one RB-50G to another.

Back on the ground after the long, wearying missions, the ravens would spend hours combining their detailed pencil notes on log sheets that became a formal report: the product of their work. One of their manuals made the point in the strongest way possible that the mission report was supremely important. "No matter how well the planning and flight phases of the ferret operation are accomplished, if the mission report is poorly written, then the labor involved on the entire operation is wasted." Turning in a sloppy report, then, would be like flying a photoreconnaissance mission with a camera that was out of focus. And like their counterparts in the fighter world, the ravens kept their own score. It had to do with the infinitely subtle art of tuning the knobs on the receivers with the exquisite care of a practiced safecracker, of massaging and caressing them as they took in all of the disparate signals, and of isolating the one or more they were after so it could be recorded. Like other occupations, there were high roads and low roads in this work. Some ravens used their hands like paws. Others did whatever they had to do to get by; to get a mission finished and chalk up another day on the way home. But others were as challenged as detectives and treated their work like a black art.

FOLLOWING THE INTELLIGENCE briefing, O'Kelley's crew had been driven to their airplane in a flight taxi, which was an enclosed trailer pulled by a jeep. It was a relatively long drive because *Little Red Ass* was parked on a remote, carefully guarded, hard stand that looked like a cul-de-sac. There, standing at attention in "formation" behind their parachutes, oxygen masks, headsets, Mae Wests, rolled-up dinghies, and the other paraphernalia of their trade in eerie shadows made by nearby lights, the crew went through the ritual of reciting what they were supposed to do in case of trouble in the air or a ditching at sea. Stan O'Kelley was a large and affable former high school football player from Napa, California, but he was also a stickler for going by the book. So they recited their lines, though not to him this time. He had not yet arrived. That was highly unusual.

"Engineer's preflight complete. Bailout through the nose wheel well hatch following co-pilot," Frank Brown said, reciting his practiced lines. "Crash land and ditch in position. Exit through engineer's escape hatch. After ditching, when aircraft stops, proceed to right raft." And on it went, one man after the next, including five of the six ravens. Five because Bentley was not there. Hours earlier, he had mentioned to O'Kelley that he had a serious eye problem, and was pleased to hear his aircraft commander tell him that he could skip the flight that night. O'Kelley had told Bentley that *Little Red Ass* would be carrying two additional men. One of them would use his seat. The two strangers were not ravens, were not known to anybody in the crew, and were not even in the Strategic Air Command.

S. Sgt. Donald G. Hill and A2c. Earl W. Radlein, Jr., were in the Air Force Security Service. Both had been to language school and spoke Russian. Their job was to monitor Soviet communication traffic in the hope of picking up a morsel or two of communication intelligence, widely known in the black world as COMINT. Perhaps more important, they would scan radio frequencies, listening to chatter between Soviet air controllers and fighter pilots who might be hunting for *Little Red Ass*, or between the pilots themselves as they closed in for an attack. Picking that up would provide early warning of potential trouble and maybe give O'Kelley some time to push the throttles full forward and get out of there as fast as he could. Hill and Radlein were there as lookouts to provide early warning that the ferret was itself being stalked by predators.

Roche had already briefed Hill and Radlein on what they were supposed to do in case of trouble. That was more than either of them got from the five secretive ravens. The specialized world of intelligence collection was so tightly "compartmented" that the ELINT guys who ferreted radar and the COMINT guys who collected communication intelligence, who eavesdropped on radio chatter, kept to themselves. They not only didn't talk shop with each other, they didn't talk anything. Not even around the base. Not even about football or movies or sushi or geishas. No one told them not to talk to each other. They just didn't. And so the two professional cultures, trapped in the social quagmire of their security clearances, remained effectively segregated.

As the crew of *Little Red Ass* and Hill and Radlein stood there on the darkened hard stand, a car carrying O'Kelley and a visitor suddenly appeared and pulled up near them. Like Hill and Radlein, the newcomer spoke Russian. Unlike the two Air Force enlisted men, however, the late arrival was a Russian who was dressed in civilian clothes and whose English was poor. That didn't matter. His Russian was excellent. The Air Force Security Service, which operated under the aegis of the National Security Agency, often sent displaced Russians on ferret missions because they were infinitely better at their native language than were Americans. The idea was to have someone on board who could hear telltale nuances that would reveal secrets or show that the plane was being stalked for an attack. (Defying common sense, excited fighter pilots *did* talk to each other as they closed in for the kill.) Americans schooled in Russian for less than a year were good enough to get the general idea of what they heard as they picked it up, and were certainly capable of translating tape recordings after they returned to their base. But, understandably, they couldn't get it all. Native Russians could. The displaced persons, or DPs, as they were generally known, were also called "sports" at Yokota and other military bases, probably because they would be handled with particular savagery if a plane went down and they were captured.

All eighteen men aboard 9653 that morning were strapped in or just sitting down by 2:15, when O'Kelley, Roche, and Brown ran through their checklists of the things that had to be done to get their sixty-five-ton plane into the air. All three had dials, levers, and switches in front, on both sides, and above their heads: master fire warning light, directional indicator, altitude and course indicators, altimeter, turn and slip indicator, radio compass repeater indicator, clock, vacuum pressure and manifold pressure indicators, tachometers, water pressure indicator lights, and more. Throttles for the plane's four engines were on the sill on O'Kelley's left, while a stand on the aisle to his right had its own forest of switches and levers for propeller pitch and synchronization, landing lights, autopilot, emergency wing flap operation, a bomb bay door indicator light and control switch, and even the windshield wipers. The nose wheel steering handle, at the top of the aisle stand, turned the plane on the ground when it was rolling. It was a pretty straightforward device that worked like the tiller on a sailboat. The emergency alarm switch—EMERG ALARM—was on the edge of the stand, just beyond O'Kelley's right armrest, and it had to be tested. There were two choices: ON/OFF. ON would set off the alarm, a claxon that sounded like the angry, attention-getting school bells that went off briefly for class change and persistently in a fire drill. This one's raucous clanging would be an order to bail out of the plane through the assigned hatch as fast as possible. O'Kelley, Roche, Brown, Czyz, Wiggins, and Keith were supposed to climb out of a hatch in the nose wheel well and hit the silk. The ravens' primary escape route was through the forward bomb bay door over which they sat. Failing that, they were supposed to work their way up front and follow O'Kelley and the others through the nose wheel hatch. This meant the fifth and last raven—ordinarily Bentley, though not this night—would be eleventh in line to get out. That was not promising. Trying to bail out of a stricken bomber, very likely one careening out of control and slamming its crewmen around like rag dolls, would be a hellish struggle.

Each of the fifteen in the regular crew had his own checklist and had to report to O'Kelley that it had been completed. He went through his own. Then he told Brown to start the number three engine: the inside one on the right wing, behind and to the right of Roche. The flight engineer ran through his own practiced ritual: "Mixture Levers—FUEL CUTOFF . . . Throttles—¼ OPEN . . . DC Voltmeter Selector Switch—SET . . . Main

Booster Pumps—BOOST NORMAL-VALVE OPEN. . . ." Brown reported that he was ready to start the engines and flicked number three's starter switch to START, then to OFF. The big black four-bladed propeller, seventeen feet tip to tip, began to turn grudgingly, as if it didn't want to be awakened. After it had turned twenty times (with Roche counting), Brown hit the ignition switch and then the primer switch, which sent electricity into the spark plugs and gasoline squirting into number three's twenty-eight cylinders. The engine coughed slowly at first, then faster, and finally settled into a loud roar, sending the fuel's burned and vaporized remnant—thick, blue smoke—pouring out of the engine's exhaust pipe in clouds that instantly turned into tumbling wisps that disappeared in the prop wash. Number three's propeller was now a blur, spinning 1,000 times a minute. Number four, outboard of number three, was next, followed by number two and finally number one, which were on 9653's left wing; the one they called port. The RB-50G was a machine that had come alive.

O'Kelley continued running through his own checklist, making sure that fourteen more things got done, including a check of the flight instruments, the alarm bell, and the master fire warning light. He saw that the ground crew had pulled away the wheel chocks. Then he released the parking brakes and eased the throttles forward until the propellers were turning 1,400 times a minute. O'Kelley told his crew to stand by to taxi. *Little Red Ass* began to move, and as it did, O'Kelley eased back on the throttles. Using the tiller, he guided the plane to the edge of Yokota's runway and stopped. He set the flaps for twenty-five degrees, brought the engines up to 2,700 rpm, and checked off two dozen more switches, dials, and gauges that had to be flipped, turned, tuned, or just watched. "Stand by for takeoff," he said into the small microphone in front of his mouth.

The plane was now sending vibrations through the bodies of every man on board and roaring so loudly that it dominated the moment. The crews of Superfortresses and other propeller-driven bombers and patrol planes that flew long missions tended to need hearing aids before other men their age. Jack Parrish, a veteran RB-50G raven, claimed years after he retired that he had impaired hearing in his left ear because of all the long flights he spent on the other side of the fuselage from the numbers one and two engines. The affliction was well known to ravens, who called it a "B-50 ear." And unlike jets, the reciprocating engines—turbocharged brutes that each contributed 2,650 pounds of horsepower in normal cruise—caused so much vibration that a pencil would be on the floor five or six seconds after it was put on a table. It felt like a low-grade quake was rumbling through a man's spine.

Having gotten clearance for takeoff from the tower, O'Kelley pushed the throttles forward and was soon rolling down the runway, his hand on the tiller that kept the nose wheel straight, between two ribbons of white lights that sped past. He let go of the steering bar when 9653 hit sixty miles an hour because the plane's own massive rudder was now slicing through the air like a fin in water and keeping it headed right down the concrete. A mile and a quarter later, he pulled gently back on the yoke, and *Little Red Ass* lifted off the runway, thundered into the warm black sky, and headed west, chasing the end of the night. It was three o'clock in the morning.

Roche reported to Wajima Homer that 9653 was on course as the plane headed out over the Sea of Japan and toward North Korea. Its cruising altitude, 5,000 feet, kept it off Vladivostok's early warning radar. But it also kept the Russians' radar off the ravens' receivers. *Little Red Ass* was supposed to have climbed to 25,000 for a better vantage point, but a malfunctioning fuel valve on one of the engines persuaded O'Kelley to level off at 20,000 feet as it crossed the line on Ed Czyz's navigation chart that was labeled "Japan Outer ADIZ." It was passing out of Japan's Air Defense Identification Zone, an internationally recognized boundary inside of which planes approaching Japan had to identify themselves and were subject to interception if they failed to do so. Now it was out of protected airspace and in the tight confines of the Sea of Japan roughly 180 miles due south of Cape Povorotny, a spit of land east of Vladivostok. Roche would later remember that 9653 continued on until it reached coordinates that put it fifty miles off the northernmost tip of the North Korean coast, not far from where Parr had shot down the Il-12 two days earlier.

Roche was appreciating the mountains rising out of the North Korean mist as the first rays of the sun touched them. Wiggins, however, was not enjoying the view at all. He was studying an aerial navigation chart which contained a rectangle over North Korea that said, very explicitly: "WARNING. Aircraft infringing upon Non-Free Flying Territory may be fired on without warning. . . ."

O'Kelley banked forty-five degrees to the northeast, then turned again, and continued on. He was now so close to Vladivostok that Roche, peering into Wiggins's radar navigation scope, saw Cape Povorotny and more of the Siberian coast to the east. The RB-50G was now in the danger zone, flying so close to the heart of the Kremlin's Pacific fleet to get the opposition's search radar turned on that it was approaching the harbor. As it did so, Warren Sanderson, Frank Tejeda, and the other three ravens busily tuned in to the radar signals that were steadily hitting 9653 and echoing back to radar operators in Vladivostok, who saw the RB-50G as an advancing white blip on their darkened scopes. Hill and Radlein were surfing through their frequencies as they searched for people talking.

Little Red Ass was now flying along the Soviet coastline. According to the Russians, it flew past Cape Gamov, which juts into Peter the Great Bay, just to the southwest of Vladivostok, then flew over Soviet territory at Ajton Island near the huge port. O'Kelley was definitely getting the Russians' attention. All the while, Hill, Radlein, and the DP were listening very carefully for any sign that there were fighters around. It was 6:15 on a gorgeous morning. *Little Red Ass* was heading back toward the Sea of Japan as Roche lit a cigarette, chatted with O'Kelley, and again took in the mountains rising majestically out of the thick mist.

"FIGHTERS DO NOT FIGHT," Antoine de Saint-Exupéry wrote in *Flight to Arras*, "they murder." The book was about his own futile reconnaissance flight against the German army advancing into France in 1940. Saint-Exupéry, an experienced pilot himself, was trying to put to rest the myth that fighter pilots behave chivalrously in combat. To the contrary, as he had good reason to know, they are professional predators. And like other predators, the essence of their work is to hit their prey by surprise, kill it, and get away. The author of *The Little Prince* was himself finally killed on a reconnaissance mission over the western Mediterranean in 1944, very likely by a German fighter pilot who came in from behind and, unnoticed until it was too late, cut him to pieces with machine guns.

It is unlikely that the pilots of the two MiG-17s who attacked *Little Red Ass*, Senior Lt. Yuri M. Yablonovski and Capt. Aleksandr D. Rybakov, had read *Flight to Arras*. But they knew their business. Their fighters carried three rapid-fire cannons that packed a very heavy punch and they came from behind to use them. Not directly behind. They knew, as all fighter pilots know, that coming in from an angle increases the size of the target and therefore the probability of scoring a kill. So they came in from the left, closing on the lumbering RB-50G as Rybakov, the senior officer, squeezed the trigger button on top of his control stick and felt his fighter shudder.

Little Red Ass shuddered, too, as Rybakov's shells slammed into it. There was a loud bang, like a car backfiring, and the bomber lurched to the left. More backfiring. O'Kelley and Roche looked to the left and saw that cannon fire was slamming into the number one engine, which was breaking up. The engine's cover, its cowling, was actually tearing off. Other rounds punched into the wing and the flap. While A2c. James E. Woods started shooting his twin .50-calibers at the MiG as it sped past, adding to the horrific racket, Brown, the flight engineer, shouted, "Feather number one." Roche cut the dead engine's throttle and turned its propeller blades sideways so they sliced into the airstream to reduce drag. That was when he saw the MiG. It streaked past his mortally wounded bomber from below and to the left, then climbed close enough in front so Roche could plainly see red stars on its silver wings. An exhilarated Sasha Rybakov leveled off about 2,000 feet above and a couple of miles in front of 9653, did a celebratory rollover, and disappeared in a dive toward the sea.

"The flap back of the engine and the cowling are all shot up," someone shouted. O'Kelley turned off the autopilot and sounded the alarm for a bailout. While it clanged, he lowered the landing gear so the escape hatch in the nose wheel well could be opened and swung *Little Red Ass* into a descending turn to the right. That's when Yuri Yablonovski let go. This time Roche heard cannon fire coming from the right, then a voice he took to be the tail gunner's shouting into the intercom, "I'm shooting at him. He's coming up and I'm shooting at him." Roche felt the plane shudder again, both from the firing of its own guns and from more cannon shells ripping into its right wing. Then he heard Brown again. "Feather number four." He pulled back the engine's throttle and feathered its propeller. Since number four was on his side, Roche could plainly see that the top of the cowling was torn away and that some of the engine it had covered had been shot off. Smashed and twisted pieces of what seconds before had been a functioning engine, jagged cylinders smeared with black oil, were hanging there, mangled by the cannon shells. He could also see that one of the feathered blades had a hole in it the size of a grapefruit. Worse, number four was on fire. Roche knew that Brown had turned on the engine's fire extinguisher because he saw carbon dioxide streaming out of the back of the engine. But it wasn't putting out the fire, which was being fed by gasoline in the wing. "Brown," Roche shouted, "get that goddamned door open." Brown struggled to open the escape hatch while O'Kelley depressurized the plane for the bailout.

Satisfied that they had done their job, Rybakov and Yablonovski turned toward home, leaving the men inside the burning bomber to try desperately to save themselves. The battle was over for the two Russian fighter pilots. But it was very much under way for those inside 9653. This, too, had been described by Saint-Exupéry a dozen years earlier: "The fighter has become a mere impartial onlooker when, from the severed carotid in the neck of the reconnaissance pilot, the first jets of blood spurt forth. When from the hood of the starboard engine the hesitant leak of the first tongue of flame rises out of the furnace fire. And the cobra has returned to its folds when the venom strikes the heart and the first muscle of the face twitches. The fighter group does not kill. It sows death. Death sprouts after it has passed."

The death of the hemorrhaging ferret came seconds after O'Kelley hit the depressurization switch. The fire in number four quickly ate through enough of the wing to break it off where what was left of the engine was still mounted. Pushed hard by the air hitting it, the outer thirty-five feet or so snapped and swung inward like a massive door on a hinge, slamming into the side of the fuselage with tremendous force. The impact probably broke off most of the plane's tail and sent the heavy radar and radio intercept receivers and recorders crashing down on the ravens.

The impact of the wing and fuselage smashing together was so powerful that Roche, whose seat belt had been fastened, was torn out of his seat. His head struck the corner of O'Kelley's instrument panel and his stomach hit the nose wheel steering bar on the aisle stand. Then he bounced into the nose. His chin was cut almost from ear to ear, his right eyelid and the corner of his left eye were split open, part of his scalp was torn open like a flap, and his face was bruised and bloody. The blood was blurring his vision. But blurred or not, he could see that he was better off than Jim Keith, the nose navigator, who lay near him. Keith's eyes were open and he seemed to be staring. There was so much blood coming from his head that Roche assumed it was bashed in. That accounted for all the blood that was spattered over the Plexiglas, on the metal frames that separated the glass panels, and on the floor. Keith was absolutely still.

Little Red Ass was no longer flying. It was spinning and tumbling in a violent, fiery free fall that created enough centrifugal force to pin Roche to the floor. Now, suddenly, he noticed that it was so quiet he assumed the engines had been ripped off. What he did hear, however, was O'Kelley ordering him to get up and bail out through the nose wheel hatch. "Roche. John," O'Kelley shouted, "just don't lie there: you got to get the hell out." Roche struggled to his feet, his parachute strapped to his back, and tried to pull himself out of the nose and back toward the escape hatch, cutting his hands and arms as he did so. He saw that the case that held his rubber dinghy had ripped open and was hanging, empty, on his left side. He looked back to where Brown and Wiggins had been, behind his and O'Kelley's seats, and saw that they were gone. He also saw bright light coming through the smoke from behind their stations. It was daylight. That meant the plane had broken apart just behind the forward machine gun turret.

Roche pulled himself back to the hatch, scrambled past the

two nose wheel tires—he would remember distinctly that one was bald and the other had treads—and dove out of the disintegrating bomber. He tumbled blindly through thick fog, yanked the rip cord of his parachute, and was jerked violently when it popped open. Then he smelled smoke. Roche saw that both the chute and his flight suit were on fire. "Oh, shit, my clothes are on fire . . . my goddamned parachute is on fire," he thought. The next thing he saw was bubbles. He later estimated that the chute opened less than one hundred feet over the water, and that what was left of 9653 landed about seventy-five feet from where he came down.

When he came back to the surface, John Roche saw that gasoline and oil were burning on the water and that the fire was moving in his direction. It was so close he could feel the heat. As he started to swim away from it, he felt drag, and remembered that his parachute was still on. One of its shroud lines was wrapped around his right leg. So he pulled his legs up to his chest, slid his thumbs into the chute's leg straps, and pulled them down his legs and over his shoes. Free of the chute, he rolled over and started to backstroke away from the fire. He also inflated his Mae West. Roche knew that the yellow rubber life preserver was supposed to keep his head above water. But he also knew that he would need something more substantial to save his life. Then, through the fog, he spotted a burning sleeping-bag mattress that had come out of someone's survival kit. He pulled it underwater to put out the flames, then tied it to his Mae West. All the while, Roche vomited blood and suffered through violent convulsions. He knew his injuries and the loss of blood were sapping his energy and that he therefore had to find something that would serve as a real raft. Slowly, painfully, Roche collected oxygen storage tanks, charred insulation material, and other debris that was floating on the calm water and tried to lash them together. As he did that, he shouted, but there was no response. Not at first.

Finally—and Roche had no clear idea of how long it took—he heard a voice coming through the mist, and he started swimming toward it. Stan O'Kelley, his hair and eyebrows singed, his nose broken, and his lips badly swollen, appeared. After looking each other over, and lying about how good they seemed, the pilot and copilot hung on to the oxygen tanks and shouted so other survivors would know they were there. At one point that morning, they heard a voice calling from within the mist, and they took turns answering, but it finally stopped.

There were other survivors out there. In fact, there was a great deal of activity in the water off Vladivostok. There were Soviet patrol boats and other naval vessels in the area. Roche would remember hearing patrol boats moving very close by. They passed so close that their wakes washed over him and O'Kelley as they prowled through the patchy mist and acrid smoke looking for survivors and anything of military value from what their leaders would soon call, quite accurately, the intruding American spy plane.

At one point that morning, three curious sharks (or one that returned twice) swam so close to them that Roche could easily see their eyes. Each time, he and O'Kelley stayed absolutely still as the large fish looked them over. Roche's .45 automatic had torn loose during the attack, but he had a .25-caliber pistol in his survival kit. What he later remembered most about the sharks was their menacing eyes, which were about a foot and a half apart, and which "stared" at them. He therefore decided to "shoot the son of a bitch in the eye" if it made a threatening move. And since he was throwing up blood and had several external wounds, an attack seemed likely. But it didn't happen. They (or it) soon lost interest in the two airmen and disappeared.

At roughly six o'clock that evening—just under twelve hours after Roche and O'Kelley hit the water—the crew of an SB-29 of the Thirty-seventh Air Rescue Squadron spotted flares fired by Roche and a green sea marker he opened, and dropped an aluminum lifeboat by parachute nearby. And that's not all they spotted. The airmen who circled Roche and O'Kelley also saw twelve Soviet patrol boats moving away from the crash site and toward shore. A few hours later, another SB-29 crew saw four men in the water within one hundred feet of each other, and two or three more not far from them. An A-3 rescue boat was dropped and seen to hit the water about fifty feet from one of the survivors. Then, with dusk approaching and fog rolling in, the rescue planes headed home to Misawa Air Base in Japan. The crew of the second would write a report stating emphatically that six or seven of the RB-50G's survivors had been seen in the water.

It took maddeningly long for the search-and-rescue aircraft to arrive because of the armistice parties at Yokota, or more accurately, because of their effect. Having celebrated Sandy's birthday the night before and gone to sleep at a reasonable hour, Jim Keeffe climbed out of bed on the morning of the 29th and noticed that the air base was quieter than it had been at any time in the preceding three years: no engines running up, no trucks grinding gears, no real activity of any kind. He walked into the combat operations building at about eight o'clock. Being a weather briefer for the aircrews, Keeffe knew that two reconnaissance planes had been working the night before: an RB-29 up in the Hokkaido area, and 9653. When he asked the acting duty officer, a major, about the RB-29, he was told that it was fine.

"What about O'Kelley?" Keeffe asked. "Well," the major answered, "we've missed two position reports." A missed position report, indicating that the plane wasn't where it was supposed to be, was a bad sign. Two missed reports was obviously worse.

"What have you done about it?" Keeffe wanted to know.

"Nothing."

"What does the contingency plan call for?"

"It's over there in the file cabinet, if you want to read it."

Keeffe looked over the contingency plan and told the major that the squadron commander had to be notified immediately if two position reports were missed, and so did Far East Air Forces Headquarters in Tokyo. When he asked whether that had been done, and was informed that it in fact had not been done, he told the major to do it. It was a measure of Keeffe's exasperation that he, a captain, was giving an order to a superior officer.

"Jim," the major answered, "everyone was partying last night. I'm not going to wake him up."

"Well, God damn it. If you're not going to wake him up, *I'll* do it."

"Suit yourself."

Keeffe hopped on his bicycle and pedaled to the bachelor officers' quarters, where the squadron commander and other officers on temporary duty lived. Even as he related the ominous news, the time for the third report to arrive came and went with no word from 9653. Keeffe and the squadron commander, a lieutenant colonel named Crane, drove back to combat operations and got the bad news from the major. Far East Air Forces was notified immediately and ordered the launch of two SB-29s, one of which would soon drop the boat to O'Kelley and Roche.

"Had this whole thing been done properly," Keeffe said many years later, the anger still there, "we would have O'Kelley, at the very least. This just fries me."

Roche, now in the water for half a day and still vomiting blood and convulsing, slipped out of his flight jacket to make swimming easier and struggled toward the boat. Ironically, during practice for such emergencies at Ramey Air Force Base in Puerto Rico, he had been the only man in the water who never made it to the lifeboat; they always had to pull him in. But this wasn't practice. Now, exhausted and near the end of his endurance, Roche forced himself to keep stroking until he reached it. Then he pulled himself up on a ladder, climbed over the gunwale, and fell into the boat, wracked with cramps in his legs and stomach. He pressed his ripped scalp firmly in place and then looked for O'Kelley, who was bobbing quietly in the water. Stan O'Kelley, in pain from multiple wounds and bitterly cold, tried to follow his copilot. Roche said afterward that he saw his skipper swim toward the boat, counting each agonized stroke: "twenty-five . . . twenty-six . . . twenty-seven . . . twenty-eight . . ." There was no twenty-ninth. The star football player from Napa High had no more to give. He rolled onto his back, according to Roche, and put his hands over his face. As Roche watched in pain and despair, Stan O'Kelley disappeared under the next wave. His body and Sergeant Brown's would wash ashore in Japan three months later.

Roche meanwhile stayed in the lifeboat, huddling in dry blankets, until late the following night. He had no way of knowing it, of course, but there was intense activity on and above the Sea of Japan as it quickly became apparent to both sides that a major incident had taken place involving aerial reconnaissance, a major shootdown right in front of Vladivostok, and survivors who were up for grabs. There were more than Soviet patrol boats scouring the area that day. There were larger vessels, including destroyer escorts, that searched the sea. Several American warships and one from Australia were also quickly diverted to the crash site. U.S.

Air Force and Navy aircraft scoured the ocean for survivors. One Navy flyer, Richard Koch, told Roche years later: "You guys just about parked it [9653] in the harbor; you guys were close enough so they could see you from shore."

When Roche saw the light from a nearby ship, he fired a flare, and as the vessel drew closer, more flares. Then he heard what had to have been the most wonderful words of his life: "Get that launch overboard." He was rescued by a U.S. Navy destroyer and was in its sick bay at 4:20 a.m. on the 30th, twenty-two hours after he landed in Vladivostok Bay. (His and O'Kelley's watches had become waterlogged and stopped at 6:20, three minutes after the attack.) Roche's scalp was immediately stitched and his other wounds treated in the ship's sick bay. He was then transferred to the U.S.S. *Princeton*, an aircraft carrier, then to another carrier, and finally flown back to Yokota. Having survived a major cold war incident, John E. Roche was now a valuable intelligence resource, something of a celebrity within the secretive aerial reconnaissance fraternity, and a political pawn.

On July 31—four days after the end of the war and two after he was shot down—Roche was driven from Yokota to Far East Air Forces Headquarters. There, he was given another medical examination and was closely questioned by Gen. Otto P. Weyland, commander of FEAF, and several subordinate officers and intelligence people. The press clamored for the surviving hero's story and was quickly fed a harrowing account of his having been shot down over international waters while on a navigational training mission.

But the Air Force was more forthcoming with the news media than it was with its colleagues in other agencies. The intelligence types tended to see their counterparts in the CIA, the Department of State, the NSA, and the Office of Naval Intelligence as obsessive and devious competitors, and they therefore kept cooperation to an absolute minimum. Secrecy, after all, amounted to an Eleventh Commandment. Captain Roche was therefore ordered to keep his mouth shut whenever he was around them. He maintained years later that he was given firm instructions not to share what he knew with anybody outside the Air Force: to tell them nothing useful. "I talked to General Weyland about this thing, you

know, and he had a bunch of guys there—CIA, or whatever—
from intelligence. Back in those days, everybody knew—hey—you
don't tell the CIA or the FBI a fucking thing. . . . When I went
back to the State Department, [it] was the same thing," he recalled. "We don't tell them a goddamned thing. The sons of
bitches aren't on our side. They [Air Force intelligence] said, 'Just
keep your mouth shut, John.' "

Roche was openly contemptuous of the Department of State,
which he considered subversive. He believed implicitly that the
civilians were so eager to accommodate America's enemies in a
misguided peace-at-any-price policy that they actually told the
Soviet Union where *Little Red Ass* would be and when. In one interview years later he maintained that he saw the patrol boats
waiting to pick up survivors before the MiGs jumped his plane:
absolute proof that a leak had led to the ambush. "They told the
Russians we'd be there," he said in another interview in June
1993, citing as additional proof the fact that the MiGs carried no
radar and would therefore have needed very precise directions.

There is evidence Soviet vessels were, indeed, waiting for the
ferret, and it very likely was marked for destruction in retaliation
for the attack on the Il-12. But the notion that the Russians were
tipped off was absurd. Ferret flights against the radar at Vladivostok were almost as regular as mail deliveries. Setting up an ambush therefore required neither a genius nor a traitor.

By the time John Roche was delivered to General Weyland on
the 31st, a public relations crusade had already begun. A picture
of the valiant flyer, the right side of his head bandaged as he
talked with Weyland, was quickly distributed to United Press and
other news organizations. Another picture of the rescued airman
that ran in newspapers around the country showed him wearing a
mouth microphone and flight cap. The hat held captain's bars. No
red ass was evident.

Charles "Chip" Bohlen, the U.S. ambassador to the Soviet
Union, delivered a well-publicized, righteously indignant note to
the famously stone-faced Soviet deputy foreign minister, Andrei
Gromyko, protesting the attack "in the strongest terms." A press
release simultaneously issued by the Department of State contained the heart of the U.S. position as it was made to the Krem-

lin: the RB-50 had been on a "routine navigational training mission" some forty miles offshore (where, it noted incorrectly, Roche had been picked up) and had therefore been the victim of an unprovoked attack.

As early as July 1947, ferret crews captured by the Russians were under orders to tell their captors they had been on a "weather mission." But the Alaskan Air Command, which was in the thick of ferreting Siberia two years later, decided the cover was not feasible because, as one memorandum put it, "a good interrogator could readily determine that the crews are not qualified for weather reconnaissance." So it was decided two years later to change the cover to a "long range navigation training mission," evidently on the assumption that getting lost was plausible for neophyte navigators. But it was a charade. The ferrets were carefully tracked by Soviet radar—which was, after all, the ferrets' purpose for being there—and the contents of a recovered plane would reveal receiving equipment and recorders, not sextants.

But that was the official line, and everyone on the inside of the operation, certainly including Roche, was expected to stick to it. Publicly admitting U.S. military aircraft violated international law by flying military missions over foreign lands (including Israel and other allies), and that they did so to collect intelligence—spying, as many would call it—was out of the question. Admitting the truth of the matter would hand the Communists an unprecedented propaganda victory and justify more aggressive countermeasures by the Russians and their Asian allies, putting the lives of the aircrews even more at risk. So the fiction was institutionalized. The established line was that planes that came under attack, as many of them did, were in international airspace and had suffered navigational errors or had been blown off course while training or doing peaceful "electromagnetic" or other scientific research.

Telegrams sent by Gen. Joseph D. Caldara, the Forbes base commander, to 9653's families the day after the attack maintained that the men were "missing on a routine training flight near Japan." That was as insensitive as it was disingenuous. Instead of at least telling families that their loved ones had been attacked by their nation's enemy for whatever reason, it was implied that the hapless airmen couldn't even overcome some glitch on a routine flight.

Bohlen's note to the Russians also said explicitly that survivors of the attack had been spotted in life rafts and Soviet vessels had been seen in the crash area. "My government," the note and the press release said, "has instructed me to request an immediate report from the Soviet authorities regarding the condition of these survivors and what arrangements are being made for their early repatriation." Newspaper editors around the country couldn't resist playing the survivor angle, since it oozed human interest. It would also prove to be a lingering embarrassment for the government.

Ed Phillips, a photographer with the *Herald-Express* in Los Angeles, went to Ruth Ann Ward's home in East Pasadena with a reporter who informed her that her husband John, the raven 4, might have been rescued by the Russians. Phillips was lucky enough to get a shot of her as she passed out. Bess Tejeda and her three young sons, Philip, David, and Michael, were posed by an Associated Press photographer gazing attentively at a radio in her mother-in-law's house in Los Angeles, evidently hanging on every word. The caption referred specifically to the Department of State's claim that the downed airmen had been picked up by Russian boats. The *Examiner* ran a picture of her flanked by the boys under a headline that said: "Downed Pilot's Family Believes He Survived Red's Air Attack."

The savvy editors of the *Nashville Tennessean* ran the survivor story on August 1 under a headline that spread across page one: "U.S. DOWNED AIRLINER—REDS," and a story in which the Russians angrily charged that the Il-12 had been shot down over China, not North Korea. It reported that Gromyko had handed his own protest note to Bohlen the previous Thursday, the day after 9653 was shot down. Other papers also carried the Il-12 piece, undoubtedly leading some readers to conclude that the supposedly unprovoked attack over allegedly international waters was simply retaliation for the deaths of the twenty-one Russians.

The Russians might have been angry. But there was no anger for the widows and children, or for the bewildered and numb parents and brothers and sisters who were the recipients of General

Caldara's telegrams. The stunned and grieving "next of kin" were left to believe that the men they would never see again couldn't even get through a routine training flight without suffering some horrible, unspecified catastrophe. It made the tragedies almost whimsical.

BESS TEJEDA HAD gotten the news, not from General Caldara, but from a reporter while she was living in a new apartment in Pomona. The first indication of trouble had come on the morning of the 30th, when she noticed a short blurb in the newspaper about a shootdown in the Far East. Calls to United Press International and the Associated Press, the two large wire services, turned up nothing. Neither did a call to the *Los Angeles Times*. She even tried UPI headquarters in New York and other local papers. In general, Bess Tejeda was assured that if her husband had been on the missing plane, she would have gotten official word from the Pentagon.

"So I never thought too much about it," she remembered years afterward. "And the kids were in bed—I had these three little boys—and the phone rang at ten o'clock at night, and this man said, 'I hope it isn't too late.' And I said, 'No, no. Why?' He said I'm Mr. So-and-so from the *Los Angeles Times.* 'Would you tell me where Major Tejeda was born?' I said, 'Yeah, he was born in Los Angeles, south central, same as me.' And he said, 'How long has he been in the Air Force?' And I said, '*Wait a minute. Why are you—*' And then I said, 'Oh, no, he was on that plane this morning . . .' And this man was so apologetic. He retreated so fast. He said, 'Oh, I'm so sorry. I thought you would have known.' I called my mother. She had been trying to call me because a telegram had just come to her house, where I was still listed as having lived, I guess. And the Tejedas, too. They lived near my mother. They had gotten a telegram as the parents. This is how I found out."

Bess Tejeda also carried pain for her young sons for years. "I went over to school the day that they were declared legally dead, which was the fifteenth of November, 1955. . . . I went over and took my oldest son out of class, and I showed him this telegram from the government," she said. "Well, he started to cry and he said, 'Just because they said that, it doesn't make my daddy dead. Just because they write that on the paper, it doesn't mean my daddy's dead.' And now I thought, he never really accepted the fact that these men did die."

Having heard years later about the likely fate of the survivors, Bess Tejeda would want to believe that Frank was killed in the crash. "I like to think that he went in the drink; that he died at the time. I kept hoping that I'd get . . . I wanted to get a telegram saying, 'We have found and positively identified Francisco Tejeda's body,' knowing then that he died at the time, because I didn't like to think of the alternative."

The wives never talked about their husbands' work, but most, like Jean O'Kelley, knew implicitly that it was exceptionally dangerous. That bred a certain amount of superstition. "We never could have a fight before they took off on a mission," she recalled after her husband's death. "You didn't because you knew maybe they weren't coming back, and you didn't want that to happen. When you parted, it was always on very calm terms."

But there could be no calmness when the news came. "You glance out the window and you see an Air Force blue car go slowly by—up and down the street—for some reason a touch of fear hits you," Jean O'Kelley wrote years later about that terrible day at Forbes. "You pour another cup of coffee hoping they won't stop. The doorbell rings—the chaplain and commanding officer are there—no one says a word. Finally you do . . . you tell them what you know has happened. . . . You know, and since you do, you feel you must make it easier on the persons bringing the bad news. Friends take the children. . . ."

Twenty years later she was back in Napa, still a widow with three grown children, working for the church and taking a night course on death and philosophy to try to make sense of what happened, or at least reconcile it. "DEATH—death, it did come—powerfully—without warning—why us?" she asked in a paper she wrote for class. "Why not the family up the street—down the block? Why us? Who had so much to still do and, after all, homecoming was only a week away. . . . God wouldn't be that cruel. Yet death came—leaving three stunned and saddened people. . . . Especially Mommy . . . who never cried."

A week after her husband's body washed ashore in Japan, Jean O'Kelley was called to Forbes. There, a major told her with astonishing cruelty, "that some people just didn't have the desire to live, and my husband was one; he just gave up and drowned. That made me mad."

She also remembered that one of her sons, who was six at the time of the shootdown and who therefore had known his father, became withdrawn and distrustful of new relationships. Anytime anyone from the military came to the door, he would try to listen in the hope that there was good news about his father. Since she was never given a chance to view her husband's body, she came to believe that it was in fact not he who had washed ashore, and that he, too, might have been taken prisoner. Years of writing to the Air Force for information produced a succession of confusing letters. The matter was under investigation, the form letters said, but nothing more came of it.

Years later, Jean O'Kelley's seventeen-year-old granddaughter, Mindi, addressed her own frustration in a high school term paper titled "The Cold War." She illustrated it with photographs of 9653 and its crew, including the grandfather she never knew, and General Caldara's telegram. Having described her grandfather's last mission, she concluded by writing that "the families of the dead were fed incredible lies that ranged from the location of the plane when it was shot down, the reason for the secrecy and injustice of their death. . . . My mother grew up without a father, no good pictures or diaries, only the love letters he sent to my grandmother when they were teenagers and her memories. I can only imagine what that would be like and it makes me extremely upset to think of how many people were in the same situation. All we can do is try to find the truth."

Jean O'Kelley also remembered that, however irrational it was, she had hated Albert Bentley because he had gotten bumped that fateful night with his eye problem and he was therefore still alive. Albert *Stanley* Bentley, Jr., for God's sake! His middle name had been her husband's first name, and "Stan" was what most people called Bentley. Back in Topeka, ironically, her kitchen window had faced Bentley's house. "Every time I'd look at that house, I'd get so mad. I couldn't stand it. The hatred just kept building up." It built to the point where she sent back a baby gift that Bentley's wife bought after the birth of a daughter.

Forty-five years later, with a telephone number supplied by Bess Tejeda Bergmann, who had remarried and was living in Pomona, Albert Bentley called Jean O'Kelley to say he would be passing through Napa. Over lunch that day in 1998, she told him about how she had hated him all those years, and about how wrong it had been. She finally came to terms with the fact of Stan Bentley's survival and her own misplaced anger.

THE EVIDENCE THAT other crew members besides Roche had survived the attack and were picked up was overwhelming. As was the case elsewhere along the Iron Curtain, the antagonists that faced each other across the Sea of Japan on July 29, 1953, worked relentlessly at collecting intelligence about each other in every conceivable way. The RB-29 near Hokkaido, the RB-50G at Vladivostok, the two MiG-17s, and other aircraft were not the only ones present in the air over the Sea of Japan that day, if electronic intrusion can be called a presence. U.S. radar operators in Japan watched one of the MiGs track and attack the ferret from behind and below, just as Roche described it to Weyland and the others. The MiG "proceeded in a southerly direction for two minutes and then turned in a northwesterly direction closing on the apparent route of the RB-50," one radar report said, even giving the stalker's altitude as 16,400 feet. The two SB-29s sent out to find the missing ferret were also closely tracked. And the Russians were not only tracking the Americans on radar but were, in turn, intercepting U.S. radio traffic.

The SB-29 that dropped the lifeboat, piloted by Maj. Edwin P. Gourley, took off at one o'clock that afternoon, six hours after the second position report failed to come in. When crewmen on the plane finally spotted an oil slick and Roche's dye marker through broken fog, they saw two groups of survivors, according to Gourley: "Two survivors at the marker dye [O'Kelley and Roche] and three to four survivors at the edge of the oil slick." He also reported that the pilot of the other rescue plane told him by radio that he saw nine patrol boats in the area. Other reports said twelve.

But according to Jack Parrish and John Wagner, a "black-bottom" RB-50G navigator who often flew penetrations deep into Siberia, there was more. Parrish and Wagner, two other lucky men, were in the crew that was supposed to have flown 9653's mission that night. But their own RB-50G developed engine trouble, so they landed in Hawaii for repairs and didn't get to Japan until a week later. O'Kelley volunteered to go in their place. Soon after their arrival at Misawa Air Base in northern Honshu, Parrish, Wagner, and others in the crew were having breakfast at the officers' club before making a "trip" over Siberia when they noticed that Gourley's crew was also having breakfast. That led to an enlightening conversation.

"They were right on the deck, the rescue crew, and they say the area was full of Russian vessels: destroyer escorts, whatnot," Wagner said, recounting what the SB-29 crew had told them. "They [the Russians] knew this was going to happen. They saw one destroyer escort—they were right on the deck—and they swore by all that's holy that they saw four, and possibly five, of our flyers being pulled out of the water and onto the destroyer escort."

Jack Parrish vividly remembered hearing the story, too. It lent credibility to Roche's claim that the Russians were waiting for them. And there was more. Parrish eventually wound up in Air Force intelligence in the Pentagon (the "Head Shed") and held several high-security clearances. There, he learned for the first time that communication intelligence had been collected constantly by National Security Agency intercept stations in Japan. He was unequivocal in claiming that the NSA listened to and recorded Russian seamen reporting by radio that they were pulling the Americans out of the water. "They were poised to do that. This thing was not just a happenstance," Parrish said, adding that O'Kelley was briefed to fly a virtual attack heading on Vladivostok to get its radar turned on. Parrish also believed that the RB-50G was shot down in retaliation for the Il-12 attack. "It was planned," he said. "They were just waiting for the next guy to come along. He [O'Kelley] was pretty deep into the bay. I didn't know O'Kelley well, but I don't think that he was the type that would have deliberately exercised them on his own. . . . We were told what to do, where to go, and what they wanted."

James M. Doyle, a Navy enlisted man who monitored Soviet traffic from March 1953 to March 1955 at the top-secret Kami-Seya Radio Facility near the Atsugi Naval Air Base in Japan, was on duty when *Little Red Ass* was attacked. He supported Parrish. In a hand-printed memo dated "Fall—1996," Doyle wrote that the ferret became lost in "heavy weather," was actually intercepted "and shot up some 44 miles inside Russian territory," but managed to make it to the sea before going down. "Subsequent intercepts indicated that two (possibly three) Soviet 'PT' type boats arrived on the scene within an hour and picked up sixteen (16) survivors and one body," he wrote. "These boats were then directed to proceed to the Vladivostok Navy Base." Another intercept described several Soviet ships hurriedly weighing anchor in Vladivostok and heading toward the northern sector of the search area, and then south, right into it. They included destroyers, minelayers, minesweepers, submarines, subchasers, and even the cruiser *Kalinin*. Meanwhile, Soviet aircraft flew observation missions, and so, of course, did the U.S. Air Force and Navy. With so many Soviet and American ships and planes roaming through a relatively small area at a moment of high tension, the scene was set for a confrontation that could easily have escalated into a sea and air battle.

While the number of survivors in Doyle's memo seems high, his account of the rescue squares not only with Gourley's, Parrish's, and Wagner's, but with that of a Russian antiaircraft gunner, Sgt. Georgi Y. Kravchenko, who watched from Russkiy Island, off Vladivostok, as the plane came under attack almost over his head. He later claimed to have seen seven parachutes blossom.

It also squares with a briefing given to President Eisenhower and other members of the National Security Council the day after the shootdown. The briefer was no less than Gen. Omar N. Bradley, the first permanent chairman of the Joint Chiefs of Staff and one of the president's former comrades in arms. Bradley told the men who sat around the long table in the White House that "one survivor was picked up and four other survivors were sighted and were believed to have been picked up by Soviet PT boats."

Ike's reaction reflected a reality that was starkly different from the ritualized lying and posturing that came out of the Department of State and the Kremlin's Foreign Ministry. "Both we and the Russians know that if U.S. planes go toward Vladivostok they are not simply on a training mission," he said. "Hence the incident was not as unprovoked as it might appear to be at first glance."

It was taken as gospel, then, that telling the truth about the circumstances of the shootdown would have subverted a greater truth: that the United States and its allies had to conduct such missions to be able to win an all-out war. No compromise was believed feasible. That in turn led to something else that was implicit: the survivors of the RB-50G, and any others who fell into the hands of the enemy, would be written off. When the United States protested, according to one highly knowledgeable individual, the Russians "told us to stuff it." It was therefore "a problem without a solution," he said.

Since the Russians adamantly denied they had picked up survivors, an unspoken understanding took hold behind the scenes on both sides that led to a kind of political puppet show that would go on for years. On October 9, 1954, the Department of State announced that Ambassador Bohlen had handed the Soviet Foreign Office a note charging $2,785,492.94 in damages for the destruction of 9653. The document added that if the Kremlin denied responsibility for the attack, as it had done repeatedly, the matter should be taken to the International Court of Justice. Finally, it demanded the release of the plane's survivors. The puppeteers knew perfectly well that the Russians weren't going to pay up, and had no intention of taking the matter to The Hague. And however heroic the prisoners were in the eyes of the few countrymen who knew what they had been doing, they were spies to their captors: spies who would be interrogated for their considerable technical knowledge and then used as forced labor. The prisoners would in no circumstance be repatriated.

TWO YEARS AFTER the shootdown, the government declared the remaining crewmen officially dead. The coming of the war in Vietnam, and then détente between Richard Nixon and Leonid Brezhnev, created new and daunting problems and prospects that were set in a context infinitely larger than the fate of Stan O'Kel-ley's crew and several others who disappeared on similar missions. It was never officially articulated, but the time came when the survivors became an inconvenience to both sides. They gradually turned into an annoyance and then a potential impediment to improving relations between the two superpowers. They became a minor obstacle to getting on with the business of the world. The argument that they had been captured was finally turned on its head by their own government, which came to insist that not a shred of evidence existed that any of them had been taken prisoner. Their plight was subsumed by history's weightier concerns and they were therefore studiously ignored and allowed to fade quietly into the cold war's twilight.

Jim Keeffe, the weather officer, retired as a lieutenant colonel. Many years after the loss of 9653, he still carried his own abiding anger about the way the prisoner issue was handled.

"I am now convinced that we were lied to by our government as to the final disposition of the other thirteen members of that crew. . . . When I took an oath of office, I made a contract with the United States Government," he said. "And what we have to realize is that government is people in this country. We are not a theocracy. There are two sides to a contract. My side is that I will obey; I will carry out my orders. The other side of the contract is that we will *never* walk off and leave people. . . . We're probably dealing with one of the blackest periods of activity of the United States government in its entire history," he went on. "In my opinion, this was heinous. They have lied to the families. They have lied to the sons and daughters. They have lied to us at the base. It is a breach of contract and it borders on criminal activity."

A SPECTRE HAUNTING AMERICA

THE RATIONALE FOR the destruction of American society was laid out in 1848 with the publication of *The Communist Manifesto*.

"A spectre is haunting Europe: the spectre of Communism. All the Powers of old Europe have entered into a holy alliance to exorcize this spectre. . . ." With those words, Karl Marx and his patron, Friedrich Engels, began one of the most influential and inflammatory treatises ever written. Their point was that capitalism—the system that was fueling the industrial revolution in Europe and the great democratic experiment in America—concentrated wealth in the hands of a bourgeois minority by ruthlessly exploiting the oppressed proletarian majority. Since the exploiters would never give up their wealth and privilege without a struggle—would not go quietly—there was no alternative but revolution. And the revolution would inevitably be destructive and bloody.

What was fundamentally new about the manifesto was that it attacked neither a religion nor a nation. It attacked one class on behalf of another. That made communism international, not nationalistic, since the downtrodden were everywhere. The impoverished and exploited masses in Europe and elsewhere had more in common with each other, according to the new doctrine, than they did with their greedy and oppressive bosses and landowners.

Not many in the West who studied Marxism and kept track of the news coming out of Russia, starting in the tumultuous winter of 1917–18 and afterward, would have doubted that Vladimir I. Lenin and his Bolshevik successors intended to spread the revolution on a sea of blood if that's what it took. The brutality in Russia, including the murders of the deposed czar Nicholas II and his family, was well known to attentive Europeans and Americans. So was the revolution's violent aftermath, which included assassinations, a civil war, and the ritualistic madness of the great purges unleashed by Lenin and then Stalin. Lavrenty P. Beria, Stalin's security overlord and coordinator of the later terrors, was a ferocious sociopath.

That is not to say the revolution didn't have partisans in the West. The best known of them, a journalist named John Reed, was in Petrograd (now St. Petersburg) when the Bolsheviks seized power and described what he saw in reverential terms in a riveting book, *Ten Days That Shook the World*. Reed, like other radical utopians, believed in the necessity of revolution years before it happened in Russia and accepted the violence as a price that had to be paid for the emancipation of the working class; that the end, as he and other radicals put it, justified the means. His coverage of a silk worker's strike in Paterson, New Jersey, in 1913 for a magazine called *The Masses* permanently changed him politically, and he spent the remaining seven years of his life working fervently for the cause. And there were others, many of them journalists and writers, who also supported communism—not necessarily the Russian variety—out of sheer altruism.

During the twenty years between the world wars, the United States went through its own upheavals, and the Reds, as they were called, seemed always to be in the shadows. Trade unionism, which was often—and usually erroneously—associated with the far left, grew substantially. And 1929 brought a depression that caused social turmoil throughout the country. Layoffs and forced migrations were facts of life, and so were bread lines and soup kitchens. The system was not effectively taking care of its citizens, as the Communist Party of the United States of America, by then a strident and highly dedicated group, repeatedly bellowed. The

CPUSA was led by a firebrand named Earl Browder, claimed from 50,000 to 75,000 members, and published its own newspaper, *The Daily Worker*.

Whatever the banter about universal brotherhood and a workers' paradise, in reality "the Party" exercised iron discipline over its idealistic members and single-mindedly tried to infiltrate the nation's scientific, political, and industrial establishment and either start "youth" organizations or co-opt existing ones. Democrats and Republicans squabbled endlessly within their own untidy ranks and between parties. But the Party exercised discipline that would have been the envy of the Marine Corps.

Herbert A. Philbrick, a young Boston advertising executive, joined the Party in 1940, then spied on it for J. Edgar Hoover's FBI, and finally turned his counterespionage work into a book and then an early television series called *I Led Three Lives*. Richard Carlson, an actor specializing in sympathetic guy-next-door types, played a naive Philbrick who gradually, horrifyingly, came to understand that he was being duped by commie-automatons who were out to take over the country and then the world. The book and the weekly programs vividly described an Orwellian organization that did not tolerate political deviation and that treated the tenets of Marxism-Leninism the way divinity schools treat the Bible.

Clandestine meetings in members' homes were described as ideological seminars in which the United States was systematically bashed and Marxism-Leninism was taught as a political catechism. "Independent thinking was not condoned," Philbrick wrote. "There was a straight and narrow line to follow, and in our discussions we would reach an impasse and progress no further every time I injected an alien thought, until the comrades were certain that my deviation on each point had been erased and a 'proper' Marxist viewpoint instilled in its place." The rigid discipline rested on the infallibility of the Party, the righteousness of the cause, and the danger posed by the ruthless, reactionary bourgeoisie, its insidious informers, and Hoover's minions.

Philbrick's revelations, which would prove to be accurate, were nonetheless a melodramatic depiction. But there were people in Washington who took the Communist threat seriously. As early as

1938, a defecting Soviet general named Walter Krivitsky warned the Department of State that agents from Moscow's State Political Administration, or GPU, were working out of the Soviet embassy in Washington and in New York. He published a series of articles in *The Saturday Evening Post* about Soviet espionage in the United States and testified on the subject before Congress. Krivitsky constantly worried that Soviet agents were going to assassinate him; he even told a member of the congressional committee that "if they ever try to prove that I took my own life, don't believe them."

On the morning of February 10, 1941, a maid found Krivitsky's body sprawled on a bed in a fifth-floor room of the Hotel Bellevue in Washington. He had been shot in the head with a .38-caliber revolver. The weapon was near his right hand, but fingerprints were obliterated by blood. Three notes, apparently written by Krivitsky, were also found. One of them, to his wife, was in Russian and mentioned his "sins." The death of Walter Krivitsky, who was born Samuel Ginzberg in the Ukraine, remains one of the enduring enigmas of the cold war's formative years.

Philbrick noted in *I Led Three Lives* that his brethren in the Party went from being "violently antiwar" before Hitler attacked the Soviet Union to favoring all-out intervention after the panzers starting rolling east on June 22, 1941. The doctrinal about-face literally happened overnight, which must have confused at least some of the faithful. "The people," he quoted *The Daily Worker* as trumpeting, "demand aid to Europe now!"

Not all the people. Most Americans were not anxious to jump into war and embrace the Soviet cause. Significantly, George F. Kennan was one of them. Kennan had served in the U.S. embassy in Moscow in the 1930s and observed Stalin's infamous purge trials. Two days after the Nazi attack, he wrote a letter to his friend, Loy Henderson, the deputy chief of the Division of European Affairs at State. Kennan said in part, "We should do nothing at home to make it appear that we are following the course Churchill seems to have entered upon in extending moral support to the Russian cause in the present Russian-German conflict." Treating the Russians like partners in defense of democracy, he went on, would actually lend an aura of morality to the Nazis.

Kennan made his case by saying that portraying the Kremlin as a protector of democracy would amount to identifying with "the Russian destruction of the Baltic states, with the attack against Finnish independence, with the partitioning of Poland and Rumania, with the crushing of religion throughout Eastern Europe, and with the domestic policy of a regime widely feared and detested throughout this part of the world and the methods of which are far from democratic. It is, I believe, no exaggeration to say that in every border country concerned, from Scandinavia—including Norway and Sweden—to the Black Sea, Russia is generally more feared than Germany."

Harry Truman noted in his own memoirs that there was an amorphous, "friendly feeling in America toward Russia," because the Russians suffered horrendous casualties fighting the Germans, and in doing so "saved us many lives." That may have been true. But whatever middle Americans felt about the Russians, the political, economic, and military establishment—the insiders—had few illusions. Kennan's attitude was shared by many knowledgeable people in Washington and London who took the Reds to be untrustworthy, pathologically suspicious, and belligerent. At one point, Churchill even threatened to stop supply convoys to Murmansk unless Royal Navy crews were treated decently there.

And, all too typically, the Kremlin stubbornly refused to cooperate in a number of important ways. It would not return three B-29s that had diverted to one of its air bases in the Far East after bombing Japan, for example, or share data on a captured German experimental U-boat with American naval experts, even though that knowledge could have helped protect convoys bound for the USSR.

One of the confiscated bombers, *Ramp Tramp*, made an emergency landing at Vladivostok on July 29, 1944, after a raid over Manchuria. Its crew naively assumed their plane would be repaired and allowed to return to their base in China. They made it home, but *Ramp Tramp* and the other two Superforts became spoils of war. Two of the bombers were painstakingly taken apart, literally bolt by bolt, with each part systematically measured and photographed. Andrei Tupolev's design bureau then used reverse engineering to produce exact copies, which would come out of the war as Tu-4s, whose long range threatened the United States.

Certainly the upper echelons at the Department of State, the Department of Justice, and the Pentagon were well aware of Communist objectives and Soviet history under Stalin. They understood that their country and the USSR had fundamental political differences that Communist dogma insisted could be settled only by violent confrontation. That being so, the American intellectual and political establishment—the members of what Columbia University sociologist C. Wright Mills would later call the power elite—also knew that it was not John Stuart Mill and Thomas Jefferson who held the estranged bedfellows together. It was Adolf Hitler. It didn't take an oracle to predict that after the Führer and his Reich had been destroyed, there would be a falling out among the victors that would reach historic and dangerous proportions.

AT THE SAME time, the men who looked sourly out at the world from atop the Kremlin Wall knew that their own country, a huge landmass in the heart of Eurasia, had been a tempting target for invaders from every direction for centuries. There had been attacks by Tatars, Mongols, Swedes, the French, the British, the Ottomans—Islam was and remained a crescent of danger that stretched from Sinkiang Province in western China to the Bosporus—the Germans, and even the Americans. Churchill's reaction to the 1917 revolution had been to call for Bolshevism to be strangled in its cradle: Allied expeditionary forces actually landed at Murmansk and then Archangel and Vladivostok in 1918 and 1919 to help White Russian counterrevolutionaries. Every schoolchild in the Soviet Union knew Americans had been part of the force that, however ineffectively, had menaced their country. The men in the Kremlin lived, as had their grandparents and their grandparents' grandparents, surrounded by covetous and often brutal enemies. The proper response seemed to lie in strength: strong leaders and strong military. The leaders took it as a fact of life that their homeland had to be militarily powerful and had to spy on and subvert the enemy at every opportunity or be devoured.

. . .

ON MAY 7, 1943, while lend-lease arms were pouring into the Soviet Union from the United States and both nations were about
halfway through their grand alliance against the Axis, J. Edgar
Hoover wrote a letter to Harry Hopkins, Franklin Roosevelt's top
adviser, noting yet another spy operation. The director of the FBI
said that a month earlier, Vassili Zubilin, a third secretary at the
Soviet embassy, had gone to Oakland to turn over money to a
leading official of the CPUSA for the express purpose of "placing
Communist Party members and Comintern agents in industries
engaged in secret war production for the United States Government so that information could be obtained for transmittal to the
Soviet Union."

Hoover sent a stream of such warnings to the Roosevelt and
then the Truman White Houses. Robert Louis Benson and
Michael Warner, the editors of *Venona*, a book that details Soviet
espionage against the United States from 1939 to 1957, note that
it is not clear how many of the warnings actually reached the
presidents or how seriously they were taken. That is correct. But
the threat was taken with utmost seriousness by those who were
responsible for combating it and collecting information on what
was seen as a growing Soviet menace: the FBI and military intelligence and, later, the CIA and the National Security Agency. The
CIA, NSA, and the military would bear primary responsibility for
collecting intelligence on the Soviet Union after the war, and
their leaders were in turn well aware of how important intelligence was to their nation's enemies.

The Manhattan Project—the program to build an atomic
bomb—amounted to a sea change where Soviet intelligence was
concerned. While traditional spying on the United States and the
West had focused on helping defeat Germany and provide short-
cuts for Soviet science and manufacturing, the atomic bomb program quickly turned the United States itself into the Soviet
Union's paramount threat. Even as the war with Germany and
Japan went on, then, the Kremlin's vast intelligence apparatus—
very much including the Party—focused on getting the bomb. If it
worked, the atomic bomb would be a weapon of Promethean pro-

portions that would change international relations profoundly. The seriousness with which the Soviets took the coming threat from the West and the nuclear espionage program can be judged by its code name: Enormous.

The seriousness was not misplaced. Whatever the American public thought of relations with its Soviet ally, Truman had no illusions about what lay ahead. He knew that after Roosevelt returned from Yalta and his meeting there with Churchill and Stalin, FDR had brooded about aggressive Soviet moves in liberated Europe. Two weeks after Roosevelt's death in April 1945, Truman himself was briefed about the atomic bomb. "If it explodes as I think it will," he said after the briefing, "I'll certainly have a hammer on those boys." He meant the Russians. Even before the war, Truman had shown no sentimentality toward them. After Germany invaded the Soviet Union, the then senator from Missouri had remarked cynically, "If we see that Germany is winning, we ought to help Russia. And if Russia is winning, we ought to help Germany. And in that way, let them kill as many [of each other] as possible."

Having gotten word that the Trinity atomic bomb test at Alamogordo had worked, Truman casually mentioned to an impassive Stalin at the Potsdam conference in July 1945 that the United States had "a new weapon of unusual destructive force." Stalin would have known about the bomb. Days later, Hiroshima and then Nagasaki were bombed. Rumors would persist for years that, in addition to wanting to end the war and prevent an estimated quarter of a million to half a million American casualties,* Tru-

---

*That number, to which Winston Churchill subscribed, has been challenged. Rufus E. Miles, Jr., a former fellow at Princeton University's Woodrow Wilson School, has made the point that Japan's military was so decisively broken by the summer of 1945 that it could put up no serious defense against an Allied invasion. The fire-bombing of Tokyo at the end of March killed or injured more people—83,000—than the Hiroshima bomb itself, which killed or wounded between 70,000 and 80,000. Miles points out that the situation was so dire by July 12 that Foreign Minister Tojo, following the emperor's instructions, ordered the Japanese ambassador in Moscow to tell Vyacheslav Molotov, the Soviet foreign minister, that the emperor wanted the war to end immediately on almost any terms acceptable to the United States. Washington was aware of this communication because naval intelligence intercepted and decoded the cables. Furthermore, an intensified bombing and a blockade through November 1 would have effectively finished off Japan. And even an invasion of Kyushu after the renewed bombing would have resulted in negligible American casualties, Miles calculates, roughly on the order of 15,000. (Miles, "Hiroshima: The Strange Myth of Half a Million American Lives Saved," *passim*.)

man authorized the use of the bomb to demonstrate the "hammer" to Stalin. Whether that is true or not, the fact that it was used at all led some Americans to help the Soviet Union get its own nuclear weapons. They reasoned that their country would be less likely to use atomic bombs again if its new enemy—the nation that was the womb of the largest utopian social experiment in history—had them as well; that there was safety in numbers.

But Soviet sympathizers in the West had to come to grips with the fact that their allegiance to utopianism was being subverted by a nation-state that, far from withering away as Marxist theory predicted, was intent on accumulating enormous power. Stalin, after all, had signed a nonaggression pact with Hitler, the patron saint of fascism. Russians had responded to the blitzkrieg, not as Communists, but as defenders of their homes and country. And they answered America's overwhelming industrial capacity, huge numbers of conventional weapons, and its nuclear capability, with dogmatic patriotism. The survival of the state was in no way mitigated by Marxist ideology. "What is vital," Kennan would write in a famous article that appeared in the journal *Foreign Affairs* in July 1947, and which he signed with an "X," "is that the 'Socialist fatherland'—that oasis of power which has been already won for Socialism in the person of the Soviet Union—should be cherished and defended by all good Communists at home and abroad, its fortunes promoted, its enemies badgered and confounded."

On the evening of September 5, 1945—twenty-two days after the end of the war—a code clerk who worked for Soviet military intelligence in the embassy in Ottawa walked out of the building with more than one hundred documents stuffed under his shirt and defected. His name was Igor Gouzenko, and the documents he carried indicated that the Manhattan Project to develop the atomic bomb and a number of U.S. agencies had been penetrated by Communist subversives. Weeks later, Elizabeth Bentley, a ranking member of the Party, began months of supplying the FBI with the names of highly placed agents within the government, including a White House aide and Harry Dexter White, the assistant secretary of the treasury. Whittaker Chambers, a *Time* magazine editor and former Soviet agent, also provided the names of infiltrators, first to Adolf A. Berle at the Department of State and then to the FBI. The Party and its sympathizers reacted with wrath, denouncing both Bentley, who was called a traitor, a liar, and a criminal by her old comrades, and Chambers, who was smeared as an "unstable, pathological liar." Both were eventually vindicated. For a while, in fact, the FBI considered using Bentley as a "double" against the Soviet spy agency but dropped the idea.

On February 22, 1946, Kennan, by then the Paul Revere of the Department of State, sent a very long, richly detailed telegram from Moscow back to Foggy Bottom warning of the danger. "We have here a political force committed fanatically to the belief that with US there can be no permanent modus vivendi, that it is desirable and necessary that the internal harmony of our society be disrupted, our traditional way of life be destroyed, the international authority of our state be broken, if Soviet power is to be secure."

That year, Churchill coined the term "Iron Curtain" to describe the growing Communist threat: a wall of obsessive secrecy and pervasive tyranny. And as if to underscore his point, Communist guerrillas in Greece who had fought the Nazis moved into the mountains in the north and began a civil war. The British had a strategic stake in the eastern Mediterranean because of Arab oil and the Suez Canal, but they came out of the war too weak to help Athens fend off the new menace. Doing so therefore fell to the United States. "The Communists, of course, thrived on the continuing conditions of misery, starvation, and economic ruin," Truman would recall in his memoirs. "Moscow and the Balkan satellite countries were now rendering open support to the EAM [Greek guerrillas]. Intelligence reports I received stated that many of the insurgents had been trained, indoctrinated, armed, and equipped at various camps beyond the Greek borders. Under Soviet direction, the report said, Greece's northern neighbors—Yugoslavia, Bulgaria, and Albania—were conducting a drive to establish a Communist Greece." And then a Communist Turkey, which not only would spread the Marxist gospel but, more important, would insulate Russians from their ancient Islamic enemies the way the Eastern European puppet regimes insulated them from the Germans and the West. Truman's response was to draw a line. He pumped a massive amount of food and materiel, including arms, into Greece as part of a new doctrine, named after him, that resisted Communist expansion by shoring up threatened countries. And he dispatched a battleship to the Mediterranean and B-29s to Great Britain.

Meanwhile, subversion boiled at home. In 1947, the Army Security Agency used the wiretapping operation code-named Venona to find out that the Soviets had an important "asset" in the War Department. It also showed the Soviet spy agency was conducting massive espionage operations in the United States, and certainly within the nuclear weapons program. Massive indeed. It was the eve of a wrenching, sobering time in American history, a time when the average citizen's simplistic view of the war—that it had been good versus evil—was abruptly changed by revelations that the evil was not entirely on the other side of some border. Suddenly, evil was right at home, among all the people, feeding off the system and trying to kill it like a cancer.

The Venona intercepts led to Judith Coplon, a Department of Justice analyst recruited by the Soviets in 1944, who was identified in 1948. She would be followed by a rogues' gallery of spies, the most notorious of whom were Klaus Fuchs (who had worked on the Manhattan Project), Harry Gold, David Greenglass, Julius and Ethel Rosenberg, and Alger Hiss. The net spread to Great Britain, where Donald Maclean of the Foreign Office and a compatriot named Guy Burgess were uncovered. Both escaped to the Sovict Union a step ahead of British counterintelligence. In the United States, evidence that Soviet agents had penetrated the defense establishment, including the nuclear weapons program, was coming from defectors like Bentley and Chambers, U.S. agents, and Venona.

The nation writhed in the revelations. The Republican right began to accuse the Roosevelt and Truman administrations of being "soft" on communism overseas—of giving away Eastern Europe—and of being dangerously lax at home. The House Un-American Activities Committee would soon put Hollywood filmmakers on a blacklist and Sen. Joseph R. McCarthy would conduct extensive hearings and blame Communists in the Department of State for "losing" China. Anyone even suspected of having Communist sympathies was branded a "pinko" or a "fellow traveler." Americans with socialist inclinations camouflaged themselves as "Progressives." There was fear in the land.

In 1950, Howard Hughes's RKO Radio Pictures released *I Married a Communist,* a pandering potboiler that tried to capitalize on the growing anti-Communist paranoia. The film did so badly at the box office when it opened that its title was quickly changed to *The Woman on Pier 13*, which implied sex and mystery. The movie was a parody of itself, but it did capture the spirit of the time. The woman in question, Christine, is a beautiful Communist seductress who seeks to lure a naive Don Lowry into the Party and also to take over the San Francisco waterfront. The Commies are portrayed like the demonic vampires in horror stories who live off the blood of their unwary, virginal victims. Then the seduced victims become vampires themselves. Here is how wise Jim Travis, who knows as much about the true nature of Communists as the character Abraham Van Helsing knew about vampires in *Dracula*, describes the peril:

"I'm not talking politics," Jim warned. "I'm talking about Commies. They're not a party of the masses. They don't want the masses. They're a party of the select few—who think they can impose on the masses their idea of what's good for them. Don, I wouldn't be lecturing *you* if I didn't think a lot of your family. There's one thing I *know*—that it's time you found out. Because they *are* a party of the few out to boss the world—every Commie has to be an active conspirator—recruit stooges—who usually don't even know they're being used. Well-meaning liberals—the underprivileged—the unemployed—and lovesick kids like *you*."

Van Helsing knew that the sign of the cross would hold a vampire at bay, but the only way to kill one was to drive a stake through its heart. In a matter of speaking, the same applied to the Commies.

BY THE END of 1946, there was little pretense that the old alliance between the USSR and the West was still intact. Large portions of Eastern Europe were under Soviet control and Communist parties were gaining footholds in a Western Europe still digging out of the debris of war. Kennan's 1947 article in *Foreign Affairs*

called for the "long-term, patient but firm and vigilant containment of Russian expansive tendencies." "Containment" was the
operative word. The old Russia had suggested that the West stop
making concessions to the Kremlin, do what it could to inspire
and support resistance to Soviet expansion, and wait for internal
weaknesses and frustrations to moderate the Kremlin's behavior.
After he returned from Moscow to Washington, Kennan quietly
metamorphosed into one of the early cold warriors. While going
to war was abhorrent to him, and he believed implicitly that history was on the side of the West, Kennan hatched a secret program, backed by CIA director Allen W. Dulles, designed to use
political warfare, including sabotage, subversion, and propaganda,
plus guerrilla warfare, to crack the Iron Curtain from within. The
idea was to make trouble for the Soviets by keeping them off balance and on the defensive. To that end, a top-secret organization
with the suitably ambiguous name of the Office of Policy Coordination was invented and given a multimillion-dollar budget.
Displaced persons of every stripe, including unrepentant Nazis,
monarchists, patriots from the countries that had been swallowed
by the Kremlin, and plain adventurers, were recruited and cob-
bled into resistance groups whose mission was to penetrate the
Communist system and weaken it from within. But quibbling
groups of émigrés, incompetent and uncoordinated planning,
plain bungling by altruistic amateurs, and tip-offs by high-level
Soviet moles such as Kim Philby turned the operation into a pathetic and usually a tragic failure. The OPC was folded into the
CIA in 1952 and quietly evaporated. The cold war had long since
been under way.

The National Security Act of 1947 created a National Security
Council that was responsible for, in Truman's words, "appraising
the national security of the United States and dealing with national security problems of common interest to all segments of
the government." The act also created the CIA to consolidate
civilian intelligence collection. It reported to the NSC. In addition, the National Defense Act, which was signed on July 26 of
that year, turned the venerable War Department into a consolidated Department of Defense that included the Army, the Navy,
and a new fully independent Air Force.

When Western military planners looked east during the winter of 1945–46, they saw the forces of communism—the forces Marx and Engels had predicted would inevitably annihilate them—occupying territory stretching from Berlin to the Bering Sea. Taken as a single political entity (which was simplistic but understandable), the Communists held the largest consolidated territory of any power in history. Planners—strategists—who had taken university-level geography would have studied Sir Halford Mackinder, and that would have made them uneasy. In 1904, the British scholar who established geography as an academic discipline wrote that Eurasia was the Earth's "world-island," and its center—western Russia—was the world-island's "heartland." Everywhere else, including the Western Hemisphere, was geographically peripheral. Who controls the heartland, Mackinder postulated, controls the world-island. Who controls the world-island controls the world. The Nazis who planned the invasion of the Soviet Union had read Mackinder and took him seriously.

Long-range strategic bombing and nuclear weapons made the world-island vulnerable to devastating attack from the air. But it still remained a vast, fearsome bastion with tremendous military and industrial potential and, by its sheer size, an intimidating neighbor and strategic adversary. No one would have taken Stalin seriously if he had been the premier of Liechtenstein. And the cradle of communism not only was huge, it had an army—the Red Army—widely respected for its bravery, tenacity, and endurance. Hitler's tanks and Stuka dive-bombers had done no better against Russian soldiers than had Napoleon's dragoons and artillery. By war's end, the battle of Stalingrad, in which the Russians suffered a million casualties turning back the Germans, was legendary. Finally, and most ominously, the guardians of the cradle were known to be working on nuclear weapons. "In the summer of 1947 the U.S.S.R. had not yet detonated its first atomic bomb," the physicist Robert L. Park has recalled, "but it had become clear by then that it was only a matter of time."

With the guns barely cool, the United States looked both east and west and thought it saw a malevolent adversary that appeared sworn to its destruction and that posed the greatest threat to the country that had ever existed. The political establishment and many ordinary Americans believed the Soviet Union had a huge army, a large and submissive population, spies everywhere, and soon would have city-busting nuclear weapons carried in aircraft and mounted on missiles. And they were convinced that immense power would be wielded by a small group of despotic ideologues led by Joseph Stalin, who was portrayed—correctly—as a ruthless mass killer. And thanks to the Kremlin's penchant for institutionalized secrecy, brought on by its own paranoia, the West faced its new arch foe with appallingly little hard information. The need for intelligence began to loom.

AT THE SAME time Stalin, his General Staff, and the men in the Politboro had only to look at the rubble of Hiroshima and Nagasaki to see that the United States had no apparent compunction about obliterating whole cities with atomic bombs. The men in the Kremlin were therefore haunted by their own spectre. The United States emerged from World War II as the most powerful nation on Earth. The "arsenal of democracy" had forged a highly mechanized army, a huge, two-ocean navy with far-ranging carriers and submarines, and an air force with bombers that could strike anywhere at will. All three services were being supplied with atomic weapons (the Army would call its short-lived nuclear cannon "Atomic Annie"). The U.S. military was now spread around the world, both in the vanquished nations and in others. Behind that wall of soldiers, sailors, and airmen was a robust economy and the most vigorous scientific establishment and industrial base in existence.

The Soviet Union, in sharp contrast, had lost at least 25 million people in what was referred to as the Great Patriotic War, and was largely a plundered and demolished wreck, at least west of the Urals. If one believed in the tenets of realpolitik, and Stalin and his ministers and generals certainly did, there would never be a better time to carry out Churchill's original plan: kill the great socialist experiment once and for all. If history held one immutable lesson for Russia, it was that the temptation for its enemy to finish it off while it was crippled would be overwhelming. Massive rearmament, the acquisition of buffer zones, and atomic bombs and the bombers to carry them were therefore given the highest priority.

The adversaries were drifting into a dangerous cycle of self-reinforcing mutual escalation. They quickly became determined to check every threat with a greater threat. An arms race of unprecedented proportion began to ratchet up relentlessly. The justification for a continuous escalation in the number and killing capacity of weapons, the incessant subversion and espionage, and the political maneuvering was an ambiguous and elusive goal called national security. But there was no national security. The more the opponents strove for national security, the more they armed and subverted, the less secure they became.

DWIGHT EISENHOWER, the Army's chief of staff at the end of the war, had been won over to airpower. As supreme Allied commander, he had seen armadas of his own and RAF bombers smash the Third Reich, and B-29s do the same to Japan from remote bases on Pacific islands. By January 29, 1946, while GIs by the many thousands were being released and weapons were being scrapped in the largest demobilization in the country's history, Eisenhower reached a basic agreement with his victorious and very proud air staff that reflected the country's abruptly changed strategic situation. The combat nucleus of the Army Air Forces would henceforth consist of three distinct commands: defense, tactical, and strategic. The Air Defense Command would protect the United States from air attack. The Tactical Air Command, or TAC, would be responsible for relatively short-range tactical air operations such as air-to-air combat, close-in ground support, and theater reconnaissance. Finally, there would be a Strategic Air Command. As its name implied, SAC would be designed to wage strategic aerial warfare: to carry high explosives or nuclear weapons over long distances to the enemy's heartland.

All three combat commands officially came into being on March 21, 1946. They were all equal rectangles on organization charts. But in reality, SAC was given a disproportionately large share of funding because everyone understood the atomic age was changing the nature of strategic warfare. The long-range bomber force was of overriding importance because in 1946 it alone was able to attack relatively quickly over intercontinental distances and well inside enemy territory. Strategic bombardment during World War II had turned the home front—the place that fed and armed the military—into a prime target. "Global reach" was the new military reality.

SAC's mission was spelled out this way: "Conduct long range offensive operations in any part of the world either independently or in cooperation with land and naval forces; to conduct maximum reconnaissance over land or sea either independently or in cooperation with naval forces; to provide combat units capable of intense and sustained combat operations employing the latest and most advanced weapons; to train units and personnel for the maintenance of the Strategic Forces in all parts of the world; to perform such special missions as the Commanding General, Army Air Forces may direct." It all came down to long-range offensive operations—heavy bombardment—and maximum reconnaissance for the collection of intelligence.

On September 14, 1946, Army Air Forces Chief of Staff Henry H. "Hap" Arnold ordered Gen. Carl A. Spaatz to chair a secret board that would consider atomic weapons as they related to the AAF. The board's report, submitted on October 23, formed the doctrinal nucleus of Air Force policy for decades to come. It asserted that the Army Air Forces ought to be directly represented in all War Department planning where atomic energy was concerned. More to the point, the Spaatz Board concluded that the only defense against atomic attack was to destroy the planes carrying the bombs in the air or on the ground. Therefore, the report went on, "We must be prepared for: (1) Preventive or retaliatory action. (2) Defense against attacks of all kinds." Preventive action meant striking first. The idea of a preemptive first strike, meaning as it did that much of the Soviet Union would effectively be turned into radioactive rubble, would horrify many thoughtful civilians for years. Yet striking first was an ancient strategy that was justified by the imperative to win. Hannibal staged a surprise attack when he took his elephants over the Alps to attack the Romans in the Po Valley in the third century B.C. The Japanese did the same at Pearl Harbor. The difference, of course, was in the nature of the weapons. The report also called for the use of forward air bases overseas for three reasons: it was better to defend against attack in other countries than in the United States; it would deny those bases to the enemy; and the bases could themselves be used for a "strategic air offensive."

The board recommended as well that the man who would represent the Air Force in all nuclear weapons and research matters be "an officer of the caliber of Maj. Gen. Curtis E. LeMay." The man who most closely fit that description was Maj. Gen. Curtis E. LeMay himself. The cigar-chomping bomber pilot was well known for masterminding the devastating bomber offensive against Japan and, more recently, for doggedly maintaining that the atomic bomb was "essentially an air weapon" whose rightful place was therefore in the Air Force.

SAC's first commander in chief was Gen. George C. Kenney, a respected veteran of the air war in the Pacific, who took charge the day SAC was formed and remained in that position for two and a half immensely chaotic years. When the Air Force became a separate service in its own right in 1947, it was caught in the demobilization, along with the other services, and it therefore was hemorrhaging skilled officers and enlisted men who wanted to shed their uniforms and grab a piece of the economic boom. Furthermore, all three armed services were stuck with obsolescent weapons and other equipment. This was particularly troubling for the Air Force because almost overnight the jet plane had turned the largest armada of fighters, bombers, and transports in the world into a collection of poorly maintained, propeller-driven antiques. On May 16, 1948, for example, 180 of SAC's B-29s were ordered to fly a "maximum effort" simulated attack against New York City. Seventy-nine of them couldn't even get off the ground. Kenney was a moderately effective, if distracted, leader who tried with some success to turn SAC toward the future. The man who succeeded him would accomplish that and more. And in the process he would himself become an enigmatic legend.

LeMay succeeded Kenney on October 19, 1948, and saw immediately that he had inherited a mess. When he got to SAC's new headquarters at Offutt Air Force Base outside of Omaha—in the center of the country and therefore the hardest place to reach by marauding enemy planes—he saw that no realistic training was being done and that bombing accuracy, even during daylight and at relatively low altitude, was abysmal. A policy of cross-training everybody so that almost everyone could do everyone else's job, instituted by Kenney because of a shortage of airmen, was a fiasco. It meant, in LeMay's characteristically blunt words, that "none of them were any good at anything." Everything, he added with rare diplomacy, "was in a state of confusion."

If Curtis LeMay could be characterized by a single adjective, it would be "focused." He came to SAC with a clear idea of his mandate based on a professional life spent in bombardment. LeMay's goal for his Strategic Air Command was therefore elegant in its simplicity and profound in its concept: create a nuclear strike force so powerful that it would deter war or win it.

Testifying before Congress years later, LeMay would say, "All responsible airmen agree that it is impossible to provide an airtight defense against a well coordinated and properly executed atomic bombing attack. . . . A substantial part of the offensive force will always get through the defenses. Therefore the primary defensive force becomes the offensive atomic strike capability of sufficient effectiveness to provide a deterrent force."

Since the offense had an overwhelming, if not decisive, advantage in nuclear war, LeMay believed implicitly in striking first. Waiting to be attacked—allowing nuclear weapons to destroy much of America's own strike force before launching a so-called retaliatory second strike—was incomprehensible to him. It was tantamount to allowing an opponent with a gun a first, uncontested shot before responding. In LeMay's view, a second strike doctrine invited war because it tempted the Soviet Union to take advantage of a punishing surprise attack that would bring the United States to its knees. This has been interpreted as meaning LeMay wanted to start a decisive, all-or-nothing war with the Soviet Union. It is an understandable interpretation. But it is wrong. The difference, a crucial one, is that LeMay wanted the United States to adopt a first strike doctrine—not simply strike first—in the belief that it would bring political advantage.

"Such a suggestion [to be willing to strike first] is absolutely necessary if the United States is to prevail in the diplomatic world," he wrote in *America Is in Danger*, published in 1968. "Many Americans shudder at the idea of our initiating a nuclear war, but they forget that it was precisely this suggestion—backed by known superiority—that gave President Kennedy the winning hand in the Cuban missile crisis. Deterrence cannot be achieved with a second-strike façade. Conceding the enemy the first blow simply invites him to find a way to smother our retaliation. . . . Deterrence cannot be assured in a no-win vacuum. It must rest not on the ability to withstand a first strike and retaliate effectively, but on the ability to launch a first strike and win if necessary."

What was required to create the most formidable attack force on the planet, in LeMay's view, was something that would come to be called "standardization." It rested on three basic principles. People needed to believe in what they were doing. There had to be progress, however slight, toward achieving an understandable goal. And effort and progress had to be rewarded. SAC adopted the aura of an elite institution in whose hands rested the survival of the United States and what was euphemistically called the free world. It followed that being in SAC was an honor. LeMay's remarks to Congress were reflected in his command's coat of arms: a mailed fist grasping the lightning bolts of war and the olive branch of peace. (Scholars of art history and others interested in symbolism would have noted that there were two bolts and only one branch, an indication of where the organization's emphasis lay.) SAC's motto, reflecting its role as a deterrent, was a public relations masterpiece: Peace Is Our Profession. LeMay thought it up.

During LeMay's nine years as commander of SAC—the longest stint of any commander—the organization was turned into the deadliest combat force of all time. Knowing that the Soviet Union's initial attack would have to be against his bases to reduce the nation's ability to counterattack, LeMay scattered the SAC installations and made security notoriously tight. Nuclear bombs ended forever the huge formations of bombers, such as those in the Eighth Air Force that filled the sky over Germany in World War II and saturated their targets. A single bomber could now do what 1,000 had done before, so there was no need for huge, vulnerable formations. Masses of bombers would not only make easier targets, but, more to the point, almost all of them would be superfluous. The new bomber force would rely on dispersion, coordination of the attack by time rather than space, and night flight for protection. Night operations put heavy emphasis on radar, both for navigation and bombing, so the relationship between the navigator and the bombardier grew closer and complex. There were frequent bombing competitions for trophies and unit citations to sharpen proficiency and stimulate morale. Practice missions increasingly took place at night and at the bombers' optimal attack altitude, which was generally high, rather than at low level, where it was easier to hit targets (and be hit).

SAC under LeMay used a tough rating system that made no allowance for excuses, according to Warren Austin, who was an electronic warfare officer in a huge RB-36D in 1952. "If you lost a mission it didn't help you if something had broken, because that was all part of the rating system," he explained years later. If chaff dispensers that were supposed to mask the plane from radar detection didn't work, "you lost the mission because the maintenance people were rated with the aircrews. And if you failed one mission you had to run three good ones to make up for it." Like a football coach who convinces his players they are championship caliber but must follow his plan and drill relentlessly to win, LeMay inspired awe in air and ground crews who tried hard not to come up short or make embarrassing mistakes. Part of LeMay's genius lay in the fact that he was painfully exacting but never arbitrary.

Brig. Gen. Regis F. A. Urschler vividly remembered being a young lieutenant and the copilot of a Fifty-fifth Strategic Reconnaissance Wing RB-47H when his aircraft and two others ran into very serious navigation problems on a flight from Shemya in the Aleutians to Yokota. The trouble, including much higher-than-forecast crosswinds, caused a critical fuel problem in Urschler's jet. The aircraft commander and pilot was nicknamed Stub because he always had a cigar in his mouth, in the air or on the ground. Urschler joked that his claim to fame was having more instrument time than anyone else in the squadron because the cockpit was always so full of smoke he couldn't see out and therefore had to fly on instruments. At any rate, Stub told Urschler to call Tokyo Airways for a high-frequency direction-finding signal so he could get his bearings. Meanwhile, the KC-97 tankers were having problems of their own taking off from Yokota and still more problems rendezvousing with the thirsty RB-47H. At one point, Urschler began thinking about running out of fuel before "hooking up" with a tanker and about the crew having to punch out (eject).

"I was a twenty-one-year-old kid who had been in SAC less than a year, and had heard all about LeMay," he remembered. "I'm not worrying about the ejection seat working. I'm not worrying about my parachute opening. I'm not thinking about my dinghy inflating or my life vest inflating. I'm not concerned about, are they going to find us in Tokyo Bay? What's going through my mind is standing in front of Curt LeMay, and him looking at me and saying, 'What happened? Why did you run out of gas?' *That's* what I'm thinking about. *That's* what's going through my god-damned mind. Better to die. Better to go down with the airplane," Reg Urschler explained, still in awe. It had nothing to do with punishment. It had to do with letting LeMay down; of being one of the guys who sabotaged—who *betrayed*—both the man and the superbly designed institution he had built by losing an aircraft because he and the others weren't as good as LeMay demanded they be. It would have been like having to tell Knute Rockne why he dropped the football on a kickoff on his own five-yard line and then stood looking at the thing while an opposing player landed on it. But it didn't come to that. Stub finally connected with the tanker, and after snarling at an air traffic controller who didn't think his approach was quite as neat as it should have been, he got the RB-47H onto the runway.

The bomber force's ultimate defense was not being on the ground on war day. As B-47s and then very large B-52 jets replaced piston types such as the B-29 and B-50, several of them were kept in the air at all times, along with their tankers and a flying command post, and they were fully loaded with bombs. Even a surprise attack or sabotage that destroyed every base before its planes could get off the ground would not go unpunished. Some bombers, unscathed, would retaliate. LeMay did everything but take out ads to make certain the Kremlin understood that fact.

Less obvious than the buildup of the bomber force itself was LeMay's drive to extend its striking range infinitely by creating a large and fully integrated in-flight refueling capability. No individual was wholly responsible for the technique, which began over San Diego Bay on June 27, 1923, when a hose was used to connect two Army Air Service de Havilland biplanes so seventy-five gallons of gasoline could be fed from one to the other. But LeMay should get credit for building the operation into what one historian has called "practically an air force unto itself, an 'invisible' foundation for the nation's original nuclear deterrent." Together with the forward bases called for in the Spaatz Report, in-flight refueling so extended the bomber force's range that no place in the entire expanse of denied territory, as the Communist bloc came to be called, was safe from attack. SAC bombers frequently flew extended missions to make the point in a way that was unmistakable.

On September 19, 1945—seventeen days after Japan surrendered—a trio of stripped-down B-29s flew nonstop from Hokkaido to Chicago, just short of 7,000 miles. LeMay was on one of them. Less than four years later, a B-50 named *Lucky Lady II* in SAC's Forty-third Bomb Wing became the first plane to fly around the world nonstop when it landed at Carswell Air Force Base outside of Fort Worth on March 2, 1949, after ninety-four hours in the air and several meticulously planned refuelings. Its crew was greeted by Secretary of the Air Force W. Stuart Symington, Air Force Chief of Staff Hoyt S. Vandenberg, and a gaggle of invited newspaper and magazine reporters. Such demonstrations were staged repeatedly, as one record after another was established, to demonstrate America's long nuclear reach.

In another life, LeMay would have excelled as a publicist, because he had a natural flair for public relations, subtle and blatantly obvious. SAC did not have aircrews, for example; it had combat crews. And *Combat Crew* was the name of the organization's own magazine. On the theory that a deterrent cannot work unless the opposition knows about it, he made certain that record-breaking flights got press coverage, and so did almost everything else that projected SAC's invincibility. Journalists were encouraged to write about SAC (as they were about the rest of the Air Force) and were taken on simulated attacks.* "Every hour of every day and night, men of our Strategic Air Command make dry-run A-bomb flights along the perimeter of the communist world," proclaimed the subhead of a *Saturday Evening Post* article. "A *Post* correspondent who flew one of these 3000-mile missions takes you along with the men who man our outermost ring of defense." Part of the routine was showing the combat crews racing to their bombers after the siren went off signaling a scramble. They had so many minutes to get rolling and into the air. Certainly all the practice was aimed at improving proficiency. But there was promotional benefit to be gained from it as well, not only where the Kremlin was concerned, but on Capitol Hill. SAC's bombers were in continuous, often bitter competition for funding with the Navy's aircraft carriers.

The beetle-browed, jowl-jawed general, a stogie always clenched in his teeth, was a complex and enigmatic man who was an inspirational father figure to his men and a frequent source of irritation to his more fastidious counterparts in the Army and Navy.

Years after LeMay's death in 1990, reverential SAC alumni still savored anecdotes about him, some apocryphal. A perennial favorite was the one about the enlisted man who warned LeMay that smoking his cigar on the flight line beside a fully fueled bomber could cause it to blow up. "It wouldn't dare," the general is said to have growled. His adoring subordinates devoured it. And his notorious, Strangelovian quips became part of SAC's folklore. He reportedly told SAC crews "There are only two things in this world [that matter]: SAC bases and SAC targets." Another time he said the most effective antisubmarine warfare was to "boil the oceans with nukes." Asked what he would do with Cuba, he was said to have answered, "Fry it." The remark he is most famously

---

*The author flew one on a B-52 out of Westover Air Force Base in Massachusetts in 1964. The flight simulated a very low-level daylight attack against a city in Illinois, and included in-flight refueling. The large eight-engine bomber swung around a racetrack before hitting its target.

quoted for, about bombing North Vietnam "back to the Stone Age," was actually written by a speechwriter. Shown a model of Dynasoar, a manned Air Force spacecraft that was never built, LeMay was said to have had only one question: "Where's the bomb bay?"

The wisecracks, apocryphal or not, became legendary. LeMay was a shrewd man and certainly no lout. He was very likely burnishing his tough image, consciously or otherwise, and therefore the image of a Strategic Air Command that would strike decisively and without hesitation if called upon to do so. He never let on publicly that he played the organ as a hobby. That would not have fit the image.

LeMay's one foray into politics came when he ran as a vice-presidential candidate with Governor George Wallace of Alabama, a staunch segregationist and right-wing extremist, who ran for the presidency in 1968. LeMay was no racist, but he responded to Wallace's deeply fundamentalist, draw-the-line Americanism. They were clobbered.

DESPITE ITS EXALTED image in the early years, SAC had a dark and troubling secret. Behind the move to swept-wing bombers and the revolutionary in-flight refueling program that would give them worldwide attack capability; behind the standardization that was setting the basis for an energetic and disciplined organization; behind the new doctrine of rigorous and realistic training, dispersal of bases, emphasis on night fighting, and assured counterpunch capacity; and behind LeMay's carefully shaped image of SAC as an omnipotent force that could turn any place on Earth into an irradiated inferno in a matter of hours, there was a haunting secret. There were few targets whose location was precisely known.

This is not to say the targeteers didn't know where Moscow and Leningrad were. But city smashing for the sake of inflicting millions of casualties and unspeakable destruction would not only be immoral, it would be militarily futile. The first rule in war-fighting strategy is to incapacitate or destroy the enemy's ability to fight back. That done, resistance ends and the war is over. But an enemy's war machine—its production facilities, army, air, and naval bases, weapons storage bunkers, military headquarters, and its entire network of defensive radars and related equipment, plus transportation networks, electrical power sources, and raw materials—can only be destroyed if the locations of its components are known. In 1946, when SAC came into being, they were virtually unknown.

In March of that year the Pentagon began producing a series of war plans, code-named Pincher, that set up a conceptual framework for an all-out war with the USSR. For planning purposes, it was assumed that the Russians would apply maximum pressure to countries on their border. The scenario created by game players had another world war starting after a Soviet miscalculation led to an invasion of Turkey which, in turn, threatened the Suez Canal. Since it was apparent that American, British, and French occupation forces would not be able to stop a Red Army invasion of Europe following the attack on Turkey, aerial bombardment would be used, since it was more destructive and less costly in lives and equipment than fighting on the ground.

Even earlier, during the closing stages of World War II, Western generals had seen that despite horrendous losses and severe shortages of weapons and other materiel, the Red Army pushed the Wehrmacht all the way back to Berlin and beyond. Coupled with Stalin's worrisome claims for large chunks of Eastern Europe at Yalta and the immediate occupation of some of it, it had seemed possible that Soviet troops advancing deep inside Germany during that spring of 1945 could have pushed on soon after the war and threatened Western Europe itself. If that had happened, the Allied air forces would have needed accurate maps of the terrain, certainly including rail lines. Within one month of Germany's surrender on May 7, 1945, then, a photoreconnaissance operation called Casey Jones was created so that B-17 Flying Fortress crews in the 306th Bomb Group could systematically carry out photomapping missions over much of Western and south-central Europe. The first experimental missions were flown at 20,000 feet on June 10, only thirty-four days after the end of the war. That's how wary the United States, for one, was of the Soviet Union.

It would be SAC's responsibility to carry the brunt of a war against the USSR by blowing up its war-making capacity, not just active military installations, deep inside the country, including in the Urals and Caucasus, with conventional bombs. The problem was that the factories and other targets had to be found before they could be "taken out" (as the targeteers and others euphemistically called obliteration). Pincher's report itself was gloomy on that score:

"The scarcity of reliable and detailed intelligence on the U.S.S.R. precludes the determination at this time of specific target systems for air attack. Any strategic bombing program established at this time would be provisional even for purposes of current planning; it is certain to be altered radically when additional information becomes available. The current lack of intelligence on the U.S.S.R. is due not only to the rigid security maintained by that country, but also to the fact that such information as is available has not yet been properly assembled. It will be possible to improve this appreciation by incorporating in it new intelligence as the information now available to the various intelligence agencies is correlated." "Available information" probably referred to captured German intelligence documents, including aerial reconnaissance photographs, and to the interrogation of German prisoners who had been inside the USSR. That was pretty much it.

Pincher's architects were concerned with more than a so-called breakout in Europe and the need to attack the Soviet Union. They also had to take into account the certainty that the Russians would simultaneously attack the United States. Looking down at the top of the planet on the kind of globe that can be found in any grade school classroom and using string to plot the shortest routes showed the routes the Soviets would have to take. Their bombers would come out of various places in far northern Siberia and cross Alaska and Canada.

And the first foreign bombs to be carried to the United States by plane would be dropped by none other than the reverse-engineered version of the trio of B-29s that landed in Siberia during the last days of the war and which were never returned: the Tu-4. To know the range of the B-29 was obviously to know the range of the Tu-4. The Air Staff therefore knew that Tu-4s could fly round-trip bombing missions from eastern Siberia to Seattle and one-way "suicide" missions all the way to Kansas. Probably the ultimate in devious attack scenarios had the Russians painting their Tu-4s to look like Air Force B-29s and flying them to Canada. Their crews would land at Canadian air bases, tell the Royal Canadian Air Force they were lost and out of gas and, after being refueled, fly "home" to unload their wares on Washington and elsewhere in a surprise attack that outdid Pearl Harbor. To accomplish the ruse, of course, hundreds of Russian airmen would have had to perfect an extraordinary level of idiomatic American English and have an acting ability worthy of Stanislavsky. (Hundreds because the bombers held ten-man crews and using just a few bombers would have been counterproductive.)

Whether the attack came by direct assault or subterfuge, it would have to start at air bases in Siberia, and most likely on the Chukotskiy Peninsula. Another likely route was out of the Murmansk area in the Soviet far north, over Greenland, and to the U.S. East Coast. Flying such missions to get a few iron bombs on U.S. territory would have been pointless. But flying them with atomic bombs would have been a far different story. That looming possibility made it absolutely imperative to be able to wipe out the bomber bases quickly and precisely. But they couldn't be hit unless they could be found. And not only the bomber bases. The Tu-4s and their successors would be protected by radar and fighter-interceptors and their operations run by control centers with coordinated communication links. The radars, the fighters, the control centers, and the communication sites also had to be pinpointed.

And if that weren't enough, there was the problem of reaching the targets even when their locations were precisely known. Weather information would be important on such missions and precise navigation would be crucial. But in 1946, navigating airplanes around the Arctic was a poorly understood art, partly because of strange geomagnetic conditions and partly because aeronautical charts of the region were next to useless. What good was a compass that pointed north when a bomber was already *at* north?

However tough SAC appeared, then, it was no better than its

aeronautical charts and the contents of its combat crews' target folders. And that was pretty bad. The reconnaissance component of SAC's dual mandate therefore started in 1946, beginning with a program that was unprecedented in American history. It was called PARPRO, for Peacetime Airborne Reconnaissance Program, and it used specially modified planes to fly along the peripheries of the USSR on photographic and electronic reconnaissance missions. Its overall name came to be Big Safari.

Where Brig. Gen. Frank A. Armstrong was concerned, the need for solid intelligence was overwhelming. Armstrong headed the Alaskan Air Command and was therefore responsible for the air defense of the region. "To provide adequately for the defense of Alaska," he wrote in November 1949, "it is essential that the iron curtain be penetrated. Since United States policy leaves the initiative for offensive military action in the hands of the Soviet Union, military preparedness goals and readiness dates are open to the choice of Soviet leaders. . . . This command believes that continuous surveillance of Northeast Siberia, if properly conducted, will yield sufficient indication of Soviet buildup to permit the command to make necessary plans and dispositions and to achieve a maximum state of combat readiness prior to a Soviet attack." Armstrong went on to ask that huge cameras with hundred-inch focal lengths be mounted on RB-29s and used for "repeat reconnaissance" missions against some twenty key Soviet coastal targets every spring and fall. Rephotographing targets was necessary to spot changes.

Gen. Nathan F. Twining readily agreed and made an interesting observation. "The lack of overland transportation, both highway and rail, in this section [of remote Siberia] makes it mandatory that all stockpiling be accomplished by seaborne carriers. As a result, it is unlikely that an airfield of any size and proportion could be located far enough inland to be out of photographic range of a camera of this size and focal length." The hundred-inch-focal-length camera was designed by James Baker, the Harvard physicist and optics genius, and it was very good. But even it could not spot objects smaller than large airplanes when used obliquely from a distance of thirty miles, because of the distorting effects of the atmosphere. The cameras did quite a bit better along the supply corridor during the Berlin airlift in 1948 because they were pointed more toward the vertical.

Unlike the high-profile braggadocio that marked the bombardment program, intelligence collecting—snooping along the Soviet frontier day and night—was top-secret. Fearing diplomatic reprisal, the Department of State absolutely refused to sanction flights over the USSR; it even insisted, over the objections of Air Force commanders, that the missions stay at least forty miles away from Soviet frontiers.

But three momentous events changed all that, and the nature of U.S. aerial reconnaissance, in short order. In September 1949, an Air Weather Service WB-29 carrying special air filters collected radioactive particles over the Pacific that showed the Soviet Union finally had "the bomb." Immediate follow-up flights confirmed it. The search for Soviet bomber bases in Siberia quickly turned from vaguely important to imperative. Within a month, the Chinese Communists led by Mao Tse-tung pushed Chiang Kai-shek and his Nationalist government off mainland China, pulling the world's most populous nation and a huge chunk of the world-island into the Communist camp. Victory was proclaimed on October 1.

Then, on June 25, 1950, the North Korean army rolled over the thirty-eighth parallel and began to push the South Korean army and U.S. occupation forces almost the entire length of South Korea. This wasn't the hit-and-run work of a band of guerrillas in Greece or the Philippines. It was a brazen, carefully calculated, well-planned attempt by Stalin's pawns in Pyongyang to grab an entire country by real war (though the old man himself is said to have had serious doubts about testing the United States in a confrontation). The loss of South Korea would not only have dramatically changed the power structure in the region, particularly relative to Japan; it would also have set a potentially calamitous precedent: that blatant armed aggression worked.

Less than a month after the invasion began, it looked as though it was working. Seoul had been overrun. Republic of Korea troops, commonly called ROKs, and the GIs had been pushed into a corner around the southeastern port city of Pusan. There they dug in, backs to the sea, and got ready to make a last stand along what was instantly named the Pusan Perimeter. The situation was likened to Dunkirk, the port in northern France where the British Army, routed by the Germans, had been evacuated in disorder in May 1940. American forces were so desperate, their hold on the peninsula so tenuous—and this speaks to the larger spectre that haunted America—that the use of nuclear weapons was seriously considered.

"The repercussions [of being pushed off Korea] would be disastrous for the United States Armed Forces, for the United States, and for the Western World," a memorandum hand-delivered to Lt. Gen. Idwal H. Edwards, the Air Force's deputy chief for operations, warned on July 12. It would have been such a catastrophe, in fact, that nuclear weapons would have to be used to prevent it. "Under such conditions it is likely that use will be directed of every available weapon to prevent the disaster. This means that we must prepare in advance to use the atomic bomb in order that, if eventually the Air Force is ordered or authorized to use the bomb, it might have some hope of saving the situation and not merely acting as a retaliation, after the fact." But Edwards didn't see nuking the "gooks" (as Koreans were called when reporters weren't around) as a panacea. Using atomic bombs against North Koreans, he ruminated, would not necessarily end Soviet attempts to exert so much "pressure" elsewhere that the United States would be drawn into fighting beyond its capability. And using atomic weapons yet again, he went on, might be bad for America's image: "At the same time," Edwards continued, "it might even stimulate consolidation of support of the Moscow regime." However tempting militarily, then, a nuclear attack against the North Koreans would carry political dangers. The writer, who signed the document "CPC," nevertheless recommended supplying ten of the bombs to the Far East Air Force immediately, along with planes that could carry them. They were not needed. The emergency evaporated, at least temporarily, when Gen. Douglas MacArthur, now in command of troops from ten nations authorized by the U.N. to intervene, flanked the North Koreans by landing at the western port of Inchon, near the thirty-eighth parallel. He trapped the invaders and swung north toward the Yalu River and China.

But the issue of using atomic bombs was raised again in November, when U.N. forces were taken by surprise and pushed back by the Chinese People's Liberation Army, which poured across the Yalu. In both cases, President Truman emphatically rejected their use; mushroom clouds sprouting in Korea would have created more problems than they solved.

Yet the Communist victory in China, the development of the atomic bomb by the Soviet Union, and the audacious attack on South Korea, coming at almost the same time, suggested to Truman, his senior advisers, and the Joint Chiefs of Staff that another world war might have been starting to rumble. They began to seriously consider the possibility that the Kremlin might take advantage of the turmoil in Asia to launch an attack against Western Europe, possibly coordinated with air attacks against the United States itself. If that happened, it would be the prelude to the final, winner-take-all phase of the cold war.

Truman publicly proclaimed a national emergency and called the National Guard to active duty in mid-December. Following a meeting with a deeply concerned Joint Chiefs of Staff, he secretly authorized two deep-penetration flights over the USSR, and specifically over the Chukotskiy Peninsula. If there *were* Tu-4s in the area—within nuclear striking range of the United States—that fact absolutely had to be known.

So did the real extent of the threat in the Soviet Union itself. It was time to start replacing conjecture and speculation with finished intelligence. Earlier that month, Truman had spent several days in closed meetings with Prime Minister Clement R. Attlee, Foreign Minister Aneurin Bevin, and other high-ranking members of the British government to discuss the Korean situation, relations with China, and the use of nuclear weapons. As he would note in his memoirs, he assured the British delegation that he had no intention of using the atomic bomb on North Korea. He carefully omitted, however, the fact that at about that time he, Attlee, and the others agreed to start a joint aerial reconnaissance program to penetrate deep into the western Soviet Union to assess the actual threat; hard intelligence had to replace all the guessing.

The United States, desperate for information in the face of a worsening threat, was starting a top-secret intelligence-collecting program of historic importance. Thousands of Air Force and Navy flyers would be sent to prowl the dangerous precincts along and behind the Iron Curtain. Many would never return.

NOR WOULD INTELLIGENCE collecting be limited to the air. The Navy had begun using submarines to keep track of the whereabouts of Japanese warships in the last war, and they would be pressed into service in the cold war as well. The Peacetime Airborne Reconnaissance Program would have a seagoing counterpart that would first use converted World War II Liberty ships that were taken out of mothballs and stuffed with electronic equipment and antennas, and then smaller, less conspicuous transports. Submarines would also be used.

Surface ships had two advantages over both airplanes and subs. They were large enough to hold many powerful receivers and two dozen or more technicians to operate them, and they could loiter for days or weeks. The light-gray vessels, sprouting antennas and radar domes, would routinely park off the Chinese, North Korean, and Siberian coasts and ply the Mediterranean and the Black Sea eavesdropping for the Navy and the National Security Agency. Others, tailing specially rigged Soviet tracking ships, would drift for days off Kamchatka like outfielders waiting for a fly ball. The "ball" would be a Soviet warhead that had been launched on a ballistic missile at the Tyuratam, Kapustin Yar, or Plesetsk launch complexes. Their Soviet counterparts, some thinly disguised as refrigerated "mother" ships for Russian deep-sea fishing vessels, continuously monitored missile launches at the Air Force's Eastern Test Range at an otherwise unknown spit of land on Florida's east coast known as Cape Canaveral. Starting in 1959, reconnaissance satellite launches at Vandenberg Air Force Base near Santa Barbara, California, would also be carefully tracked.

The spy ships' disadvantage would lie in the fact that they were large, slow, and defenseless, which made them easy prey. And two of them did become prey in quick succession.

The first, the U.S.S. *Liberty*, became the unwilling star of a sensational international incident in June 1967, at the time of the

Six-Day War between Israel and the Arabs. It was a crystal-clear day with unlimited visibility and the ship was in international waters, flying the Stars and Stripes. Israeli reconnaissance planes carefully looked the *Liberty* over and their pilots and the ship's crew waved to each other. Then, without warning, Israeli fighters appeared. They strafed and bombed the ship in a ferocious low-level attack. Following the air attack, Israeli motor torpedo boats fired five torpedoes at her, one of which hit amidships, killing twenty-five sailors instantly. Two U.S. aircraft carriers in the Mediterranean responded to the *Liberty*'s call for help by launching fighters.

At that point, the White House ordered the carriers to recall their fighters, and when the admiral in charge of the carriers called the White House to confirm the order, he was told first by Secretary of State Robert McNamara and then by President Lyndon Johnson that he was indeed to order the planes to return, that the president did not want to embarrass an ally, and that Johnson didn't care who was killed or what happened to the *Liberty*. The fighters were recalled. Thirty-four sailors died in the air and sea attacks and the ship was left a scorched, bullet-riddled, bombed-out derelict.

In a page that could have been taken from peripheral airborne reconnaissance encounters with Communist fighters, Johnson went on television to announce that ten sailors had been killed in a "six-minute accidental" attack by the Israelis. The Israelis themselves claimed they thought the *Liberty* was Egyptian. But Secretary of State Dean Rusk and Adm. Thomas Moorer later said the attack was no accident, and so did two Israeli officers and some of the ship's survivors. Surviving sailors were ordered not to discuss the incident with anyone, under threat of court-martial. No congressional investigation was undertaken. And a Navy investigation of the crew's actions was allegedly a whitewash in which the right questions were not asked and evidence was suppressed.

To this day, the surviving crewmen of the *Liberty* are bitter because, in the words of one former Navy intelligence officer, "Someone killed thirty-four Americans and got away with it. What's more, its own government covered up the truth and helped them get away with it."

The submarine operation, which began soon after World War II with periscope peeping and sonar soundings, was formalized in 1959. Variously called Binnacle, Bollard, and Holystone, among other names, it would be directed mostly against the Soviet Union, with special attention paid to the large port facilities at Severomorsk, Murmansk, Petropavlovsk, and Vladivostok, but also with regular sweeps along the coasts. As would be expected, Soviet subs spied, too. The Russians often crossed the Pacific and made runs from Seattle down to San Diego, which was the Vladivostok of the West Coast. Others did the same thing at Norfolk, Virginia, another large naval base, and at Groton, Connecticut, where General Dynamics' Electric Boat Division made ballistic-missile and fast attack submarines.

Like their Air Force counterparts, U.S. spy subs carried electronic intelligence specialists to intercept coded communication, missile telemetry, and ferret shipborne radar, plus a handful of Russian-speaking communication specialists who eavesdropped on radio traffic. And also like the Air Force, they represented two distinct cultures that were as tightly compartmented as the subs in which they worked.

There would inevitably be political similarities, too. Like aerial and, later, space reconnaissance, the submariners would become ensnared in a bitterly contentious power struggle between their own Office of Naval Intelligence, the CIA, and the NSA. The National Reconnaissance Office (NRO), which was created in 1961 to buy and run the spy satellites, would have a counterpart for the spy subs: the National Underwater Reconnaissance Office. The fight for control of the NURO, like the war over the NRO, would for a time become almost Kremlinesque.

But also like Air Force and Navy airmen, the men in the submarines would distinguish themselves throughout the cold war and afterward, often working closely with reconnaissance planes. One operation alone, described by Sherry Sontag and Christopher Drew in their heavily researched, best-selling *Blind Man's Bluff*, spoke to the intelligence and bravery of the men who reconnoitered the Russians at dangerously close quarters. That was the saga of James Bradley, the director of undersea warfare in the Office of Naval Intelligence, who concocted a brazen plan to tap an underwater communication cable that ran between the Soviet missile submarine base at Petropavlovsk, under the Sea of Okhotsk, to Vladivostok and Moscow. And it was done by sailors on a submarine named *Halibut*, who, with others at sea and in the air, wrote a chapter in their nation's history that was as vital as it was publicly unacknowledged.

As the shadows of the cold war began to lengthen, with each side pitted against the other in realms that extended from one hundred fathoms under the sea to one hundred miles in space, the need to collect intelligence with aircraft flying manned reconnaissance missions grew urgent. But it was as dangerous as it was imperative. Fighter and bomber crews practiced constantly but flew no combat. They were in the cold war. But Air Force and Navy reconnaissance crews routinely flew into the teeth of the enemy on operational combat missions. For them, the cold war was very hot indeed.

FIRST BLOOD

THE BATTLE OF BRITAIN was lost before it started.

Beginning in 1936, as the German General Staff rearmed in preparation for what would become World War II, reports reached Berlin that 350-foot-high masts, generally in clusters of three and with horizontal crossed lattice antennas mounted midway up and at the top, were being built along the southern and eastern coasts of Britain. The first was erected at Orfordness, 250 miles northeast of London, and was taken to be a radio communication antenna. But then another went up at nearby Bawdsey, followed by others at Dover and Canewdon. By the end of 1939 twenty of them, called Chain Home towers, would sprout in a ragged line from the Isle of Wight to the Firth of Forth, near Edinburgh.

Gen. Wolfgang Martini, who headed the Luftwaffe's communication command, knew about the antennas relatively early and was mystified by them. Individually each did, indeed, look like a radio antenna. But all of them were strung out facing the continent like radar towers positioned to warn of an air attack against the British Isles. The curious general would get no help from the British, of course. They *were* radar towers. The British had been working hard to perfect radar since 1935, but the last thing they would do with the top-secret research was give it to the Germans, against whom it was likely to be used. Research on radar was also being done in the United States and in Germany itself. Scientists and their military patrons in all three countries were well aware that being able to see clearly over long distances at night and in poor weather would start the most profound revolution in warfare since the invention of the airplane.

By the spring of 1939, the British had put in place a secret air defense system that was almost entirely dependent on using radar to locate and count enemy aircraft sixty miles off the British coast and relay the sightings to an underground communication center at Uxbridge. There, the invading formations would be plotted on large table maps. Uxbridge would then telephone instructions to scramble Royal Air Force fighter squadrons so the bombers could be intercepted before they reached their targets.

Martini knew nothing of this, of course. What he did conclude, however, was that the masts were unquestionably some sort of radar antennas. Yet they were completely different from the two major types of radar being developed in Germany: a medium-range early warning system named Freya and a shorter-range, ground-controlled intercept system called Würzburg that directed antiaircraft guns and fighter-interceptors. Both German systems used dishes, not spindly masts, to collect return signals. Perplexed, Martini told Hermann Göring, who headed the Luftwaffe, and other senior officers that it was vital to pick up the British radar signals so they could be analyzed and, if need be, countered. No airplane could do the job properly, he continued, since they were too small, could not stay up long enough, and couldn't stay motionless as the signals came in. What was needed, Martini added, was dirigibles; maybe six of them. That idea went nowhere. The Third Reich's production lines were straining to produce fighters, bombers, and transports, Martini was told, and could not be diverted to manufacture colossal airships like the *Graf Zeppelin*.

But, the disappointed general was told, he could have the *Graf Zeppelin* itself. So that stately airship, a 776-foot-long sister of the ill-fated *Hindenburg*, was fitted with an array of high-frequency and ultrahigh-frequency radio receivers and cathode-ray tubes that were supposed to show what the British radar signals looked like: intercept them so they could be analyzed. A brace of antennas in the form of thin aerials were rigged under *Graf Zeppelin*'s long gondola to collect the radar pulses the way radio receivers pull in radio signals.

And so the world's first airborne radar reconnaissance mission, and certainly one of the most bizarre, began on a night at the end of May 1939, when the *Graf Zeppelin*, with General Martini aboard, slipped its moorings at Frankfurt and headed out over the North Sea. Hours later, it reached a position near Bawdsey and then turned north to fly parallel to the coast, just out of sight of land. As it did so, the technicians at the receivers carefully turned the knobs on their receivers as they tried to pick up the British signals. But what they got, no matter how carefully they tried to tune in, was loud crackling static that revealed nothing.

Their targets, however, did quite a bit better. The radar observers at Bawdsey and Canewdon who were looking at their own cathode-ray tubes that night were transfixed as they watched the largest blip they had ever seen move slowly north, along the coast. They telephoned their sighting to Uxbridge, which, according to procedure, began to plot the visitor's progress on its map table. The size of the blip left no doubt that it was a dirigible, and its route up the coast also left no doubt that it was doing what the British called a "radar interrogation."

Onward through the night the great fat spying cigar droned as its operators tried without the slightest success to take the pulse of the British radar. But the British certainly took theirs. The *Graf Zeppelin* was picked up by one radar site after another, each of which meticulously tracked its position. And not only was the great Nazi dirigible tracked, but its radio transmissions were intercepted by British intelligence. At one point, the clueless Germans reported home that they were over the North Sea a few miles off the coast of Yorkshire. This caused some hilarity at Fighter Command, since its radar plots clearly showed that the *Graf Zeppelin* was in fact in the clouds right over Hull, a city on the Humber Estuary that was twenty miles inland. "We were sorely tempted to radio a correction message to the airship," one amused RAF officer recalled years later, "but this would have revealed we were actually seeing her position on radar, so we kept silent." Finally, unaware that he had not only provided valuable practice for the RAF's radar and radio intercept operators, but that he had revealed his country's acute interest in Great Britain's air defenses, the disgruntled Wolfgang Martini ordered the *Graf Zeppelin* to return to Frankfurt.

A second attempt was made on August 2, less than a month before the Wehrmacht invaded Poland in the opening round of World War II, but it also failed. This time, however, there was a standoff. The Germans yet again could not find the British radar signal, but the radar operators could not find the Germans, either. The *Graf Zeppelin* was sighted by a number of people on the ground, however, as it flew north just outside the three-mile limit. And they watched as it finally glided at less than 1,000 feet through broken cloud cover over the Royal Navy base at Scapa Flow way up in the Orkneys. It then turned for home on the evening of August 3, possibly with reconnaissance photographs of British warships, but yet again without radar intelligence.

After the London *Daily Telegraph* reported the intrusion, Germany issued an official communiqué denying that its dirigible had violated British airspace. That caused some amusement in Britain. Berlin maintained that the luckless airship had neither left Germany nor approached the coast of England. "There can be no question of an intention to fly over or near British territory," the communiqué stated. Then, in a reference that must have produced double takes in the RAF, it baldly added that there had been severe storms over the North Sea and that it was possible the *Graf Zeppelin* had been "blown off course." Both zeppelin radar reconnaissance missions came up empty. But that second foray established its place in the history of the enterprise by providing a durable pretext—a "cover" in the language of the trade—for a ferret that was caught where it wasn't supposed to be: foul weather was responsible.

Equipment trouble is one explanation for the *Graf Zeppelin*'s failure. More likely, it was because German radar operated on relatively short, high-frequency wavelengths of up to fifty inches, while the British version worked on very long wavelengths that would have been unbelievable to the Germans: roughly ten yards. It is therefore conceivable that it simply never occurred to General Martini to have his men search that end of the frequency band. For whatever reason, Germany started the Battle of Britain in July 1940 profoundly ignorant about the RAF's ability to use its fighter-interceptors efficiently by sending them directly to their targets with the help of radar. The Luftwaffe therefore essentially left the Chain Home system alone. It was mauled as a consequence. In effect, the Battle of Britain was over before it began.

THE USE OF RADAR and the development of ways to counter it, together with the parallel use of radio for communication and radio interception and false orders broadcast on radio, amounted to an entirely new way of conducting conflict: electronic warfare. They and a whole kaleidoscope of other methods of using electronics for war fighting were pushed relentlessly by both sides during the period that led to the war and throughout the war itself. The ancient ritual of legions of gladiators locked in combat, sword to sword and muscle to muscle (or bomber to bomber and bayonet to bayonet) was forever altered by what Winston Churchill called "the Wizard War." It was intense scientific competition that was fought, not on battlefields and oceans, but in the remote world of scientific laboratories and engineering divisions. For the first time, for example, a flight of attacking bombers could be thwarted not by men in fighters shooting guns at them or by antiaircraft batteries on the ground, but by projecting the radio beacons the bombers relied on for navigation somewhere else. This was called "meaconing." It accounted for the loss of a number of German bombers. One bomber crew landed in Devonshire, according to Churchill, because its navigator thought he was over France. Crew and bomber were captured without a shot being fired.

On the night of October 22–23, 1943, as RAF Wellington bombers bore down on the German city of Kassel, Luftwaffe night fighters directed by ground controllers using the Freya radar took off to intercept them. The voices of the controllers were usually calm as they steered the fighters toward their quarry. But not that night. As the minutes passed, the voices over the pilots' earphones became excited, then apparently confused, then chaotic, and finally enraged. The pilots concluded, correctly, that they were listening to two controllers: a real one and a "ghost."

"Don't be led astray by the enemy," the infuriated real controller shouted into his microphone. "In the name of General Schmid, I order all aircraft to return to Kassel."

"The Englishman is now swearing," the English ghost replied calmly.

"Dammit," shouted the near-apoplectic German. "It's not the Englishman swearing, it's *me!*"

It was the beginning of Operation Corona, in which British ghost controllers broadcast fake messages to German night fighter pilots from three high-powered transmitters at Rugby. During the next six months, the increasingly frenzied Luftwaffe pilots were sent to defend empty skies or ordered to land at remote airfields because their own bases were allegedly under attack or socked in by thick fog. Soon, the suspicious and uncertain pilots were left to wonder whether they were in fact being diverted to bases that really were under attack. And while they wondered, their fuel gauges dropped. Corona amounted to only a small fraction of the wizard war, which started in the 1930s and never ended.

The RAF itself ferreted radar continuously, going after not just the Freyas and Würzburgs, but an airborne type called Lichtenstein that guided the night fighters. As early as July 1942, the British picked up what they thought was airborne radar, and even named it Emil. Wellington bombers on "wireless investigation" duty tried seventeen times to lure German night fighters into the sky over the Netherlands so they would turn on their radar, but without success. On December 3, 1942, one of them did manage to draw German radar-equipped fighters, but in doing so, it met a fate that would be shared by its successors long after the war ended. It was so badly shot up by the night fighters it was ferreting that it crashed into the English Channel. Before it did so, its crew radioed back details about Emil.

"This was a secret war, whose battles were lost or won unknown to the public, and only with difficulty comprehended. . . . No such warfare had ever been waged by mortal men," Churchill recounted in his history of World War II. "The terms in which it could be recorded or talked about were unintelligible to ordinary folk. Yet if we had not mastered its profound meaning and used its mysteries even while we saw them only in the glimpse, all the efforts, all the prowess of the fighting airmen, all the bravery and sacrifices of the people, would have been in vain."

1ST LT. ROGER IHLE, one of the new breed of American electronic warfare officers, became one of the first U.S. wizard warriors when he studied radio communication at Harvard and MIT and then attended the new Radar Countermeasures School at Boca Raton, Florida, in 1943. He, 1st Lt. Matthew Slavin II, and two other officers formed only the second group to complete the specialized training. Ihle and Slavin returned to Boston from Florida and were handed three boxes of "top-secret" radar intercept equipment and ordered to take it by Pullman train—public transportation—to Wright-Patterson Field outside of Dayton. "It was so primitive," Ihle would recall many years later, "that what we had was all amateur radio stuff, the old Hallicrafters SR-27, I think it was: a ham radio receiver." He and Slavin got the boxes to the air base, located their B-17F, and fastened the equipment to a shelf opposite the cramped radioman's position. Besides the receiver, there was an oscilloscope for analyzing pulses and an experimental receiver for higher frequencies that didn't work very well. The pulse analyzer recorded radar signal strength, Isle said, "and that was the way we got an approximate location on the radar sets."

The B-17F was painted black and named *Archangel*. With the exception of its color, which theoretically made night missions safer, and Ihle, Slavin, their three secret boxes, and stub antennas, *Archangel* was a standard Flying Fortress that also carried bombs. "It was a military crew. About half the crew," he said with dry humor, "were people who had been sentenced to the Air Force for stealing cars, writing bad checks, and whatnot."

Archangel was assigned to the Fifteenth Air Force in the Mediterranean. It left Ohio in early autumn 1943 and headed for a British air base at Blida, Algeria, with Ihle and Slavin on board.

Since it didn't have the range to make it across the North At-
lantic, *Archangel* took a southerly route through Puerto Rico,
Trinidad, Brazil, Ascension Island, Liberia, and Casablanca in
Morocco.

Life at Blida was basic. "We didn't have quarters or anything
like that because they weren't ready for us. So we slept on the pad
underneath the wing of our aircraft, serviced it ourselves, and
flew the missions," Ihle recalled, adding that *Archangel* had to be
hand-fed. "We would fill the bomber with gasoline out of five-
gallon cans and strain it through a chamois filter."

They ranged all over the Mediterranean, searching for Freya
radars day and night. Daylight missions were flown at the rear of
formations of B-17s on bomb runs. It was dangerous work because of the constant possibility of attack by fighters or ground
fire. The black Flying Fortress would also take off alone half an
hour before sunset and prowl for up to eight hours, until the gas
got low. Night operations were especially dangerous because they
were flown at 500 feet. That kept *Archangel* out of enemy radar's
direct beam while providing enough beam spillover so Ihle,
Slavin, and the other radar spotters could take their readings. The
terms "raven" or "crow" were not yet in general use for radar intercept officers, Ihle explained. "We were known as freaks." The
black bombers often had to weave through mountainous islands
in the Adriatic and off Sicily in the dead of night, he added, and
the crews could barely see mountains towering above them to the
left and right. The planes themselves carried no radar so navigation meant eyeballing the area very carefully and, as Ihle put it,
"dodging islands." Three of the six bombers in his group were lost.
One crashed into a mountain in the Pyrénées. That much was
known because six months later its crew's dog tags were returned
by a Basque shepherd, Ihle said. "The navigator got lost," he continued, matter-of-factly. "He went into a mountain." It was not
uncommon, especially in the Adriatic, off the Yugoslav coast.
"You'd go down there and all of a sudden the plane would bounce,
turn, swerve, and you'd look out, and here was a big island underneath you." The other two Fortresses, like Saint-Exupéry's
camera-carrying P-38, simply disappeared over water without a
trace; without leaving so much as an oil slick.

"We had to figure out everything from scratch," Ihle said, "because nothing had ever been done in this field. We were the beginners. Nobody knew how to operate this stuff [at night]. We just worked it out so, for reconnaissance, we'd have to do it at a low altitude underneath the radar, or get in as close as we could to shore while staying out far enough so we couldn't be dropped by gunfire."

Since the Fortresses had no direction finders, he and the navigator would simply note on the navigation chart where the radar signal was strongest. It was truly seat-of-the-pants, groundbreaking work. The radar's exact location was fixed by sending a photo-reconnaissance plane into the area to try to get pictures of antennas.

"I had the unlucky job of writing all that stuff up after we came home from missions. And so we'd write it up and send it to the communications officer of the Fifteenth Air Force. What he did with it, I don't know," Ihle remembered. After nine months, he was transferred to Fifteenth Air Force Headquarters in Bari, Italy, where he helped devise radar countermeasures for the bomber force. "We installed 5,000 radar jammers in B-17s and taught the radiomen how to operate them. And we installed chaff dispensers in every aircraft." Chaff, an old staple used to thwart enemy radar, is a cloud of precisely cut metallic strips that hides planes in what appears on the radar screen as an electronic blizzard.

As Allied ground forces pushed the Germans back up the Italian peninsula, *Archangel* flew on regular daytime bombing missions with other B-17s and dropped its own bombs. But *Archangel*'s pilot was used to flying alone and at night, not in large formations, so he tended to wander around, much to the exasperation of the other pilots in the formation, who were trained to keep their positions. "They always stuck us way back on the tail end. We were the last aircraft on the outside. That," Ihle added, "was the place that always got attacked by fighters."

The idea of using linguists to warn of an enemy attack in the air, a practice that came into widespread use in the cold war, started in the skies over Axis Europe. "We had these German-speaking boys we had monitoring all of the aircraft frequencies of the Germans, so when they heard the Germans starting to scramble, why, they told the [American] fighters what was happening, and they [fighter-bombers] swept in under the bombers and wiped out the airfields," Ihle explained. "We did this two days in a row, and the third day, there wasn't an aircraft on the field. Everything that could fly was gone."

Ihle was told originally that his overseas tour would be two to three months. It lasted two and a half years, he said. "Then they came in one morning and said, 'You wanna go home?'

"I said, 'Yeah, sometime.'

" 'Go home, pack, there's a B-24 leaving in an hour.' So I got on board a brand new '24 and came back to the States. It was after Germany surrendered."

Looking back at the creation, Roger Ihle seemed amazed that any of it had worked at all. "The thing is, they went into everything sort of halfway, and not with adequate equipment, and no training. There wasn't any training that we had [before going into combat]. We had to train ourselves through what we did, and we tried to pass it on to people coming in later: what we knew and what we did and what happened," he remembered. *Archangel* was an appendage of the Fifteenth Air Force when it went to North Africa, not an integral part of it, so even getting spare parts was difficult in those first days because there was no unit to which to charge them. It was only later, when the other five Fortresses arrived early in 1944, that the six crews were turned into a coherent unit: the Sixteenth Reconnaissance Squadron. It was a problem not only in the Mediterranean but in the Eighth Air Force in England and in the Twentieth Air Force in the Pacific.

"Advanced training is probably the best thing that they can have. The equipment isn't so important as the training and discipline, because you have to be able to concentrate on what you're doing even when you're under fire," advised Roger Ihle.

PHOTORECONNAISSANCE was a different matter altogether. Advanced training was not the problem for the men in the camera-laden planes who searched for radar antennas around the Mediterranean and elsewhere. Cameras, after all, had been used in reconnaissance long before there were pulse analyzers and jammers. Cameras were around before there were airplanes.

The value of photographs of the enemy taken from the air, exposing (as it were) all the people, weapons, and supporting equipment that could not be seen from the ground, provided so obvious an advantage to war fighting that cameras were put on balloons and even on kites before a heavier-than-air machine even got off the ground. A camera-carrying twenty-foot-high kite was used by the Army's Ninth Infantry Regiment on Governors Island in New York as early as 1895, and a strikingly clear photograph of the Capitol in Washington, with the House and Senate office buildings under construction, was taken by balloon in 1907. One of the first "official" military aerial photos was taken from a Wright Flyer racing a Baltimore-bound train near College Park, Maryland, four years later.

All of the belligerents used aerial photography from the start of the Great War. By 1917, in fact, the U.S. Army Signal Corps had opened a School of Military Aeronautics at Cornell University in Ithaca, New York, and began the formal training of flying photographers and photointerpreters. George W. Goddard, an artist and amateur photographer who enlisted in the school so he could become a pilot, was derailed by a major who told him, "We need aerial photographers more than we need pilots." Goddard, who was to revolutionize aerial photography and retire from the U.S. Air Force as a brigadier general, became a member of the first class to train commanders of aerial photography sections. Many of his instructors were Britons and Frenchmen with combat experience.

An impressive map of the entire battlefront, from the English Channel to the Swiss border, was mounted on a wall in Cornell's Schoellkopf Hall and was kept updated as the stagnant war continued. (Given the static nature of the fighting, that would not have been especially difficult.) "The map showed in great detail the first, second, and third German trench systems, no-man's-land, and the first, second, and third English, American and French trench systems. Each day," Goddard would recall, "the students would interpret the various pictures with the assistance of the French and British instructors who were familiar with the particular areas along the battle lines." The Germans, who already excelled at optics, had their own high-quality photographs of the front.

During the 1930s, the U.S. Army evolved four enduring uses of airplanes to collect information. The first and most primitive was visual observation, essentially as it had been done from balloons by the Army of the Potomac. Pilots and observers were used in direct support of ground forces. They located and watched the enemy and radioed information to their own side for artillery spotting, counterattacks, bombardment, and other action. The second, photomapping, used cameras to create accurate maps of large areas for use by war planners. Useful information would include the location of highway and other transportation systems, terrain features such as mountains and rivers, and the layout of cities and towns. The third collected operational intelligence. This was the system that was supposed to describe in detail the enemy's strengths and weaknesses, military and civilian. Locating air bases and finding aircraft so they could be counted and studied are two examples among many. Bomb damage assessment, in which places that had been bombed were photographed to see whether follow-up attacks were necessary, was another.

And as German, Italian, and Japanese expansionism slowly became more evident, both sides developed what in effect was the predecessor of SAC's Peacetime Airborne Reconnaissance Program, though it was done by civilians as well as soldiers.

In fact, where photoreconnaissance between the wars was concerned, an inventive Australian adventurer named Sidney Cotton was undoubtedly the king of spies. Cotton took three cameras with five-inch lenses and set them so that one pointed straight down and the other two faced outward. Then he mounted them in the belly of a twin-engine Lockheed 12A that was painted a pale duck egg green which made it disappear against the sky. He mounted the cameras behind tight-fitting metal ports that were almost invisible on the ground. Starting in 1939 and continuing well into 1940, Cotton, posing as a businessman, crisscrossed Europe in his plane and photographed eleven-and-a-half-mile-wide swaths of territory dozens of miles long from 20,000 feet and higher. He provided the RAF with invaluable photographs of German port facilities and military installations, likely trouble spots in the Mediterranean area, and, since Germany and the USSR had a nonaggression treaty, Soviet oil facilities in Baku that could potentially supply Hitler's war machine. By then—early 1940—Cotton's operation was called the Photographic Development Unit and was using three stripped-down Spitfires carrying extra fuel tanks. The PDU soon became the RAF's Photographic Reconnaissance Unit, which went through the war collecting intelligence and doing bomb damage assessment. It was an RAF Spitfire that turned up the first Freya radar.

Cotton's German counterpart, a Luftwaffe officer named Theodore Rowehl, did the same thing. He had an HE-111 twin-engine bomber modified to look like a Lufthansa airliner and sent it around Europe on the pretext of trying to find suitable routes for regularly scheduled air service. Since everyone was trying to get along with Hitler, Rowehl's camera-carrying bomber was received cordially just about everywhere it went. It worked the south of England, the French side of the English Channel, the North Sea coast, and the Baltic coast as far as Leningrad.

Meanwhile, improvements in photoreconnaissance equipment paralleled the boxes carried by the ferrets. By the time Hitler attacked Poland, twin-lens stereoscopic cameras to provide a three-dimensional effect for photointerpreters had long been in use. Color film, which added a whole dimension to photointerpretation, was a newer development. So was the strip camera, developed by Goddard after he saw a camera at a racetrack in California that was used to determine winners in photo finishes. A photograph taken obliquely or vertically from a low-flying plane would be blurred for the same reason trees seem blurred when seen from the side window of a moving car. The answer was to use a film strip synchronized to move at a speed relative to that of the plane as the target was photographed. Since plane and target would in effect be moving at the same speed, it was as if both were motionless. Night photoreconnaissance was helped by the development of an electronic flash system. Finally, the Trimetrogon camera was invented to extend side coverage. Like Cotton's arrangement, it used a vertical camera and two obliques. Unlike it, the Trimetrogon saw all the way from horizon to horizon as well as straight down, meaning that activity on the far periphery of the picture could be seen as well as what was going on under the plane itself.

Aerial reconnaissance came of age in World War II as all of the major powers, including Japan and the Soviet Union, came to fully understand the value of collecting intelligence and assessing damage. Targets could then be reattacked if necessary. Virtually every type of U.S. combat aircraft was modified to carry cameras, and some, like Roger Ihle's B-17, to carry electronic intelligence gear as well.

And photointerpretation developed into an art form in its own right. As war fronts moved across Europe, the Pacific, and the Middle East, film processing and interpretation moved with them in the form of mobile units that took the film right off the planes for developing and analysis. Interpreters soon learned that an absence of snow on rooftops in winter meant the buildings were heated and therefore in use; that the first paths shoveled in snow at military installations usually connected officers' quarters and the latrine; that explosives bunkers had drive-through access; that radars were always surrounded by security fences; and an encyclopedia of other deductions based on the sort of logical association given in standardized examinations:

Extending a runway from 5,000 feet to 10,000 feet is being done to:
      (*a*) provide employment for construction workers.
      (*b*) clear trees that are dangerous obstacles.
      (*c*) accommodate bombers or other heavy aircraft.
      (*d*) use up an excess supply of concrete.

The answer is (*c*). Being heavy, bombers require longer runways than fighters, and so do transport planes. The three other choices are possible but highly implausible on the face of it.

It was British photointerpreters, in fact, who first spotted German V-2 ballistic missiles lying on their sides near their launch towers on Peenemunde in June 1943. Less than a year later, intensive photoreconnaissance of the Normandy area, some of it "on the deck"—just above treetop level—by camera-carrying P-38s (called F-5s), paved the way for D day. And on the big day itself, 116 photo and visual missions were flown, producing almost 10,000 prints for Eisenhower and his strategists. By war's end, photoreconnaissance had become a thoroughly integrated and indispensable part of strategic warfare.

There was a haunting epilogue to photoreconnaissance in World War II. Thirty years after the war, Dino Brugioni, one of the legendary CIA photointerpreters who briefed President Kennedy during the Cuban missile crisis, got to wondering whether the Auschwitz-Birkenau concentration camp in Poland had ever been photographed by reconnaissance planes. So he went to the Defense Intelligence Agency film library and pulled up photographs of the I.G. Farben Buna Synthetic Rubber Plant and the area that surrounded it. Brugioni knew that slave laborers from Auschwitz had been used to make rubber for the Third Reich. Sure enough, the death camp turned up in several photographs of the area near the factory. What would appear to the untrained eye as a line of dots connected to a rectangle the way a tail is connected to some microorganism appeared to Brugioni—correctly—as a line of prisoners going into the gas chamber–crematorium. Many other details, including barracks, a rail line, two gas chambers, guard towers, and other lines of prisoners became apparent to his highly trained eye.

THE AIRCRAFT THAT did the reconnaissance were mongrels from the standard gene pool, not specially bred creatures. Since the reconnaissance plane's job was to get home with intelligence, not engage in combat, speed and maneuverability counted. Relatively short-range operations were therefore handled by converted P-38s, P-51s, and British Mosquitoes. Deeper missions, and especially those using heavy equipment, were flown by more vulnerable bombers: A-20s, B-17s, B-24s, and B-25s.

As World War II wound on, everyone in aerial reconnaissance began to see that flying at high altitude increased the safety margin. Three dedicated reconnaissance planes were therefore proposed to the Army, all of them capable of flying higher than fighters and bombers. The F-15A Reporter was developed by Northrop Aviation from its large P-61 Black Widow night fighter. Only thirty-six were built; an order for another 175 was canceled at war's end. As early as 1943, Republic Aviation designed a bullet-nosed, highly streamlined, four-engine reconnaissance plane it called the XR-12 Rainbow. The XR-12 was large enough to carry a full spate of cameras in three compartments and its own processing and developing laboratory. This meant finished, usable photographs would be ready even before it landed.

Meanwhile, Howard Hughes designed and built his own entry: a graceful, twin-boomed, very streamlined high flyer called the XR-11. The prototype had propeller failure in an early test flight and crashed in Beverly Hills in 1946, seriously injuring the aspiring movie mogul. A second XR-11 flew the following year. By then, however, the war was long over, defense appropriations were way down, and the jet fighter had changed military aviation decisively. All three planes therefore died in their infancy. The new Air Force, and the Navy, too, would have to make do. Where long-range reconnaissance was concerned, that would mean the Air Force's redoubtable B-29 and the Navy's PB4Y Privateer, a rugged four-engine patrol plane designed and manufactured by Consolidated Aircraft during the war and based on its B-24 Liberator heavy bomber.

"FROM STETTIN IN the Baltic to Trieste in the Adriatic, an Iron Curtain has descended across the Continent," Churchill said in his short, immortal speech at Westminster College in Fulton, Missouri, on March 5, 1946. The master orator and rhetorician was right as far as he went. But he did not stretch the curtain far enough: it ran across the top of the world. Sixteen days later, as the Strategic Air Command was born, the United States of America and the Union of Soviet Socialist Republics faced each other warily from opposite sides of a curtain that extended around the world.

Whatever it was called, Soviet secrecy enveloped the territory into which it was expanding, and that alarmed the United States and Great Britain. The need to penetrate the curtain started almost immediately and grew to a near-frenzy by the end of the decade.

Even during the last stages of the war, there were no illusions in Britain or the United States about what the end of the conflict would bring. One distinct possibility, at least from London's and Washington's perspective, was a Red Army that rolled through Germany and kept heading west. However begrudgingly, the Russians were admired as tough, disciplined fighters who relied more on grit and muscle than on technology. So early in June 1945— barely a month after the end of the war in Europe—the Army Air Force's 306th Bomb Group started photomapping large sections of Western and south-central Europe, very much including rail lines, in the Casey Jones operation. Regular B-17 bomber crews were taught the rudiments of aerial photography by specialists from the Nineteenth Photo Squadron in Italy, given cameras, and sent out to create a detailed map of terrain that might have to be defended against the Red Army.

On October 15, 1945—six weeks after the surrender of Japan—a Navy PBM Mariner patrol plane from Fleet Air Wing One got to within a mile of Port Arthur in Manchuria, which had just been occupied by Soviet forces. The plane was there to monitor Japanese ships evacuating troops from China, look over a beached and abandoned Navy PBY Catalina flying boat, and pick up whatever it could on what the Russians were doing. Just after it turned for home, it was caught by a propeller-driven Russian fighter and shot at. The fat blue patrol plane made it back to Japan with the distinction of having drawn the first fire by a Russian interceptor in the Far East. The curtain to the cold war was going up.

Four months later, the Navy did it again. This time, one of its planes flew over Dairen, near Port Arthur, and was intercepted by two Soviet fighters. According to the Navy, the patrol plane was not hit and made it safely home. After "high government officials" leaked word to the news media that the plane's pilot had become confused and thought he was over a Chinese city, the Navy said that the pilot would be disciplined. What it did not say was that Dairen was the site of a large radar installation that was marked as a priority target for ferreting.

So was the radar at Big Diomede Island, which was just inside the Soviet side of the Bering Strait, and which therefore looked squarely at Alaska. The island was ferreted three times between March 8, 1946, and January 31, 1947. No Russian fighters chased the ferrets, but Moscow vehemently protested the intrusions. Following the script worked out by the Germans for the second *Graf Zeppelin* mission, the United States replied that the overflights were accidental and had been caused by poor weather over the Bering Strait (all three times).

The Russians, who were notoriously xenophobic (with good reason), were not fooled. They easily followed the ferrets on their radar and saw, in each case, that the planes flew patterns that could only be used for reconnaissance. It was a very small jump to the suspicion that all foreign aircraft, no matter what their ostensible reason for flying near Soviet frontiers, were up to no good. The increasing number of aircraft in all guises that prowled along the edges of their vast country, and occasionally "wandered" over the edges, could mean only one thing: intelligence was being collected that would make them vulnerable to an all-out nuclear attack by the only nation in the world with atomic bombs. It was therefore considered vital to keep the spies at bay. Every plane, military or civilian, large or small, that ventured close to the Soviet Union or its proxies was presumed to be collecting intelligence.

So the Kremlin used its fighters as a pitcher uses beanballs: to keep the opponent away from the plate. The Russians were so wary of being spied on from the air that they attacked an Air France DC-4 as it flew down the corridor from Frankfurt to Berlin on April 29, 1952. MiG cannon fire raked the airliner, wounding two passengers, before its pilot made it to Berlin. The Russians immediately charged that the DC-4 had violated East German airspace and had ignored orders to land. The Allies responded by insisting that the plane had been where it was supposed to be. More to the point, the protest note said, firing on unarmed planes in peacetime was "inadmissible and contrary to all standards of civilized behavior." That was true enough. Left unsaid, however, was the fact that the corridors leading to Berlin were routinely used by Allied planes carrying cameras with very long lenses and signals-intercept gear. Nor were flour, milk, butter, and other comestibles the only things carried by the C-47s, C-54s, and C-97s that flew into and out of Templehof airport around the clock during the Berlin airlift.

AT THE SAME TIME, the Russians had no intention of limiting their part in the great game to defense. They had their own intelligence to collect, and they did so aggressively, first with cameras and later with pulse analyzers and other ferret hardware. Soviet aircraft flying from Vladivostok to Tokyo between 1945 and 1947 repeatedly flew out of the air control corridor over Japan to reconnoiter military installations and the Seventh Fleet. They did the same thing over the American occupation zone in West Germany. In a number of instances, the Russians ignored orders to get back into the flight corridor and instead took evasive action. Soviet aircraft penetrated Swedish airspace in August 1946 and again in November 1947. Both flights went over the heavily fortified military base at Karlskrona. The Swedes, who were never as neutral as they let on, flew their own penetration flights into Soviet airspace on July 17 and 26, 1951. The following year, they lost planes to Russian fighters, one of them an unarmed DC-3 over the Baltic.

THE FAR NORTH, which was the only feasible bomber route before in-flight refueling took hold, was a bleak, mysterious wilderness that menaced flyers and their airplanes. Weather conditions were often abominable and affected every aspect of operations in the Arctic, from physiological and psychological problems among individuals to nightmarish mechanical trouble. And trying to navigate in a place where time zones converged, magnetic compasses went haywire, and landmarks were buried under snow was always potentially perilous. There was often no clear distinction between snow-covered land and mountains, ice-covered ocean, and the glaring white sky. It could be like flying into a milk bottle.

Strategic factors, some real and some imagined, made Arctic operations even more difficult. For one thing, the polar region was useless to SAC as an attack route if the bomber force either couldn't get off the runways or couldn't find its way to the targets once it got into the air. Flying techniques to overcome those problems had to be worked out in spite of the locale and, of course, because of it.

Meanwhile, the intelligence vacuum quickly filled with visions of swarthy Slavs carving out advanced bases in northeastern Siberia, the ominously named October Revolution Island and Bolshevik Island off the north coast of Siberia, Franz Josef Land, the Murmansk area, and, for all anybody knew, even on land—if there was land—on islands in the Canadian Archipelago. There were SAC planners every bit as paranoid as their Russian counterparts who were convinced the Russian brown bear was in reality a polar bear that was everywhere.

Simple logic said that there was no point in creating a bomber force to be stationed in a godforsaken place from which it couldn't function. The first unit formed by the new Strategic Air Command was therefore not a bombardment squadron but a photoreconnaissance one. The Forty-sixth Reconnaissance Squadron was created in June 1946 and was promptly sent to Ladd Field outside of Fairbanks in the Alaska Territory with late-model B-29Fs. It was technically part of a wide-ranging operation that called for understanding the Alaskan, Aleutian, and eastern Siberian regions so they could be used successfully as bases and successfully attacked, respectively. Northern Greenland was also to be extensively reconnoitered and mapped so bombers based there, at Thule Air Base, could hit western Siberia. The whole operation was code-named Project Nanook.

The B-29Fs, which had been built to carry bombs across the Pacific, were stripped of their gun turrets and had extra fuel tanks installed in their bomb bays to increase range. There were several other major modifications, including the installation of Trimetrogon and long-focal-length cameras, radar scope cameras with large film capacities, and larger-than-normal astrodomes for the critically important navigators. Streamlining the bombers and reducing their weight increased their ceiling from 31,850 feet to 35,000 feet, an altitude no Soviet fighter could reach, at least at that time. And bright red was painted on every plane's tail and wingtips so they would be easier to spot if they crashed on the ice or snow. Since air/sea rescue aircraft in Alaska, notably C-47s, hadn't anywhere near the range to search for a downed reconnaissance plane, it would be up to the Forty-sixth itself to search for the missing crew.

The Forty-sixth was assigned the job of developing an accurate navigation system around the polar area, doing detailed weather studies, surveying and mapping the Arctic, studying polar magnetism, testing the endurance and efficiency of ground and air crews under the "stress" of extreme weather conditions, inventing ways to make the planes fully usable year-round, and scouring northeastern Siberia for enemy bombers and any other threat that turned up. When all that had been accomplished, or at least was under way, SAC's premier squadron would be expected to train bomber squadrons to navigate and work in the Arctic in preparation for war day. One of the units would be the renowned 509th Bomb Group, which had A-bombed Japan.

Major Maynard E. White, who commanded the Forty-sixth, was a security maven. He warned his nineteen crews that there were enemy agents in Fairbanks, and possibly even at Ladd Field, and careless talk could mean a crew might not return. "If you hear anyone, and this includes members of other flights, talking about missions or asking you any questions that even hint at what we have discussed here today . . . make sure you can identify them and then report the incident to me any time of the day or night." He explained the squadron's mission in minute detail, and that included the forays it would be making over Siberia. That bent the "need to know" rule. But in fact it was precisely the security issue that White had in mind. "The reason I am telling you all this classified information," he went on, "is to keep you from speculating. Now you don't need to speculate." White theorized that if his men knew exactly what they were in for, there wouldn't be much talk about it, and that would help the security situation. What they were in for was the combing of Siberia with their Trimetrogons: penetrations, many of them deep, in search of Soviet army units, munitions depots, and, mostly, the dreaded Tu-4s and any other bombers that threatened the United States.

On August 2, 1946, one of the B-29Fs (now referred to as F-13s) flew the squadron's first long-range mission, a "pioneering" one according to the unit's history, which lasted twelve hours and five minutes. Ten hours and twenty minutes of that flight were flown during icing conditions. And it was midsummer. In the dead of winter, when the temperature dropped to fifty degrees below zero Fahrenheit, the planes' tires would stick to the ground; brakes, gear boxes, and oil lines froze; and batteries had to be removed from planes that were parked outdoors for more than four hours. At any rate, from then on F-13s scoured the region while learning how to function, on the ground and in the air, in the worst flying conditions in the world.

The Forty-sixth, soon to be renumbered as the Seventy-second Reconnaissance Squadron, found that there were no air bases in the Provideniya Bukhta area of the Chukotskiy Peninsula. But airfields, storage depots, and barracks did turn up at Velkel, Anadyr, and Lavrentiya. "They were building airfields in the northern areas of Russia, and along the coastal areas, they were building submarine bases and airfields that we suspected were for offensive purposes," Fred Wack, a radar man and veteran of those early missions, recalled.

Wack said the missions over Siberia, some of which lasted for more than twenty-four hours, amounted to endurance tests. "After about thirteen or fourteen hours you think that you can't go any further but you continue to work at it," he explained. He and his crewmates popped Benzedrine to stay awake. After about seventeen hours, he added, he and the others became so numb from fatigue that "it really didn't matter anymore." All of the missions, regardless of duration, were flown in absolute radio silence. Several reported after landing back at Ladd that MiGs tried to shoot them down, but like dogs jumping and snapping at someone in a tree, they couldn't get high enough to get a bite.

As was the case with other units, the men of the Forty-sixth received little in the way of medals or other documented recognition for their work because it was official policy to deny it was being done. Medals were awarded for specific reasons and almost always were given in public. That was anathema to the intelligence fraternity. One crew, which flew a series of missions around the Kamchatka Peninsula with hundred-inch-focal-length cameras in late 1949, was quietly given Distinguished Flying Crosses and Air Medals, neither of which required elaborate explanation.

While it reconnoitered all over northeastern Siberia, the Forty-sixth also made some fundamental scientific contributions to understanding the Arctic, including its shifting magnetic pole, and developed a grid navigation system that simplified Arctic flying because it focused on getting from one geographic box to another without relying on magnetic compasses.

The first SAC electronic intelligence operation was getting under way at the same time. Believing the Soviets could be audacious enough to set up radar in the far reaches of Greenland, two ravens, 1st Lts. John E. Filos and Henry C. Monjar, were sent to Bluic West Eight Air Base in Greenland in a jury-rigged B-17G in early September 1946 to prowl over the world's largest island listening for enemy radar. There were no Russians on northern Greenland. Or if there were, they were fishing, not operating a radar station.

But most of the action in the north was still in Alaska. On October 15, 1946, with the Forty-sixth having been flying photo-reconnaissance missions for all of ten weeks, General LeMay showed up at Ladd with several high-ranking Air Force officers to look over the operation. He was then the deputy chief of staff for research and development and two years away from heading SAC.

During a reception that evening, LeMay pulled Maynard White into a corner and spent four hours grilling him about Project Nanook and its forays over Siberia. Mrs. White interrupted twice with plates of finger food but was politely ignored by the visiting general from "the lower forty-eight." He wanted to know, in particular, whether White thought it feasible for B-29s to fly from Alaska right across the breadth of the Soviet Union, land in Western Europe, and then fly back again. Because of his intimate knowledge of B-29s, LeMay knew the 5,000-mile missions would have required midair refueling, which would have involved two planes, not one, and therefore would have complicated the mission enormously.

Curtis LeMay got no useful information out of security-conscious Maynard White. Whatever his uniform, White reasoned, LeMay wasn't in SAC and therefore wasn't cleared for such a briefing. He therefore played dumb and politely told his guest that he really didn't have enough information to be able to discuss the matter. The fact that LeMay even raised the question indicates how desperate the Air Force was for intelligence.

Less than a month later, White was summoned to another meeting with LeMay, this one at Mitchell Field on Long Island in New York. Now the general wanted to discuss the feasibility of using specially designed, long-range, very-high-altitude aircraft to do the trans-Russian reconnaissance instead of B-29s. A concept was germinating in LeMay's mind. It would eventually be called the U-2.

Meanwhile, the Forty-sixth kept flying. Three of its far-ranging planes crashed. One of them, *Kee Bird*, bellied into an ice field in Greenland. The plane got its name from a mythical bird, invented by the Air Force personnel at Ladd, that supposedly stayed in Alaska all through the bitter winter when smarter birds flew south. The Kee Bird would trudge around in the snow, ruffling its feathers, and mumbling, "Kee-Kee-Rist but it's c-cold!"

Another of the Forty-sixth's far-ranging crews, this one flying over Siberia with the cameras on, had an adventure that belonged in a movie. As they flew right over an air base, the men in the Superfortress were astonished to see they were surrounded by Soviet planes. But no one was shooting at them. Then someone noticed that all the other planes looked exactly like their own B-29. It quickly became obvious, however, that there was one striking difference, though it was only skin-deep. The other "B-29s" didn't have red tails and wingtips. They had red stars. The flabbergasted Americans realized they were looking at a gaggle of Tu-4s. Enemy bombers! And when the crews in the Tu-4s saw the B-29, they obviously believed they were looking at one of their own bombers (or else it was Be Kind to American Reconnaissance Planes Day). The camera-laden interloper slipped away unnoticed and made it back to Ladd without a scratch.

In April 1947, White's squadron took on the added assignment of flying long ferret missions between Anchorage and Tokyo. That sent the planes and their new ravens down the length of the Siberian coast and then, after a week to ten days in Japan, back up again. The crews from Ladd were soon joined by other units,

Air Force and Navy, as the effort to get the measure of the radars all along the Siberian coast accelerated. There would be so many of them that flying the route got to be called a milk run. Sometimes the milk suddenly turned sour.

"Electronic reconnaissance flights should be made as often as possible with the equipment and personnel available," Maj. Gen. Charles P. Cabell, the Air Force's director of intelligence, told the Alaskan Air Command in a top-secret directive written on July 26, 1948. "Frequent repetition of search lines is considered essential." Specifically, ferret crews were supposed to locate enemy radar installations, determine their purpose—controlling fighters for an intercept, early warning, so-called gun-laying antiaircraft control, and so on—and get the "technical characteristics of the signal."

For your information, Cabell added, "intercept data has established the location and characteristics of some 39 European stations comprising a well defined Soviet chain of radar activity. In the Far Eastern area there have been eleven stations reported which have been established as to location." They started at Wrangel Island off the Chukotskiy Peninsula in northeastern Siberia, went through Diomede Island in the Bering Strait, down the coast through Petropavlovsk and Vladivostok, and ended at Dairen in Manchuria.

A year later, Lt. Gen. Lauris Norstad, the Air Force's deputy chief of staff for operations, sent an even more explicit order to LeMay at SAC headquarters at Offutt. It told LeMay in detail that SAC was now responsible for the Electronic Reconnaissance Program: "The Joint Chiefs of Staff have directed that 'an aggressive program to obtain the maximum amount of intelligence concerning foreign electronic developments shall be carried out as a safeguard to the national defense.' "

The memorandum figured importantly in the Peacetime Airborne Reconnaissance Program because it established the basic organizations that would conduct worldwide photo and electronic reconnaissance operations for years to come. Norstad moved the 324th Strategic Reconnaissance Squadron, Electronic, out of the Ninety-first Strategic Reconnaissance Group and into the Fifty-fifth Strategic Reconnaissance Group. He also assigned the

Ninety-first responsibility for photoreconnaissance and the Fifty-fifth for electronic reconnaissance, though the Fifty-fifth would do photoreconnaissance as well. The Fifty-fifth had done photoreconnaissance when it was activated, hence its motto: *Videmus omnia*, "We see all." The Ninety-first was born as the Army Signal Corps' Ninety-first Aero Squadron in August 1917 and sent to France as an observation unit supporting ground troops. The Fifty-fifth was organized as a fighter group on the eve of World War II and was turned into a reconnaissance group in 1947 and then into a wing the following year.

Norstad also directed that once the Ninety-first had switched from RB-50Bs to jet-propelled RB-47s, the RB-50Bs would be converted from photoreconnaissance to RB-50G ferrets and turned over to the 343d, which had been the 324th. The ill-fated *Little Red Ass* was one of those RB-50Gs.

The Peacetime Airborne Reconnaissance Program—PARPRO—worked only the periphery of the Iron Curtain and was therefore distinct from the overflights. In the latter, RB-29s on eighteen- to twenty-four-hour flights between Alaska and Japan suddenly darted into Siberian airspace to photograph and ferret targets deep inland. Still other penetrations flew right out of Japan itself. PARPRO missions often flew breathtakingly close to Soviet and other denied territory but did not make penetrations. The missions were flown relentlessly.

"We only knew when we were called into a briefing that we had been selected for the next ferret mission," Richard J. Meyer, a retired Air Force lieutenant colonel and a veteran of the Seventy-second Reconnaissance Squadron, explained in 1994 in reference to deep penetrations. "I think that the thing most locked into my memory is the concluding words of each ferret mission briefing: 'Gentlemen, there is no possible search or rescue capability on this mission. In the event you go down and survive to be captured, every effort will be made to effect your return, but no result can be promised.' "

All aircrews got a week of survival training. The reconnaissance crews got a couple of extra weeks, apparently because the frequency of their overflights made a crash landing in denied territory far more likely. The program had to do with surviving both mother nature and their captors. The outdoor training took place at Stead Air Force Base, near Reno, and at some other bases, including Forbes. Political preparation was given at a number of places, also including Forbes, and it was realistic in the extreme.

The airmen were ordinarily left in the wilds of Nevada, the "survival forest" at Forbes, or elsewhere for a week with a day's supply of rations. They were expected to make shelter out of their parachutes or find it locally and live off whatever vegetation and animals they could kill and cook. After a couple of days, some of the ravenous airmen even ate ants and rodents. Many who went through the course maintained, through firsthand experience or hearsay, that porcupines are inedible, cooked or not. Rabbit stew, on the other hand, amounted to fois gras.

If they were captured, the airmen were under orders to give their captors a cover story about the "long range navigation training mission." It was essentially the same cover story the government would give their loved ones. But there was far more to practicing survival at the hands of captors than mouthing glib cover stories. Reg Urschler, the RB-47H copilot who dreaded having to tell LeMay that he had run out of fuel over the Sea of Japan, had an experience that was more or less typical of political survival training. He recalled that he and the others in his crew were told to report to Forbes as if they were going to fly a regular mission. Instead, they were separated individually or in groups of two or three, blindfolded, and taken into a building. There they were stripped to their shorts, given a blue laundry bag with a rope cord, and squeezed into wall lockers that were too short for them to stand and too narrow for them to sit. So each man stayed in a half-sitting position all day and into the next while someone occasionally beat on the locker with a billy club and demanded that he and the others "say your number." The retired brigadier general smiled one day many years later as he remembered that when one man in his crew did not respond to the order, the locker door was opened and the "captors" saw that he had the laundry bag cord around his neck and seemed to have hanged himself. The airman had pulled a practical joke on his tormentors. "That-a-way, Jack," his fellow prisoners cheered.

Interrogation was realistic and went from the threat of physical force to very subtle mental manipulation. And it always came when they were already physically exhausted. Robb Hoover, an RB-47H raven and another veteran of the Fifty-fifth, said, "they really messed with your mind." In one survival training exercise, his crew was supposedly shot down over Albania. He remembered his captors wanted to know what he knew about Albania. There was a temptation to tell them, to "show off." But spilling the beans about Albania could lead to spilling the beans about the mission. The lesson, Hoover explained, was not to "act like a Boy Scout; not to show off." Answering their questions too quickly was definitely not a good idea, he continued. "Take your time."

SURVIVAL TRAINING MAY have helped the crewmen of the *Turbulent Turtle*, but it is unlikely. Whatever happened to them, their mission fundamentally changed the rules of the Peacetime Airborne Reconnaissance Program.

Turbulent Turtle was a Navy PB4Y-2 Privateer in Patrol Squadron Twenty-six. VP-26's home was the Patuxent River Naval Air Station in Maryland. But in April 1950, four of the squadron's Privateers were on rotational temporary duty at Port Lyautey, French Morocco. The planes were stuffed with hardware for electronic intelligence collection and were based in Morocco because the Navy was responsible for reconnaissance in the Mediterranean and Black Sea areas. Although the Air Force ordinarily covered northern Europe, including the Baltic, the boundaries there, as in Asia, were far from rigid. So VP-26's Privateers ranged as far north as the Baltic, too. They flew their missions under the guise of courier planes carrying diplomatic pouches around Western Europe, Scandinavia, and, in particular, the Baltic and the Adriatic. Since it was common knowledge that the large planes carried electronics technicians, and since C-47s and C-54s were more adapted to carrying mail than maritime patrol aircraft—it didn't require a lumbering battle-ax to deliver mail—no one was fooled by the ruse.

In early April, VP-26 received orders to send one of its Privateers up to Wiesbaden, West Germany, from where it was to ferret Latvian radar. It landed at Wiesbaden late on the night of the 6th.

Like other large reconnaissance planes of a certain age, *Turbulent Turtle* had been designed to carry bombs and a dozen machine guns. But like its Air Force counterparts, the RB-29s and RB-50s, its bomb bay now held electronic warfare specialists and their ubiquitous black boxes. But unlike the Air Force bombers, *Turbulent Turtle* carried no guns because of its thin cover as a mail courier. It ordinarily carried an eleven-man crew. On April 8, however, it flew with only ten because Stephen J. Zaklan, an enlisted electronics technician, was grounded at Wiesbaden with hepatitis. That day, unknowingly, Zaklan joined the ranks of the select few who dodged death by missing a doomed mission. Lt. John H. Fette, the aircraft commander, and nine others were less fortunate. Fette was in the Naval Reserve and had 1,800 hours in Privateers, many of them in the Philippines in World War II. He was considered to be the best patrol plane commander in VP-26 and was renowned as one of its toughest check pilots. But that wouldn't help.

Fette took off from Wiesbaden in midmorning that Saturday and headed north to Bremerhaven. Then he banked to the right, skirted Copenhagen, and headed out over the Baltic toward the Latvian coast.

At 2:20 in the afternoon, a routine Air Force radio position check failed to raise the Privateer. Late that night, the Air Force Flight Service in Frankfurt, which kept track of all military air operations in Europe, notified the Navy that 59645 *Turbulent Turtle*'s serial number—was seriously overdue. Procedure called for aircraft from the missing plane's own squadron to help with the search, so before dawn the next morning, the other three Privateers were sent from Morocco to Wiesbaden to join the search. Carefully, secretly, the Privateers, joined by twenty-five Air Force planes, searched a wide swath of the Baltic off Latvia for any sign of the missing plane. They turned up nothing.

The Swedes had better luck. A few days after the search was called off, a Swedish fishing vessel found a life raft floating near Gotland Island, roughly halfway between Sweden and Latvia. It was reported to have had shrapnel holes in it. Then a British freighter found another raft forty-five miles southeast of Stockholm. Both rafts were positively identified as belonging to *Turbu-*

lent Turtle. They had dye markers attached to lifelines at regular intervals, a practice peculiar to VP-26. The supply compartments on the raft picked up by the British were open and empty, suggesting that at least some of the crew might have survived the crash and been captured.

Nor was there any doubt as to what had happened. Swedish intelligence intercepted unambiguous orders from Soviet ground controllers to fighter pilots to shoot down the American reconnaissance plane. The taped command was quickly passed on to U.S. intelligence. The Swedish connection, which worked on a number of levels, was one of the best-kept secrets of the cold war. Sweden was given powerful Air Force and Navy cameras for use in its own aerial reconnaissance program, for example, and it shared the pictures with its benefactors.

News of the attack was broken—no, trumpeted—by Moscow three days after it occurred. Andrei Y. Vyshinsky, the Soviet foreign minister, handed the U.S. ambassador to the Soviet Union, Adm. Alan G. Kirk, a short but vituperative protest note on April 11. In it the Kremlin identified the downed plane as a "B-29 type, a Flying Fortress" that penetrated twenty-one kilometers into the USSR. Fighters were sent after the intruder, the note went on, and when it refused to land at a nearby air base and instead shot at the interceptors, it was attacked. It then turned toward the sea and disappeared.

The part about refusing to land, then being reluctantly attacked, and finally heading back out to sea like a wounded bird would become standard boilerplate for such demarches. But the last paragraph was written to send the United States a new and unambiguous message: "The Soviet Government announces its resolute protest to the Government of the United States against this gross violation of the Soviet frontier by an American military plane, which at the same time constitutes an unheard of violation of the elementary rules of international law." Whatever the mistaken reference to a B-29, which in any case would have been a Superfortress, not a Flying Fortress, it was clear that it had been the Privateer that was attacked.

The shooting down of *Turbulent Turtle* marked a turning point in relations between the two antagonists. The message was that

the Kremlin had had enough of U.S. planes ferreting radar, eavesdropping on communication, dropping spies, and taking pictures
along and even inside Soviet borders. The sanctity of the USSR
(which claimed a twelve-mile limit) would from now on be
fiercely protected. Any intruder that ventured too close to its territory could therefore expect to suffer the consequences.

Being world-class propagandists, and having staked out the
moral high ground in their note, the men in the Kremlin immediately went on the offensive by sharing it with the news media.
Caught off guard, "high defense officials in Washington" said the
missing Privateer was unarmed and had been on a round-trip
training flight to Copenhagen, later described as a "weather research flight."

Ten days after *Turbulent Turtle* vanished, the Department of
State counterattacked with its own note (copies of which were
duly distributed to the newspapers). All U.S. military aircraft, including the unarmed Privateer, fly with strict instructions to avoid
foreign territory unless they have permission to be there, the note
said. Then State proclaimed its own right to the moral high
ground in what was the opening broadside of a series of ritualized
and sanctimonious ripostes that would become standard fare for
years: "The Ambassador of the United States has been instructed
to protest in the most solemn manner against this violation of international law and of the most elementary rules of peaceful conduct between nations. The United States Government demands
that the Soviet Government institute a prompt and thorough investigation of this matter in order that the facts set forth above
may be confirmed to its satisfaction."

Like the Russians, the news media in the United States found
the official explanation for the last flight of *Turbulent Turtle* un-
persuasive. "The American Privateer presumably was engaged in
some sort of reconnaissance, whether 'insolent' [as the Russians
charged] or otherwise, whether over Russian-occupied territory or
not," *Newsweek* noted. "The aircraft was equipped with radar and
photographic equipment and contained three electronic specialists in its ten-man crew," it added. "Moreover, it was operating in
a militarily fascinating area."

Washington Post columnist Marquis Childs maintained that the

Russians thought the Privateer was carrying new reconnaissance equipment that extended its collection range. Drew Pearson, the leading investigative journalist of the era, pointed out in the *New York Mirror* that publicizing the fact that three of *Turbulent Turtle*'s crewmen were electronics specialists advertised its mission even before it took off. The Russians knew it was full of "high-powered radar and electronics equipment," he scolded. And a third columnist, the widely respected Walter Lippmann, wrote in *The Washington Post* that the Soviets knew the Privateer carried "important electronic equipment" and set a trap for it in order to grab it, and that the trap had obviously failed. A second reason, he explained, was political:

"The affair lends considerable weight to the view that the Russians are intent first of all upon making their own territory invulnerable to American airpower. If they could make it invulnerable, then the Red Army would be virtually unopposed around the periphery of the Soviet Union. This Baltic incident is meant, I believe, to convince the Russian people and also the people of Europe that the Soviet Union has achieved an air defense."

Indeed it had. President Truman, who was surprised by the incident and its political fallout, immediately ordered a thirty-day suspension of ferret and other electronic intelligence flights starting on April 17. But on May 5, Omar N. Bradley, chairman of the Joint Chiefs of Staff, sent a memorandum to Secretary of Defense Louis A. Johnson saying the benefit of the flights was eminently worth the risk and urging that they be continued. He was also careful to note that "special electronic airborne search projects" had been going on for years "without a formal statement of policy but on the basis of an informal working agreement between the Navy and the Air Force." That would now change.

Writing on behalf of the Joint Chiefs, Bradley suggested that Special Electronic Airborne Search Projects, known as SESP, "be resumed with the least practicable delay." The document went on to outline the extent of the ferret program, noting at one point that planes operating "adjacent to the USSR or its satellites be armed and that their crews be instructed to shoot in self-defense." Truman, who studied the memorandum after Johnson forwarded it to him, penned in the margin, "Good sense, it seems to me."

Furthermore, Bradley continued, flights by individual aircraft will, "to the maximum extent possible, be scheduled so that the portion(s) of the flight near particularly sensitive or heavily defended areas will be under cover of darkness or weather" and they should fly no closer than twenty miles. "Approved 5/19/50," Harry Truman wrote under Bradley's signature.

THE RESTRUCTURING OF ferret operations and their sanctioning by the White House was profoundly important, not only militarily, but politically. The increasing fear of an expanding Soviet military threat growing within that country's vast domain, especially with its newly acquired nuclear weapons, meant the Western alliance absolutely had to be able to strike decisively by air. And that, in turn, rested squarely on getting past the radar. The ferreting requirement, as well as the need for photoreconnaissance, far outweighed the inevitable diplomatic confrontations that were bound to make headlines when an incident such as the downing of *Turbulent Turtle* occurred.

First blood had been spilled. There would be more. There would also be prisoners who vanished behind the curtain. *Turbulent Turtle*'s rafts were indeed a clue that their occupants had been picked up by Russians. Credible eyewitness reports that American Navy flyers had been seen in a Soviet prison surfaced a few years later. In one, an American who was released from one of the gulags told Department of State investigators that a Yugoslav had told him of meeting eight American airmen who claimed to have been shot down over the Baltic. The American, John Noble, reported they had told the Yugoslav they had been picked up by a Soviet coast guard boat. The Yugoslav himself was located in West Germany in May 1955 and corroborated Noble's story. He could not identify the Americans by name, but he told of talking to one crewman who stated emphatically that he had been shot down over the Baltic and was serving a twenty-five-year sentence for espionage.

And there were other reports. A Norwegian, Bjorn Willy Gunerinssen, told his government that while he was held captive in the prison at Vorkuta, there were persistent rumors of U.S. Navy flyers being there, as well. Gunerinssen said the rumors had grown much stronger by 1954. Still others corroborated the suspicion that crewmen from an Air Force RB-29 ferret shot down by MiGs over the Sea of Japan on June 13, 1952, were also prisoners in the Soviet Union.

The reports were taken so seriously that on July 17, 1956, the United States sent a highly publicized note to the Soviet Foreign Ministry accusing the Russians of holding at least ten officers and enlisted men from the two planes. The protest said the United States was "compelled to believe" information about detained airmen who were in various Soviet camps because of eyewitness accounts from "persons of various nationalities freed from Soviet Government imprisonment during the last several years." One injured naval airman had been seen at a camp near Taishet in eastern Siberia and at a collective farm. Others from *Turbulent Turtle* were reported to be in the Vorkuta area, the note continued. A tenth man believed to be from the RB-29 complained in a hospital in the Far East that he had been "wrongfully" convicted by the Russians.

"While the foregoing specific cases involve the crew members of two aircraft, it may well be that the Soviet Government has in its custody members of the crews of other United States aircraft," the note went on, "particularly crew members of aircraft engaged on behalf of the United Nations Command side of the military action in Korea since 1950." The note included the names of the twelve men on the RB-29 (which it studiously called a B-29). At least two of them, a major and a master sergeant, had indeed been pulled out of the water by Russians. By the time the note was written, however, both had been brutally killed.

Large-scale reconnaissance was under way. And so was the means to stop it.

MORE BLOOD

THE ATTACK ON *Turbulent Turtle* heralded a new and ominous stage in the quiet but relentless air war that was playing out in the deep shadow of the cold war. It was a clear signal by the Kremlin that the "spies" who constantly prowled along its frontier, and often violated it, would be kept at bay by whatever force was necessary. The Union of Soviet Socialist Republics was proclaiming that it was surrounded, but it was not defenseless. Warning had been served: anyone who came looking for illicit information could expect to be bloodied.

Eleven weeks later, on June 25, 1950, North Korean infantry and tanks abruptly spilled over the thirty-eighth parallel and overran South Korean positions. The cold war suddenly turned hot. Taken in a larger context, the invasion of South Korea was seen by American strategists as being another manifestation—and a blatantly bold and obvious one—of worldwide communism's relentless, insidious war on Western democracy.

"I told my advisers," Truman wrote a few years later, "that what was developing in Korea seemed to me like a repetition on a larger scale of what had happened in Berlin. The Reds were probing for weaknesses in our armor; we had to meet their thrust without getting embroiled in a world-wide war." Less than five months before the invasion, in fact, Truman authorized development of the hydrogen bomb.

Meeting the North Korean invasion meant rushing poorly equipped U.S. Army units that had gone soft from easy occupation duty in Japan into the fiery breach. It also meant rallying the United Nations to stop the advancing Communists in what was euphemistically called a "police action." (The term invariably provoked snickers from GIs whose bloody battles at Pork Chop Hill, the Choson Reservoir, and elsewhere seemed to them like a real war.)

Korea was the eye of the storm during the summer of 1950, but it was a storm that extended elsewhere as well. With U.S. and other NATO troops, including Greeks and Turks, committed to the defense of South Korea, it was feared that the Russians would use the distraction to grab territory in Western Europe, Turkey, or Iran through a combination of military aggression and subversion. And if that led to a general war, no one in the Department of Defense doubted still more Russians would come pouring out of eastern Siberia to strike at the forty-eight states themselves.

Collecting intelligence everywhere, therefore, became a desperate matter. Strategic intelligence collection divided into two generic areas, though they overlapped. The first, which was dominated by the CIA, had to do with making long-term estimates of Soviet and other nations' capabilities in everything from food production to energy output to weapon development, testing, and inventories. The second, which was almost completely dominated by the Air Force and the Navy, had to do with the requirements of actual war fighting. Unlike the CIA, for example, SAC did not need to know how much uranium the Soviet Union was enriching (although it did know). What SAC needed was very accurate and constantly updated information on what its targets were—including uranium enrichment facilities—where they were located, and how they could be "taken out" with minimal loss of aircraft.

SAC's core mission was to destroy the enemy's capacity to destroy the United States and its allies. That meant airfields, missile installations, naval facilities, weapons storage bunkers, and the national and regional command headquarters themselves—where

Capt. O'Kelley's RB-50G was shot down on July 29, 1953. M. Sgt. Francis Brown and A2c. James Woods (top) were lost, as was O'Kelley (upper left). Capt. John E. Roche (upper right) was the only survivor. The plane itself is shown taking off on a mission. Most of the crewmen enjoyed a night out in Japan before they disappeared

WESTERN
UNION

W. P. MARSHALL, President

10B64 KB383
K.TKA461 GOVT RX PD=FORBES AFB TOPEKA KANS 30 655P MC=
MARGARET K O'KELLEY=
          1036 SPRING ST NAPA CALIF (REPORT DELIVERY)=

BPAF 6772. IT IS WITH DEEP REGET THAT I OFFICIALLY
INFORM YOU OF THE MISSING STATUS OF YOUR HUSBAND
CAPTAIN STANLEY K O'KELLEY. STANLEY WAS REPORTED
MISSING ON A ROUTINE TRAINING FLIGHT NEAR JAPAN ON THE
29TH OF JULY 1953. A VIGOROUS SEARCH OF THE AREA IS
BEING CONDUCTED BY EVERY FACILITY AT THE DISPOSAL OF
THE UNITED STATES GOVERNMENT ANY FURTHER INFORMATION

WILL BE TELEGRAPHED TO YOU IMMEIDATELY. PLEASE ACCEPT
MY SINCERE SYMPATHY FOR THE ANXIETY THIS MAY CAUSE YO.
STANLEY'S MOTHER AND FATHER HAVE BEEN NOTIFIED BY
TELEGRAM=
          JOSEPH D CALDARA BRIG GENERAL USAF COMM=

Margaret and Stan O'Kelley in San Francisco on their honeymoon in April 1944 when he was a lieutenant in the Army Air Forces. Nine years later he was shot down on a ferret mission off Vladivostok and died at sea. The telegram, typical of others, was misleading

Mary Dunham Nichols's husband, John, was shot down north of Hokkaido on October 7, 1952. His Annapolis class ring was returned by a Russian forty years later and hangs on a gold chain

She was given the flag that draped her husband's coffin before he was buried at Arlington National Cemetery on August 1, 1995, as her daughter, Suzanne, and grandsons looked on

This RB-50G was originally designed as a bomber, not as an intelligence collector. It and fourteen others were extensively modified to collect signals from enemy radar. One of them, Little Red Ass, was attacked and shot down near Vladivostok on July 29, 1953

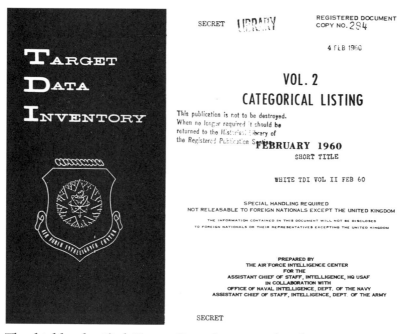

TARGET DATA INVENTORY

REGISTERED DOCUMENT
COPY NO. 284

4 FEB 1960

VOL. 2
CATEGORICAL LISTING

This publication is not to be destroyed. When no longer required it should be returned to the Historical Library of the Registered Publication Section

FEBRUARY 1960

SHORT TITLE

WHITE TDI VOL II FEB 60

SPECIAL HANDLING REQUIRED
NOT RELEASABLE TO FOREIGN NATIONALS EXCEPT THE UNITED KINGDOM

THE INFORMATION CONTAINED IN THIS DOCUMENT WILL NOT BE DISCLOSED
TO FOREIGN NATIONALS OR THEIR REPRESENTATIVES EXCEPTING THE UNITED KINGDOM

PREPARED BY
THE AIR FORCE INTELLIGENCE CENTER
FOR THE
ASSISTANT CHIEF OF STAFF, INTELLIGENCE, HQ USAF
IN COLLABORATION WITH
OFFICE OF NAVAL INTELLIGENCE, DEPT. OF THE NAVY
ASSISTANT CHIEF OF STAFF, INTELLIGENCE, DEPT. OF THE ARMY

SECRET

The highly classified Target Data Inventory *listed every target in the Communist bloc, including many hundreds of radar and other air defense sites by function, location, and vulnerability to attack*

The RB-47H, another bomber adapted to ferret radar, was vastly superior to propeller-driven aircraft because of its speed. (Inset) Robb Hoover, a former raven, shows Brig. Gen. Regis Urschler (ret.), who was an RB-47 copilot, where the ravens' compartment was

This Fifty-fifth Strategic Reconnaissance Wing RB-47H was intercepted by Yak-25 fighters as it ferreted over the Laptev Sea in the summer of 1966. Its crew (from left to right) is Lt. Col. James Taylor, Lt. Richard Tucker, Capt. Thomas Reed, Capt. William Lewis, Capt. Robb Hoover, and Capt. Errol Hoberman

Curious MiG pilots often came in close and "tucked in." This MiG-19 was one of the three that intercepted an RB-47H over the Baltic Sea on September 24, 1962. The MiG pilot took a picture of the American jet while its pilot, John Drost, took this picture of him

Wang Wei, a Chinese pilot who was killed in 2001 when his fighter collided with a Navy reconnaissance plane, enjoyed flying dangerously close to foreign planes. Months earlier, he was photographed brazenly holding up his e-mail address for the Americans to copy

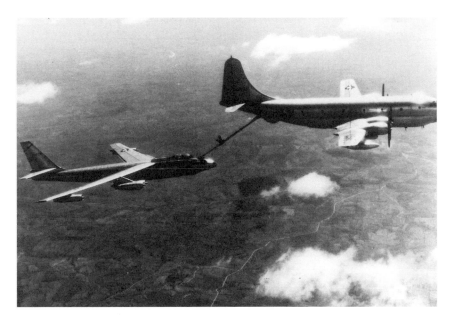

Gen. Curtis E. LeMay ordered SAC to develop aerial refueling capability to increase its planes' range. The top photograph shows a KC-97G refueling an RB-47E, which collected photo intelligence. Below, another tanker is filling—"gassing up"—a SAC RF-84F Thunderflash, another camera-carrier

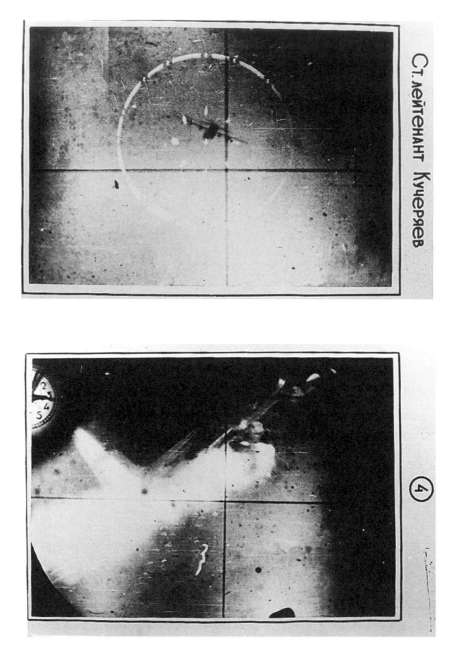

This rare Soviet gun camera film shows a U.S. Air Force C-130 reconnaissance plane being stalked and then wracked by MiG cannon fire over Armenia on September 2, 1958. All seventeen crew members were killed. The MiG pilot's name, Senior Lt. Kucharyaev, appears on the film

the politicians and officers who gave orders worked—were at the top of the hit list. They were closely followed by all other military installations and their support structure, from food warehouses to tank factories. SAC was also supposed to inflict so much collateral damage to so many other places, such as power plants, major roads, and waterways, that the enemy would be unable to function as a society, let alone wage war.

The targets numbered in the many thousands, and keeping track of them quickly grew into a highly secretive and complicated military specialty. Each was listed in minute detail in a *Target Data Inventory* and a *Bombing Encyclopedia*, both of which were compiled by the Air Force Intelligence Center in Washington in collaboration with Army and Navy intelligence and the CIA. All the information in those collections went into the target folders that Air Force and Navy attackers were primed to use when they were sent to war. This was the heart, the epicenter, of the intelligence collection process. It was in these constantly updated reference systems that all the information collected around the world by ferrets, aerial photography, eavesdropping, and garden variety spying was funneled, sifted, strained, and crystallized into precise details about where all the targets were, what they did, how they were defended, and what it would take to obliterate them.

The encyclopedia listed targets' names, geographic coordinates, function and output, and transportation routes (how they were connected to the other parts of the overall defense web). It and a huge file called the Strategic Library Bombing Index were menus of mayhem that contained every target of any value everywhere on Earth. And that data, in turn, not only went into the target folders used by Air Force and Navy bomber crews but, later, into the brains of the missiles that hid in silos and lurked underwater. The folders were compiled by the Air Staff's Strategic Vulnerability Branch. Other target intelligence, certainly including what the ferrets brought back, went directly to Offutt so it could be incorporated directly into the folders, or to the Air Force Foreign Technology Division at Wright-Patterson Air Force Base outside of Dayton, which specialized in understanding the opposition's weapons capability in detail.

The *Target Data Inventory*, which was updated three times a year, justified its existence up front: "Its purpose is to provide standardized target data for target planning and coordination. It is a means for the dissemination and maintenance of essential information on the identification, location, relative importance and physical vulnerability of those Sino-Soviet Bloc installations and complexes which have been evaluated as possessing current or potential target significance."

By 1960, both volumes of the *Target Data Inventory*, or *TDI*, would total well over 1,000 pages and list every conceivable target by the many thousands. Volume I listed them alphabetically. Volume II arranged them by category. And the categories far transgressed the narrow interpretation of "military." They included everything that could conceivably be militarily useful, down to factories that made helmets and the sources of water soldiers and civilians drank. Orphanages and mental institutions would not make the list, but much else did, including air defense bases, guided missile airframe factories, chemical and biological warfare research facilities, railroad bridges, assorted navy supply depots, "exotic" fuel storage depots, freight and passenger terminals, locomotive repair facilities, radio stations, "populated places," and even viaducts.

The significance of every target was rated according to six criteria in descending order of importance: "Air Offense, Long Range—the capability to support air attack on the Continental United States; Air Offense, Medium Range—the capability to support air attack on US overseas and Allied installations; Air Defense—the capability to support defense against penetration of Soviet Bloc air space by US and Allied aircraft; Land Operations—the capability to support the conduct of land warfare; Sea Operations—the capability to support sea operations"; and finally War Support, which related to industrial, economic, political, and even psychological support of the military.

Soviet air defenses were a lower priority than offensive capability in the air, meaning it was more important to prevent the Russians from bombing the United States and its allies than it was to bomb Russian targets. But the difference was esoteric. The way to prevent such an attack, according to SAC doctrine, was to destroy as many Russian bombers and missiles as possible before they got off the ground. That meant breaking through their air defenses and clobbering the offense the way defensive linebackers break through the offensive line to hit quarterbacks before they throw the ball.

Soviet air defense would itself be divided into fighter, missile, and antiaircraft gun facilities, weapon storage bunkers, command and personnel areas, the airfields themselves, and the various kinds of radar. SAC's targeteers tried to make the strike points on airfields so precise, to take one target category, that the coordinates for where the bomb or missile was supposed to hit crossed at the "center of runway" for airfields with one runway; "midpoint of a line joining the center of the runways" where there were parallel runways; and "midpoint of the intersection" where runways crossed. The coordinates were supposed to be accurate to within 1,000 feet. That required a very high order of photo intelligence. To take another class of targets from hundreds: each of the 696 "Radar Sites, Early Warning, Fixed" that ringed the USSR and were scattered inside its borders in 1960 would be given a single line in the *Target Data Inventory* that told the attackers everything they needed to know to blow it up.

The radar station at Vladivostok was divided into categories that ran across the page: its primary location and general area; its name; a *Bombing Encyclopedia* number—0291E06172 (E for electronic)—which would tell where it was on the World Aeronautical Chart and give information on the site itself; coordinates (43 minutes, 16 seconds north latitude, and 132 minutes, 1 second east longitude); a number that gave its significance (001000, meaning it was an air defense facility of primary importance); a numerical designation providing additional information; and a PV, or physical vulnerability number (in this case, 09Q5), which told the initiated how the site would react to being hit by the blast wave from a one-kiloton nuclear bomb or from one of more than twenty kilotons. (The fate assigned to some air defense control centers was grim: "at least severe structural damage to buried and semi-buried reinforced concrete framed buildings and associated damage generally as follows: severe earth and debris damage to the building contents including communications equipment, radar equipment, plotting boards, etc., and utilities.") Finally, the site's country was listed: UR, for USSR.

All that intelligence, plus the radars' vital signs supplied by the ferrets, were what photoreconnaissance was supposed to bring back. But it came at great cost during the Korean War and afterward, largely because the men who were sent out to collect the information did so in hand-me-down airplanes that had been designed for other purposes.

IT HAD BEEN understood almost since the birth of aviation that speed and altitude conferred an extra margin of safety to the aviator. It was the low-flying bird, or the one on the ground, that became prey for hawks, cats, and other predators. The one that soared survived. While keeping its propeller-driven RB-29s and RB-50s active, the Air Force therefore began converting faster jet fighters and bombers for reconnaissance. Lockheed's already old but reliable RF-80C Shooting Star was pressed into service for tactical reconnaissance in direct support of the ground war in Korea, and so was Republic Aviation's RF-84F Thunderflash.

North American Aviation's MiG-killing F-86 Sabrejet was fitted with a forward oblique twenty-four-inch camera and a pair of twenty-inch cameras in a compartment under the pilot's seat. That version was called the RF-86A. The speedy fighters not only handled tactical reconnaissance, but occasionally went on deep forays into Manchuria and Siberia on strategic missions. Sabres fitted with four 200-gallon drop tanks to extend their range, and two distortionless cameras that photographed a near-panoramic swath of territory, were sent on high-flying penetration missions in search of air bases at Vladivostok, Sakhalin Island, Dairen, Khabarovsk, deep into Manchuria, and almost 1,000 miles into the Soviet Union.

The fuel was so precious that the camera-carrying Sabrejets were towed to the head of the takeoff runway and then started so they wouldn't waste a drop. Sudden forays into Manchuria during the Korean War began when one of the fighters accompanied a crowd of regular gun-wielding Sabrejets into MiG Alley, which ran along the southern edge of the Yalu, looking for a dogfight.

The unarmed reconnaissance jet would then slip away from the formation when a fight started, streak over the Yalu at more than 600 miles an hour and at around 50,000 feet, and head north in search of air bases and other photo opportunities. They flew at times when they wouldn't leave white contrails. Seen from the ground, contrails looked like long chalk lines on a blackboard and would give them away. At that altitude the Sabrejets were easily tracked by search radar, but they were too high for the MiG pilots to see and they were therefore not attacked. Because they flew alone over long distances and at high altitude, looking for "a needle in a haystack," as one veteran put it, pilots had to be exceptional navigators.

Later, the same basic missions were flown by the Sabrejet's successor, the F-100 Super Sabre, out of Turkey and over the Caucasus region in an operation called Slick Chick. As in Asia, the key to surviving the penetrations was surprise, speed, and staying in enemy airspace for as short a time as possible.

George Saylor, a Sabrejet recce pilot from Montgomery, Alabama, flew in a squadron that called itself the Honeybuckets. The term referred to the pails of human excrement used by South Korean farmers to fertilize their rice paddies. The pilots in the squadron were told their operation was higher than top secret and that meant telling no one. "You signed a paper that you wouldn't reveal it in any way," Saylor revealed after the work was declassified in 1996. "The story they handed out was that we were studying winds aloft."

None of the camera-carrying Sabrejets was lost in action, but there were some close calls. Melvin Vojvodich recalled years later that he was chased by about fifty MiGs one day as he made a beeline for the Yellow Sea. "I found out that it's a good thing that even if fifty of them are chasing you and firing like crazy, only one can get on your tail at a time."

With a single notable exception, the propeller-driven B-36, the long-range strategic reconnaissance mission was shifted to the new jet bombers, which were quickly modified for their new role. The first of them, North American's RB-45C Tornado, had straight wings that carried four engines. It was nicknamed the "Lead Sled" by those who flew it because of its difficult flying characteristics in some situations. And it was especially vulnerable to flak. One Air Force report claimed "even the slightest rip, tear, or battle damage affects the [RB-45's] operational characteristics." But the Tornado's virtue was that it could fly at a little more than 500 miles an hour, or roughly 150 miles an hour faster than the plodding RB-50, and could climb to 40,000 feet. The problem was that MiGs could fly even faster.

Great Britain's first jet bomber, the English Electric Canberra, was also built under license by the Martin Company in Baltimore and called the Night Intruder. The first U.S. Air Force Canberra, which was called the B-57, was made in England and became the first jet to cross the Atlantic nonstop on February 21, 1951. U.S. reconnaissance versions, called the RB-57D and RB-57F, had exceptionally long wings and could deliver high-quality photographs or collect electronic intelligence from as high as 64,000 feet. Canberras on reconnaissance in both the Old World and the New would gain a special place in the annals of the cold war.

Boeing's sleek, swept-wing B-47, which first took to the air on December 17, 1947—the forty-fourth anniversary of the Wright brothers' flight at Kitty Hawk—was also adapted to several reconnaissance missions beginning in 1953. The Stratojet, as Boeing called it, was a marvel of its time because it looked like a very large fighter, handled like one, and could reach a maximum speed of 600 miles an hour. It had an impressive range of 4,000 miles, could be refueled in the air, and in its bomber version was used by LeMay to set distance records that were unabashedly designed to intimidate the Russians.

The exception to the all-jet reconnaissance bombers was Convair's gigantic RB-36D, the intelligence-collecting version of SAC's B-36D Peacemaker, which was conceived to carry monster-sized nuclear weapons to the Soviet heartland. "Peacemaker" alluded to the plane's deterrent role, as in SAC's motto, "Peace is our profession."

The first of the mammoth bombers arrived at the Twenty-eighth Strategic Reconnaissance Wing at Rapid City Air Force Base, South Dakota, on June 2, 1950. It was 162 feet long and used six powerful propeller engines that pushed from the back of its 230-foot-long wings, plus a pair of turbojets slung under each of them. The Peacemaker's wings were so thick at the root they had passageways that could be entered from catwalks on either side of the bomb bay. Inside the wings, crewmen could work on fuse panels, fuel and oil valves, and electrical terminals, and make in-flight repairs. They could even operate the plane's flaps and lower its landing gear manually in case of an electrical or hydraulic problem.

RB-36Ds carried either electronic warfare equipment for signals intelligence collection, including ferreting, or fourteen cameras, most of them huge. Roger Ihle, who had flown ferret missions on the B-17 *Archangel* around the Mediterranean in World War II, was called up again during the Korean War and eventually wound up on an RB-36D. He claimed, correctly, that the plane's photographic capability was awesome. "They had every kind of camera I think was ever invented," he said. "They could take forward obliques, verticals, side obliques, rear obliques. They had everything covered, photographically." Gen. George W. Goddard, the Air Force's master camera designer, wrote years later that the RB-36D's size meant that for the first time there was no real weight restriction on the cameras. He and James Baker, the Harvard optics genius and another leading light in photoreconnaissance, therefore developed a scanning camera with a forty-eight-inch lens that weighed nearly a ton. One of them, installed in an RB-36 flying over Fort Worth at 34,000 feet, shot a picture over a golf course that clearly showed two golf balls and a caddy holding the flag.

The lumbering beast cruised at 225 miles an hour, which was nothing to brag about. But it made a valuable strategic reconnaissance plane because it could get up to 45,200 feet and had a range of 7,500 miles. And even that considerable distance was extended when someone thought of turning the RB-36 into a mother ship carrying a speedy, hitchhiking fighter that was itself provided with its own brace of cameras. The idea, born out of the sheer desperation of the moment, was to carry the fighter—an RF-84F—in the modified bomb bay of the RB-36D and release it just outside enemy territory. The swept-wing fighter was then supposed to dash over the border, get pictures of the target from 25,000 feet, and then race back to the mother ship, which would lower an H-shaped trapeze. The Thunderflash's pilot would inch closer and closer to the trapeze until he connected with it and would then be pulled into the mother ship's belly for the flight home. Ten of the huge bombers and twenty-five RF-84Fs were modified to work together and actually went into service for about a year. But operational difficulties and the arrival of the RB-45Cs, RB-47s, and RB-57Ds ended the bomber-fighter marriage and, ultimately, the use of the RB-36D itself.

During their relatively brief career as reconnaissance planes, however, the RB-36Ds' size and range made them valuable because they could fly what were then enormous distances at very high altitude. They were unexcelled at photomapping and were therefore assigned the job of mapping populated areas of North Africa and much of Western Europe. One of the Twenty-eighth Strategic Reconnaissance Wing's Peacemakers actually mapped all of Portugal on one pass flying at 23,000 feet.

They also collected intelligence, photographic and electronic, on far-ranging missions over the North Pole, along the periphery of the Soviet Arctic and Siberia, and on penetrations in the days before the Soviet radar ring was complete. Missions were flown over the North Pole "to irritate the Russians," Ihle quipped with his dry sense of humor. They were flown to ferret and photograph, as he well knew.

In 1952, when the Twenty-eighth was staging out of England to map Europe and North Africa, it was ordered to ferret the Russians' new five-frequency radar, which was code-named Token by the Air Force. An RB-36D was therefore sent across the Baltic, high over Poland, and on to Vienna with a full complement of ravens and a Russian linguist named George Varhov. The flight, which gave the Poles, Czechs, East Germans, and some Russians their first look at a B-36 radar blip, collected "most if not all the five frequencies that SAC wanted," the pilot later reported. Varhov monitored the chatter on the ground, as he was supposed to, but couldn't get it all because he spoke a different dialect of Russian than the controllers. He did note, though, that they were "quite excited." That was putting it mildly. They were watching by far the largest blip they had ever seen, a blip that represented a potentially enormous bomb load. Or at least they watched the lumbering monster until it jammed them.

RB-36D penetrations were done rarely and very cautiously. The plane did indeed leave an unmistakable blip on radar scopes, and its maximum altitude was easily reached by MiG-17s, which could climb to 54,500 feet. There were reportedly several over-flights of the USSR itself in late 1950 and into 1951. But these were scaled back and then stopped as the MiG-17s went into service. The conservative mission planning paid off: no RB-36 fell to Communist fire.

But the planes' propeller engines were notoriously tempera-mental and several were lost on training missions, five of them in the Twenty-eighth. Like a number of other reconnaissance offi-cers, including Stan Bentley, Jim Keeffe, John Wagner, Jack Par-rish, and Stephen Zaklan, Roger Ihle owed his life to having been bumped from a flight. In mid-March 1953, Brig. Gen. Richard E. Ellsworth, Rapid City Air Force Base's commander, decided to lead a flight of updated RB-36Hs on a long practice mission to the Azores and back. Since generals are not regular members of flight crews, Ihle was ordered to sit out that particular mission to make room for his commanding officer. All twenty-three men in that crew were killed when the bomber flew into a mountain in Newfoundland in miserable weather on the way home. The South Dakota base was renamed in honor of General Ellsworth on June 8, 1953. President Eisenhower was there. So was Ellsworth's widow, Maryann, who still looked stunned and disbelieving be-hind her veil.

MEANWHILE, THE JETS were going operational. Thirty-three RB-45Cs were manufactured by Douglas under contract with North American. The first of them rolled off the assembly line in June 1950, when the Korean War started, and a detachment of three was sent right to the Ninety-first Strategic Reconnaissance Squadron at Yokota Air Base.

One of those Tornados became the first long-range jet recon-naissance aircraft to be shot down when it was jumped by MiG-

15s about forty-five miles east of Andung, China, on December 4, 1950. Andung is just across the Yalu from Sinuiju, North Korea, near where the plane crashed. Its pilot was Capt. Charles E. McDonough of New London, Connecticut, who was also the commander of the detachment. The copilot was Capt. Jules E. Young of East Rochester, New York, and the navigator was 1st Lt. James L. Picucci of New York City.

The downing of McDonough's plane was one of the more mysterious and tragic incidents in a shadow war that was haunted by them. The Tornado carried a lone passenger that day. He was a forty-six-year-old Air Force colonel named John R. Lovell, and his presence has remained unexplained to this day. Lovell was a West Point graduate, a former member of the U.S. Olympic boxing team, and a highly knowledgeable intelligence officer who had served in World War II. Jack Lovell worked directly for Maj. Gen. Charles P. Cabell, who not only headed Air Force intelligence in the Pentagon, but who had close ties to the CIA and would go on to become the agency's deputy director after the Korean armistice. Cabell wanted to send the RB-45s based in Japan over the Soviet Union as well as over North Korea, and Lovell himself was heavily involved in their operation at Yokota.

Full, or "bird," colonels did not fly on combat missions over enemy territory very often, and certainly not officers like Lovell, who knew a great deal about U.S. intelligence collection in the region. But a longtime colleague of his said later that he was the kind of guy who would have wanted to fly a mission, even a dangerous one, because the experience would have helped him plan other missions.

To compound the mystery, Lovell inexplicably carried a top-secret Soviet order-of-battle document that day which listed details of Soviet aircraft and the Russian military presence in the region, and which even contained photographs of senior Soviet officers, including Stalin's son, Vasily, who was the commander in chief of the Soviet Air Force in the Moscow district. Strategic reconnaissance crews were absolutely forbidden to carry personal items such as wallets, let alone military secrets, on missions. They carried only the dog tags around their necks, a Geneva Convention card that proclaimed, for whatever it was worth, that they were entitled to be treated humanely, and the cloth blood chits that offered a reward for their repatriation in the language of the region. But Lovell was toting a briefcase full of prized intelligence when he climbed into McDonough's Tornado.

On December 5, the day after the RB-45C was shot down, Lovell's wife, Mary Jo, received a telegram claiming the plane had simply disappeared. For years afterward, the four airmen were presumed lost. That is where the matter would have ended except for persistent research four decades later by Rand Corporation staffer Paul M. Cole; McDonough's daughter, Jeanne Dear; and Lovell's daughter, Nancy Dean. Both women would launch their own investigations after Boris N. Yeltsin announced in 1992 that his country had indeed captured twelve Americans on reconnaissance missions. Dear would be stunned to find her father's name on a list of U.S. flyers held by the Soviet Union. Like many other wives and children, Dear and Dean would write to their congressmen, attend hearings in Washington, and pore over every record they could lay their hands on. As in other reconnaissance shootdowns, however, their government would maintain in a long-standing charade that their fathers had disappeared without a trace; they were officially unaccounted for. Missing in Action.

The U.S.-Russia Joint Commission on POW/MIA Affairs and a subordinate support organization called the Defense POW/Missing Personnel Office, or DPMO, established shortly before Yeltsin's startling announcement, confirmed that there was no record whatsoever of any of the four men on the Tornado.

In fact, two MiG pilots got hits on the RB-45C as it inexplicably lost altitude. (They later cut cards to decide which of them would get credit for the kill. Aleksandr F. Andrianov, the commander of the fighter group, drew the lucky card.) No one knows what happened to Young and Picucci. They simply vanished with hundreds of other American servicemen, almost undoubtedly crashing and dying in their plane. But both McDonough and Lovell managed to parachute out.

McDonough was dreadfully unlucky. Not only was he shot down but his parachute landed on the Tornado's smoldering wreckage, severely burning him. Yet he managed to climb out of his chute and make his way into the hills before night fell. He spent that long, bitter cold night alone in the rugged countryside, just south of the Yalu, shaking in misery and trying to avoid capture. By morning, Captain McDonough was in excruciating pain from the burns and had severe frostbite. Gravely wounded, hungry, and suffering from gangrene, he set off to find help, finally stumbling on a Korean family and begging for food. They knew the penalty for protecting enemy soldiers and they therefore promptly turned him in.

According to a document found in the Soviet General Staff archive at Podolsk in 1993 by Paul Cole, the delirious airman died during a long and agonizing interrogation two weeks after he was shot down. "I am informing you that the pilot from the shot down B-45 aircraft died en route and the interrogation was not finished," Marshal Stepan Krasovskii, the senior Soviet military adviser to the Chinese, wrote to Marshal Pavel Batitskii, the chief of the General Staff in Moscow. McDonough's condition and death were corroborated by Hamilton B. Shawe, Jr., a captured Air Force pilot and prisoner of war who had spent three days with him in a partly demolished prison near Sinuiju.

Not only would Jeanne Dear and Nancy Dean learn through Krasovskii's memo and the interview with Shawe that Captain McDonough had died of his wounds and exposure while in captivity, but a former Soviet Air Force political officer named Col. Pavel Vasilyevich Fironov would turn up and explain what had happened to Lovell. Fironov was in the room during Jack Lovell's two-and-a-half-hour interrogation by the North Koreans and described the colonel's grisly murder.

Lovell's rank made it clear to Fironov that they had bagged a very important American and that further, careful questioning could be profitable. But that didn't happen. Fironov recounted years later how Lovell, a victim of the North Korean Communist temperament, was killed. In effect, he was murdered by the same reflexive paranoid aggressiveness, the same temper out of control, that eventually would send North Korean fighters ranging unnecessarily far out to sea to attack an unarmed U.S. Navy reconnaissance plane with thirty-one men on board, as well as naval vessels to capture the *Pueblo*.

Lovell's chief interrogator was the commander of the North

Korean air force (which, his title notwithstanding, had no planes to speak of at the time). What set the general off, suddenly ending any possibility that Fironov was going to leave the room with at least some scraps of decent information, was the fact that the defiant Lovell would not stand and show appropriate respect for his chief interrogator. The American colonel, the general barked shrilly, was a captured spy, an intruder on North Korean territory, and an officer of inferior rank. Lovell asked Fironov, who spoke excellent English, to ask the general to spare his life because he had a daughter, and also because executing him would violate the Geneva Convention. Had it not been so senselessly brutal, the scene could have come out of Gilbert and Sullivan.

But it was no operetta and Lovell was not to be spared. The general was far more concerned with losing face than with finding information. As Fironov looked on in disbelief, the stammering North Korean worked himself into an uncontrolled rage. Finally, shaking with fury, he ordered that a sign be made saying "War Criminal" and had it hung around Lovell's neck. The execution order was Lovell's forced march into town.

Jack Lovell stood in the center of a desolate village in a remote part of the world in the dead of winter. There, the former Olympic boxer who had kissed his daughter good-bye on Thanksgiving Day, less than two weeks before, as he headed for the Far East, was reviled by a crazed mob of villagers. They shouted at him and cursed him in a language he did not understand. Then they beat to death the only American they had ever seen or could get their hands on, with fists and sticks, and left his broken, bloody body where it fell.

THAT MONTH, DECEMBER 1950, was an alarming one for the White House. Gen. Douglas MacArthur's brilliant flanking action at the port of Inchon in mid-September had cut off the North Koreans who were squeezing U.N. forces at the Pusan Perimeter. The invasion force then swung north and spearheaded a drive all the way to the Yalu. The entire Korean peninsula seemed firmly in the U.N. command's control. Then disaster struck. Chinese troops poured across the Yalu and by sheer numbers pushed the U.N.

forces back down the peninsula in very bloody fighting, some of it hand-to-hand. Stunned GIs reported facing human waves of enemy soldiers who came at them with no apparent regard for their lives. That, of course, was not true; they had very high regard for being shot for cowardice by their own officers.

With the U.N. allies engaged in bitter fighting against the People's Liberation Army, and losing ground by the day, Truman began to worry that the deteriorating situation in Korea could tempt the Soviet Union to launch a simultaneous surprise attack by land against Western Europe and by air against the United States in an attempt to crush the West once and for all. He therefore authorized two deep-penetration flights over the Chukotskiy Peninsula in far eastern Siberia to see what, if anything, the Russians were up to.

The aircraft picked for the missions was the swept-wing, all-jet, RB-47B Stratojet. Its speed and agility made it the best possible choice. But the operation literally went up in smoke on the apron at Eielson Air Force Base in Alaska even before it started. In August 1951, the plane that was supposed to fly over Chukotskiy on the first of the penetrations caught fire as it was fueled and had to be written off. Its enraged commander demanded, without success, that someone in the ground crew be court-martialed for the costly mistake. Both missions were canceled. It would be a year before another aircrew tried to sneak into the sky over Chukotskiy.

The penetrators had better luck over China, which was repeatedly overflown (though increasingly by Nationalist Chinese crews from Formosa). Capt. Stacy D. Naftel, who flew an RB-45C in the 323d Strategic Reconnaissance Squadron out of Yokota, flew one of the most memorable missions of his career over China on the night of the Fourth of July, 1951, to take one example.

That night Naftel left Yokota, crossed the Sea of Japan, and then flew over North Korea just south of Pyongyang. Then he crossed Korea Bay, banked to the right over Dairen—Chinese airspace—and followed the railroad 500 miles to the northeast, over Fushun, heading for Harbin in Manchuria. Typically, Naftel and his crew had been given the coordinates for the target they were supposed to radar-photograph, but they had no idea what it was. At any rate, it was near Fushun that he and his copilot, 1st Lt.

Edward Kendrex, noticed what looked like Roman candles exploding off their right wing. Since the Tornado was at roughly 35,000 feet, the explosions were "hellishly high" for antiaircraft fire. Naftel banked the plane, looked straight down, and saw nothing but blackness. But the "Roman candles" kept going off, so he told Kendrex to look behind them.

"My God, Stace," Kendrex said. "There are about seven aircraft back there in echelon. They've all got their navigation lights on." They were MiG-15s and they were lined up behind and to the right of the RB-45C. The Roman candles were 20-millimeter tracers or exploding shells. The first MiG in line fired at the Americans until it was out of ammunition. Then it dropped down and came up behind them and to the left. Next, like an aerial shooting gallery, the second MiG in line tried to hit them. "This went on for some time," Naftel would report dryly.

"In the meantime, we went into a series of corkscrew maneuvers, varying heading and altitude, trying to shake them and spoil any stability they might have at that altitude," Naftel continued. "We were riding the red line [indicating maximum speed] and I can't remember at what speed the RB-45 was red-lined, but we were right on it and maybe sometimes a little over. Whenever I'd feel the aircraft start to shudder, I'd ease off or pull up some. . . . The navigator, Bob Dusenberry, called me on the inter-phone urging me to give it the gun, and I replied, 'Bob, the engines are on the limits now.' Anyway, this went on for—I think we recorded about twenty-nine minutes of attack time altogether.

"The MiGs didn't have any problem staying with us," Naftel went on. "I think—and it's my supposition—that they probably ran low on fuel because they were expending a lot more than they normally would, trying to get us lined up in their sights. Incidentally, this was the first time, according to information I was given, that our intelligence sources found out the Chinese had the capability for night airborne interception."

The Tornado finally reached Harbin, photographed the assigned target on radar, and headed for home. Naftel landed back at Yokota five hours and fifty minutes after he took off and saw that he had 300 gallons of fuel in the tank: a relative thimbleful that would have about filled the fuel lines, he added. Neither he nor Kendrex nor Dusenberry was ever told what the target was, but years later they learned it was probably a medical research center at which experiments on prisoners of war and other inmates were performed, and which was marked for possible destruction. "The only fireworks we saw that Fourth of July," Stacy Naftel vividly recalled, "were provided by the enemy."

BY THE AUTUMN OF 1951, with the war in Korea raging, the ferrets worked along the Chinese and Soviet coasts continuously. On November 6, the Russians demonstrated again that reconnoitering their coastal defenses could have deadly consequences. That day, MiGs jumped a U.S. Navy P2V-3W Neptune patrol plane in VP-6 at Atsugi Air Base and shot it down near Cape Ostrovnoi. The attack came so suddenly that the crew hadn't even time to send out a Mayday distress signal.

The next day, a Soviet protest accused the United States of violating Soviet territory. The demarche, reminiscent of the Privateer note the previous year, read like a form letter ordered up from the Kremlin secretarial pool: "Upon the approach of the two Soviet fighters with the intention of forcing the American plane, which had violated the Soviet state frontier, to land on a Soviet airport, the American plane opened fire on them. The Soviet airplanes were forced to open return fire, after which the American airplane went off in the direction of the sea and disappeared."

The MiG pilots undoubtedly did try to force the Neptune to head for an air base in the area since it was a valuable prize politically as well as militarily. But U.S. aircrews were repeatedly warned about it and told they were not to let themselves be herded to a landing on Soviet territory in any circumstance.

Robb Hoover, the Fifty-fifth Strategic Reconnaissance Wing alumnus, spoke for the Navy as well as the Air Force when he said emphatically that every pre-mission briefing ended with the point being underscored. "Under no circumstances will you allow yourself to be forced to land in enemy territory," the briefing officer would say. "And if fighters come out after you and try to, through whatever coercive techniques, force you to follow them, force you to land in Russian, or what we consider enemy territory, you will *not* comply with their instructions under any circumstance." Then, Hoover continued, the briefing officer would act as if he was polling jurors. He'd go to each man in the crew and put the question to him: "Do you understand what 'under no circumstances' means?" It was implicit that fighting their way out, even at the cost of being shot down and killed, was preferable to being captured with their plane and ferreting equipment intact. Not only did the Pentagon dread having its electronic countermeasures equipment fall into the hands of the enemy, but it was as sure as sunrise that plane and crew would be paraded in front of the international press as spies, bandits, pirates, and provocateurs.

The United States countered that the Neptune was forty miles out to sea when it was attacked, and first claimed it was on patrol duty and then that it was on "weather reconnaissance." If true, it could only mean that the Department of Defense had a peculiar, obsessive, and long-standing fascination with the weather at Vladivostok. But, as usual, it was not true. Gen. James H. Walsh, the director of intelligence at SAC, not only called it an "electronic reconnaissance aircraft" in a letter to the Air Force director of intelligence on December 3, but indicated that it had been doing the same work as the RB-50Gs at Yokota. That meant ferreting.

A Rand Corporation analysis of the Soviet note, which it correctly called "stereotyped," and the fact that MiG pilots were again awarded medals in public for an attack, led the Air Force think tank to conclude that the Politburo wanted to make it absolutely clear that the shootdown was not the random work of overexuberant, trigger-happy fighter pilots who happened on a target of opportunity. The note all but said explicitly that the shootdown and others like it were state policy. In other words, any military aircraft that came too close to the Soviet Union would be earmarked for destruction. "Now in the Far East, as in the Baltic, the Soviet Union served dramatic notice by deed rather than words," the analysis noted, "that air intruders would be forced to land and, if they 'resisted,' shot down."

The ten men on the Neptune that went down on November 6, 1951, were listed as missing and unaccounted for by the Pentagon. But, as with *Turbulent Turtle* and many other shootdowns to follow, there was compelling evidence that at least some of them were pulled out of the water and imprisoned. Years after the cold war, a Russian named Vladimir Trotsenko recounted seeing American flyers in Military Hospital 404 in Novosysoyevka in the Soviet Far East in November 1951. In 1996, after the collapse of the Soviet Union, the former paratrooper openly talked about four Americans, one of whom had an arm in a cast and who kept slowly repeating, "America: San Francisco, Cleveland, Los Angeles, Chicago." Lt. (jg) Samuel Rosenfeld, who was in the Neptune's crew, was from San Francisco. He was reliably reported to have been taken prisoner. Others in the crew were from Ohio, elsewhere in California, and Illinois, though according to Navy records not the other cities named by the American. Trotsenko, a spry and clear-headed sixty-eight-year-old in 1996 when he made his statement, added that the man with the broken arm would point to another man in a body cast and make a cradling motion to indicate he had small children back home. The date and the location of the hospital coincided with the downing of the Neptune.

Patricia Lively Dickinson, whose brother Jack D. Lively was an aviation machinist's mate and crewman on the Neptune, would spend years trying to find out whether Lively had been captured. Her parents believed it implicitly until the end of their days, she said in 1994. "We just never believed Jack was dead. They [her parents] thought they'd find him and bring him home," Mrs. Dickinson remembered, adding that the Pentagon was "keeping a lid on this for whatever reason." But then she gave the reason, however obliquely. Jack had once told her he flew over Vladivostok so often he knew it "like the back of his hand." That wasn't far-fetched, since Vladivostok was frequently overflown, usually in the dark or in moonlight and with the radar cameras on for precise navigation.

Stacy Naftel did his last Vladivostok mission in broad daylight in early August 1951 in a truly audacious bit of flying. With all its standard photographic cameras going, Naftel slammed the throttles in his Tornado full forward, suddenly broke out of low cloud cover at about 800 feet, and thundered right up the length of the harbor with all four engines roaring and black smoke pouring out of the exhausts. The Russian sailors were taken completely by surprise as they cleaned and maintained their ships.

"We sure caught the attention of a lot of the deckhands on the Soviet warships and freighters anchored there," Naftel recalled years later. "They were really scrambling as we completed our run and pulled back up into the overcast." The Russian gun crews were too startled to get off a shot, let alone hit him. Just the same, Naftel climbed out as fast as he could and headed home thankful for the clouds that concealed him.

Unlike other aviators, and certainly those in photo reconnaissance, ferret crews tended to be wary of clear skies because they felt dangerously exposed. Richard Meyer, who flew RB-29 ferret penetrations with the Seventy-second Strategic Reconnaissance Squadron, explained that "the flights that penetrated far inland were the ones that were considered the most dangerous. If you were discovered, the only hope would be a cloud formation large enough to duck into before you were intercepted. It was a very vulnerable feeling to see all clear weather and no clouds in sight."

THE BRITISH, MEANWHILE, were working their end. And they had jets, too. Some were RB-45Cs provided by the U.S. Air Force with the agreement that the RAF would use them to penetrate the western Soviet Union. The others were the stubby-winged, twin engine Canberras.

British squadrons first reconnoitered the Russian military during the Crimean War, before the battle of Balaclava in October 1854. Those squadrons were in the Light Brigade, of course, and they were blown to pieces by Russian artillery along with most of the rest of the "Noble 600." In the 1850s, as in the 1950s, British and Russian imperial interests came into direct conflict. The first time, Czar Nicholas I tried to annex Turkey and was thwarted by Queen Victoria. The British worried that a Russian presence in Turkey would threaten their lifeblood: extensive commercial and political interests in the eastern Mediterranean. They were still worrying about it a century later, so the wariness continued, as did the reconnaissance.

The RAF formed a top-secret reconnaissance outfit in the

spring of 1951 with a typically murky name. The Special Duty Flight, as it was called, could have delivered mail or spare parts. Squadron Leader John Crampton, who headed one of the first RAF units to fly Canberras, was put in charge of the SDF. Aircrews led by Crampton went from Sculthorpe Royal Air Force Base in relatively secluded Norfolk to Barksdale Air Force Base in Louisiana in early August 1951 on the pretext of conducting British-American air refueling trials. They spent ten days there familiarizing themselves with the B-45. Then they went to Lockbourne Air Force Base in Ohio for advanced training in the RB-45C. Crampton and the others returned to Sculthorpe late that fall with four Tornados. Procedure called for keeping one airplane ready as a backup in case a mission requiring the entire flight was needed and one of the other three was grounded.

Not coincidentally, there were already eight RB-45Cs at Sculthorpe, plus as many KB-29P tankers, and they were American. They belonged to the Ninety-first Strategic Reconnaissance Wing, which was on temporary duty out of its home base at Lockbourne. The Ninety-first was making a minutely detailed photo mosaic map of the Rhine Valley from the English Channel to Switzerland. The map was supposed to help NATO repel a Warsaw Pact attack by giving ground forces a clear picture of the terrain they were fighting on and by providing an accurate reference for fighter-bombers supporting them or strategic bombers trying to destroy territory captured by the Warsaw Pact forces. The maps would also be used to program the guidance systems on the Redstone and Jupiter ballistic missiles that were soon to be deployed in Germany and Italy for the defense of Western Europe.

Hal Austin, a SAC bomber pilot who rotated to Sculthorpe several times, did photomapping with RB-45Cs in the early 1950s. He would also fly a lone daylight photoreconnaissance mission over the USSR in 1954 that was so brazen it went into the program's folklore.

"We typically flew ten-hour missions," Austin said. "We'd take off, go over and do some photo work over Europe. And then a KB-29 tanker would meet us, we'd take on 6,000 gallons of gas and go at it again." Daylight penetrations of the western Soviet Union by RB-45s were absolutely forbidden since the area was heavily defended. Everyone was mindful of what had happened to McDonough's Tornado in Korea the year before. "The rules were to stay a minimum of fifty miles [from the frontier] and our commander added another fifty, so our rules were to stay 100 miles away from Eastern Europe."

Going in—penetrating—would be the RAF's job. Certainly it was physically perilous work. But it was also politically dangerous. In October 1951 the British Conservative Party won a general election, so Winston Churchill replaced the Labour Party's Clement R. Attlee as prime minister. Yet there were still Labourites in Parliament who were sympathetic to the cause of Soviet socialism, which they steadfastly believed was utopian. So Churchill approved the RAF overflight program knowing that if one of the planes came down on Russian territory, Labour MPs in an embarrassed and angered House of Commons undoubtedly would force a vote of confidence to bring down his government. But he balanced that possibility against the desperate need for radar pictures of Soviet military targets that would help SAC and RAF bombers in the event of war. Showing a depth of character that was already legendary, Churchill signed off on one of the most daring reconnaissance missions in history.

John Crampton flew a high-speed, high-altitude test run along the Berlin corridor on the night of March 21, 1952, to see how the opposition would respond. It didn't. On April 16, he and one of his crewmen were told by Bomber Command briefers that the Special Duty Flight was going to fly not one sortie over the heavily defended region, but three, and they would be done simultaneously. That made sense. Flying the missions at the same time would deny Soviet air defenses a chance to prepare for follow-on penetrations, which would have increased the danger to the second and third crews that went in. It had been well established during the massed air attacks on Germany that the first bombers over the target had an advantage, while those that followed were subjected to more ferocious attacks because the Luftwaffe and antiaircraft batteries had more time to prepare for them, more time to find their range.

Lines on a large wall map in the operations room showed Crampton that one Tornado would enter the Baltic states through

Germany in the dead of night. Another would radar-map Belorussia. The third would reach the heart of western Russia—within sight of Moscow itself—then bank right and head for the Ukraine. In each case, they would radar-map Long Range Aviation bases, which were the Soviet equivalent of SAC bases, and the fighter bases and antiaircraft batteries protecting them.

Security being as tight as it was, the other two crews had been given no clear idea of what Bomber Command had in store for them. But Crampton soon set them straight. Flight Sgt. Robert Anstee, an RB-45C copilot who had managed against great odds to survive more than fifty bombing missions over Germany, remembered being appalled when his pilot and navigator showed him the flight plan. "I thought at the time, 'Oh my god, what have they let us in for? Why? Why us? Why did we get lumbered with it?' "

The three Tornados, wearing red, white, and blue RAF roundels, took off from Sculthorpe very late on the afternoon of April 17, refueled over Denmark, climbed to 35,000 feet, and broke into enemy airspace together. Refueling just before they crossed the border not only extended their range, it increased their speed, since their four turbojets had more fuel to burn for higher thrust. Like everything else, fuel consumption based on speed and altitude was calculated meticulously.

The Soviet air defense system came alive. Radars went on, orders were issued, and MiGs were scrambled. And as the Russians reacted frantically, antennas in West Germany and Norway listened attentively. Crampton flew the longest leg, down to the Ukraine, and therefore had to refuel not only going in but as soon as he made it out. The flight lasted a grueling ten and a half hours. All three planes made it back to Sculthorpe with their radar imagery and without a scratch, in spite of the MiGs that had hunted for them throughout the flights. The three crews were awarded Air Force Crosses, which did not bear citations, and Crampton was personally congratulated by LeMay when he returned to Lockbourne in May.

The audacious triple penetration caused a serious shakeup in the Soviet air defense force that had the predictable effect of making future penetrations, and even peripheral reconnaissance flights, even more dangerous. The overflights so angered and frustrated the Kremlin that a special commission was set up to investigate the nation's obviously vulnerable air defenses. The fact that the commission included Lavrenty P. Beria, Stalin's widely feared security chief, suggests that Stalin, the Politburo, and the General Staff were enraged and frustrated by their country's airspace being violated with impunity.

THE DEEP PENETRATIONS would have cast a dark cloud over Stalin and the men in the Kremlin, as they did over Nikita Khrushchev and Leonid Brezhnev years later. The defenses that were in place along their country's long frontier had been successfully thwarted yet again by the enemy's prying spy machines. There were a number of reasons for the rage. Certainly the Russians were deeply concerned about the military situation; indeed, with survival itself. The intruders were collecting useful information that would put their homeland at grave risk in the event of all-out war. It was also clear that where bombers carrying cameras, radars, and listening devices could go, so too could others carrying atomic bombs. However many regiments of infantry and armor were in place to repel an invasion, nuclear weapons made porous air defenses tantamount to being fully exposed. A plane that could photograph Red Square could drop an atomic bomb on it. That was the new reality. No place, including the Kremlin itself, was safe from annihilation. Suddenly, there was nowhere to hide.

Sergei Khrushchev put it very well years later when he recalled his father's reaction to a plan by Dwight Eisenhower for an Open Skies policy in 1955 that would have allowed each side's reconnaissance planes to monitor the other's military facilities as a confidence-building measure. "For my father at that time it was the same fear [as the United States had]. . . . Just after the summit [in Geneva in 1955] he brought home the brochure that was yellow and contained photographs that showed what American aerial photography can do: he was always interested in new things. . . . I asked him, what is your opinion, can we accept this [Open Skies]? He said it was not possible because the Americans are really looking for targets for a war against the U.S.S.R. When they understand that we are defenseless against an aerial attack, it will push the Americans to begin the war earlier." Collecting information that was militarily useful, that would have led to the destruction of their country, was an activity the Russians could confront and oppose fairly calmly. But there was a dimension to the overflights, and even to the incessant peripheral missions by planes that prowled along their borders, that was psychologically painful for them. Being watched at will from high above sovereign territory—having foreigners in effect take your picture or eavesdrop on your conversations even when you tried your hardest to prevent it—showed that the nation wasn't all that sovereign. It amounted to a violation not only of territory but of the very sanctity, the essential dignity, of the national spirit. It was ultimately the powerlessness, the nakedness, the feeling of being mocked, that provoked the Russians' abiding rage.

The Soviet sense of impotence would have been there even if the RAF had been the only transgressor. But the deal that was struck between the two old wartime allies and ethnic cousins gave the U.S. Air Force and Navy the responsibility for working the Soviet Far East, both off shore and over land. This they did continuously.

On May 28, 1952, five weeks after the Special Duty Flight's triple penetration, Far East Air Forces Bomber Command cut an order authorizing the Ninety-first Strategic Reconnaissance Squadron to "conduct and report visual, photographic and electronic reconnaissance" of enemy territory, "maintain an all weather operational capability," and fly "special reconnaissance missions." The directive ended by prohibiting reconnaissance crews from flying within fifty miles of the Soviet or Manchurian border "except as authorized" by Bomber Command itself. The prohibition against getting closer than fifty miles was evidently intended to keep overeager crews from being shot down while going after low-priority targets. But high-priority targets, particularly air bases and radar, were something else. Authorizations to get in close to them were plentiful, since there was no alternative.

"In the beginning, the only way you could get any reconnaissance was along the periphery or to penetrate with aircraft," explained John Bergen, a career Air Force intelligence officer who spent eight and a half years in SAC and did stints in both the National Security Agency and the Defense Intelligence Agency. "And because of the nature of strategic warfare, you'd expect them to put their best radars, their newest radars, their newest surface-to-air missile systems, their newest fighters, along the periphery to counter the U.S. bombers when they came in and got to their homeland," Bergen went on, sketching the bigger strategic picture. "So you would expect along the periphery, where they expected the bombers to penetrate . . . they would put their long-distance, early warning, ground-controlled intercept radars netted together in some sort of fashion so they could control their fighters, their surface-to-air missiles, and provide for an early warning, and then attack guidance, for the fighters and information for the surface-to-air missile sites to shoot down the bombers before they dropped their weapons."

Peripheral flights and penetrations were separate operations but were complementary, Bergen continued, with information from one helping the other. Ferreting coastal radar on peripheral flights, for example, helped penetrating aircraft get past the radar. Overall, the idea was to be able to know "how good they really were as opposed to how good they were from a theoretical standpoint. You could tell when you were detected, how far out, how low they could go, how high they could go. What were their operational capabilities—their *real* capabilities—as opposed to their theoretical capabilities?" Sometimes, he said, multiple coordinated missions were flown against the Russians with varying numbers of planes flying different patterns. That way, "you could present a problem to them," as he put it, and see exactly how they responded.

Almost from the start, the intelligence community tried to systematize collection. "You establish criteria," Bergen added. "You want to hear early warning radars at least once a month, so you would plan your missions accordingly. There were radars we updated every time we flew, particularly on the periphery, say in the Baltic area. An early warning radar might be once a year. A surface-to-air missile [radar] you needed to see at least once every three months. And border ones are so critical, so threatening, you might want to hear them—look for that particular radar—every time you flew a mission." The same applied to photography. Many targets, certainly including submarine bases and nuclear weapons facilities and test sites, were continuously rephotographed.

BETWEEN APRIL 2 and June 16, 1952, the Navy and Air Force teamed up to both ferret and photograph radar sites and air bases by flying inland along the Siberian coast from Kamchatka to Wrangel Island in the Soviet Arctic. The Navy aircraft, a P2V-3W Neptune, was fitted for ferreting and could find, identity, and take the readings of radars and radio communication equipment over a wide range of frequencies. The Air Force plane was an RB-50 carrying cameras. Working under maximum security—strict radio silence was kept even during takeoffs and landings—the pair penetrated fifteen to twenty miles inland as many as nine times. The Navy plane flew at 15,000 feet and used its direction-finding equipment to pinpoint installations for the higher-flying Superfortress to photograph. As was the case with other overflights, the intruders were not shot down. In fact, incredibly, the Neptune was intercepted by MiG-15s over the Bering Sea near the St. Lawrence Islands and even over Soviet territory and was not attacked. Raking the plodding twin-engine patrol plane with cannon fire, as happened to several other Neptunes, would have been easy. But these MiG pilots carefully looked over and photographed the American aircraft and held their fire.

THE CREW OF a Ninety-first Strategic Reconnaissance Squadron RB-29 that was flying a surveillance mission off Vladivostok on June 13, 1952, three days before the last Navy–Air Force penetration, was not so lucky. The plane, No. 44-61810, took off from Yokota at 10:07 that morning under the command of Maj. Samuel N. Busch. It made a routine "coast-out" report twenty minutes later indicating it was on its way westward and was routinely tracked by radar until 1:20 p.m. It then suddenly disappeared, carrying its twelve-man crew into apparent oblivion.

The RB-29 was shot down by MiG-15s. That much was clear to the Air Force, if not to the families of the men on board. The fate of the crew, in fact, quickly became another of the lingering enigmas of the twilight war.

According to a report sent to Soviet Air Force Gen. Vasily Stalin by Admiral Nikolai G. Kuznetsov the next day, the RB-29 came to within two to three miles of land as it flew over Valentina Bay, the ferrets' regular patrol point. A pair of MiG-15s scrambled from Unashi Air Base for an intercept. Following procedure, the two MiG pilots tried to turn the intruder inland. Also following procedure, Busch would have none of that, so he tried to head back out to sea. Kuznetsov reported that the RB-29 opened fire on the MiGs, which would have been exceptionally stupid and was undoubtedly not true, and that the MiG pilots returned fire. The reconnaissance plane burst into flames, he went on, and crashed about eighteen miles off shore.

Roland Robitaille, an enlisted man who took part in a search for Busch's plane the next day, remembered years later that the briefing officer at Yokota told the crew of his rescue plane that the Russians had already been warned not to interfere with the search. The warning to the Russians was prudent because, as the young airman put it, his plane was so close to Vladivostok he could plainly see an airfield north of the port. And when he looked down, he saw the missing RB-29, still floating high in the water. The fact that he saw the airfield and the downed reconnaissance plane at almost the same time clearly shows that it went down right in front of the naval base. Busch "must have made a perfect ditching. All men aboard should have escaped injury unless some were hit by gun fire," Robitaille explained. Then someone else saw that the two doors to the life raft bays above the RB-29's wings were open and the bays were empty. Finally, he added, a faint wake could be seen from the area of the RB-29 that led "directly to Vladivostoch [sic] with no vessels in sight." The crew of another rescue plane even spotted one of the rafts. It was by then a familiar scene: all of the appearances that some or all of the crew had gotten out of the plane and been captured and spirited away. And that's exactly what happened, as events almost fifty years later would show.

By October 1955, a number of airmen who had helped search for Busch's plane and who had themselves been shot down over

Korea during the war and captured, reported that their Communist interrogators had questioned them closely about a Major Busch. Lt. Col. Richard A. Steele of the Air Force's Personnel Services Division doggedly followed up by sending them letters specifically asking about the Busch connection. At least two acknowledged that they had, indeed, been questioned about him.

"During my imprisonment with the Communist [*sic*] I was asked several times about Major Samuel Busch," Edwin D. Combs answered. "The reds knew that we were in the 91st with Major Busch and quite often asked me what Major Busch's duties were with the Sq. especially if Major Busch's crew ever flew any missions other than Korean missions." The idea, commonly practiced by interrogators around the world, was to collect enough scraps of information so Busch himself, when confronted with them, would think his inquisitors knew more than they did know. Then, in theory, he would acknowledge what they told him and elaborate.

William E. Koski, who was living in Miami in 1955, answered Steele in a letter dated January 26, 1956. "As you are aware, the communists asked me numerous questions about Major Busch, expressing enough interest in him, to the exclusion of any of his crew members as to indicate to me the likelyhood [*sic*] of their holding the Major a prisoner," Koski wrote. "They asked about Busch and only about him, which to me jived [*sic*] with the communist radio report that had been monitored in Japan on 13 June, stating that one officer airman had been picked up.

"As you know," Koski continued, "the search mission did locate a life raft, safe indication that there were survivors. Since the raft could only have been launched from the rear entrance door or the mid-upper raft compartments, why should the A/C [Busch, the aircraft commander] who would have to crawl through his escape window to get out of a ditched B-29, be the only one to make it, with the exclusion of 10 or 11 other men?" Why indeed?

The radio news report certainly jibed with a Radio Moscow broadcast on the morning of June 16, 1952—three days after the shootdown—reporting that a surviving officer had been pulled out of the water by a Russian boat two days earlier. By October, however, Far East Air Forces was knocking down the Russian report. It said the broadcast had nothing to do with the downed RB-29, but instead concerned biological warfare propaganda and a B-26 that was reported missing on January 14. What the B-26, a twin-engine light bomber, was doing over the Sea of Japan anywhere near Vladivostok was not explained.

Typically, the authorities knew exactly what had happened. Yet loved ones were systematically deceived in the name of national security or the requirements of diplomacy. On June 15 the Air Force announced that wreckage tentatively identified as that of a missing B-29 (again, not an RB-29) had been sighted in the Sea of Japan "about midway between Korea and northern Honshu." While acknowledging that 44-61810 was attached to the Ninety-first Strategic Reconnaissance Squadron, the Air Force maintained it had been on a "routine survey mission" and that the "cause of the accident is undetermined."

Despite overwhelming evidence that the RB-29 had been shot down, and circumstantial evidence that it was over or very near enemy territory and that crewmen had been seen alive, the Air Force insisted that the reconnaissance plane had vanished. Less than a year later, a Japanese prisoner in the Khabarovsk labor camp in Siberia reported that there had been "twelve or thirteen" U.S. airmen with him. A subsequent report stated that an officer from an RB-29 was seen in a Soviet hospital north of Magadan in Siberia in October 1953.

But the sighting reports went for nothing because reconnaissance crewmen who were held by the Communists amounted to a problem without a solution where the White House was concerned. To seriously take on the Kremlin over its holding of the flyers would open a can of scorpions, not merely worms. In the first place, Eisenhower would be inviting attacks—however unjustified—from Democrats to the far right accusing him of not being aggressive enough to get the boys (as they were always called) released. He would be branded a weakling. Second, pushing too hard could have provoked the Kremlin into publicly airing all it really knew about the Peaceful Airborne Reconnaissance Program, supported by plentiful signals intercepts, radar tracks, and even photographs of the black-bellied, antenna-sprouting recon-naissance planes taken by MiG pilots. Finally, there was the pos-sibility of armed conflict.

Col. Philip J. Corso, a senior military intelligence adviser, would report to Eisenhower in 1953 that as many as 1,200 Amer-ican POWs, almost all of them captured in the Korean War, had been shipped to the Soviet Union for imprisonment and interro-gation. "Based on what I know of Soviet policy," Corso told the president, "these boys will never come back alive." Eisenhower agreed and told the Department of Defense that more public protests would be not only useless, but potentially dangerous. "The fear of general war with the Soviet Union and China tied our hands," the colonel later recalled. "We never said anything to the families," he added. "We didn't know what to say."

Ignoring the issue would have been one thing. But it was fol-lowed by a policy of deliberate disinformation. Assistant Secretary of State Thurston Morton told the Senate in August 1953 that "to the Department's knowledge there are no United States soldiers in the category of prisoners of war being held in the Soviet Union." A month later, Gen. G. B. Erskine, a marine and an as-sistant to the secretary of defense, said explicitly that there was evidence a "small number of Air Force crews are probably held by the Soviet Union." But, Erskine added, "it would be undesirable to pass that information on to their relatives since it would lead them to believe that they might still be alive." It was the Penta-gon's position, then, that the next of kin of the missing flyers had to be kept ignorant for their own good.

But someone in the Department of State either never got the word or decided to ignore it. On July 17, 1956, *The New York Times* reported that the U.S. embassy in Moscow told the Soviet Foreign Ministry that the United States believed at least ten U.S. airmen were in Soviet prisons, and that some of them were from Sam Busch's crew.

The *Philadelphia Daily News* picked up the *Times* story and, in journalistic tradition, put a local angle on it, since Busch and two of the others on the plane, 1st Lt. James A. Sculley, the copilot, and S. Sgt. Miguel W. Monserrat, were Philadelphians. Under a headline proclaiming "Flier's Mother Prays For His Safe Return," the paper ran a human interest piece describing Mrs. Leah Busch, Sam's mother, walking to her synagogue "with head bowed" to pray for the safe return of her son. "I've always felt that he was alive," Busch's mother was quoted as saying repeatedly. "I've hoped and prayed daily for his return." As events would show forty-three years later, Samuel Busch did indeed survive the attack and was captured. But he was not going to come home.

AS THE KOREAN WAR ground on, Air Force and Navy planes flew almost continuous reconnaissance missions throughout the entire region, and Soviet air defenses literally rose to meet the challenge.

On the afternoon of October 7, 1952—four months after 44-61810 was shot down—a sister RB-29, 44-61815, was also blown out of the sky by MiGs. It, too, was attached to the Ninety-first Strategic Reconnaissance Squadron at Yokota. Unlike Sam Busch's aircraft, this one, named *Sunbonnet King*, carried a crew of eight and was officially on a "routine photo-mapping mission" over northeastern Hokkaido. Make that *extreme* northeastern Hokkaido, an area where Japan and the Soviet-controlled Kurile Islands come together. The Kuriles are strung out like stepping-stones that lead to the Kamchatka Peninsula and its then-feared naval and long-range bomber bases.

By two o'clock, *Sunbonnet King* was cruising 15,000 feet over the Nemuro Strait, which separated forces whose countries, that day, were gearing up for a possible all-out war while the one in Korea slowed to a stalemate. The strait, narrow as a bullet on the air navigation chart used by 1st Lt. John R. Dunham, *Sunbonnet King*'s navigator, marked the edge of Japan's outer air defense identification zone. At that moment Dunham, Capt. Eugene M. English, Jr., the plane's commander, and the six others in the crew were being tracked by both "friendly" and "unfriendly" radars on either side of the strait. At precisely 2:15 p.m., the men who were watching *Sunbonnet King* on American radar at Nemuro, on the northern lip of the spit of land that juts toward the Kuriles, saw a second blip approach and then appear to merge with it.

The Air Defense Control Center at Misawa Air Base immediately warned Captain English and *Sunbonnet King*'s pilot, 2d Lt. Paul E. Brock, that an unidentified "bogey" was near them and asked if they could see it. They could not. At 2:22 English matter-of-factly radioed back that *Sunbonnet King* would stay in the area for another hour.

Exactly eleven minutes later, the men in the Nemuro station heard this frantic call from the RB-29: "Mayday. Let's get the hell out of here." It was the last transmission to come from *Sunbonnet King*. Repeated attempts by Nemuro and the Ninety-first at Yokota to contact the plane went unanswered. At 2:34—one minute after the call for help—four Thunderjet fighter-bombers and an SA-16 Albatross amphibian rescue plane were scrambled at Misawa and headed toward the reconnaissance plane's last known position. They would find nothing when they got there.

But Goto Yosamatsu, a Japanese fisherman, saw the whole thing. He had been caught fishing in disputed waters by a Soviet patrol boat on June 21 and was doing six months' "penal servitude" on tiny Yuri Island when *Sunbonnet King* was attacked. At 2:30 that day, he would recall, the sound of an airplane overhead made him look up. "I sighted a very large four-engine aircraft flying northeastward at an altitude of approximately 3,000 meters. At that time, I thought to myself, 'Why Russia has large aircraft, too.' " Since Yuri Island was occupied by the Soviet Union, and the American reconnaissance plane was flying to the northeast when it passed overhead, it was heading even deeper into hostile airspace.

"Just then," Yosamatsu continued, "a very small aircraft . . . made a nose dive with great speed from above the larger one." It fired at the four-engine plane, he added, and so, apparently, did shore batteries. Finally, the big plane "raised its nose way up, and for an instant assumed a position as if it were going to make a loop. At that instant the tail section broke off and began to fall." Hit by machine gun fire from a propeller-driven LA-11—the last piston-engine fighter to fly for the Soviet Union—and possibly by flak from antiaircraft guns on the ground, *Sunbonnet King* began to disintegrate. The fighter's pilot, a Ukrainian named Boris A. Zhiryakov, watched the RB-29 explode in midair. Then he headed for home.

Vasily Ivanovich Saiko, a twenty-four-year-old sergeant in the Soviet Maritime Border Guards, also saw *Sunbonnet King's* end. Saiko, who came from Ust-Donetsk in the Rostov region due south of Moscow, saw the RB-29 hit the water three or four miles out in Yuri Island's bay. It came down, he later recalled, with a great roar. Saiko's ship steamed to the crash site. When it got there, small boats were sent out to collect anything of value, including survivors. Strong winds were blowing over the dark, oil-stained water, and it was clear that the American "RB" had disappeared under the waves. Saiko and two other seamen in one of the boats saw that papers and debris floated on the surface. Then they saw a body they believed was the plane's pilot floating in the tangled lines of his parachute. The three of them at first thought he was alive.

When they pulled up next to the body, Saiko grabbed his legs. But the boat was rolling and pitching so violently that Saiko himself lost his balance and went overboard. Entangled in the parachute shrouds himself and choking on seawater, the Russian seaman was finally pulled back on board. So was the American. It was then that the Russians made a gruesome discovery. Not only was the airman dead, but the top of his head had been shorn off, along with his face. Saiko and the others turned back toward the patrol ship with the body and the papers they collected and soon had both on board. The body was wrapped in a tarpaulin.

The next day, Vasily Saiko was ordered to help take the decapitated American to the island in a launch. It was on the short trip to the dock that Saiko caught sight of a large gold ring on one of the corpse's fingers. Impulsively, he looked around to make sure no one was looking and then quickly pulled off the ring and slipped it into his pocket. It was a fine souvenir, Saiko reflected, and no doubt one that the soldiers who would carry the American's body off for burial would also find attractive. Furthermore, he knew perfectly well that if he turned it in, it would find its way into the pocket of one of the officers. So Vasily Saiko kept his valuable souvenir and mentioned it to no one.

The ring did not belong to *Sunbonnet King's* "pilot." It belonged to Lieutenant Dunham, the navigator, and it was his class ring from the U.S. Naval Academy, class of 1950. Since there was no Air Force Academy in those days, the Air Force readily accepted volunteers from both Annapolis and West Point, and Dunham had been one of them. He had entered the Air Force on June 2, 1950, immediately after graduation. A little more than two years later, he left a widow named Mary and a five-week-old daughter, Suzanne, back in Easton, Maryland.

The body of John Robertson Dunham was buried on Yuri Island. The Soviet Union admitted firing at the RB-29 after it violated the state frontier but, typically, denied knowledge of the fate of its crew. Dunham was posthumously promoted to captain, and in November 1955 he was declared officially dead in a "Casualty Report (Non-Battle)" that listed his cause of death as an "aircraft accident (military)." Yet again airmen who were killed by the enemy while on a dangerous—and not high-priority—foray were assigned to the lengthening roster of hapless accident victims.

After he left the Maritime Border Guards that autumn of 1952, Vasily Saiko became a student at Rostov River College, where he studied ship piloting and navigation. He would recall forty years later that he was "in great distress" during his student days, meaning he was often broke. The ring, he would point out, was fifty grams of pure gold and was engraved in a way that was exotic by Russian standards. He claimed he was even offered a car for it by a rich Georgian. But he steadfastly refused to barter away his cherished souvenir.

"I always had a feeling that I had to return the ring. There had to be the pilot's relatives somewhere who didn't know anything about his fate. However, at that time the relations between our countries were hostile, and that was an obstacle. Therefore, I was afraid to turn for help to the American Embassy in Moscow. I understood that nothing good would come of it. I could only make trouble for myself. But times changed for the best."

They certainly did. When those times came, Vasily Saiko would finally return John Dunham's ring to his widow. And Dunham himself, almost alone among the Air Force and Navy airmen who were shot down on cold war reconnaissance missions, would be returned as well.

WIZARD WAR

WHATEVER THE DANGERS of the war in Korea, the possibility of armed conflict in Europe, and subversion nearly everywhere else, strategists on both sides of the Iron Curtain knew that the ultimate act of ideological confrontation was nuclear war. Each opponent therefore concentrated on developing the capacity to annihilate the other. As a close second, each tried to ward off its own horrific destruction, and reconnaissance was the first line of defense.

Harry Truman's two overarching military priorities were therefore the development of atomic and then thermonuclear weapons and the means to use them to attack Communist targets. As early as July 1949, with a small stockpile of large and immensely complicated atomic bombs on hand and preliminary research on the even more complicated H-bomb under way, Truman asked the National Security Council to figure out what the United States needed to fight a full-scale war with the Reds. "As a result of my request," he later wrote, "the Special Committee [of the NSC] brought this important conclusion to me: the production of atomic weapons should be stepped up. At the same time, they recommended that the newly developed B-36 bomber be given a priority second only to atomic weapons, for the B-36 was designed as a long-range plane capable of delivering our new type A-bomb on any target in the world." Eisenhower would carry on that policy and assign the highest national priority to four ballistic missile programs. Two of them, Atlas and Titan, would be intercontinental.

There was no doubt by the time the Korean War started, then, that atomic and hydrogen bombs and warheads would inevitably be the weapons used in another world war and that there were two basic ways to send them over long distances: in bombers and on missiles. The Navy meant to have both. The admirals argued that supercarriers could launch A-bomb-carrying strike aircraft off enemy coasts and were mobile enough to make poor targets. And submarines carrying missiles would be virtually unstoppable. The appropriations battle between long-range Air Force bombers such as the B-36 and then the B-52, and the Navy's huge Forrestal class aircraft carriers and missile-carrying nuclear submarines propelled interservice rivalry to a new height of rancor. Adm. Hyman G. Rickover, the "father" of the nuclear submarine, was the Navy's Curtis E. LeMay.

Meanwhile, the threat was amorphous but real. The Soviet long-range bomber force had atomic bombs and Tu-4s that could carry them to the United States. It was developing jet bombers and was known to be working hard to develop its own (not souped-up German) long-range ballistic missiles. It didn't take a Karl von Clausewitz to conclude the time was rapidly approaching when the United States would be vulnerable to a devastating surprise attack. Every policy maker in Washington vividly remembered the trauma of December 7, 1941. It was a time "when the Pearl Harbor surprise attack was still very much on everyone's mind," Richard M. Bissell, Jr., recalled years later. Bissell, a courtly, bespectacled Yale economist, would soon figure prominently in his country's all-out effort to pry strategic weapons secrets out of the opposition's treasure chest.

LIKE KHRUSHCHEV, EISENHOWER was justifiably frightened by nuclear weapons and was awed by their capacity to destroy. At a National Security Council meeting on August 4, 1955, whose main subject was war gaming, target selection, and civil defense, Secretary of Defense Charles E. Wilson raised the possibility of the Russians sending a colossally powerful hydrogen bomb to the United States by ship or submarine. That prompted Ike to ask how much force it would take to knock Earth off its axis. Robert C. Sprague, a Department of Defense scientist, answered that the matter was under study but that a hydrogen bomb detonated offshore could start a tidal wave 200 feet high that might be powerful enough to start the whole planet wobbling in orbit. "We finally will get destruction of such magnitude that you can't talk about defense," the president told the twenty-five men in the room.

How much would it take to make the Earth radioactive? he wanted to know. One thousand megatons would be close to tolerance, someone else answered, and 10,000 megatons would surely be enough if the bomb went off in the atmosphere. Everything would be poisoned. Scientific advances in nuclear weapon technology, Ike mused, would "soon get to the point where no one can win." When the time came that each side could fire 1,000 missiles at the other, he quipped, "I personally would want to take off for the Argentine." There would be no refuge on the Pampas, either.

The Russians, of course, were also worried about a horrible surprise. Having been double-crossed by the Nazis, who signed the nonaggression pact in 1939 and then launched a savage invasion of the Soviet Union two years later, the Russians counted the SAC bombers and attack carriers surrounding them and understandably brooded that their own Pearl Harbor was looming. Stalin therefore pressed on with his country's nuclear weapons program and both bombers and missiles. After the old despot's death in 1953, and following the party purges in which Khrushchev politically eviscerated Georgi Malenkov, Nikolai Bulganin, Vyacheslav Molotov, and other rivals, he stepped up these programs. But there was no point in trying to catch up to NATO with conventional bombers, Khrushchev decided. He would leapfrog to ICBMs.

U.S. intelligence tracked the Soviet strategic war programs as closely as possible. As early as December 1946, a military intelligence program aptly called Wringer had begun wringing details about the Soviet Union out of thousands of repatriated European and Asian prisoners. Much of the information was about Moscow's nascent missile program and came from a handful of repatriated engineers and hundreds of technicians who had worked on the German V-2 program and then been captured by the Red Army along with some of the missiles themselves. (The U.S. Army grabbed about one hundred unassembled V-2s in the Soviet occupation zone, virtually under the noses of the Russians, in an operation that was worthy of Ian Fleming.) The Germans told their American and British interrogators that the V-2 amounted to a starter missile for a homemade product and that the chief designer of the Soviet missile was a genius named Sergei P. Korolyov.

The Soviet Union's premier test facility, U.S. and British intelligence officers learned in 1952, was a place called Kapustin Yar near the Volga, east of Stalingrad. The site, in the far south, was picked because Earth's velocity is greatest at the equator; the farther south a rocket is launched in an easterly direction, the more shove it gets from nature (which is why Florida was chosen for the American launch facility). But Kapustin Yar was also selected because it was remote, which enhanced security, and far enough inside the country to discourage reconnaissance flights. Discourage them, but not prevent them.

It is axiomatic in the intelligence world that no one goes to the enormous expense and trouble of developing long-range missiles to carry the equivalent of sticks of dynamite. Big rockets, even when they are purportedly designed for space launches, are taken as indicators that really nasty weapons are also in the works. So it was with Kapustin Yar and, a few years later, with the giant launch center at Tyuratam, deep in Kazakhstan. (Tyuratam was called the Baikonur Cosmodrome after a town 170 miles away in an effort to deceive the West, and many still call it that.) The really nasty weapon, an atomic bomb, had been successfully tested in 1949. It went with the ballistic missile as an arrow goes with a bow.

"We just can't ignore it," Robert Amory, the CIA's deputy director of intelligence at the time, recalled someone saying about work at Kapustin Yar. "This is going to be a major new thing, this missile development, and we've got to get on top of it in the beginning and judge it." Both the agency and the Air Force badly wanted pictures of Tyuratam, but the Air Force was unwilling to fly a mission to get them. Amory has quoted Air Force chief of staff Gen. Nathan F. Twining as saying it couldn't be done.

So the Americans went to the RAF, which had flown the triple penetration with RB-45Cs in April 1952. One of the sorties was John Crampton's epic run from West Germany down to the Ukraine. The British agreed to reconnoiter Kapustin Yar. That dangerous mission, along with others whose targets were Soviet naval facilities along the Black Sea and "over the fence" photographs inside East Germany and elsewhere in central Europe, were collectively named Project Robin. The "fence" was slang for the Iron Curtain—forbidden territory.

Although Robin remains highly classified to this day because of obsessive Ministry of Defence secrecy, a number of insiders, including Amory, former CIA historian Donald Welzenbach, and George W. Goddard, the Air Force camera designer, have confirmed it. The Kapustin Yar penetration almost certainly involved a modified Canberra B2 bomber belonging to the RAF's 540 Squadron at Sculthorpe, which flew photoreconnaissance missions. The plane was fitted with "wet" wings, meaning they were loaded with fuel for the long flight, and a hundred-inch camera designed by James Baker. The camera, mounted to snap oblique pictures, was apparently so powerful that it took clear test shots of St. Paul's Cathedral in London from off the Dover coast, a distance of seventy-five miles.

Sometime during the summer of 1953, the camera-carrying Canberra took off from Giebelstadt in West Germany, crossed into East Germany, and entered Soviet airspace. Then, like Crampton's Tornado, it banked to the right and thundered south. This time, however, the RAF bomber followed the Volga.

Soviet radar tracked the intruder throughout its flight and fighters were scrambled to shoot it down as it made its way to Kapustin Yar. As the Canberra continued on toward the missile facility, it gradually gained altitude because its fuel burned off, until it was above 48,000 feet. One Russian fighter pilot, Lt. Mikhail Shulga, later told of his frustrating attempt to get his cannons trained on the British bomber. The ground controllers who watched the moving blip on their radar kept telling him to look higher. Then Shulga spotted his quarry. When he reported that to the controllers, they ordered him to test his cannons. He did so as his MiG inched higher in the thinning air. But it was no use. The Canberra's stubby wings were grabbing more air than the sharply angled, swept-back wings on Shulga's fighter, which wanted to stall in the thin air. "They said, 'Do it again.' I tried again. 'Can't you reach it?' 'No, I can't.' "

Shulga may not have been able to hit the Canberra, but apparently others did. When it landed in Iran hours later, it had cannon holes to show for the adventure, as well as a couple of hundred "fair" photographs of the missile facility, according to Amory. "The whole of Russia had been alerted to the thing," he added, "and it damned near created a major international incident." The CIA and the Air Force were so pleased with the pictures of Kapustin Yar that they wanted more. But Amory reported that the RAF in effect said, "God, never again."

Meanwhile, the Air Force had become so impressed by the Canberra that it awarded a contract to the Martin Company to produce an American version called the B-57A. Except for the fact that the pilot and copilot sat in tandem in the B-57A instead of side by side under a bubble canopy as in the RAF aircraft, the planes looked identical. A reconnaissance version called the RB-57A was produced with cameras in a bay behind the bomb bay. The first sixty-seven of them were sent to the 363d Tactical Reconnaissance Wing at Shaw Air Force Base in South Carolina by April 1954.

Whatever the Air Force thought about its version of the Canberra, George Goddard considered it a "dog." He suggested that its stubby wings be substantially lengthened, which would give it far higher altitude, and that a more powerful camera be installed. The new modification, called the RB-57D, had huge 106-foot-long wings and more powerful engines that did, indeed, give it real altitude: 60,000 feet. Twenty of the high flyers were built as stopgap strategic reconnaissance planes and were used in both Europe and Asia. But they came with problems, the most notable being the long wings' tendency to buckle where they joined the fuselage. None are known to have had accidents in the air, but at least one RB-57D suffered an embarrassing collapsed wing on the ground. Those who flew them loved them anyway.

AMERICAN SAILORS, MEANWHILE, were being killed flying close-in reconnaissance missions on the other side of the world. One of the most ferocious incidents occurred on January 18, 1953, near the port of Swatow. Since it was directly across the Formosa Strait from the Nationalist Chinese bastion on Taiwan, it was a heavily defended installation. That day, a Navy P2V-5 from VP-22, the patrol squadron based at Atsugi, was shot out of the sky by Chinese antiaircraft fire while it was ferreting. The fact that it was brought down by ground fire indicates that, like the Vladivostok flights up north, the Neptune was flying low and very close to its target so it could get the Chinese search radar turned on. It certainly succeeded.

The Coast Guard responded to a Mayday call from the shot-up Neptune by sending a PBM-5 Mariner to the site of the ditching to pick up survivors. The fat, twin-engine amphibian landed in eight-to-twelve-foot swells to pick up eleven of the Neptune's surviving thirteen-man crew. Then the rescue plane itself came under furious fire from shore batteries on nearby Nan Ao Tao Island. By then, its own crew was calling for help. The Mariner's pilot had to choose between staying where he was while the guns on Nan Ao Tao zeroed in on his plane, eventually blowing it to bits, or risk taking off in the very rough sea. He decided to get out of there, which was the right call, but the heavy flying boat foundered in the high sea and crashed.

The shootdown of the Neptune was turning into a full-blown catastrophe, with two crews under fire. Frantic calls for help brought the destroyer *Halsey Powell* to the scene under full steam, and also another Mariner, this one from the Navy's VP-40. The Chinese blazed away at them, too, as sailors on the destroyer managed to pull ten of the nineteen downed airmen out of the water. Seven were from the Neptune; three from the Mariner.

The second Mariner drew machine gun fire as it circled the crash site. And another destroyer, the *Gregory*, was hit by still more fire from the shore batteries as soon as it arrived on the scene.

The People's Republic of China, perhaps taking its cues from the Russians but more likely driven by its own territorial imperative, had fought tenaciously to keep the ever-probing Americans at bay. Like the RB-29s and RB-50s, the propeller-driven Neptunes and Mariners had not been designed for such work, and their brave crews were suffering the consequences. They would continue to do so.

The next day, January 19, Dwight Eisenhower was inaugurated president. He would have been briefed on the massacre soon afterward.

THE B-47—BOEING's sleek Stratojet—was to the Superfortress and the Neptune what a sports car is to a delivery truck. With sharply swept wings and tail and six General Electric jet engines, the B-47Bs that came into SAC's inventory beginning in mid-1951 were truly futuristic. They cruised at more than 500 miles an hour and had a top speed of about 600 miles an hour. Their maximum altitude was roughly 40,000 feet. What is more, unlike the Canberra and the propeller-driven bombers, the Stratojet was so automated it had only a three-man crew. The B-50 had eleven or twelve, four of them to operate the guns that protruded from it on all sides. Since the B-47 was designed to fit into the new bombing doctrine—to attack targets alone, not in a large formation—it had only a pilot, a copilot, and a navigator. The copilot, who was behind the pilot under a long Plexiglas canopy, sat on a swivel chair so he could face backward to operate the plane's only guns: a pair of .50-caliber machine guns at first, and later, two 20-millimeter cannons.

The B-47's primary mission was to extend SAC's bombing capability around the world by mating it with the tankers in the large air-to-air refueling operation LeMay started early in his tenure as commander in chief of SAC. But everyone knew from the beginning that the Stratojet's speed, range, maneuverability, and dependability would make it a fine reconnaissance aircraft. If the B-47 could penetrate Communist air defenses with nuclear bombs, it could penetrate them with cameras (and vice versa, as the Russians well knew).

Twenty-four of the B models were therefore converted to RB-47Bs in 1953 and 1954 by mounting eight cameras and related equipment in their bomb bays. They were succeeded by 255 RB-47Es, each carrying eleven cameras, and by specialized sisters: RB-47Hs, which carried three ravens and their amplifiers and other hardware in the cramped bomb bay to do ferreting; ERB-47Hs, which did very specialized electronic intelligence work with only two electronic warfare officers; and RB-47Ks, which handled both photo and weather reconnaissance.

But during the spring of 1952, with delivery of the first RB-47B still more than a year away, the Air Force found itself in an intelligence crisis. Hard information came in reporting that numbers of Soviet Tu-4s had begun flying into and out of air bases at Mys Schmidta on the Chukchi Sea, at Providenyia on the Chukotskiy Peninsula, and, farther west, on tiny Dikson Island on the shoreline of the Kara Sea. Fears that the Tu-4s would be stationed in eastern Siberia went back to 1946, when the Forty-sixth Reconnaissance Squadron was formed at Ladd Field in Alaska for Project Nanook, but only a few of the Russian bombers had turned up.

The new reports, however, were considered credible. Provideniya juts well into the Bering Sea across from Alaska and was close enough to fly one-way missions to the entire United States. The reaction to a Soviet long-range bomber force at Provideniya in 1952 would have been roughly the same as the reaction to intermediate-range ballistic missiles in Cuba ten years later. So the Pentagon and the CIA wanted pictures and therefore asked the White House to approve overflights of those areas and from Provideniya down to the Kamchatka Peninsula.

In anticipation of approval, the Air Force ordered two of the B-47Bs modified to carry the necessary cameras on July 5. On August 12, Secretary of Defense Robert A. Lovett sent President Truman a memorandum from Gen. Omar N. Bradley, chairman of the Joint Chiefs of Staff, and Walter Bedell Smith, the director of Central Intelligence, requesting both overflights. Truman understood the importance of the intelligence. But, like Churchill, he also understood the folly of pushing his luck. He therefore signed off on the northern overflight but not on the one over Kamchatka. And ever attuned to international politics, he only approved the northern mission on condition that Dean Acheson, the secretary of state, approved it as well.

That done, the Air Force issued mission orders and authorized the two B-47Bs to be flown to Eielson Air Force Base outside of Fairbanks. The operation was now referred to only as Project 52 AFR-18 and was given a security classification so tight that only three Air Force generals in the Pentagon knew about it (one of them being LeMay and another being Brig. Gen. James H. Walsh, the director of intelligence).

Lt. Col. Donald E. Hillman, a veteran World War II fighter pilot with 145 missions and at that moment the deputy commander of the 306th Bombardment Wing at MacDill Air Force Base in Florida, was picked to lead the mission. It had been the 306th that photomapped parts of Europe in the Casey Jones program in 1945.

Project 52 AFR-18 was so secret that the two B-47Bs and a pair of KC-97 tankers flew to Eielson by way of Rapid City Air Force Base in South Dakota, where the Twenty-eighth Bombardment Wing and its B-36s were stationed. That was supposed to make the flight look like a training exercise even to most of the crewmen involved. Only when all four planes reached Eielson were the rest of the crewmen told about the overflight.

During the six-day layover at Rapid City, Brig. Gen. Richard E. Ellsworth, the base commander, talked Hillman into giving him a ride in one of the B-47Bs, then very exotic airplanes. With the general strapped into the copilot's seat behind him, Hillman pushed the Stratojet's throttles full forward and started down the runway. A third of the way into the takeoff roll and with speed building quickly, Hillman looked at his instrument panel and was horrified to see that the plane's flaps were up. Without the flaps down, he knew, "our takeoff could not succeed and would end in a disastrous fireball when we ran off the end of the runway at 200 knots." The Stratojet was now going too fast for an abort—too fast to stop—so Hillman frantically pulled down the flap handle and then watched the flap indicator creep slowly downward: "very slowly downward!" Don Hillman would vividly remember looking at grass when the bomber, its flaps finally down, climbed into the air at the edge of the concrete. "Project 52 AFR-18, and the lives of its primary crew, nearly ended in Rapid City, South Dakota," he would later write. General Ellsworth's life would have ended, too. The incident could have been called an ill omen for the general, who was killed less than six months later when his RB-36H crashed into a mountain in Newfoundland.

The mission itself began just after sunrise on October 15 when the two KC-97s left Eielson and headed for Point Barrow, on Alaska's north end. There were about ten hours of daylight at that latitude in mid-October and the meteorologists were calling for clear skies all along the route over Siberia. They were wrong.

Hillman and Col. Patrick D. Fleming, flying the other B-47, followed the tankers an hour later. Both bombers were topped off in the Point Barrow area. Then the KC-97s turned for home and the B-47s flew on in radio silence. When they were over the Chukchi Sea due east of Wrangel Island, Fleming, following the plan, broke off and went into a racetrack pattern. His job was to relay any communication between Hillman and Eielson and, in the event Hillman had to abort, fly the mission himself.

Don Hillman, now alone, guided his Stratojet past the northern end of Wrangel Island and on to Ambarchik, on the East Siberian Sea, where he banked to the left and headed south. There were no reconnaissance targets in the region. But by flying so far westward, then turning and approaching the targets from the west, it was hoped Russian radar operators on the Chukotskiy Peninsula would think the blip coming at them from well inside their own country was friendly. It was a good plan. And it almost worked.

With the B-47's ground-mapping radar and cameras on, Hillman raced toward his five target airfields, and was annoyed to see that he was flying over two-tenths scattered cloud cover and some haze. Since a sizable amount of fuel had already been burned, the bomber climbed past 40,000 feet. It was after they finished taking imagery of the second of the five targets on their list that the radar warning signal went off. The device worked like "fuzz busters" that warn of police radar; it picked up the radio beam, or signal, and sounded an alarm in the crew's headsets. Maj. Lester E. Gunter, the copilot, swiveled his seat behind Hillman until he faced the tail, where the twin 20-millimeter cannons were mounted. Gunter was supposed to fire at anything threatening.

A few minutes later, Gunter spotted Soviet fighters. He used the intercom to tell Hillman and Maj. Edward A. "Shakey" Timmons, the navigator who sat in the nose, that fighters were trailing them from below. Gunter could plainly see that the silvery specs were trying desperately to catch up, but they had taken off too late to do that, very likely because the ruse of coming from the west had delayed the ground controllers' reaction.

Now that the American plane was widely known by the Russians to be an intruder, and other interceptors were very likely scrambling ahead, Hillman broke radio silence to give Pat Fleming his position and situation. Since the air base at Provideniya, the last stop on Hillman's target list, was the headquarters of the regional MiG regiment, an attack there was very probable. But it never came.

Hillman flew over the coast of the Chukotskiy Peninsula and out of Soviet airspace and headed straight back to Eielson, where he landed well after dark. Fleming followed a few minutes later. Hillman, Gunter, and Timmons had flown for seven and three-quarters hours and traveled 3,500 miles, 800 of them over hostile territory. Their film was rushed to Eielson's photo lab, where it was processed and duplicated. The originals—both the camera film and that taken of the radar images—were flown directly to Washington and turned over to CIA analysts. The conventional cameras were obstructed by the cloud cover. But the radar delivered. No armada of Tu-4s poised to strike America could be found. There was no threat, and an examination of facilities at the five installations showed they were not even equipped to pose one. At least not then.

Both crews were awarded Distinguished Flying Crosses in April 1953 for their exploit, but not publicly. By then, Hillman had been rotated to SAC Headquarters at Offutt Air Force Base. One day soon after his arrival, he was called into LeMay's office. SAC's commander in chief got up from his desk, closed the door, and personally pinned a DFC on Don Hillman. Seeing a puzzled expression on the colonel's face, LeMay broke into a rare smile. "It's secret," he told Hillman.

Project 52 AFR-18 was so successful the Air Staff almost immediately requested White House approval for more overflights. The mission also had two unintended consequences. The ease with which it was carried out forced the Russians to move a second MiG regiment into the region. And communication intercepts revealed that the commander of the region's air force was sacked for incompetence.

IT WAS NO accident that the nobility of the bombers—the B-47s— flew high over the USSR searching for fighters and other bombers, while creatures of a lower caste—the RB-29s, RB-50s, and RB-45s and the Navy's PBMs, P4Ms, and P2Vs, the Mariners, Mercators, and Neptunes—worked close-in ferret missions off China and the Soviet Pacific. They even penetrated those places as well as North Korea and North Vietnam.

The division of labor within the Air Force was the result of LeMay's single-minded belief that SAC's (and therefore the Air Force's) paramount responsibility was to prepare for a strategic war against the Soviet Union. To achieve that goal—to be battle-ready—meant sharply focusing SAC's human and material resources on all-out war. He therefore not only instituted a revolutionary, realistic training regimen, but launched a modernization program that led to the B-47, the B-52, the KC-135 Stratotanker, and a variety of missiles, both ballistic and bomber-borne.

That being the case, sending his best bombers to Korea for bombing and reconnaissance amounted to squandering scarce resources, and LeMay therefore refused to do it. This set up an early conflict between SAC and the Far East Air Forces. Since FEAF was responsible for Air Force operations in Korea, where a war was going on, and elsewhere in East Asia, it wanted B-47s and RB-47s stuffed with the latest electronic countermeasures hardware. But LeMay knew his bomber crews could not practice for nuclear war, could not keep their edge, if they were routinely dropping ordinary "iron bombs" on North Koreans. He was also loath to compromise the B-47's performance capability and the latest ECM equipment—"assets" that would be vital for jamming Soviet radar in nuclear strikes—by wasting them in a war he considered utterly trivial compared to the one he was preparing to fight. He therefore stubbornly rejected an FEAF request for his Stratojets and tankers.

But the generals in Japan were fighting a real war, and whether or not it equated with Armageddon, they worried increasingly that their bomber and reconnaissance crews—SAC crews—were being chewed up by the MiGs.

"Without wishing to appear unduly alarmed," an alarmed Brig. Gen. W. P. Fisher, who commanded FEAF's bombers, wrote to Maj. Gen. John B. Montgomery, SAC's director of operations, in late January 1953, "the whole feeling here is that these guys are beginning to develop a real overall air defense team which is making our margin of security in operations slimmer all the time. If they ever crack that last link and get an all-weather capability of pressing an accurate firing attack, the B-29 business is really going to get rough."

It was already rough. On March 15, a Fifty-fifth Strategic Reconnaissance Wing RB-50 flying under cover of the "weather observation" ruse was jumped by MiGs as it ferreted the Soviet naval installation at Petropavlovsk. One of the MiGs fired at the bomber without scoring a hit, and the RB-50's central fire control gunner, T. Sgt. Jesse Prim, returned the fire, also without hitting the target. The MiG came in fast, Prim later recounted, "and flames and smoke from his guns were plainly visible. The minute I began firing, the Soviet jet broke its attack and dove underneath us. It came up on the other side, curved away from us, and flew home." The MiGs did, indeed, turn back to Kamchatka and the SAC bomber headed for Alaska.

Typically, the U.S. protest maintained that the RB-50 was one hundred miles north of Petropavlovsk and "at least 25 miles" from Soviet territory. It neglected to mention why the United States had an obsessive interest in collecting weather data around Siberia and did so with armed aircraft. Just as typically, the Russians answered by insisting the bomber penetrated thirty miles into their territory and got close to Petropavlovsk itself.

Sen. Ralph E. Flanders, a Vermont Republican and a member of the Senate Armed Services Committee, suggested that the Air Force might have been "a little reckless" in flying so close to Soviet territory. Then the senator wondered aloud if Siberian weather could be observed at a safer distance. Nah. Four months later, O'Kelley, Roche, and the others on *Little Red Ass* would go down in yet another attack by MiGs.

IT WAS ROUGH for the Navy, too. On January 4, 1954, a P2V-5 with the call sign Three Cape Cod was ferreting off Dairen when it disappeared under circumstances that to this day remain not only mysterious but suspicious, and which the Navy has steadfastly covered up.

The Neptune, which carried a crew of ten, was attached to VP-2 at Iwakuni Air Base in Japan and was piloted by Lt. Jesse Beasley. It took off from there at 2:26 that afternoon and headed west to the North Korean coast, then down to the demilitarized zone separating the two Koreas, across MiG Alley, and over the Yellow Sea. Its apparent destination was the Manchurian coast around Dairen, where it was supposed to ferret radar, possibly in conjunction with a submarine. The area was overcast to 5,500 feet and there were snow squalls, making visibility poor.

Several hours into the mission, Three Cape Cod reported back to Iwakuni that it had engine trouble and was heading home. Its transmissions soon ended abruptly and it disappeared without a trace. Exactly what was wrong with one or both of its engines remains a mystery. The Navy would later insist that the radio log of messages going back and forth between the crippled patrol plane and its base showed it reported a "rough" engine. The word implies mechanical failure. But it is ambiguous. The log also showed that Three Cape Cod's last transmission, made at 11:14 that night, was "We need aid."

Jesse Beasley's widow was officially informed that her husband's aircraft was on a "training flight" when both of its engines failed and it ditched somewhere in the Yellow Sea. Another letter claimed it had been in a military aircraft accident. But military training flights are not deliberately flown at night and in bad weather.

Forty years later one of Beasley's sons would begin a dogged investigation into what happened to Three Cape Cod that led to a very different conclusion. Charles "Satch" Beasley, a Tennessee aircraft mechanic who had his own pilot's license, managed to penetrate a smoke screen laced with doctored records, missing documents, and what Beasley called "double speak" to find that Three Cape Cod was almost undoubtedly attacked by Chinese MiG-15s as it was ferreting radar at or near Dairen. What happened after the attack is itself an incredible saga of courage, suffering, and tragedy.

But before Satch Beasley came to understand the range of possible causes of his father's disappearance in the crippled Neptune that fateful night, he would have to penetrate what Churchill called a "bodyguard of lies." He would learn that phrases such as "mechanical mishap," "hazardous duty," and "lost at sea" masked possible deadly encounters not only with enemy planes but with friendlies as well. When Beasley asked the man who had been VP-2's operations officer whether his father was shot down, he was told, "Anything is possible" and "Your dad was dealt a bad hand that night." The former operations officer told someone else that "Lieutenant Beasley and his crew were in the wrong aircraft, in the wrong place, at the wrong time." Period.

Beasley's detective work would reveal several bad hands. The P2V-5's engines were fifty hours past the 500-hour high-failure mark. The "training" mission took place in an area where there had been previous MiG attacks, the last one being only eighteen days before Three Cape Cod went down. The plane itself was equipped with an ultra-high-frequency radio that was incompatible with the very-high-frequency radios used by the Korean-based Air Force controllers who monitored the Neptune on radar. This meant the Navy plane couldn't communicate with its own air defense system. Worse, the plane's identification-friend-or-foe apparatus, commonly called IFF, was not operating. It was supposed to transmit a continuous signal telling all U.S. radars, on land, sea, and in the air, that the plane was "friendly" and therefore should not be attacked. With Three Cape Cod's IFF not working, however, radar in South Korea picked it up as an unidentified blip coming from the direction of Red China. And the blip was coming in below 400 feet in poor weather on a nearly moonless night.

After meticulously poring over records, using his own knowledge of airplanes and navigation, and talking with knowledgeable veterans, Beasley finally concluded that his father decided he couldn't make it back to Iwakuni on one fully functioning engine, so he decided to try a landing at an air base in South Korea. Three Cape Cod approached the South Korean coast at very low altitude for one of three reasons or all of them. Flying on the deck was standard procedure to keep enemy fighters from attacking from below. In addition, piston engines, unlike jets, are more fuel-efficient at low altitude. Or the Neptune could have been there because it couldn't get higher on the one engine.

Just as in the movies, the crew had to toss things overboard to lighten the limping plane. Two of the things they seem to have thrown out were the navigator and the radar man. Within two days, searchers located both bodies relatively far from where the Navy claimed the plane ditched. And they were at opposite ends of a small island group, a clear indication they had been jettisoned several minutes apart and had not floated from the crash site.

The officer who wrote the investigative report of the incident almost a month later claimed, "The autopsy reports stated that there was no evidence of fractures or of any other injuries that may have produced death on either of the recovered bodies. The findings in both reports concluded that the primary cause of death was exposure to cold and immersion." Yet a report from the air rescue squadron that searched for Three Cape Cod said explicitly that the body of Loyd B. Rensink, the radar man, was recovered by the destroyer U.S.S. *Tingey* and it had the "left side of head of body smashed in."

Three Cape Cod, now with eight crewmen on board and one of its engines dead or dying, apparently flew over the South Korean coast in darkness and at very low altitude. Beasley fought poor visibility as he headed for what was probably the air base at Wonju, thirty miles south of Seoul.

Whatever Beasley's visibility problem, he was himself clearly visible on radar at an Aircraft Control and Warning Squadron. What the men on the ground saw was a blip that registered as a low-flying bomber coming from the direction of Communist China and heading right for a military air base. What is more, the intruder did not respond to voice interrogation and, more damning, gave no IFF signal. Following procedure, the air controllers seem to have vectored a Marine fighter that was already in the air and on patrol to investigate and if necessary intercept the intruding "bogey." Another pilot flying patrol in a night fighter high above the Marine aircraft at that moment later claimed he saw a large, circular, orange-colored glow suddenly appear far below. He reported it as an explosion and noted the time as 11:15: one minute after Three Cape Cod's last transmission. It could have been one of the Neptune's jettisoned wing tanks. Or it could have been the Neptune.

Satch Beasley last saw his father on Christmas Day, 1953, when he was given a three-speed bicycle as a present. His dad spent much of the day teaching him to ride it. The next day, Lt. Jesse Beasley and the rest of VP-2 left the Whidbey Island Naval Air Station in Washington State for Japan. Ten days later he was reported missing on the "training mission."

Satch heard the news when he pedaled home from school for lunch and found strangers in the apartment and his mother red-eyed. Another woman, the pregnant wife of Three Cape Cod's plane captain, was crying inconsolably. His mother told him his father was missing and one of the uniformed men in the room informed eight-year-old Charles Beasley that he was now "the man of the house." Over the next few years, the little man of the house would watch in sorrow as his mother had a series of nervous breakdowns that required days of attendance by doctors and relatives each time. Throughout, she believed her husband had been captured by the Chinese, and for years she tried without success to pry information out of the government in Beijing. She did no better with her own government. The Navy continued to maintain Jesse Beasley had been the hapless victim of double engine failure and had disappeared roughly 200 miles off the Korean coast.

In 1994 an increasingly frustrated and disillusioned Satch

Beasley mounted a full-scale campaign to prove that the ten men on Three Cape Cod died heroes' deaths and were not the hapless victims of a freak training accident. But the Navy wouldn't budge. He sent the evidence he turned up to the Pentagon and urged that a serious investigation of the incident be launched. The Navy responded by doing what its ships do in dangerous situations at sea: it made smoke for concealment.

"We will require additional time . . . to complete our review of the material before responding to your request," the faceless bureaucrats told Beasley. "We have, again, requested assistance from the Deputy Assistant Secretary of State (POW/Missing Personnel Affairs) to determine if your father's aircraft mishap falls within their area of responsibility. Unfortunately, we will require additional time. . . ." *Mishap?*

Gen. Robert L. Jones, a deputy assistant secretary of defense and the head of the Defense POW/Missing Personnel Office (DPMO), who was responsible for tracking prisoners of war and those missing in action, adopted the Navy's line. In a letter to Beasley's congressman written in December 1999, Jones blithely maintained, despite clear evidence to the contrary, that "there is no credible evidence that Lieutenant Beasley's loss incident was the result of anything other than aircraft mechanical malfunction." There was no apparent attempt to reconcile engine failure with the fact that the bodies of two crewmen were found far from where the plane should have crashed, that two reports on Rensink were contradictory, and that one of them claimed his head was smashed in.

So the Navy slunk away from the messy and potentially embarrassing problem by handing it to DPMO. And DPMO in turn obediently supported the Navy by pronouncing, astonishingly, that Beasley had no case. It was part of a persistent pattern of denial and deception deeply rooted in the secretive intelligence culture itself and in the defense establishment's stubborn unwillingness to dredge up potential problems it didn't want to have to confront.

There was a mare's nest of motives and combinations of them that applied to all shootdowns. Secret operations had to be protected for the safety of the crews and continuation of the missions. The Pentagonians dreaded being pressured to retaliate after they admitted an attack had taken place. They also wanted to minimize pressure by families to recover men taken prisoner by the Communists or the remains of those who had been killed. And since Three Cape Cod, like any number of other ferret flights, probably violated another nation's airspace, they didn't want international legal complications. Finally, and perhaps most fundamentally, losing an aircraft amounted to a failure of some sort and there was a persistent, though unarticulated, fear that mistakes could be brought to light that would ruin careers. The same senior officer class that bore ultimate responsibility for the operations made the secrecy rules. The rules were rationalized— correctly—on national security requirements, but by clear implication they also had to do with career security requirements.

Satch Beasley was a mere speck on that scale. But for him and his sister Sarah, who worked so hard to bring closure on their father's death to their aged and ill mother in the face of unyielding official opposition, there was the painful feeling that he was betrayed by his own country for the sake of simple expedience. And they were far from alone.

ANOTHER P2V-5 NEPTUNE in VP-19 at Atsugi had the dubious distinction of performing its mission so perfectly that it got a clear picture of the radar used to shoot it down. At a little after 6 p.m. on September 4, 1954, the plane was ferreting Vladivostok's ground control intercept radar, which it had succeeded in getting turned on, when it was jumped by two MiGs being vectored by that very radar.

The plane's pilot, Cmdr. John B. Wayne, would later recount in the arcane language of the business how the electronic countermeasures operator "picked up an unusual ECM contact with a frequency of 2825 MC [megacycles], a PRF [pulse repetition frequency] of 1200 and a PW [pulse width] of 0.6 us." That may be gobbledygook to the uninitiated, but taken with data on the radar's range, height capability, and width of coverage, it was as clear as the instructions in an automobile owner's manual. "Several other stations which had been on the air shut down," Wayne continued, "and it is believed now that this radar was used as a ground controlled intercept radar for the fighters which later attacked us."

The first inkling there were MiGs around came from the gunner in the plane's top turret, who announced, "We have company," just as a MiG made a firing pass from behind. Wayne turned hard right while simultaneously pushing the Neptune's steering column forward. That sent the patrol plane into a steep dive, losing nearly 3,000 feet a minute, as it headed for cloud cover and the sea. Wayne was following standard defensive procedure, which called for flying the plane down to the deck—right above the water—so the fighters couldn't attack from below.

The MiG pilot also turned hard to the right and dove away. Then a second firing pass was made, this time with the Neptune shooting back as its altitude dropped. The third attack scored. The plane was hit in its left wing by several slugs, one of which was a high-explosive shell that blew away a foot-wide chunk of wing outboard of the engine. Crewmen peering at the Neptune's port side told Wayne that fuel was spurting out of the hole.

The MiG pilots were apparently unaware of the damage they had caused, and instead of pressing the attack to finish off the Neptune, they joined up in formation and headed westward to their base. Meanwhile, the fuel in the torn wing caught fire. When it had burned a third of the way through, Wayne dropped to 400 feet, ordered his crew to get to their ditching stations, reduced power, lowered his flaps, and made a perfect landing on a calm sea. But the tail section broke off anyway.

Water poured into the flight deck immediately as crewmen scrambled to get out of the fuselage and onto the wings. Within thirty seconds of hitting the water, the Neptune's nose went down, throwing the nine crewmen who were on its wings into the water. A tenth, Ens. Roger H. Reid, was still inside trying to get a life raft to the men on one of the wings when the plane sank. He went down with it. The nine survivors spent the night in a raft and were picked up and flown to Misawa in SA-16 amphibians the next morning.

Following the script, the Department of State maintained the Neptune was forty miles out to sea when it was attacked. An immediate protest was sent to the Russians, who were billed $1,355,650.52 in damages, and the matter was referred to the U.N. Security Council and eventually to the International Court of Justice at The Hague. Each move was accompanied by a detailed press release.

The protest complained that "without prior signal or warning, Soviet fighter aircraft of the MiG type, at least two in number, came up behind the Neptune aircraft, approaching it in an offensive, hostile firing position, with the glaring sun behind the fighters, and then, having determined that this was a United States Neptune, still without any prior warning opened fire upon the Neptune several seconds after 6:12 o'clock shooting numerous rounds of ammunition at it from the rear in a manner calculated to effect the Neptune's immediate destruction." The bit about coming out of the sun may have been borrowed from hackneyed pulp fiction and movie staples of the Randolph Scott genre in which the cowardly bad guys attack with the sun behind them. The implication was that American fighter pilots studied the Marquis of Queensberry Rules in flight school.

Also following the script, the Kremlin responded with one of its standard, all-purpose protest notes alleging that the Neptune was inside the Soviet frontier, that the MiGs were there "to propose that it immediately leave," that the Americans shot first, and that the intruder again "withdrew in the direction of the sea."

In a speech before the U.N. Security Council on September 10, Ambassador Henry Cabot Lodge, Jr., said the attack six days earlier had been only one of a series of similar, unprovoked shootings that constituted a pattern. A "series," certainly; "unprovoked," hardly. Lodge challenged the USSR to negotiate in good faith, either face-to-face or through the International Court of Justice.

His counterpart, Andrei Y. Vyshinsky, parried by accusing the Americans of "peeping into other people's gardens" in search of military secrets, and specifically of using radar to detect Soviet installations. He also used the occasion to flail the United States with other, similar incidents going back to the attack on the Privateer (which he, too, erroneously called a B-29 Flying Fortress) on April 8, 1950. And in the boilerplate Russian rhetoric of the time, he went on to charge that the United States had only put the incident on the Security Council's agenda in the first place to alarm public opinion and increase international tensions.

MEANWHILE, FAR OFFSTAGE and in the deep shadows, the quiet but relentless duel between the intelligence collectors and their heavily armed opponents went on around the clock. While Foggy Bottom and the Soviet Foreign Ministry publicly hammered each other over the shootdowns, secret encounters, some of them deadly, occurred almost constantly. It was not altogether unusual during the mid- and late 1950s for reconnaissance planes to return to bases in Japan with damage from gunfire, sometimes light, sometimes very heavy. Larry Holdridge, a naval aviator at Iwakuni in 1958 and 1959, has said there was frequent scuttlebutt in the officers' club about the mysterious Neptunes parked on the flight line that were said to go on long signals and photographic intelligence missions. Some of the forays were costly. "One P2V returned to the base with major damage to the aft fuselage and empennage," he said years later. "The consensus of opinion on the base was that it was attacked by a MiG and, of course, was unarmed. One crew member was killed," Holdrige continued, adding that the sailor was rumored to be an enlisted man and an equipment operator. "I wonder if his family had the comfort of knowing that he was one of many unsung cold war heroes? Possibly not, due to the classified nature of the mission." Most definitely not.

NOT ALL NEPTUNES worked for the Navy. Seven of them did it for the CIA in Air Force "clothing." The agency and the military services often clashed over roles and missions—turf—and that certainly applied first to aerial and then to space reconnaissance. In 1954 the CIA bought five new P2V-7s from Lockheed's Advanced Development Company, the renowned "Skunk Works" that would soon develop the U-2 and then the A-12 and SR-71 supersonic reconnaissance planes, and reconditioned two others that belonged to the Navy. Neptunes were picked because they had already proven to be durable and adaptable to intelligence collection.

Furthermore, Navy facilities to service them stretched around the world. The problem was that the Navy refused to allow the "secret seven" to fly with its markings or under its cover for fear it would get smeared if one of them went down where it didn't belong (including the Caribbean, which the agency monitored). The Air Force was more cooperative, however, so the heavily instrumented dark blue planes were painted with "U.S. Air Force" on their sides and called RB-69As.

Working in a program first called Cherry, and then Wild Cherry, the CIA reconnaissance planes ranged around the world on widely differing operations that included dropping propaganda leaflets and spies, retrieving packages and spies with the Skyhook aerial retrieval system, monitoring communication, and doing photoreconnaissance. Two of the still-secret planes flew out of Wiesbaden and used their hidden cameras, side-looking airborne radar, and communication intercept equipment to collect intelligence along the periphery of the Warsaw Pact nations. The other five were based in Formosa and Japan, from where they regularly worked targets in China, making penetrations at low altitude and at night. All five were lost between 1960 and 1964, three of them to enemy fire, one in a probable accident over China, and the fifth in another accident while on its way to South Korea.

Accidents, in fact, claimed the lives of many reconnaissance crews. This was partly due to the geographical and weather conditions in which some outfits such as the Forty-sixth and then the Seventy-second Reconnaissance Squadrons flew in Alaska and elsewhere. It was also because the missions themselves tended to be very long and were often flown at night.

One especially gruesome accident happened at Offutt at 2:30 on the morning of February 26, 1952, when an RB-50G carrying the usual crew of sixteen from a three-month ferreting stint out of Yokota crashed while landing. Three factors, none of which would have been a problem by itself, combined to cause a deadly disaster.

The pilot, Maj. Zane Grey Hall, had not slept well at Hickam Air Force Base in Hawaii, where the crew stopped for an overnight layover after an eighteen-hour flight from Japan. He lost sleep because he and his crew were billeted with other men who talked all night. Then, with fatigue setting in, he had flown fifteen more hours on the last leg. Hall was therefore exhausted as he got clearance from the Offutt tower to land on Runway 12. With flaps full down and the bomber approaching the runway at 140 miles an hour, as it was supposed to, Hall peered ahead. Now the second factor came into play. Both of Runway 12's green center lights were out, leaving two high-intensity green threshold lights to mark where the runway began. That threw off Hall's depth perception. Finally, Runway 12 began on top of a steep hundred-foot-high embankment.

An instant before the Superfort was supposed to come down on the runway, Hall realized in horror that it was too low and wasn't going to clear the embankment. He and 2d Lt. Frederick J. Straub, the copilot, yanked back on their steering wheels simultaneously. But it was too late. The main landing gear snagged the embankment five or six feet below the surface of the runway. Then the tail skid caught it. The plane bounced roughly fifty feet into the air over the end of the runway. Its left wing dipped straight down, scraped the concrete, and ripped off. The left side of the fuselage itself came crashing down onto the runway, slid about 900 feet, and finally stopped with the right wing almost twisted off and lying on top of the upper gun turret and a nearby escape hatch.

1st Lt. Edward W. Parker, one of the RB-50G's two navigators, was sitting with his back against a brace in his forward compartment when the plane caught the edge of the embankment and then slammed into the runway. He wasn't belted into his seat and therefore was thrown so violently against the black boxes and cabin wall that his shoulder broke and his liver was punctured. When what was left of the plane came to a stop, Parker struggled into the pilot's compartment, where he found Hall pinned under debris. Straub, the copilot, was nowhere in sight. Parker put out a small fire and helped pull Hall's leg out of the twisted metal. At that point, a sergeant came running up to the plane and helped both of them through a broken window. He learned later that 1st Lt. Jerome Medford, the other navigator, had all of his ribs broken but still managed to crawl out of another window to safety.

The five ravens in the bomb bay were not so lucky. "I heard one of the fellas crying for help," Parker remembered years later. But he couldn't help. There was no telling whether only one of the five was still alive or others were as well. The only way out for them was to crawl through a passage to the rear bomb bay. The other emergency exit, the hatch near the top turret, was blocked by the right wing. Parker staggered to the side of the runway in near-darkness and collapsed. That's when he heard the fire trucks and ambulances.

The standard medical report issued after the crash stated unequivocally that the seats of all five ravens had been torn loose, the men were covered by their own heavy electronic countermeasures equipment, and that fuel "was pored [sic] on five fatalities and almost immediately ignited, thus causing fatal burns without regard to other injuries these individuals may have sustained."

But that's not the way Parker remembered it. The base firefighters had no way of knowing this particular B-50 was a ferret and therefore had five men, not bombs, in its bomb bay. So they followed standard procedure. They pushed large hoses into the bomb bay and filled it with foam to keep the bombs from exploding. Ed Parker maintained many years later that the thick foam suffocated at least one of the ravens and possibly as many as four others.

"Well," Parker went on, "the wives aren't going to be too happy to hear this. The wives were told they were killed on impact. But I know that at least one of them was alive. It was that foam nozzle that killed him."

Eight years later Parker, by then a raven himself, was scheduled to fly on a ferret mission in an RB-47H based at Brize-Norton Air Base in England. But he was pulled off the mission because his wife had come down with rheumatic fever and he was needed back in Topeka to take care of the children. The plane was attacked by MiGs over the Barents Sea and was shot down on July 1, 1960, in a major incident. The three ravens were killed. He therefore joined Jim Keeffe, John Wagner, Jack Parrish, Steve Zaklan, Roger Ihle, and others who were in the Lucky To Be Alive

Club because fate kept them off doomed aircraft. To the end of his days, Ed Parker put this motto on every piece of correspondence he wrote: "I'd rather have luck than skill, any day!"

WHATEVER THE PUBLIC thought about the end of the war in Korea, another unheralded but often deadly war raged in the skies around the Communist bloc. The next year, 1954, the pace of "peacetime" reconnaissance missions against the Communists and the fury with which they were challenged grew precipitously. Both sides settled into an ongoing confrontation. The United States was determined to collect intelligence at all cost and the Chinese and Russians were equally determined to make the operation as costly as possible. Reconnaissance missions were now mounted almost around the clock and run-ins between the opponents were frequent.

The Air Force and the Navy tried to reduce casualties by providing fighter escorts for the reconnaissance planes, or at least trying to coordinate operations so fighters were in the area whenever possible. On January 22, for example, a Tornado was jumped by eight Chinese MiG-15s over the Yellow Sea. They were chased off by sixteen F-86F Sabrejets carrying wing tanks that extended their range. One of the pilots even bagged a MiG. And during the Korean War, to take another example, RB-45Cs flying out of Japan sometimes crossed "MiG Alley," the corridor along the Yalu that separated North Korea and China, on special overflight penetration missions. Every time one of the planes did that, it was escorted by Sabrejets.

The Chinese tried to protect their airspace with such ferocity that at 8:45 a.m. on July 23—in broad daylight—they shot down a Cathay Pacific Airlines DC-4 airliner carrying twelve passengers and a crew of five from Singapore to Hong Kong. With one of its four engines burning, the plane ditched off Hainan Island. As a sharply worded demarche from the Department of State noted, three Americans were killed, two of them children of the "tender ages of 2 and 4 years," and three other Americans were wounded, including a six-year-old.

An account of the incident that appeared in *The New York Times* gave a clear picture of the fear with which foreigners approached Red Chinese territory. After a rescue plane reported seeing four people in a raft, a Navy PBY Catalina amphibian was sent to help rescue survivors. It later landed in Hong Kong "and reported it had sighted 'rafts' and had circled them but did not put down because they were too near Communist waters for a United States military aircraft. A second United States Navy plane continued to circle the rafts while a civilian flying boat from Hong Kong was called to make a rescue attempt. It was felt that the civilian plane could intrude on Red waters with greater safety."

Three days later, two piston-engine U.S. Navy AD Skyraider attack bombers from the carrier *Philippine Sea* that had joined the search for survivors were themselves attacked by two Chinese LA-7s. The Lavochkins were beefy propeller-driven Russian war surplus fighters. Both were destroyed by the Skyraiders. The Navy attack planes' presence off the Chinese coast fueled China's own protest note. The attack on the airliner, in fact, was ignored. Having charged that the Skyraiders attacked two Chinese planes on patrol over Hainan Island, the note got down to basics. The rhetoric is worth recalling because it gives the flavor of the time:

"The above constitutes yet another outrageous act of aggression on the part of the United States imperialists in utter disregard of all law and order.

"For several years the United States imperialists occupying China's territory Taiwan have been providing the Chiang Kai-shek gang with large numbers of aircraft, naval vessels, and all kinds of munitions and water material, and directing and supporting the Chiang Kai-shek gang to harass constantly China's coastal areas and islands, to drop secret agents over China and to practice piratical interception and robbery of merchant ships of various nations sailing to China for trade.

"More than this, the United States naval and air forces have on many occasions invaded directly China's territorial waters and territorial air." They certainly got that last part right.

It was neither the first time nor the last when an airliner was either mistaken for a masquerading spy plane or simply shot down by overzealous fighter pilots. The Russians shot up an Air France DC-4 in the Berlin corridor in late April 1952 and wounded two passengers before it safely reached Berlin. A year later, Ralph Parr shot down the Il-12, no doubt deeply angering the dead officers' colleagues and putting them in a vengeful mood that may have led to the attack on *Little Red Ass*. And thirty years after that, another Russian pilot mistakenly shot down Korean Air Lines Flight 007 when it strayed over Sakhalin Island. The pilot of the Su-15 fighter that sent two missiles into the jumbo jet, killing all 269 people on board, later claimed he thought he was firing at an RC-135 missile intelligence collector in a program called Cobra Ball. So, apparently, did his ground controllers.

THE MISSION OF high-level intelligence professionals is to collect information, with priorities set by time and resources, in as many dark corners as possible. They therefore monitor friends as well as opponents to keep track of important developments in an uncertain world. Sometimes they share what they collect with allies. France is a case in point. So is Israel.

During the early spring of 1954, the Foreign Legion was fighting a desperate, losing battle in French Indochina against Ho Chi Minh and the Vietminh forces trying to push France off the peninsula. That April and early May, a climactic battle was fought at Dien Bien Phu, in what was to become North Vietnam, and U.S. Air Force reconnaissance planes were sent there to assess the situation for both Washington and Paris. John Wagner and Jack Parrish were on the crew of one of the RB-50Gs that was ordered to fly to the beleaguered fortress from Clark Air Force Base in the Philippines to monitor radar and communication traffic. They got an eyeful: a nighttime sound-and-light display they would never forget.

"It was like daylight," Wagner said years later. "This is at night at 10,000 feet. We boxed it. We flew around it [the fortress] to pick up whatever we could as far as radar pulses on any of their weapons, to find out whether they had sophisticated weapon homing devices," meaning radar-controlled antiaircraft guns, he explained. Since he was one of the navigators, Wagner was in the plane's Plexiglas nose and therefore had a front row seat—a "great view"—of one of the fiercest battles in the wars against French colonialism. Dien Bien Phu stands to this day as a metaphor for a grim, bloody fight to the finish.

"The sky was lit up like daylight," he said again, still marveling at the spectacle. "General Giap . . . had hauled scores of heavy weapons over the mountains of China on the backs of coolies into the Dien Bien Phu area. The French didn't think it could be done." The crew of the RB-50G never caught sight of the fortress itself, but the pyrotechnics were awesome. "All we saw was a tremendous fire fight. I couldn't believe it. It looked like World War II all over again. And they're pulling these heavy weapons into this fortress area and they were decimating the French. We flew a circle around there and then we got out."

Parrish called it a "milk run," a "nice flight." He, too, said the exploding shells, the sudden, large flashes of light clearly indicated that a battle of epic proportion was happening. "We knew what was going on, which sobers you in a hell of a hurry. And we knew there were people down there getting shot and killed; a lot of them, not just a few." One of the reasons Wagner, Parrish, and the others thought the mission was a milk run was that they were unaware they had accidentally penetrated nearly thirty-five miles into Red China. They only discovered their mistake after they returned to their air base and their radar imagery was analyzed.

In one respect, the flight that night was not only anything but a milk run, but it bore out the old adage that what can go wrong will go wrong. Before they left Clark, Albert J. Lauer, the aircraft commander, and his crew were given strict orders to break radio silence only if they spotted a large number of naval vessels. "If you see any heavy naval activity," Wagner remembered being instructed, "break radio silence and call in the clear because this will foretell probably a Soviet naval invasion by ship of Indochina." They were also briefed that the U.S. Seventh Fleet was 200 miles to the south.

"Well, when we came out over the water, we saw big, big ships down there." Lauer, following instructions, broke radio silence and described the whole armada, giving a detailed summary of the number and position of the ships in plain English. It was only after they returned home that they discovered they had radioed the position of the Seventh Fleet, which was not where the intelligence people thought it was. "I in effect gave away the position of the Pacific fleet," Wagner recalled, laughing at the thought that he and his crew had the rare distinction of having flown a reconnaissance mission for the opposition (if it was listening). There was, of course, no reprimand.

Another aftereffect of that mission deeply galled Wagner even decades later. None other than Pierre Mendès-France wanted to award the Croix de Guerre to him and to the others in the crew for outstanding heroism while helping French forces. But, John Wagner explained with a trace of anger still in his voice, the premier was overruled by the Air Force because of the publicity that would accompany the decorations. "So everything was shoveled under the rug."

As the French were aided by U.S. reconnaissance, they were also targeted. Ten years after Dien Bien Phu, when President Charles de Gaulle pulled France out of NATO, created an independent airborne strike force called the *force de frappe*, and began a nuclear weapons testing program, the CIA began to monitor developments as a matter of routine. When the original French nuclear test site in the Sahara was lost after Algeria won its war of liberation in 1962, a new test site was established on Mururoa Atoll in French Polynesia the following year. The roughly twenty-mile-by-ten-mile chunk of coral was picked because its truly remote location seemed to ensure a high degree of security. But Mururoa was easily within range of a U-2 that had practiced the difficult and dangerous business of taking off and landing on an aircraft carrier for just such an operation. In May 1964, a quietly momentous time for U.S. aerial reconnaissance, a U-2G took off from the carrier *Ranger* and photographed the test site from an altitude so high it was invisible to naked eyes on Mururoa. Combined with other intelligence, including seismic detection of the explosive force and air sampling of the radioactive particles from the mushroom cloud, an accurate picture of the French weapon came together. It was not shared with the French Atomic Energy

Commission and it certainly would not have earned the U-2 pilot a Croix de Guerre.

MEANWHILE, THE AIR FORCE had been working the opposition. Dien Bien Phu fell to the Vietminh on May 3, 1954, ending French colonial rule in Indochina. Five days later, on the other side of the planet, Capt. Harold R. Austin and his RB-47E crew pulled off one of the cold war's epic overflights, a penetration so audacious that it is indelibly etched in the folklore.

Austin had been based at RAF Sculthorpe while photomapping Western Europe in RB-45s in April 1952. That was when John Crampton's flight of Tornados flew the triple penetration and the squadron leader himself roared close to Moscow itself in the middle of the night before swinging south to the Ukraine. The RAF crews had radar-photographed several Soviet air bases that night.

Two years later, Hal Austin was flying in the 324th Strategic Reconnaissance Squadron, which a couple of weeks before had deployed from Lockbourne Air Force Base to Fairford RAF Base near Oxford with eight of Lockbourne's ninety spanking new RB-47E photoreconnaissance aircraft. He was going to penetrate a region other than Crampton's. But that wasn't the only difference between the two missions. The Americans were going to use standard visual cameras, meaning they were going to fly in broad daylight. Everybody in the business knew daytime penetrations were the riskiest.

To be sure, Austin would be flying a better plane than the old Tornado. But contrary to what he and his two crewmen would be told at the briefing, the Russians who wanted to kill him would not be flying MiG-15s. They would be flying newer, improved MiG-17s. Austin would be the first pilot to fly a B-47 over the Soviet Union on a daytime photoreconnaissance run, and although he had no way of knowing it beforehand, he would return with several mementos.

The mission started by literally testing the air. Early on the morning of Thursday, May 6, six of the eight RB-47Es took off from Fairford and headed north toward Spitsbergen. They refueled from KC-97s off the Norwegian coast and carefully kept station all the way. In SAC, keeping station meant each group of three planes would fly in a V formation, with the two planes bringing up the rear following the leader to the right and left a mile back. The navigators in the two rear Stratojets would set their positions on the lead airplane. The second group of three would fly the same formation two miles back and 500 feet lower. Keeping station would figure importantly for Austin's penetration. The round-trip went as briefed. All six RB-47Es reached Spitsbergen, took its picture, and returned to Fairford.

The Soviet air defenses did not get unduly worked up about the flight to Spitsbergen. That was understandable, considering that exactly one week earlier, on the night of April 29, the RAF had been at it again. A flight of RB-45Cs had been "over Moscow" itself, as Austin would put it. By comparison, the practice run to Spitsbergen had amounted to no threat at all. And that, of course, was the plan.

Two days later, on the morning of Saturday, May 8, all six crews were ready to repeat the flight north. But the eighteen pilots, copilots, and navigators at the briefing were told there was to be a change. Three RB-47Es would head for Spitsbergen exactly as they had on Thursday. The second set of three would break off and head east at a point a little more than halfway to Spitsbergen. Then they would cut over the northernmost reaches of Norway and Sweden and keep going until they were one hundred miles north of Murmansk. At that point, the briefing officer explained, they were to turn and head for home.

After the briefing, Austin, his copilot, Capt. Carl Holt, and Maj. Vance Heavilin, the navigator, were quietly told to go to the target study room, where LeMay's bomber crews went over navigation charts and other material they needed to reach their targets. There, in the protected confines of the small chamber, two colonels they had never laid eyes on—one from SAC intelligence and the other from operations—confronted them. "Let me have your target maps," Austin, his voice still inflected by his Texas Panhandle roots, would remember one of them saying. They were the maps that were to have been used on that day's mission. None of the three had laid eyes on the maps yet, but Hal Austin would guess years later that they probably called for the three deviating

RB-47Es to leave the Murmansk area and head south on a pe-ripheral practice mission over Sweden, Norway, and probably West Germany.

Then Austin, Holt, and Heavilin were each handed a different set of maps. One of the colonels pulled out a strip map and laid it on the table. It was narrow and showed the line of flight, extend-ing one hundred miles on either side, that would take them over their real route. It was an attention grabber. They were supposed to cover 700 miles of Russian territory, starting at Murmansk and then heading south to Archangel. From there, the incredulous air-men saw, they were to turn southwest and fly on to Onega and then head due west and out of denied territory. According to the strip map, they would pass north of Helsinki, just to the north of Stockholm and Oslo, and would leave Scandinavia near Bergen and fly on to Fairford.

"We started going over this strip map," Austin said, "and these guys were talking like tobacco auctioneers" as they laid out the mission. " 'Got nine airfield targets, and here's your route of flight.' And they had it all laid out, airfields marked on a map. And someplace real early in the briefing, he [one of the briefers] told Vance Heavilin, my navigator, he says, 'If anything happens to you guys, you eat this sucker.' " So there it was. They were under or-ders to fly over nine Soviet air bases in daylight—bases that were sure to be defended in spades—photographing them as they went, and then sprint for home without getting shot to pieces.

The six RB-47s took off in radio silence. The control tower op-erators knew the takeoff sequence and flashed a green light to each bomber at five- or six-minute intervals. One after another, the planes thundered down Fairford's runway trailing black smoke. Since he was the leader of the second group of three, at least at that point, Austin was fourth in line. The weather was beautiful, so the six Stratojets, still maintaining radio silence, had no trouble connecting with their tankers off the Norwegian coast exactly as they had done two days earlier. "We top off the fuel," Austin said. "We're plumb full."

The pilot of the RB-47E behind and to Austin's right, flying the number two position, had been told that at one point he and Austin were to "swap leads," but he had not been told why. Now, still heading north one hundred miles off the Norwegian coast, Austin eased his throttles back and dropped into the right-hand slot, while the pilot who had been there moved up and into the lead. Austin was now bringing up the right rear side of the second group: a tail-end Charlie.

When the six of them reached their turning point at the northern edge of Norway, the lead flight reversed direction, just as it had on Thursday, and started heading back to England. The leader of the second flight carefully followed, swinging his jet smoothly to the left until it, too, was pointing toward home. And he fully expected the two planes behind him to do the same. But Austin didn't. At that point, he abruptly broke right and banked away hard, heading south toward Murmansk very much on his own. The flight leader, having no idea what had gotten into Austin's head, or whether his plane had suffered some calamity, was stupefied.

"Jimmy Valentine almost broke radio silence," Austin would recall. "He thought we'd lost our cotton-picking minds when he realized that we had not made the turn with him and instead were going south."

The lone RB-47E cruised over Murmansk at 40,000 feet. It was a little high given how much the plane weighed because of all the fuel it still carried, but one of the two colonels had ordered them to penetrate at that altitude because it would complicate the job of the interceptors. "The MiG-15 and the MiG-17 are very unstable gun platforms at 40,000 feet. The higher you get, the more unstable they are." They didn't have radar-controlled guns or any of that stuff on those airplanes, he had said. "The MiGs did look-and-shoot. That was the capability they had. . . . In the intelligence briefing, he mentioned that 'you'll only have MiG-15s to worry about. You can outrun 'em at 40,000 feet.' We asked about MiG-17s," Austin remembered. He, Holt, and Heavilin were assured by the colonel from SAC intelligence they didn't think MiG-17s had been deployed; they didn't have to worry about them. Wrong.

As they flew north of Murmansk, where the first two large target airfields were, Heavilin turned on the radar camera and three K-17 Trimetrogons, one of which shot straight down, while the other two took oblique pictures for horizon-to-horizon coverage. The actual target pictures of the air bases were taken with K-38s, which had thirty-six-inch focal lengths. All of the cameras stayed on during the entire time the plane was over Soviet territory.

Holt turned on the rear-looking radar that would target pursuing enemy fighters for the two 20-millimeter cannons in the tail. About then he looked back and saw that the Stratojet was leaving heavy white contrails in the clear sky. And that's not all he saw. Twenty minutes into Russia, with the first two air bases photographed, he reported that some planes were coming up on their left rear. But they never even got close. Austin guessed they were unarmed MiG-15s sent up to look them over.

Continuing on, they photographed a third air base between Murmansk and Archangel and two more at Archangel itself. That's when Holt spotted a second group of planes that also came up from the Stratojet's tail end. "Hey, these guys are coming up to our altitude," he warned on the intercom. But the newcomers made no firing passes, either, which led Austin to conclude they too had been on a training mission and were just trying to check out the penetrator. But these MiGs definitely had gotten closer to their altitude. A few minutes after the second group fell away, Holt spotted yet a third flight, this one with six fighters. Like the second group, and those that followed, they came up on the RB-47E's left side. They tracked it for six or seven minutes and then also fell away, as Austin, taking instructions from Heavilin in the nose, swung the bomber around until it was flying toward Onega to the southwest. The Russians were obviously tracking them closely now on fire control radar and straining to get close enough for a shot.

Flying at 40,000 feet was a trade-off. The thin air at that altitude may have turned MiGs into unstable gun platforms, as the colonels back at Fairford had predicted, but it also robbed the Stratojet of speed. Its six turbojets developed more thrust and more speed at lower altitude because the air was thicker and they therefore had more of it to eat.

With five of the nine air bases photographed, the RB-47E headed toward number six, which was about one hundred miles ahead. Austin and Heavilin had just settled into that leg of the mission when Holt came on again. This time there was an edge of intensity in his voice.

"Wait a minute," the copilot said. "Here comes another batch of airplanes." They were being chased by a fourth group of fighters. But now Carl Holt did not see six fighters together. "What we did see," Austin remembered, "was all of a sudden we've got something going above and below the airplane. I could see it, and I said, 'Holt, what the hell's going on back there?' He said, 'They're making fighter passes at us.' It turns out, what I'm seeing is tracers; tracers going both above and below the airplane. They're *shootin'* at us." For an instant, Austin thought ruefully about the "intelligence weenies" who had positively assured them there would be only MiG-15s and that in any case 40,000 feet would make them unstable for accurate firing. The fighters gave every indication of being stable enough.

"You better turn around and get those damned guns ready, man," Austin told Holt. "We're gonna need to start to use 'em back there." By then a second fighter—a MiG-17—had made a pass, spraying cannon fire laced with tracers past their plane. But Holt couldn't get his own cannons to work, which was an early and well-known affliction of RB-47s. "Kick it or something," Austin told his copilot. They both knew that if Holt couldn't get the plane's only gun to work, the next MiG would be climbing into their tail pipes, as he later put it.

When a third MiG came in for a firing pass, the cannons finally let out a short burst for a few seconds, so the MiG pilot prudently broke off the attack and dropped out of range of the bomber's flashing stinger. The rest of the MiGs in that flight, and in two others that followed, gave the Americans a wider berth. Word had gotten around that the lone intruder would shoot back.

Austin said years later that LeMay asked him why the MiGs hadn't shot him down. "My answer was very quick: 'They were not willing to come up our tail pipes.' There was no doubt in my mind that if they'd been willing to come up our tail pipes, they would have shot us down. But they were unwilling to do that" because they thought the cannons would fire dependably and they therefore kept a respectful distance.

Curtis LeMay, the world's preeminent bomber maven, knew

fighter pilots almost invariably attack from somewhere behind or to the side of their prey because it increases the element of surprise and gives them more time to line up for a good shot. He also knew fighters cannot shoot backward and attacking them from the rear is therefore a lot safer than going head-to-head. Nonetheless, he responded with one of his patented quips. "Well," he told Austin, "I'm convinced that all fighter pilots are cowards, anyway."

Meanwhile, a sixth air base had been photographed and Austin now concentrated on turning to approach the seventh. Holt's attention fixed on yet another MiG that was turning in for a firing pass. It was like being under continuous attack by sharks. As Austin banked and slid into a forty-five-degree turn to the left for the approach to the next target, the Soviet fighter, its cannons ready, came in from the left rear. Its pilot therefore had a substantial part of the RB-47 in his gunsight, since it was turning right into his fire zone. So he squeezed the firing button with his thumb.

Only one of the rounds that came out of the three cannons hit the Stratojet. But it was what the air combat fraternity calls a golden BB: a lucky shot. It slammed into the upper left section of the wing about ten feet from the fuselage, leaving a three-inch hole where it went in. It continued on, puncturing the retracted flap under the wing and tearing a jagged hole in it that was nine inches by six inches and shaped like South America. Finally, it smashed into the fuselage itself, where it exploded near one of three main fuel tanks, sending shrapnel in all directions.

All hell did not break loose. In fact, the only indication Austin, Holt, and Heavilin had that they had been hit was the loss of the intercom. But that was bad enough. The three of them had been keeping up a steady stream of chatter, with Heavilin giving Austin continuous, precise turning instructions so they could photograph their successive targets, Holt warning of each MiG attack, and Austin responding to both of them as was necessary. Now all three were deaf, out of contact. And the noise level inside their plane was "severe," as Austin put it.

The fifth and sixth MiGs in the group attacked in turn. But they didn't score and, evidently low on fuel, headed back to one of the newly photographed bases. Meanwhile, Austin continued to roll out. But he had to get the heading to the next target from Heavilin even though the intercom was dead. So he shouted back at Holt to crawl down to the nose and find out what the navigator wanted him to do. Holt squeezed out of his seat and made his way down the narrow aisle and into the nose, where he got turning instructions from Heavilin, and relayed them to Austin. They were over the next airfield. Austin held the aircraft absolutely steady as the cameras rolled on.

He was now convinced he no longer had an altitude advantage. "Enough of the 40,000 feet crap," he thought. He pushed the control column forward and dropped to 36,000 feet, picking up some speed.

By then, Holt had made his way back to his seat just in time to see yet another group of six fighters closing on them. The newcomers, apparently having been told that the Stratojet had used its guns, hung back, well out of its cone of fire. Just as the RB-47 was taking pictures of the last of the nine air bases, a sixth and last group of MiG-17s came in. The Russians were obviously infuriated. But Holt was then back in the aisle passing messages back and forth between the pilot and the navigator and was therefore literally in no position to cover their rear. He and Austin braced for more cannon fire while Heavilin pored over his charts. They were almost over Finland.

"This guy came up on our right wing, sat out there, and he kept dipping at us," Hal Austin said as he thought about that last MiG pilot. "Dipping his wing like he's gonna come in on us. And I swear we were close enough to shake hands. . . ." But Austin, Holt, and Heavilin were graced. The MiG pilot either had no ammunition or he had an abundance of respect for his lone, intrepid foe. "And finally," Hal Austin, still amazed, would recall, "he's settin' there level, and he gives me a hand salute. I saluted him back. He peels off and that's the last I saw of him." By the time the two pilots exchanged salutes, they were well into Finnish airspace.

One Helsinki newspaper reported that Laps in northern Finland had heard jets shooting and surmised there had been a battle between American and Russians planes. The story ran in *The Columbus Dispatch*, which covered Lockbourne Air Force Base, on May 16. It quoted an Air Force spokesman as saying no American planes had been in the area.

By the time they left Norwegian airspace, Austin and his crew were forty to forty-five minutes behind schedule and dangerously low on fuel. He climbed up to 43,000 feet and eased the throttles back. He couldn't establish contact with England because the radio was badly damaged, but he could barely hear through static that a tanker waiting to refuel them off Stavanger, Norway, was leaving the carefully planned rendezvous point and returning to its base.

They were getting edgy. "Now, Carl Holt is beginning to panic a little bit," Austin said, adding that his copilot worried they wouldn't be able to prove they had done the mission if the plane, cameras, and film went to the bottom of the ocean.

Using his call sign, Austin started requesting help every three or four minutes as his stricken plane crossed over the North Sea, bearing down on Brize-Norton, the nearest RAF base. He had no idea whether anybody heard him. A hundred and fifty miles out, he told Holt and Heavilin they were going to start down, and set his engines at idle. Then the three of them got lucky. As it turned out, only one channel on the radio was working, but a friend and KC-97 pilot named Jim Rigley happened to be on runway alert at Mildenhall at that moment and heard Austin's familiar voice.

Knowing Austin had a matter of minutes left to stay in the air, Rigley asked the tower for permission to take off immediately. It was denied. There was an emergency with a fighter in the pattern, he was told, and it would take six minutes to resolve. Rigley responded by bringing his four Pratt & Whitney Wasp Majors up to full power and barreling down the runway and into the air. Then he headed for where he thought he would find his friend.

Minutes later, Austin spotted the fat silver tanker, headed for it, and connected. The fuel gauges in the B-47E were like the ones in old cars, Austin said: they wiggled back and forth when there was fuel in the tank. But they weren't moving at that moment. "Holt swears that the gauges were no longer wiggling when I went under Rigley," Hal Austin added, smiling.

A large crowd was waiting for Austin, Holt, and Heavilin when they finally rolled to a stop back at Fairford. Typically, word had quickly gotten around that there had been some kind of an incident. With the canopy raised, a ladder was rolled up, and the Stratojet's crew chief was the first to climb it to greet his pilot and copilot. He was therefore the first to see the ugly hole made by the cannon shell.

"What the hell did you hit?" he asked Austin. It was the first real indication that the plane had been damaged.

"It was not a seagull," Austin answered, straight-faced, as the film canisters were unloaded and taken to intelligence.

Rigley was slapped with a violation by the base commander almost as soon as he landed and was reminded that control tower operators had the last word on takeoffs and landings. The mark on his record was overruled by LeMay.

Four months later, back in the States, Hal Austin, Carl Holt, and Vance Heavilin were each awarded two Distinguished Flying Crosses with oak-leaf clusters by LeMay, who pinned them on Austin and Holt himself. Heavilin was by then stationed in Florida.

"This should be a Silver Star," LeMay said once again. "But for a Silver Star, I've got to tell too many people in Washington. So here's two DFCs in lieu of a Silver Star." As usual, secrecy—the ubiquitous national security—took precedence over publicly recognizing a mission that was as successful as it was dangerous.

Still, it was the greatest day, after the greatest mission, of Hal Austin's life.

THE RAVEN'S SONG

THE 7499TH SUPPORT GROUP, which prowled along the Iron Curtain as part of an operation called Big Safari, epitomized the reconnaissance game. Its number was arbitrary, "Support" was ambiguous, Big Safari had nothing to do with lions and zebras, and many of its planes were designed to carry passengers with luggage, not ravens with black boxes. But that's why it flew the most successful covert reconnaissance operation of the cold war. It was composed of three units: the 7405th Support Squadron, based at Wiesbaden, West Germany, and the 7406th and 7407th Support Squadrons, based at Rhein-Main, also in West Germany. The 7499th, the umbrella unit, was headquartered at Wiesbaden with the 7405th until 1975, when it moved to Rhein-Main.

The 7499th began "border patrol" operations along the Iron Curtain at the end of the 1940s with a few old RB-17s that were fitted with rudimentary electronic intercept equipment. Starting in 1955, it became part of the Big Safari program, which itself started in 1952. Officially, the 7499th was one of the many units that studied "electromagnetic wave propagation" around the world. That is indeed what it did. But to say so is like saying an artist paints pictures. It is true but utterly ambiguous. And that, of course, was precisely the idea. In fact, Big Safari was and remains a unique logistical program in which highly specialized reconnaissance sensors and other equipment are fitted to various planes for specific kinds of missions.

The mission of the 7499th Support Group was to intercept enemy communication traffic, ferret radar, and test advanced electronic warfare equipment in Eastern Europe and the western USSR. The equipment itself—what was used and how it was used—came under Big Safari's jurisdiction.

The 7406th and 7407th Support Squadrons flew C-130A Hercules turboprop transports and the jet-propelled, extended-wing RB-57Fs, respectively. The latter, a General Dynamics–produced near-twin of Martin's stretched-wing RB-57D, was an unabashed reconnaissance aircraft whose stretched wings gave it an obvious altitude advantage over other reconnaissance planes, at least until the U-2 arrived in 1956. Any military aviator, certainly including Russians, who saw an RB-57F had no doubt about its mission, and therefore the mission of the 7407th.

The 7405th was different. If it had been automotive instead of aeronautical, its carefully protected section of the air base at Wiesbaden would have looked like a used car lot. There were RC-54 transport planes, spookdom's version of Donald Douglas's ancient DC-4, a propeller-driven crate that had been designed at the end of the 1930s for transcontinental airline use. The DC-4 had a younger first cousin, the four-engine DC-6, and it too worked for the 7405th as the C-118. There were also twin-engine, propeller-driven Convair T-29s, which had been developed right after the war as "flying classrooms" to train Air Force navigators and radar operators. Like any smart aircraft manufacturer, Convair sold passenger-carrying models of the T-29 to the airlines, foremost among them American Airlines. The four used by the 7405th made an average of a dozen flights a month along the Berlin corridors, taking pictures as they went. There were also previously owned B-26 Invaders, handsome and relatively fast twin-engine ground attack planes that served in World War II and Korea.*

Most of this motley collection of flying machines did electronic interception of one sort or another. But the star of the stable was an RC-97 that took pictures with the largest camera ever used in U.S. aerial reconnaissance. It was called Pie Face and it was Big Safari's first major project. Pie Face weighed 6,500 pounds with its mount and had a lens-to-film focal length of 240 inches. In other words, its lens was twenty feet long and could therefore take oblique photographs—slanted sideways—of objects seventy miles away in clear weather. Each photograph was eighteen inches by thirty-six inches and came from the largest roll of film ever special-ordered from Kodak. The huge camera was used about twelve times a month along the Berlin corridors.

Unlike most reconnaissance planes, those belonging to the 7405th had no telltale radar bulges, antennas, or other external paraphernalia that would give them away. They therefore appeared innocuous. An RC-97 belonging to the 7405th looked like a transport plane. It looked so much like a transport, in fact, that the men who flew it tended to call it a C-97 even though it was technically an RC-97 because of its real mission. One of the planes carried a forty-eight-inch panoramic oblique camera, a twelve-inch panoramic vertical camera, a vertical infrared scanner, a forward-looking infrared system, and four electronic intercept stations. The camera ports were hidden behind sliding external panels and the domes were fully retractable. All sensors, including electronic eavesdropping equipment, were secreted below the deck in RC-97s. The planes could therefore carry real cargo and unwitting passengers while collecting intelligence. The C-130s carried their sensors in fake cargo containers.

Naturally, the men of the 7405th wanted to believe they were fooling the opposition. But they weren't and they knew it. Of all the planes that flew the corridors leading into and out of Berlin, only those from the 7405th asked to be allowed to navigate on

*The Douglas B-26 was also known as the A-26 during World War II because Martin built the B-26 Marauder, another twin-engine attack plane. The Douglas version was given the B-26 designation after the war, when the Marauders were retired. This has created some confusion.

their own, followed routes that were different from other aircraft, routinely wandered 500 feet from their assigned altitudes, and made random flight patterns. The deviations were carefully noted on the ground. Furthermore, both the Russians and the East Germans took their own telephoto pictures of the ambling aircraft at below the 10,000-foot maximum altitude that clearly showed open camera doors. And it couldn't have taken counterintelligence specialists at Templehof Airfield long to conclude something suspicious was going on when as many as fifteen men emerged from one of the planes, had lunch, and then climbed back in and left to return to West Germany without delivering either passengers or cargo or leaving with them. The cover was so obviously transparent that the crews called themselves the "Berlin for Lunch Bunch."

Sending anything that flew for the 7405th on penetration missions, even shallow ones, in Eastern Europe's heavily defended skies would have amounted to murder. (China, which was regularly penetrated by other units using RC-54s and other ungainly machines, including the CIA's bastardized RB-69A Neptunes, was another story, because its defenses were much thinner.) So the planes worked the curtain from the safe side.

Donald Gardner, a raven who flew in the 7405th from September 1955 to September 1959, "monitored" East Germany, Czechoslovakia, Hungary, and also Yugoslavia and Albania, the last two in an RC-54 over the Adriatic. He also staged out of Incirlik in southern Turkey to join the gang of Navy and other Air Force units that infested the Black Sea looking for Soviet naval activity (including shipbuilding) and fresh scraps of radar and communication data. Gardner got as far east as the Yerevan region of Soviet Armenia, a place that would figure prominently—and very publicly—in the 7499th Support Group's history in the late summer of 1958.

There was a stark, though not immediately apparent, difference between the reconnaissance crews and their brethren who flew fighters in the Tactical Air Command, interceptors in the Air Defense Command, and bombers in SAC. Except for the two "hot" wars, first in Korea and then in Vietnam, the fighters did not actually fight, the interceptors did not actually shoot down aircraft attacking the United States and its allies, and the bombers did not actually bomb the enemy. They practiced. (In the case of SAC, thanks to LeMay, they practiced incessantly.)

Reconnaissance, however, was profoundly different. Whether they took photographs, ferreted radar, intercepted communication, or eavesdropped on missile telemetry, recce crews—on and under the sea as well as in the air—created life-threatening situations just by virtue of what they did. Since they couldn't do their jobs unless they got close enough to their armed quarry to invite attack, reconnaissance crews were effectively the only units in the armed forces that continuously engaged in actual combat operations. Others practiced fighting the bear and the dragon. But out of sight of the rest of the world, the recce crews actually tweaked their tails, and many were severely mauled for it.

Unlike outfits such as the Ninth, Fifty-fifth, and Ninety-first Strategic Reconnaissance Wings, which could be sent anywhere, the 7499th Support Group was confined to Europe. That's because testing new equipment was a major part of its job. Big Safari was a flying laboratory for new electronic, communication, and photographic intelligence gadgets of all sorts. Since the Soviet Union installed its best radar and other defenses along its frontier and those of the Warsaw Pact buffer states that separated it from NATO, it made sense to test the stuff there, especially since NATO forces were close at hand to ride shotgun.

Like other versions of the cargo-carrying C-54 Skymaster, Gardner's RC-54 had a pilot, a copilot, and a navigator. But behind the flight crew, six ravens worked the various radar frequencies. Gardner was one of them. And like its slightly larger RC-118 descendant, the RC-54's glaring weakness was that it was as slow and defenseless as a turkey (and flew like one). On the other hand, it was used precisely because, unlike a retreaded bomber, it was a low-profile, relatively unprovocative bird that didn't look threatening. And having been designed to carry forty or more passengers in comfort, it was practically the *Queen Mary* compared to Superfortresses and Stratojets.

Big Safari flights were almost always long, safe, and monotonous. They plied up and down the length of Eastern Europe ferreting one radar station after another and eavesdropping on communication with constantly improving hardware. "Most of our equipment was all new stuff," Gardner explained. "It was experimental, and if it was good, if it proved out, it would be made standard and put in, like, the RB-47."

Gardner and the others also made the Berlin milk run a number of times, and like many of their predecessors who flew during the airlift in 1948 and 1949, they routinely collected intelligence. "There were flights up the corridor. I've gone up there in a B-26. You take a black box with you—a receiver—and you just mark the signals as you go up. You just turn on the thing and record everything you get, up and back: air traffic control, or fire control, and stuff like that."

As elsewhere, the reconnaissance planes themselves were often closely tracked by Russians stationed in East Germany, both from the ground and in the air. One time a plane on a photographic intelligence mission came back with a picture that showed signs on the ground reading "Merry Christmas." (Later, reconnaissance satellites would pick up less cordial expressions stamped in the snow at the Tyuratam missile launch facility by Russians who knew one or two expletives in English.)

Being monitored by Communist radar and planes was old hat and fully expected. But Gardner did have one experience that rattled him and that offered a rare glimpse at another dimension of the game he was in. And it happened, not at 10,000 feet, but on terra firma.

It was, and remains, standard practice for counterintelligence operatives to establish the credentials of "walk-ins," as defectors are called. They do that to sort out military, political, or intelligence turncoats who have valuable information from, say, dentists (unless the dentist happened to be Nicolae Ceaușescu's or Walter Ulbricht's). Gardner remembered being at one briefing with several other military officers while a defector was trying to establish his credentials under close questioning. "This defector—I think he was East German—looked around and he looked at me and said, 'That's Lieutenant Gardner.' He would say, 'This is Colonel So-and-so, Major So-and-so.' He pointed at two of us and said, 'They're working at Wiesbaden Air Base.' It's amazing," Don Gardner said. "You're taken aback." The opposition clearly had its own

agents at Wiesbaden, Rhein-Main, and other installations, perhaps in the units' personnel offices, where records and photographs were kept. "Amazing," he said again.

Big Safari (its unclassified name) grew through the years as
new situations, some of them starting abruptly, developed. Relative to traditionally ponderous and red tape–bound Air Force operations, Big Safari was designed to react quickly by marrying
highly specialized equipment to changing technical requirements.
Throughout the cold war and afterward, the program would use a
small staff to adapt or create everything from specialized radar interception gear, to unmanned reconnaissance drones used in the
war in Vietnam and afterward, to the high-flying RB-57F, to a series of heavily modified RC-135s that are the military reconnaissance equivalent of the civilian Boeing 707. Wearing blisters,
bulges, bulbous noses, and other custom protrusions that concealed a variety of specialized communication and intercept antennas and assorted radars and other equipment, the RC-135s
would fly through the end of the century and into the next in
highly specific programs named Cobra Ball, Rivet Ball, Rivet
Joint, Rivet Quick, Rivet Amber, Rivet Card, Combat Pink, and
Combat Sent, among many others.

DON GARDNER AND his colleagues who flew ferret missions called
their work routine. It was. But the routine called for thousands of
hours of monotony that could be interrupted by sudden, terrifying
encounters. It was like wandering through a lovely forest for
hours, then turning a corner and running into the bogeyman. Violence and sudden death stalked reconnaissance missions and
were themselves part of the routine. Some embraced it. Some
shrank from it. No one ever forgot it was always in the air.

Robb Hoover, the raven who started in RB-47Hs and who is
known throughout the SAC reconnaissance fraternity as an affable and thoughtful man, knew exactly how his job fit into the
command's overall war plan and the requirements of national defense. He understood that ferreting could be done indifferently.
Or it could amount to an art form.

"A PRF in effect gives a sound—a pulse repetition frequency—

and if it's 1,000 pulses a second, that has a certain sound to it, almost akin to the sounds of a piano. The different keys on a piano resonate or ring in a certain frequency. These PRFs, these radars, do the same thing. And if you listen to them long enough," he explained, they can be recognized instantly even without equipment. "You just need to hear it once or twice—drrring . . . drrring . . ." When that happened, Hoover continued, he would know that a given frequency was 900 or 950 pulses a second. And that told him what radar he was hearing. "I presume that it's a Flat Face radar." (Like other military equipment, Soviet radars were given code names such as Flat Face, Fansong, Spoon Rest, Knife Rest, Hen House, Crown Drum, Skin Head, Fire Can, Scan Can, Dumbo, Mushroom, Yo Yo, and, of course, Token.) "I can look in the data I'm carrying with me, my tasking book, and see that we have a known radar, a Flat Face, at that location. The whole thing took me maybe a couple of seconds. I didn't have to go through a long thing. And so I can quickly dismiss that [radar] as irrelevant. I don't want to divert my attention to there. I want to focus my attention on much higher-priority signals that may not be there."

Finding the higher-priority signals—new targets that could be added to the inventory—was how Robb Hoover and others kept their own scores. In 1964, with the war in Vietnam heating up, Hoover ferreted on a Fifty-fifth Strategic Reconnaissance Wing RB-47H that flew out of Yokota and sniffed around the Gulf of Tonkin, three and a half hours to the southwest. It was before the Soviet Union supplied the North Vietnamese with the V-750 surface-to-air missile, commonly called the SA-2 in the West. The missile's existence was a long-established fact. One had shot down Francis Gary Powers four years earlier; another had destroyed Maj. Rudolf Anderson's U-2 over Cuba during the dangerous missile crisis in the autumn of 1962. Still others sprouted around air bases and other targets throughout the Warsaw Pact. The V-750 was a dependable antiaircraft missile, and since the United States was heavily dependent on planes to support the ground war, it was reasonable to suppose the weapons would be sent to North Vietnam.

Hoover's and the other ravens' job was to find out as soon as possible whether the guys in the fighters and bombers were going to have to deal with the deadly weapons. They would do that stuffed in the semidarkness of the RB-47H's windowless bomb bay, caressing the knobs on their receivers and listening to endless chirping and tweetering thirty or thirty-five miles off Haiphong.

"Our intelligence people said, 'The highest priority you have is to see if one of these radars would show up in the Hanoi area.' That would be an extremely high priority because it could be a precursor indicator that they're thinking about bringing in the SA-2 missiles. And then," Hoover added, smiling at the notorious absurdity of some orders, "they give me ten other priorities. Well, I only have one receiver. And if I'm looking for thing A, many times I can't look for thing B and thing C." For the hour that the RB-47H stayed over the Gulf of Tonkin on that mission, Hoover therefore kept his APR-9 receiver tuned to pick up the one small frequency band that would betray the presence of an SA-2 radar. It worked, too.

"And in fact, I *did* intercept—I think it was in October '64— that radar. I got a very short intercept on it. I was up [tuned] just long enough where I could take a couple of these direction find-ing cuts that went right up the Red River Valley toward Hanoi." He recorded the brief signal and brought it back to Yokota. "They were very excited," he remembered. "I think that the first SA-2 missile shootdowns of our aircraft were in the spring of '65. It was a precursor sign, another little piece of the puzzle, that they'd be bringing in that SA-2 missile."

Being the first to ferret the deadly antiaircraft missiles was in-tellectually rewarding. But there was more to it than that. There was also a visceral, deeply self-defining, almost transcendental as-pect to ferreting an enemy. For Hoover, it was like bullfighting. There was certainly a technical challenge. But what provided the excitement, what got the adrenaline going, was to see how close he could come to the horns without getting gored.

"We'd fly our missions and they'd launch their fighters, and they'd come up next to us, sometimes almost overlapping our wingtips. Well, this gave us a great opportunity because we could see how efficient they are in launching their fighters. How good are their tactics? How are they controlling the fighter? What kind

of GCI [ground-controlled intercept] radar are they using? Sometimes the fighters would turn on their airborne intercept radar
and come right up our tail," Hoover explained with his character-
istic smile. "That was, in one way, a bonanza. Very exciting.

"And if they got close enough, in a firing position right on our
tail, some number of yards which I can't recall anymore—perhaps
1,000, something like that—they would go from the search radar,
which had this kind of boogie beat to it—tick-tick-tickety-tick . . .
tick-tick-tickety-tick—and then the Soviet fighter pilot would lock
his radar on." Hoover made a fluttering, high-pitched sound by
exhaling with his tongue behind his upper front teeth. "And when
you heard that, it was electrifying because then you knew he was
locked on you at a distance where he could shoot you down. All
he had to do was move his thumb. And that's it. If you're out there
at the far end of the stream, in the upper reaches of the Soviet
Arctic, you know there isn't going to be anyone who's ever going
to be able to get to you and offer you any help, or chase them
away, or do anything else about them. So sometimes," Robb
Hoover continued, "if they were too threatening in those activities, we could fall back on the time-honored 'discretion is the better part of valor' and fold up our tent and go back home."

But Hoover also had empathy for his adversaries (at least for
those who didn't fly fighters). Ostrov Vize, which has an early
warning radar, is a tiny island halfway between Franz Josef Land
and North Land just below the eightieth parallel in the Arctic
Ocean. Whenever he was in the neighborhood, Hoover would
ponder the isolated souls who were manning that radar. "I kept
thinking that there are some poor Russian radar operators trying
to work on that godforsaken, barren little island. Usually, they'd
be icebound that far north. I used to wonder: 'How long are those
guys up there? Is that a one-year tour of duty?' " In Hoover's opinion, being stuck on such a forlorn and bitterly cold rock month after month so they could spot an attacker that would never come,
or even his RB-47H, and routinely relay its whereabouts to the regional headquarters was a truly lousy job.

So Hoover decided on one peripheral flight to ferret the Ostrov
Vize radar—a very boring, well-established radar—out of sympathy and respect for the miserable souls who were down there

tracking him. They would never know it, of course, but it was Hoover's way of lending a little dignity to their existence. "I will record your radar," he told himself. "I will turn it in to my intelligence people, and they may tell me, 'Robb, this is the 178th time we have intercepted the early warning and height-finding radar at Ostrov Vize.' Okay, fine. I hope I was providing him some justification for his miserable assignment."

CARLOS C. CAMPBELL never met Robb Hoover. But he fully shared the experience of collecting intelligence in dangerous places. Campbell put in thirty-two months as a navigator and air intelligence officer in VP-22, a reconnaissance squadron based at Iwakuni Air Base, near Hiroshima, from 1960 to 1962. The unit's primary assignment was ASW—antisubmarine warfare—but it also "rigged" enemy surface vessels: it took close looks at what was on their decks and photographed them for analysis.

The pictures were then scrutinized by a new breed of analyst who specialized in what the CIA somewhat self-mockingly called "cratology," or the study of crates. The theory was that a disassembled MiG-19 or SA-2 missile or T-54 tank or any other military hardware would be shipped in a wooden crate built expressly for that weapon. Once the size and shape of a crate containing the fuselage of an IL-28 light bomber was known, for example, the odds favored every other crate with those exact specifications also containing an IL-28 fuselage. But everybody in intelligence knew cratology was far from an exact science. The opposition could have used IL-28 fuselage crates, complete with markings in Cyrillic, to transport anything from assault rifles to vodka if they knew the Americans would be rigging them.

Like Hoover and others, Campbell understood the levels of the game. He also understood from firsthand experience the recurring danger that went with collecting information an armed enemy did not want him to have. Campbell was jumped a number of times and remembered them vividly.

"When it happens to you, you want to do your job," he said. "You don't want to let yourself down. You don't want to panic. You use humor, and you also have this mind-set where you think you're bulletproof. And here you are. You want to live. You don't want to kill people. But it's a crew, and the crew has been trained to work as a unit, and you don't want to be the one guy to screw up."

Seeing an enemy fighter close up was unnerving because the situation suddenly became dangerous and unpredictable. "There were a few seconds when you got numb. Then you just came out of it. When you see a snake or something like that, you get a little feeling through your body: 'I don't want to be here.' And then, all of a sudden, 'I've gotta get out of here.' You go through it the first time, and it doesn't happen again."

Campbell's Neptune often flew to the northern tip of Hokkaido, then cut toward the Siberian coast, and then down past Olga Bay, where there was a submarine base, and on to Vladivostok. It always got "dicey" there, not so much because of the Russians, but because they would sometimes continue flying on to the coast of North Korea. North Korean fighter pilots, like Communist Chinese fighter pilots, had particularly nasty reputations. Unlike the Russians, who were usually restrained where the use of cannons and missiles was concerned, and who occasionally even showed respect for the adversaries, the North Koreans in particular would in effect cross the street to get a good bite.

"The North Koreans were really bad-asses. They'd shoot first and ask questions later," Campbell remembered. "The only flight that I had where we thought we were going to head west, as the expression goes, is when we were jumped by a North Korean MiG. We knew he was trying to shoot us down because we could pick up his fire control radar on our electronic countermeasures system," Campbell said, echoing Hoover. "He had locked on us and was trying to shoot us down." Following procedure, the pilot dropped to 500 feet. "That foiled them because they couldn't get under the P2V." And since instruments are unreliable unless a plane is flying straight and level, he added, the North Koreans didn't want to risk flying into the ocean by trying to maneuver beneath or even around the patrol plane at that altitude.

The game was played more subtly, with more nuance, with the Russians. Being attacked by North Koreans was a given, a foregone conclusion. Flying near Soviet fighters was most often, though not always, like being in water with a languid barracuda or in a room with a dozing pit viper. You could probably get away if you backed off slowly, didn't make any sudden moves, and didn't do anything provocative (pointing machine guns at fighter pilots tends to provoke them).

"Most of the time, they would harass us," Campbell said of the Russians. "It was almost like a bit of a game. We're flying straight and level and they would go up like this, and then they would pick us up. We're flying here, and they would do these kinds of maneuvers," he added, turning his left hand into an imaginary Neptune and his right into an imaginary MiG that is flying alongside the P2V. Then his right hand peeled, flew away, and swung back in until it was right off the imaginary Navy patrol plane's wing again. (Using hands that way is a primal means of expression for combat airmen the world over.) "They would always try to get us to turn in toward the coast, because the closer you got to the shoreline, the more legitimate their hostile actions would be. Then they could shoot you down. They could orbit you. Try to make passes at you. They could make life somewhat miserable. Tactically, you have to go lower and slower, and the one thing you want to do to show that you're taking nonhostile action is turn away from the coast. Once you turn away from the coast, they're going to leave you alone."

Enemy fighters were not the only menace faced by Navy patrol crews. VP-22 and other antisubmarine squadrons would barge right into the middle of Soviet antisubmarine exercises whenever they could. It was like crashing the other gang's party. "They would put their guns on us and they would track us with their guns. . . . We'd kind of give them a little space. We'd make enough runs to get as much intelligence as we could without doing something stupid."

Thirty-five years later, Carlos Campbell sat in his comfortable living room in Reston, Virginia, and brought a perspective to his early days in the Navy that only the passage of years could put in focus. A picture of his daughter, Kimberly, who was a physician, stood on top of a bookcase across the room.

"Keep in mind," he explained, "we're kids. We're twenty-two, twenty-three. I'm sixty-one now. There's no way in the world I would have done in my forties what I did in my twenties. When you're in your thirties, and you've got a family, you're very cautious. We didn't like flying with any of the, you know, what we called 'older pilots.' They were extremely cautious. They didn't like bad weather. They didn't take any risks. They wouldn't go down [on the deck]. Flying is a young man's game, even in a patrol squadron, so of course we took risks."

Like Hoover, Carlos Campbell had an intellect that allowed him to empathize with the opposition; he could put himself in its place. There was not the slightest doubt in his mind, for example, that U.S. reconnaissance crews had been captured by the Russians. The cold war, he said, was a *war*, and while the downed American airmen were heroes to their own countrymen, they were invasive and potentially deadly enemies to the Russians and were treated accordingly.

Campbell wondered aloud how the people of the United States would have reacted to frequent reports that Soviet long-range bombers, possibly carrying nuclear weapons, were prowling very close to both coasts. "How would United States citizens act if, every time, they knew that a Bear or a Bison [bomber] came down our coast and it was on the evening news? 'Well, today a Russian bomber with nuclear weapons on board flew within thirty miles of the United States . . .' We'd get very anxious. . . . Go back to the shootdowns. They get ten warm bodies and they bring them back to normal life and health—not that you'd ever be normal mentally—and they incarcerate them. There are a lot of people—thirty, forty, fifty Americans—and you think they're going to let anybody out? It's not going to happen."

THE FIRST RB-47 WAS shot out of the sky on the morning of April 17, 1955, as it photographed and radar-mapped the southern end of the Kamchatka Peninsula from over water. It was an RB-47E from the Fourth Strategic Reconnaissance Squadron at Eielson and was on one of the routine milk run flights to Japan when it was jumped by MiG-15s and shot down. The incident was ominous because it was the first time one of the fast, swept-wing jets was clobbered. More ominously, the MiG-15 that did it was no longer the top-of-the-line fighter. MiG-17s—one of which had punched a large hole in Hal Austin's RB-47E the year before—were by then operating throughout the Soviet Union, while MiG-19s and Yak-25s, the large, twin-engine, radar-equipped, all-weather interceptors that were called "Flashlight" by NATO, were in the wings (in a manner of speaking).

The Russians, who tracked the bomber on radar throughout its fatal flight, later admitted it had not violated their airspace. But they shot it down anyway as it flew thirty-two miles east of Cape Kronotski. Years later, after the end of the cold war, the Russians also reported that the U.S. search-and-rescue planes, which they monitored, spent four days looking for the three downed crewmen in the wrong place. Their fate remains unknown.

TWO MONTHS LATER, it was the Navy's turn again. On June 22, 1955, another P2V-5 ferret was jumped by MiGs, this time over the Bering Sea, as it started back to its station on Kodiak Island after monitoring radar along the Chukotski Peninsula and looking for Soviet ships to photograph. But the incident was different from most of the others in one fundamental respect. The eleven crewmen, some of them severely shot up and burned, made it home and described in vivid detail the terror they had lived through.

Charley Baker Three, as this particular mission was called, left the Kodiak Naval Air Station at around dawn and climbed to 10,000 feet as it cut across southwestern Alaska. It spent the rest of the morning ferreting off Provideniya. Donald E. Sonnek, an aviation ordnance man who was responsible for the plane's guns and bombs, would one day recall that Charley Baker Three was only the second Neptune to fly that particular route. The week before, he said, the crew on its predecessor had spotted something worrisome. High above and behind them, they reported in their debriefing, they had noticed long, white, graceful contrails. That, Don Sonnek explained, meant they were being stalked by MiGs.

The MiGs were there again at a little after 11 a.m. on June 22, just as Charley Baker Three turned and started for home. Sonnek was sitting next to a large window on the right side of the plane, idly reading a manual. "I looked out the window, and a MiG come by like that." He quickly radioed the pilot, Lt. Richard F. Fischer, and reported what he had seen; just then three glowing tracers sailed silently by. "They're firing on us," he told Fischer and Lt. (jg) David M. Lockhart, the copilot. "I could see the guy sitting in there, just as plain as day," Sonnek said about the pilot of the first MiG. "He wasn't looking at me, he was looking straight ahead. I suppose he was radioing the other guy and saying, 'Hey, these guys are sleeping.' He could see that none of the guns were being manned."

With the dark blue twin-engine patrol plane growing larger in his gun site, the "other guy" pressed the firing button and felt his MiG shudder as its three cannons sent rounds tearing into the Neptune's left engine and fuselage. The Russian stayed right there, raking the patrol plane, as Fischer, following procedure, shoved his control column forward to lose altitude.

Thaddeus Maziarz, another enlisted man, had been thinking about the newborn son he had not yet seen when the attack began. Now he watched as flames poured out of the left engine and licked at a five-foot gash that exposed one of the P2V-5's wing tanks and charred spars. The wheel well was also on fire; Maziarz could see the fire moving toward the fuselage itself. At least there was no danger of fire in the right wing tank. No danger because it was gone. Sonnek had watched as the first MiG shot it off and had seen it tumble away. Maziarz peered through the smoke in the cabin. He saw that the needles in the gauges showing the amount of gasoline in the wing tanks was dropping fast. He also saw that there were shrapnel holes in a nearby life raft he could have shoved his fist through.

Charley Baker Three was hundreds of miles from Kodiak, it had turned into a torch that could explode at any moment, and the life raft looked like a Swiss cheese. Ted Maziarz sucked in his breath as his burning plane skimmed fifty feet over the Bering Sea. It was so close to the water its prop wash was leaving wakes.

Some of the cannon shells that had punctured the fuselage had exploded, sending shrapnel in all directions. Sonnek and Martin E. Berg, another ordnance man, were knocked to the floor by the violent impact of the ammunition going off. Sonnek managed to pull himself to his feet. Then he felt something warm and gooey running down his left arm. When he took off his flight jacket he saw he was bleeding from a shrapnel wound. He didn't know there was another metal shard in his lower back. Don Sonnek would carry both chunks of metal for the rest of his life, souvenirs of his encounter with Russians at very low altitude. Berg couldn't get up, so Sonnek picked him up, and the two of them struggled toward the front of the plane. Berg's back was peppered with cannon fragments. Eddie Benko, one of the two radar men, had the tip of an unexploded 23-millimeter cannon round in his arm. Ens. David Assard, a navigator, saw that his left hand was shattered by yet another cannon round.

It was Saint-Exupéry all over again. The two cobras—the MiGs—were heading back to their base at Provideniya while their stricken victim struggled to get home, badly shot up and burning, at a perilously low altitude.

Fischer, who was not wounded, knew there was no chance of nursing his severely crippled plane back to Kodiak. So he decided to head for St. Lawrence Island, which had the virtues of being close and friendly.

"There was fire all over and I put my hands over my face," Sonnek remembered. The smoke was so thick he couldn't see his crewmates. "Where the hell are these people?" he wondered aloud.

"The wing's gonna fall off, the wing's gonna fall off," Maziarz shouted. As a chief petty officer, he was the Neptune's plane captain and was therefore in charge of all enlisted ranks.

"What do you want me to do, Chief," Charles Shields, the radioman, shouted back, "hold it on with my hands?"

By then, Shields was sending continuous Mayday signals and giving Charley Baker Three's position. Everyone was at his ditching station. Sonnek braced his back against the forward wing spar that connected the wings through the fuselage. He was looking through the window again when he suddenly saw that the blue water had given way to the coast of St. Lawrence Island. "Holy crow," Sonnek thought, "there's nothing but rocks coming up." He anticipated the deep, grinding crunch that would come as the jagged rock formation tore into the Neptune's belly, right under where he sat, and quickly chewed upward.

But Fischer, looking ahead, could see a flat pasture beyond the rocks and he used all the energy his plane had left to reach it. As soon as he was over tall grass, Fischer made sure the plane's rudder was holding it straight and chopped the throttles, killing both engines. Carefully working the wheel and pedals, he eased his burning Neptune into a perfect belly landing.

"I've made rougher landings on runways with some of them young pilots we trained," Sonnek said. "He smoothed it right in, nice and slick. We come to a stop and we got the hell out of there." He popped the nearest hatch and scrambled out onto the wing. When his hands came down on the wing, which was blistering hot, there was a flash of more pain. Sonnek did not realize it at that moment, but both of his hands were so seared, so severely burned, that the flesh on his fingers had melted and fused. But even in the din and terror of the crash landing, even with the excruciating pain in his hands and elsewhere, Don Sonnek knew he was much better off outside the plane than inside. Hot ammunition was now exploding in there and flares were going off. His crewmates, wounded or not, were scrambling as fast as they could out of every opening they could find and heading straight for a water-soaked ditch nearby. It was better than "getting my rear end burned," he would later explain to justify his mutilated hands.

The eleven of them stayed in that cool, wet ditch and watched the Neptune's riddled carcass burn and shudder from the explosions. Four of the eleven survivors, including Fischer, got out unscathed. Sonnek and the other six were given morphine so they felt no pain. Not at first, anyway.

Then the Eskimos appeared. They came in two skin-covered, motor-driven boats and said prayers for the airmen before taking them to Gambell, their village. While their rescuers contacted Elmendorf Air Force Base, outside of Anchorage, the crewmen of Charley Baker Three told each other that, given the circumstances, they looked pretty good. But according to Sonnek, it was only when they went into the bathroom of the local school looking for water to drink, and looked in the mirror, that they saw the truth. "Chuck [Shields] walked in first, and he looked. Then he turned around to me and said, 'you damned liar.' " Some skin was hanging off their heads. Some was so badly scorched it smelled like the charred meat it was. Sonnek's hair had melted into his head.

The survivors were flown to Elmendorf on an Air Force C-47 and the seven who were wounded were hospitalized. The doctors surgically separated Sonnek's fingers and grafted new skin onto all of his right hand so he would not have to spend the rest of his life with hands that were as webbed as a duck's feet. And the edges of his ears were so badly burned they had to be trimmed. But that was for the best, one of the surgeons told Sonnek in an apparent effort to cheer him up, because they were too big anyway. For the rest of his life, Don Sonnek's left ear would ring, both hands would hurt, and scars on his arm and back would conceal the metal souvenirs from his last patrol.

At a news conference six days after the well-publicized attack, John Foster Dulles, the secretary of state and brother of CIA chief Allen W. Dulles, went on the offensive. He accused the Russians of "a willful violation" of international law by "trigger-happy" pilots who attacked the P2V-5 over admittedly narrow international waters. Referring to the mission itself, Dulles blatantly lied, as was customary. "It's a plane which makes that flight for the purpose of observing vessels in distress and things of that sort," he told the reporters. "That has no relationship to any kind of military activity and, as I say, it's a routine flight." Meanwhile, news photographers were allowed to take pictures of the wounded crewmen in their hospital ward. Sonnek, stripped to his waist and sitting cross-legged in bed, used his bandaged hands to describe the attack. His face was covered with nasty burns. He made *Life* magazine and newspapers around the country. So did his Neptune, whose fire-gutted remains offered dramatic testimony to the ferocity of the attack.

Perhaps the grisly pictures or an upcoming summit meeting or both persuaded the Russians to soften their usual stance after similar incidents. The Kremlin not only offered an unprecedented apology for the attack, but equally unprecedented, it paid half of the estimated damages with a check made out for $724,947.68. The Department of State had asked for payment in full, but diplomacy is about compromise. By meeting the reparation demand halfway, the Russians took responsibility for shooting down the Neptune. By refusing to pay the other half, they were making the point that there would have been no attack in the first place had the patrol plane not been snooping where it was, and that responsibility was America's. Split the difference.

THE NEED FOR intelligence was considered so urgent in 1955 that reconnaissance crews were systematically being sent into harm's way, and their toll was rising accordingly. That year, two innovative programs were launched to save Air Force and Navy lives. One of them was misguided and failure-prone. The other was majestic.

The first, originally called Project Gopher when it was conceived in 1950, and later Grandson and Genetrix, was a joint Air Force-Navy-CIA operation that was supposed to collect photographs over the Soviet Union by using huge balloons carrying refrigerator-sized cameras in gondolas. The program was plagued from the beginning by developmental problems. General Mills, for example, fabricated the balloons themselves using faulty polyethylene. The giant breakfast cereal maker therefore had trouble meeting its production requirement.

And since the Strategic Air Command was responsible for strategic reconnaissance, Genetrix was turned over to LeMay for implementation. His immediate reaction to being told he was in charge of an armada of balloons has gone unrecorded, but it was undoubtedly memorable. Official cover was provided by a Navy meteorological program called Moby Dick that sent a stream of balloons across the Pacific.

Genetrix was launched in January 1956 when the first of 516 of the balloons rose from West Germany and floated eastward. The launches from there, as well as from Scotland and Turkey, continued for six weeks. The Russians, long since inured to the Pentagon's apparent fascination with their weather, protested to the United States and Turkey that the flights were "inadmissible" and constituted a "gross violation" of their airspace. To further make the point, they also shot down as many as they could. Then, in early February, they staged an elaborate display of fifty camera systems, related communication equipment, and some of the shriveled balloons themselves at a news conference in Moscow. It presaged the Francis Gary Powers extravaganza by four years.

The Department of State responded with another elaborate note claiming some weather balloons might have accidentally wandered into the Soviet Union and that they were scientifically important. But the note also assured the Kremlin that the flights would stop. Eisenhower and Dulles decided the project had been of dubious value all along and had become an embarrassment.

Genetrix operations were officially ended on March 1, 1956. Of the 516 launches, 399 became operational; 44 actually reached the Pacific on prevailing winds and were mostly retrieved by trapezes hanging out of C-119 transports sent to snatch the balloons as they floated down. Forty produced photographs, whose value was subject to widely differing interpretation. Richard M. Bissell, Jr., and Herbert R. "Pete" Scoville, Jr., both of whom were heavily involved in the CIA's technical intelligence collection program at the highest level, were disparaging of Genetrix. Scoville called it a "disaster." LeMay would have agreed.

Genetrix was easy to terminate because the other program, the majestic one, promised to be sensationally effective. Its heart was a manned, high-flying, jet-propelled glider designed to fly over the USSR at altitudes that could not be reached by any Soviet fighter of the time. It was called the U-2. Beginning in July 1956, it would start a true revolution in aerial reconnaissance. In the process, it would save the lives of countless airmen who no longer would have to fly dangerous deep penetrations at altitudes that made them vulnerable to attack. But initially the U-2 was a photoreconnaissance aircraft, not a ferret, so the electronic intelligence collectors continued to be sent in harm's way. And some would continue to get captured and killed.

IF TROPHIES HAD been awarded for angering the Russians, Project Home Run would have gotten the big one. During the seven weeks between March 21 and May 10, 1956, sixteen RB-47E photoreconnaissance planes and five RB-47H electronic reconnaissance planes supported by spares and twenty-eight KC-97 tankers flew an astonishing 156 missions over Siberia. The jets were from the Tenth and 343d Strategic Reconnaissance Squadrons and were on temporary duty at Thule Air Force Base in Greenland, where temperatures typically dipped to thirty-five degrees below zero Fahrenheit. They flew from there over the top of the world in absolute radio silence and collected pictures, radar intelligence, and communication intercepts over a 3,500-mile-wide swath of territory that stretched from Murmansk on the Kola Peninsula all the way to Provid'eniya on the Bering Strait. The missions collected invaluable intelligence on air bases, radar stations, the nuclear test site on Novaya Zemlya, and timber, mining, and nickel smelting operations in the vast region.

And as if the ongoing penetrations weren't provocative enough, Project Home Run's finale was a so-called massed overflight on May 6–7 in which six of the camera-carrying RB-47Es flew abreast in broad daylight, crossing the coast near Ambarchik at 40,000 feet. From there they streaked south at full throttle, photomapped the area, and then headed out over Anadyr and the Bering Strait for a landing at Eielson Air Force Base in Alaska.

"To this day," aerospace historian R. Cargill Hall wrote more than forty years later, "the SAC Thule missions remain one of the most incredible demonstrations of professional aviation skill ever seen in any military organization at any time."

Whatever the rationale for sending six bombers going full-bore and in formation over Soviet territory, Russians watching their blips on radar could reasonably have thought it was the beginning of war day; that they were coming under nuclear attack. As it turned out, only three or four attempts were made to intercept the intruders, none of them successful. That failure, plus the intelligence return itself, showed Siberia was in fact very porous and poorly protected. No one knew it better than the Russians themselves, and it gnawed at them. Campbell's point was that such operations understandably frustrated and angered the Russians precisely because they proved their homeland was vulnerable to a potentially devastating attack. Taken in that light, America's heroes were Russia's dangerous and contemptible spies.

The Russians delivered a strong protest to the U.S. embassy a

week after the six-plane overflight. On May 29, the Department
of State answered it with a note explaining that "navigational difficulties" in the Arctic might have caused unintentional violations
of Soviet airspace. If that was indeed the case, the note added, it
was regrettable. One hundred and fifty-six instances of navigational difficulties in seven weeks. Khrushchev must have seethed.

THE FIRST DEADLY incident in 1956 came just after midnight on
August 22, and once again it was the Navy's turn. This time, however, the attacking fighters were not Russian. They were Chinese.

The aircraft was a Martin P4M-1Q Mercator, and was one of
six belonging to VQ-1, the electronic warfare squadron at Iwakuni
Air Base in Japan. Mercators were developed to replace the slug-
gish Privateers. All nineteen that were built to fly operational
missions were fitted specifically for electronic countermeasure
operations. They had two propeller engines and, to "enhance sur-
vivability," two jets mounted near them. This one, like the others,
carried eight new APR-4 and APR-9 receivers and several intercept antennas. And, also like the others, this P4M-1Q worked not
only for the Navy but for the National Security Agency. It and its
sisters were so secret they had other units' identification letters
and numbers painted on their tails, were given arbitrary identification numbers that were changed monthly, usually used Neptune squadrons' call signs, and flew only at night and with lights
off.

At 12:25 a.m., under the kind of full moon crews on such
flights usually dreaded, the Mercator, wearing identification number 187642 (it was really 124362), was caught by Communist
Chinese MiGs as it ferreted radar at 6,000 feet 32 miles east of
Wenchow and 150 miles north of Formosa in the Shanghai area.
The only word that the plane was being shot at came from its pilot, Lt. Cmdr. Milton Hutchinson, who radioed forty minutes after his last regular position report that he was "under attack by
enemy aircraft." He quickly repeated it and tried to add something, but the transmission to Japan abruptly ended. It was the
last word from the Navy patrol craft.

Within hours, the Chinese broadcast the news that their fighters had damaged a "Chiang Kai-shek" plane near the Chushan Islands but that it had disappeared. The reference was to the despised Nationalist Chinese on Formosa. As usual, the Seventh Fleet quickly sent planes and ships to the area to search for the downed airmen and report on what had happened. A destroyer turned up the body of one of the Mercator's sixteen crewmen, PO Albert P. Mattin, as well as two fuel tanks, one wheel, and, yet again, empty life rafts. Two days later another destroyer found the body of Lt. Cmdr. James W. Ponsford.

Since the United States did not recognize the People's Republic of China, and therefore had no diplomatic relations with Peking, the British were asked to act as intermediaries in trying to get information from the Reds on the fate of the plane and any survivors. As long-standing custom required, the letter from the British chargé d'affaires in Peking to Chang Han-fu, the Chinese Communist vice-minister for foreign affairs, studiously referred to the missing Mercator as having been on a routine flight.

Whatever the plane's mission, Chang answered by insisting that he knew nothing about either it or any survivors. That was a lie. But then he got to the point, which had to do with the American puppet on Formosa, the real source of his rage: "However, I would like to inform you of another event which was made public on the 23rd of August. After 0/00 hour [midnight] on August 23, a Chiang military plane was discovered over the sea south-east of Shanghai intruding over the Ma An Islands. Aircraft of the Chinese Air Force immediately took off," he wrote, and damaged the intruder, which headed for the open sea. "As is well-known," Chang continued, getting to the point, "the war acts of harassment and destruction carried out by the military planes despatched [sic] by the Chiang Kai-shek clique to intrude over the mainland and the coastal islands have become even more frequent during the past year. Our Air Force has often fought with these Chiang military planes and shot them down, damaging them or driving them away. As for this Chiang plane which intruded over the Ma An Islands, our Air Force took the same action and damaged it. It goes without saying," Chang added, "that these Chiang planes are all aircraft of the American type."

Eisenhower was well aware of U.S. reconnaissance forays

around the world. The strategist in him certainly understood the need for reconnaissance and accepted the loss of the Mercator. But Eisenhower the politician was as exasperated as Chang Han-fu, not just because the Navy ferret had been caught and destroyed—that had to be expected—but because no plausible cover story had been prepared ahead of time. Ike's mood at a National Security Council meeting a week after the shootdown was described by Col. Andrew J. Goodpaster, his military aide and confidante:

"The President said what he particularly objected to in connection with the Navy plane incident was the fact that the Administration had no story prepared in advance, and that State and the [armed] Services 'quarreled for a week over what they should say.' A cover plan should have been ready before the incident occurred. He said we are 'between the devil and the deep blue sea' in this matter because if we say that our plane was in the clear, the people of our country are entitled to demand to know why we do not do something about this incident, whereas if we say the plane crew made an error, this statement is alleged to be 'throwing off' on the Navy. He thought it was very unsatisfactory that this Administration, after three years, had no cover story ready for this matter."

And Ike could also see the situation as the enemy saw it. "The President said that if planes were flying twenty to fifty miles from our shores," Goodpaster continued, "we would be very likely to shoot them down if they came in closer, whether through error or not." Soviet ferrets did eventually come in closer and would be carefully escorted down both coasts. None would be shot down.

Mattin's and Ponsford's were not the only bodies recovered from the shootdown. The remains of AT1c. William F. Haskins and AT3c. Jack A. Curtis, both enlisted technicians, were turned over to the British by the Chinese in Shanghai and were later autopsied. No shrapnel fragments were found, leading medical authorities to conclude that they had been crushed to death when the Mercator hit the water.

An official report of the incident stated that "the condition of the bodies indicated that they had been subjected to a crash of great impact. . . . It was the opinion of qualified medical authority that the broken condition of the bodies that had been recovered was such that there would have been no survivors of a crash as violent as that which caused the injuries." That hypothesis would have earned a failing grade in medical school.

Within a year of the shootdown, very credible reports reached Japan that at least three survivors had been picked up by Chinese patrol boats in the immediate vicinity of the crash. A month after the shootdown, a Japanese apparently was told by a crewman from one of the boats that three Americans were pulled out of the water alive and three were pulled out dead and were cremated. One of the three who were rescued also died of his wounds. But another was slightly injured. The third was said to have been seriously wounded and was hospitalized.

Then, independently, Air Force intelligence corroborated the story told by the Japanese. At least two reliable sources inside Communist China reported that two of the P4M-1Q's crewmen were indeed being held in Peking and Shanghai under relatively comfortable conditions. In a secret air intelligence information report, "Information on Surviving Crew Members of the Downed US Naval Aircraft," written on March 25, 1957, Capt. Henry D. Chiu of Air Force intelligence made a compelling case that they were indeed alive and well. "Both prisoners have been examined by a doctor twice a month and have received favorable treatment," Chiu wrote, adding, "The said crew leader has not yet undergone formal investigation but he has been submitting personal notes weekly to the military sub-committee." Chiu himself was a veteran of the Republic of China Air Force who had been persuaded by Gen. Bruce Holloway to join the U.S. Air Force with a captain's commission. His knowledge of both Chinese and military aviation made him particularly valuable.

In another report, Chiu noted that both men were being allowed to move freely but were not permitted at speak with anyone except their keepers. The sources described one of them as being "well-built, lean and taller than average. Oval-faced, slightly raised cheekbones and thin lips. Doesn't speak much. The letter 'J' was on his memo-book." The other was reported as being "relatively round-faced with a ruddy complecion [sic]. Height was not tall and was rather stout-looking. Dark bearded and light freckles on both sides of the nose. Has a cheerful disposition." Using those descriptions and studying photographs of the Mercator's crew, Henry Chiu determined that the "chicoms" were holding Lt. (jg) James B. Deane, Jr., and either AO2c. Warren E. Caron or AT2c. Leonard Strykowski. There is no record of the case being pursued and neither man was ever heard of again.

ON SEPTEMBER 10, 1956, barely two weeks after the loss of the Mercator, yet another RB-50G went down over the Sea of Japan with a regular crew of sixteen. All of them, as well as the plane itself, vanished without a trace. Responsibility for the mishap was quickly assigned to God.

The aircraft was in the 6091st Reconnaissance Squadron at Yokota and was flying a regular ferret mission in absolute radio silence, as usual. It disappeared somewhere between western Honshu and Vladivostok, the electronic warfare fraternity's perennial favorite East Asian target. Given the fact it was on that mission, and therefore was much closer to the Soviet naval base than to Japan, it was almost certainly attacked and destroyed by MiGs. Air Force Security Service electronic intercepts, which included Soviet communication traffic that night, strongly suggested that the RB-50G was intercepted.

Meanwhile Emma, the worst typhoon of the season, was winding down in the general area after causing heavy destruction and more than fifty deaths in Japan, Okinawa, South Korea, and the Philippines. At its worst, the storm was 600 miles across and had 155-mile-an-hour winds. When it became clear by 10:30 that night that the RB-50G was seriously overdue, and in fact would have run out of fuel an hour earlier, someone got the idea of using Emma as a cover story.

Reporters in Tokyo were told by a representative of the Far East Air Forces that the missing RB-50 (not RB-50G, which would have provided a morsel of real information to the cognoscenti) was a typhoon-hunting weather observation aircraft that was supposed to help predict Emma's path by flying into its center and dropping instruments to record wind velocity, barometric pressure, temperature, and other data. In response to a reporter's question, the Air Force spokesman discounted the idea that the plane might have been shot down.

In reality, by the time the RB-50G left Yokota, Emma had shrunk to eighty miles across with eighty-mile-an-hour winds. Furthermore, its crew was given the customary weather briefing. They therefore knew where the storm was, had some idea of its severity, and unquestionably avoided it. Ordering an RB-50G into a storm like Emma would have been a career ender for the commanding officer who did it. Yet the men who disappeared that night have officially been credited, not with losing their lives under fire in defense of their country, but with being the pathetic victims of a storm they couldn't handle. This carried the clear implication they had dubious flying skills, which was not true.

THE ANCIENT GREEKS had a name for the bewitching female whose seductive song lured mariners at sea to their deaths: siren. Her counterpart in aviation also has a name: meacon. It means a radio beacon transmitted so a navigator who is using it to stay on course is misled. Locking onto a radio beacon for navigation is roughly the same as a blind person using a familiar sound coming from a known location to get around without losing his or her way. Deliberately making the familiar sound in a different, dangerous location could cause the blind person to have a serious accident. In the world of electronic countermeasures, deliberately luring an airplane off course, perhaps to be ambushed, is known as meaconing. It is how an Air Force C-130 on a communication intercept mission ran into MiG-17s over Soviet Armenia on the afternoon of September 2, 1958. The fighters were waiting for it.

The rugged four-engine transport belonged to the 7499th Support Group's 7406th Support Squadron based at Rhein-Main. But it was on temporary duty at Incirlik Air Base outside of Adana, in Turkey's deep south. Officially, 50-0528 was part of a "worldwide Air Force project to study the propagation of radio waves transmitted by U.S. radio stations." The Russians, as usual, were not fooled.

The C-130s regularly flew from Incirlik to Trabazon on the Black Sea. From there they turned southeast and continued on to

Van. The planes would then turn and head back to Trabazon, then turn again for Van, then back to Trabazon and so on, flying a "racetrack" circuit back and forth between the two cities before returning to Trabazon one last time and then heading home to Incirlik. Any Russian who believed the blips on radar that went back and forth along the same monotonous track, day after day, were planes studying U.S. radio wave propagation would buy Red Square (or, if he could get out, the Brooklyn Bridge). It was *Soviet* radio waves the Americans were "studying."

The boxy, red-tailed turboprop was one of ten C-130s that had been painstakingly converted to carry advanced communication intercept equipment while appearing to look like any of the C-130s the Air Force regularly used for hauling troops and cargo around the world. The masquerading transports were in an operation called Sun Valley, which was in turn part of the Big Safari test and evaluation program.

Like the requirements of the whole intelligence collection process, as well as the reaction of the Soviet Union that fateful day and in its long aftermath, the central object in the larger political drama—the C-130—was itself a supremely deceptive device. If the ten spook aircraft were going to pass for flying trucks, for example, they could have no telltale blisters that would give them away to Soviet photointerpreters as carrying special antennas.

So the engineers at the TEMCO plant in Greenville, Texas (now the secretive E-Systems that is preeminent in such work), came up with an inspired idea. They designed fake fiberglass fuel tanks that looked exactly like the real ones but which held spiral direction-finding antennas. Like real wing tanks, which held 450 gallons each, the dummies were fifteen feet long. Not only that, but a small reservoir behind each cap actually held fuel, so any snoop on the ground who removed it would see and smell the real thing. The cargo section itself was turned into a soundproof compartment to hold eight or more communication intelligence specialists and their various consoles. And the ramp at the back of the fuselage, which was used to load and unload the real cargo carriers, was bolted shut so the area could be used for in-flight maintenance and repair.

That was the way 56-0528 was configured when Capt. Paul E.

Duncan pulled back on his control column and climbed gently into the air over Incirlik at 12:21 that Tuesday afternoon. There were four other officers on board and twelve enlisted men, eleven of whom worked for the Air Force Security Service and therefore also for the National Security Agency. The flight's secondary purpose was to familiarize another pilot and navigator with the well-traveled route. Duncan himself had flown the mission on his own familiarization flight two or three days earlier. But the regular navigator, 1st Lt. Ricardo M. Villareal, had done it at least ten times, meaning at least fifty circuits between Trabazon and Van.

Duncan reached Trabazon at 1:42 p.m. and radioed his position to Incirlik. Then he turned the C-130 to the southeast, heading straight for what he and the others in the cockpit thought was Van. The track they thought they were on would have put them no closer than eighty-five miles from the Soviet Armenian frontier. Weather conditions below were poor, with rain showers and low visibility, so Duncan was unable to see conspicuous reference points. He was therefore flying on instruments at 20,000 feet. Behind him, the eleven airmen, their headsets on, worked the receivers in search of useful intelligence.

Villareal, the prime navigator, saw that his radio compass was locked onto the Van beacon and so he was apparently on course. But he was not on course, at least not for Van. The transmitter there had been having problems for at least twelve years and was notoriously unreliable. The C-130's radio compass was now pointing toward a powerful 50,000-watt broadcasting station at Yerevan in Armenia. Villareal, Duncan, and the others still believed they were headed for the Van beacon when they flew past the Turkish village of Kars and over the Soviet border.

Three MiG-17s were waiting for them. As NSA technicians monitored and recorded the conversations between the MiG pilots and their controller, the fighters gradually, carefully, crept up on the Hercules and positioned themselves for the attack. One flew off each of the transport's wings. The third, flown by a senior lieutenant named Kucharyaev, pulled in behind and below it, in punch position. On the ground seven Turks, one with binoculars, saw a sight they would never forget.

"Two zero one, I am attacking the target," Kucharyaev told the others as he fired a missile at 56-0528. It missed. Then he fired another. It scored a direct hit on the forward fuselage.

"Target speed is three hundred [kilometers, or 180 miles an hour]. I am going along with it. It is turning toward the fence [the border]."

". . . the target is burning."

"There's a hit."

"The target is burning, five eight two."

"The target is banking."

"It is going toward the fence," one of the attackers said as Duncan tried desperately to turn the crippled plane back toward Turkey.

"Open fire."

"Two one eight, are you attacking?"

"Yes, yes, I . . ." Another senior lieutenant, named Lopatkov, then turned in toward the transport from the right and raked it with cannon fire as it banked to the left in a shallow dive. The cannon rounds were exploding in the cabin, where the COMINT technicians had been listening attentively only moments before, and flames were now pouring out of 56-0528.

"The target is burning."

"The tail assembly is falling off the target."

". . . eighty-two, do you see me? I am in front of the target."

"Look!"

"Oh?"

"Look at him. He will not get away. He is already falling."

"Yes, he is falling. I will finish him off, boys. I will finish him off on the run."

"The target has lost control. It is going down."

"Now the target will fall."

It took exactly 130 seconds, start to finish, to destroy 56-0528, and the Turks saw the whole thing. The plane fell in rugged terrain near Talia, a town on the slopes of Mount Alagoz, twenty-four miles from the border and roughly thirty-five miles northwest of Yerevan. Whatever the MiG pilot thought he saw, the C-130's tail did not fall off in the air; it was virtually the only recognizable part of the burning rubble that stayed intact after it hit the ground. The first Russians on the scene reported that the Hercules turned into an inferno and could not be approached for hours. After it cooled, they carefully poked through the charred debris for anything militarily useful. They also took photographs that included the blackened remains of some of the crewmen. One of them clearly showed a foot.

The C-130 was not the first plane to stray over the "fence" within range of Yerevan's powerful transmitter that year. On June 27, a C-118 on a courier flight from Wiesbaden to Tehcran, with Peshawar, Pakistan, as its final destination, also took a mysterious turn over the border after it reached Van during stormy weather. It too was shot down by MiGs. Five of the nine crewmen bailed out. The other four crash-landed the plane and then destroyed it to get rid of its cargo. The documents almost certainly contained details of U-2 operations, which were staged out of Wiesbaden and Peshawar, among other places, including Incirlik. All nine crewmen were carefully interrogated and then released on the Soviet-Iranian border on July 7.

When he was questioned by his own side, the C-118's navigator reported he had definitely "homed" on Soviet stations, thinking they were Turkish. He, too, had been meaconed. So was Don Gardner of the 7405th Support Squadron, who often flew that route and maintained he also had heard the enticing call of the siren at Yerevan. But since he and his navigator were expecting it, they resisted the temptation to follow the voice of doom.

The C-118 and C-130 incidents were profoundly different. The Russians—renowned chess players—flatly denied they had shot down the C-130, even though they knew the United States believed they almost certainly had. The deception was part of the war of nerves that ran through the fabric of the cold war. The remains of six of the crewmen were returned but the Russians steadfastly insisted they had no knowledge of the fate of the other eleven.

Moses Fields spoke for the families of others who were missing in shootdowns before and after the destruction of 56-0528 when he wrote to Eisenhower on May 10, 1960. His son, A2c. Joel Fields, was one of the eleven.

"Mr. President I am sure that you are aware of the fact that even a knowledge of my son's death is better than knowing nothing of his fate. I am a father. I love my son. But I do not know how to give my love to him, whether in grief or in anxious prayer for his safety. Certainly every man is entitled to know this much about those he loves.

"My son went into the service of his country, as did the sons and daughters of many citizens, with a loyal conviction that his country merited his very life. I do not quarrel with this. I share the conviction. Even now I am not bitter. I simply want to know. My mind has been clouded, my heart torn in two for almost two years. Dare I ask for a reply?"

The reply came from Col. William G. Draper, an Air Force aide to Ike, who told Moses Fields that nothing more had been learned. "You are assured that you will be immediately notified when anything pertinent to the status of your son is revealed."

The Russians repeatedly denied they had the eleven missing airmen, dead or alive. A long diplomatic note made the point in May 1959. As happened after other shootdowns, the note contained a rebuke to the effect that the tragedy would not have happened in the first place if the American plane had been on its own side of the fence: "Those who give the orders for such flights of American airplanes should bear the responsibility before the relatives of those who perished and before the whole American public."

Khrushchev responded to an inquiry by Eisenhower on October 1, 1959, with a letter, heavy in platitudes, about the Soviet government showing "the most thoughtful approach to the destiny of human beings," which flatly denied that the Americans or their remains were in the Soviet Union. He referred to the C-130 as having "crashed."

The Soviet first secretary's answer was especially galling because the U.S. embassy in Moscow had by then picked up a two-part series describing the attack in the newspaper *Sovetskaya Aviatsiya* (*Soviet Aviation*) that ran on September 19 and 20, 1958, less than three weeks after it happened. The first part, "The Target Is Detected," appeared under a picture of four ground controllers diligently plotting the course of the intruder. The prose, as usual, was Orwellian: "It was plotted by the senior plotter, Private

First Class Borshchenko, who has a rating of excellent in combat and political training. This diligent and disciplined fighting man recorded the course of the 'enemy' with short precise chalk marks." The second part, "A Swift Attack," paid gleeful tribute to the bravery, skill, and intelligence of the pilots who had protected the homeland from a mysterious enemy that was not otherwise identified.

The eleven missing airmen remain one of the cold war's unsolved mysteries. It was odd that six bodies were returned and eleven were missing, and to this day there are contradictory reports on their fate. Their bailing out was absolutely discounted. Neither the Turks nor the Russians reported seeing parachutes. And given the fact that the transport suffered a direct hit by a missile and was severely mauled by cannon fire and had turned into an inferno within seconds of the attack, escape was virtually impossible.

One plausible explanation appeared in a CIA information report containing "unevaluated" material that was distributed on November 7, 1958, two months after the attack. In it, a group of villagers were described as having run to the crash site and tried to rescue survivors. "However, when they approached the aircraft, an explosion occurred and they were forced to remain in the background and let it burn. When the flames had died down, probing revealed a total of 18 bodies, 12 of these burned beyond recognition."

Another explanation came early in 1960 from Georgians who lived in the Caucasus. They quietly told a representative of the U.S. embassy who was visiting their mountainous region that the bodies of all eleven airmen had been riddled with bullets and had therefore been completely destroyed to hide the fact they had been shot down. That information was reported to the White House, but the president did not share it with the grieving survivors.

RECOGNITION FINALLY CAME on September 2, 1997, when the men of 56-0528 were publicly honored at the dedication of a National Vigilance Park, complete with a facsimile of their C-130A, at National Security Agency headquarters at Fort Meade.

7 A PRISON CALLED LUBYANKA

THE UNITED STATES of America was afflicted with deepening angst as the 1950s moved to their exhausting and painful end. The exhilarated nation that had emerged from World War II as the planet's only nuclear power, an unrivaled military colossus, and a technological leader with the highest standard of living on Earth, saw with growing apprehension that its security was seriously eroding.

At home, Sen. Joseph McCarthy's tumultuous hunt for Communist infiltrators both inside and outside government left a residue of shattered careers in the Army, the Department of State, Hollywood, and elsewhere. The process of hunting down the miscreants, of turning over rocks to find bugs in living black and white on television, had at once captivated and upset the nation, which was still in turmoil after the spectacle subsided. Suspicion lingered across the land.

At the same time, increasingly restive black Americans came to realize they had had enough of de facto segregation and started to form a national movement that soon popularized a new political expression called "civil rights." Most white Americans took segregation, explicit or subtle, for granted. That now changed dramati-

cally. On December 1, 1956, the Rev. Dr. Martin Luther King, Jr.,
led a black boycott of the Montgomery, Alabama, bus system, in
which African-Americans were forced to ride at the back of the
vehicles. (They also attended segregated schools, were kept in
separate military units, used "colored only" public toilets, and suffered other daily indignities most of their white neighbors readily
accepted.) The buses were desegregated three weeks later, but the
success sparked a wider civil rights drive throughout much of the
South that ran into bitter, often violent opposition. In the wake of
the McCarthy hearings, television viewers could watch black
demonstrators being attacked by angry whites and police dogs, Alabama Governor George Wallace snarl that segregating the races
was good for both of them, the recovery of the bodies of three
white, Northern civil rights workers who were murdered in Mississippi, and federal troops enforcing school integration in Little
Rock, Arkansas.

The news from overseas brought no relief. The Communist
menace seemed to lap at America as relentlessly as the ocean at a
beach. Twice in 1956—in Poland in June and in Hungary in October—uprisings against Communist rule were put down with the
brutal use of soldiers and tanks. That July, Gamal Abdel Nasser
ordered Egyptian troops to seize the Suez Canal. Israel responded
by invading the Sinai Peninsula and Britain and France followed
suit by landing at Port Said. The fighting stopped only after Eisenhower persuaded all three allies to declare a cease-fire. Nasser's
determination to control the canal was only one manifestation of
the far wider war against colonialism that was being waged from
Indochina to Algeria and from one end of Africa to the other.
Fearing the loss of its economically important colonies, France, in
particular, fought stubborn, ferocious wars in both Indochina and
Algeria. It didn't capitulate to Algeria's FLN until 1962.

While America's allies—Britain, France, Belgium, and the
Netherlands—were being dislodged from their colonies by force
and otherwise, the Communists moved relentlessly on. In the
generally simplistic view of the time, the nationalist leaders in
what were then called the underdeveloped or less developed
countries were taken to be unwitting Communist dupes at best
and dedicated Marxist-Leninist agents at worst. In either case,

many Americans and Western Europeans were easily persuaded that the inevitable outcome of the wars of national independence would be to put the "liberated" countries in the Communist camp. The hard-won victory over the fascists to make the world safe for democracy suddenly seemed to be menaced by the radical left.

Millions of alarmed Americans held the view that all the trouble in places like the Belgian Congo, the Dutch East Indies, and French Indochina was caused by dedicated subversives who were trained and controlled by the infinitely devious and diabolical Russians.

Jack Webb, an actor who played a tough Los Angeles police sergeant named Joe Friday in an early television series called *Dragnet*, made a documentary for the Department of Defense purporting to show Russians practicing to look and sound like Americans so they could infiltrate the United States and take it over. The film, called *Freedom and You*, showed a supposedly "typical American town, shrouded in secrecy and protected by utmost security, deep behind the Iron Curtain." The town, protected by barbed wire and complete with a church and a drugstore, was stocked with teenage Communist agents-in-training who looked exactly like the boy and girl next door and who practiced being Americans every day.

"Frightening, isn't it?" Webb asked. "From all appearances, this community could be in Iowa, California, Tennessee. But appearances are deceptive. You might call this a college town, Communist-style." Webb spoke in the menacing tone he might have used to get a killer to confess on *Dragnet*. The scene showed bobby-socked teenagers hanging out at the drugstore soda fountain while the kid behind the counter, wearing the traditional white cap and apron, made what could have been malteds or ice cream sodas. It was a scene out of Archie Comics. "As part of a plan to destroy our free way of life," Webb explained, "these young Communists are studying the economic, political and religious institutions that are the very heartbeat of America. They're studying *you*!" Whew!

That was a studied piece of Pentagon propaganda designed to validate weapons programs such as strategic bombers, atomic submarines, and aircraft carriers. But the threat was real. Soviet policy from Stalin on, as noted by George F. Kennan, was to arm massively, tightly control the proletariat, create and occupy buffer states in Europe and the Balkans that would blunt a Western attack, and relentlessly subvert the West and steal its secrets. Fidel Castro's victory over the corrupt Batista regime in Cuba in 1959, followed by his sudden declaration of unity with the Soviet Union, profoundly shook Washington because he provided its deadly enemy with an operational base that was a mere ninety miles from the United States. In the chess argot so loved by Russians, Khrushchev wasn't pushing pawns in Europe; he was using a dangerous castle to move the length of the board. And that castle was shortly to carry intermediate-range ballistic missiles.

To all those abiding dangers was added yet another, this one in an entirely new dimension: space.

On October 4, 1957, incredulous Americans could look at the night sky and see a white dot named *Sputnik* moving across a background of stars. Unknown to most people in the West, and certainly to most Russians, a small team of dedicated scientists and engineers in the Soviet Union, some of them brilliant, had labored for years to get the world's first successful spacecraft into orbit. Led by Sergei Korolyov, later known as the legendary chief designer, the group created "bottom-up" rocket and space programs—"bottom-up" in the sense that, far from being encouraged and nurtured by their government, they were actively opposed by Stalin and the military for wasting precious resources in a blatantly trivial attempt to explore other worlds.

The United States saw none of that when *Sputnik* sailed silently overhead, nor for decades to come. What it did see, however, was yet another dangerous encroachment. That very day, General Electric was promoting an eleven-cubic-foot-capacity refrigerator that held seventy pounds of food and had automatic defrosting, magnetic safety doors with adjustable shelves, fruit and vegetable compartments, and even an automatic butter conditioner.

Such appliances, as well as cars with tail fins and television shows such as *Leave It to Beaver*, were suddenly taken as metaphors for a society that had become too contented and self-indulgent for its own good. Most Americans were astonished to see that the space age had been started by a nation they thought was technologically backward.

In the coming days, while Khrushchev boasted about an achievement he himself had not understood until it hit the Western press, rueful news media and many politicians turned their wrath on Eisenhower. Ike was roundly lambasted for being an amiable but distracted penny-pincher who had effectively handed the Reds yet another victory, this one witnessed by the whole world. The White House grimly maintained that the United States was not in a race to space with the Soviet Union (it hadn't been, but now it assuredly was) and that the embryonic American space program was in no sense inferior to the opposition's. As events would soon show, that was correct. While Khrushchev tried to wring every propaganda advantage he could out of a series of firsts—first living creature in space (Laika the mutt), first man, first woman, first space walk, first formation flight—the United States built a top-down program that was so solid, so precision-driven, it would be able to land men on the Moon six times without a single in-flight casualty. The Russians couldn't do that. But few Americans knew it. Meanwhile, each space program drove the other, with developments in one forcing the other to react. It was exactly the same in the military, and certainly in the realm of reconnaissance.

JACK PARRISH, THE raven who flew ferret missions near and sometimes over Siberia in the early 1950s, went on to serve a long stint in Air Force intelligence in the Pentagon. He spent five and a half years there, working on advanced systems, much of the time with the CIA. Parrish therefore developed an exceptionally broad perspective on his profession.

He saw that both antagonists in the cold war were locked in a reactive spiral that was mutually reinforcing. It was the rough political equivalent of Isaac Newton's classic third law of motion: for every action, there is an equal and opposite reaction. In technical intelligence collection, for every "measure," there was an equal and opposite countermeasure.

"One of the things that I've seen in the recon business is that we both push each other," Parrish said one day in his home in suburban Maryland as he reflected on a dimension of the cold war that extended beyond flying missions. He and his buddy, John Wagner, flew in Operation Quiz Kid, which ferreted the renowned five-frequency Token radar. Parrish was respectful of Token, a device that could have guided his killers right to him. "The Russians would never have had to have the Token radar if we hadn't succeeded in adopting tactics and airplanes that could overwhelm what they had prior to that. So they came up with Token radar, which was a very beautiful radar."

They also came up with hefty, radar-toting, long-range fighters designed to hold Parrish, Wagner, and other Western "spies" at bay and, with surface-to-air missiles, mangle as many SAC and RAF bombers as they could before their homeland was obliterated. Andrei N. Tupolev's and Semyon A. Lavochkin's engineers could read in American and British aviation magazines that some of SAC's B-52s carried "stand-off" missiles named Hound Dog (designed to stay on the "scent") that could be launched 600 miles from their targets. RAF Vulcan and Victor bombers could launch their own thirty-five-foot-long, nuclear-tipped Blue Steel missiles from 400 miles out.

The Soviet Air Defense Forces knew most of the attackers would come over the high Arctic and would have to be engaged there before they released their hellish weapons. The idea, which formed part of the core of both sides' war scenarios, was to stop the attackers as far as possible from the homeland. To do that, the Tupolev and Lavochkin design bureaus came up with the largest fighters in the world. Tupolev's was a twin-engine, eighty-five-foot-long brute that had a maximum speed of 1,200 miles an hour, a ceiling of over 65,000 feet, and a range of 2,000 miles. The Tu-28, or Fiddler, as NATO called it, was so big that when it went into operation in 1961 it was mistaken for a bomber by Western intelligence.* At eighty-eight feet, Lavochkin's delta-wing La-250 was even larger. Five Anacondas, as the huge, ungainly fighters were called by their design bureau, were built and tested. But they were

---

*It was also known as the Tu-128.

plagued by accidents. Two crashed, two were scrapped, and one survived to be put on display at the Soviet Air Force Museum.

The Tu-28 was armed with four of the largest air-to-air missiles in the world. They were called the AA-5 Ash, and they found their target either by riding a radar beam or by sensing heat coming from its exhaust. AA-5s were almost eleven feet long and could hit planes nineteen miles away with high explosives.

Robb Hoover got a look at AA-5s up close while ferreting off Amderma, the site of a large fighter base at the southern edge of the Kara Sea. Tu-28Ps came out to escort the American reconnaissance plane and pulled in close enough so there was no mistaking the message: they would also be there to greet the B-52s that came to turn their country into radioactive rubble. Hoover was awed by the AA-5. "I actually got to see one of those," he said. "It's the biggest missile I've ever seen under a wing." The feeling that came over him as he looked at it, up close and ready to fire, he added, is best described by the French word *frisson*: a sudden, involuntary shudder of excitement that can come from being terrified.

The Mikoyan-Gurevich design bureau responded to the prospect of two supersonic, high-flying American bombers that never made it to service—North American's B-70 Valkyrie and an attack version of Lockheed's SR-71 Blackbird reconnaissance aircraft—with its own high flyer. The hefty MiG-25 could reach a blistering Mach 3, or three times the speed of sound, and climb to 75,000 feet at 30,000 feet a minute. The "Foxbat's" speed and altitude capability also made it a good reconnaissance aircraft, with Israel being one of its targets.

And as Jack Parrish well knew, the Russians ferreted radar and eavesdropped, too. Like their opponents, they modified off-the-shelf bombers and transports to handle long-range operations. Dalnaya Aviatsiya, the Long-Range Aviation bombing force, and Aviatsiya Voyenno—Morskovo Flota, the naval air arm, both relied on the Tu-16, roughly the equivalent of the B-47, for electronic and communication intelligence.

But the king of Soviet intelligence collectors was and remains the massive Tu-95. It is called "Bear" by NATO, but "Mastodon" would be more like it. The colossal bomber has the distinction of being the only turboprop combat plane in the world and, with four pairs of huge counterrotating propellers mounted on swept wings, remains a freak that defies design theory, since swept wings are supposed to fly too fast for propeller engines. Yet the lumbering giant's 4,000-mile range and twenty-four-hour endurance make it an ideal electronic warfare "platform" (as the Pentagon aptly puts it). Unlike other Soviet reconnaissance aircraft, Tu-95s ranged almost all over the world in the 1970s and well into the 1980s.

Bears made their international debut when a pair of them flew nonstop from Murmansk to Cuba—ferreting Greenland and the U.S. East Coast along the way—in April 1970. From then until 1981, when Tu-95s were permanently stationed in Cuba, an average of five ferret missions a year were flown along the eastern seaboard. Similar operations were routinely flown off Alaska, western Canada, and the U.S. West Coast. Air Force fighters— F-15 Eagles stationed in Alaska, for example—would scramble when a lone Bear appeared on radar from the direction of Siberia. They would escort it in formation as it headed south, ferreting coastal radar, as some of its crewmen waved to the Americans who watched them. Navy Phantoms and, later, Tomcats did the same thing. Procedure called for one fighter to come in close to inspect the huge bombers while one or more others hung back in punch position. An attempt to attack the closer fighter would have triggered a swift and lethal counterattack by the others. The Russians knew it and never made a move that would have been suicidal. To the contrary, the colossal silver bombers with their red stars were routinely photographed with still and movie cameras by fighter pilots who wanted souvenirs.

As late as the fall of 2000, Russian aircraft were ferreting the carrier *Kittyhawk* in the Sea of Japan. Meanwhile, U.S. intelligence reported that some Tu-95s were being moved to Anadyr Air Base near the Bering Sea and three others were flown to the Tiksi Air Base in north-central Siberia. It was concluded that the Bears were once again being called on to ferret radar in the Aleutians and elsewhere in the region, possibly in anticipation of the antimissile system the United States was considering building. The Bears would be safe enough provided they stayed over water.

But it was a far different matter for American prowlers in the cold war. With the crews of piston-engine bombers and patrol planes, and even jet bombers, being bloodied on peripheral missions against the Soviet Union and China, and with penetrations being as dangerous as they were desperately necessary, Richard S. Leghorn pondered ways to steal the cheese without getting caught in the trap. Leghorn was obsessive about reconnaissance. He was an MIT graduate who had commanded the Sixty-seventh Reconnaissance Group in World War II and had flown photographic missions in support of the Normandy invasion on June 6, 1944. As early as 1946, with the wartime alliance between the United States and the Soviet Union already crumbling and SAC being formed, Leghorn maintained that the nation needed to develop a consistent, ongoing aerial reconnaissance operation that would collect vital intelligence even in time of peace. The idea of conducting military reconnaissance when no war was going on was radical in 1946. It was to become the Peacetime Airborne Reconnaissance Program. And the key to achieving it, Leghorn knew, was being able to get to very high altitude.

Leghorn was recalled to active duty in 1951 and put in charge of the Reconnaissance Systems Branch of the Air Force's Wright Air Development Command in Dayton. There, he fought to stretch the Canberra's wings so it could fill the high-altitude reconnaissance gap until a plane specifically designed for that mission could be built. The result was the high-flying RB-57D. But it wasn't built without a bureaucratic war and compromise. The Air Research and Development Command, to which Leghorn reported, insisted the plane be built for combat. That was the rule. But it meant the stretch-wing Canberra had to carry armor and other hardware that added weight. It amounted to tying an anchor around its tail. The finished RB-57D therefore couldn't get above 64,000 feet any more than Leghorn could get above the rules. So he transferred to the Pentagon early in 1952, where he worked for Col. Bernard A. Schriever in the development office.

BETWEEN 1951 AND 1955, a small galaxy of brilliant scientists, engineers, and managers coalesced to form the nucleus of a new

U.S. aerial reconnaissance program. It is fair to say they were to strategic intelligence collection what the founding fathers were to the republic itself: a singular group of imaginative and far-sighted individuals whose interrelationship was synergistic.

In 1951, the Air Force requirement for targeting information inside the Soviet Union led it to create a special civilian organization to study ways of collecting the data. The group was headed by Carl F. P. Overhage, an Eastman Kodak physicist, and included James G. Baker and Edward M. Purcell of Harvard; Allan F. Donovan from the Cornell Aeronautical Laboratory; Edwin H. "Din" Land, the founder of the Polaroid Corporation and inventor of the camera that bore his name; Stewart E. Miller of Bell Laboratories; and Richard S. Perkin of the Perkin-Elmer Company, which made large lenses. Leghorn was the Air Force liaison officer.

The Beacon Hill Study Group, as it was called, spent weekends visiting Air Force bases, laboratories, and companies around the country collecting the latest information and proposals on technologies that could be applied to aerial reconnaissance. One of the more imaginative suggestions, eventually rejected, was for an "invisible" dirigible: a giant, flattened airship with a blue-tinted, nonreflective coating, which would cruise slowly along Soviet borders at 90,000 feet taking pictures as it went.

The Beacon Hill report was published under tight security on June 15, 1952, two days after the RB-29 commanded by Maj. Samuel N. Busch was shot down near Vladivostok with twelve men on board. Busch and most of his crew were captured. Ironically, the Beacon Hill report made a number of recommendations, including the development of a high-altitude reconnaissance plane that would stay out of reach of the kind of Soviet interceptors that caught Busch's plane: "To avoid political involvements, such aerial reconnaissance must be conducted either from vehicles flying in friendly airspace, or—a decision on this point permitting—from vehicles whose performance is such that they can operate in Soviet airspace with greatly reduced chances of detection or interception." No plane in service, certainly not Boeing's modified bombers, was capable of working over Soviet territory for long without inviting a political catastrophe. The thought of the Russians displaying a plane, and possibly its crew, they had shot down deep inside their own territory was a nightmare.

The Beacon Hill group essentially turned into the Intelligence Systems Panel in July 1953—the month before the Russians detonated their first H-bomb—which called for an airplane that would fly above 70,000 feet. Donovan whittled the requirement to a fine point. The high flyer had to be a light single-engine sailplane that would cruise high above the target area with cameras.

That aircraft already existed, at least on paper, and was called the CL-282. Its designer was Clarence L. "Kelly" Johnson, the engineering genius who headed Lockheed's Advanced Development Projects division, known throughout the industry as the Skunk Works. Johnson conceived the reconnaissance plane as a much slower, long-winged version of his supersonic F-104 Starfighter. He offered the CL-282 to the Air Force, but it was turned down because the airmen were already buying RB-57Ds and funding the preliminary design of another twin-engine reconnaissance aircraft called the Bell X-16.

LeMay, who was always worried about the primacy of his bomber force, was briefed on the CL-282 in July 1954. Halfway through the presentation he stood up, took his cigar out of his mouth, and said that if he wanted high-altitude photographs he would put cameras in his B-36s (which he did). He added that he had no interest in a plane without guns and then left the room, muttering that the whole business was a waste of his time. It's not that the head of SAC was against reconnaissance. To the contrary, his targeteers depended on it. But he didn't want funding for what he derisively called "boutique" airplanes—finicky specialty items—to come out of his bomber and missile budget. LeMay remained unalterably convinced that very large numbers of bombers and missiles were imperative for the defense of the country and anything that siphoned funds away from them had to be resisted at all cost.

By July 1954, fragmented intelligence reports that the Soviet Union had flight-tested a large four-jet intercontinental bomber, the Myasishchev M-4, were making their way back to Washington. It was named "Bison" by NATO and was the equivalent of the B-52. Eisenhower had become sufficiently worried about a surprise attack by A-bomb-armed M-4s that he convened yet another group to study that contingency. It was called the Technological Capabilities Panel and was headed by James R. Killian, Jr., the president of MIT. The TCP was subdivided into three committees: one for offensive capability, one for defensive capability, and one for intelligence. Its report, "Meeting the Threat of Surprise Attack," was presented at a top-secret session of the National Security Council in the White House on Valentine's Day, 1954.

The intelligence committee, chaired by "Din" Land, suggested that a plane capable of flying at record-breaking altitude be developed as quickly as possible to get the measure of Soviet military capabilities and the industrial base that supported them. It also suggested that earth satellites, as the not yet existing machines were called, be developed as intelligence collectors that would cruise so far above enemy territory they would be impervious to attack. Land, Baker, and the others also knew that reconnaissance machines circling Earth at an altitude of perhaps one hundred miles would have an unexcelled view.

Kelly Johnson lobbied hard and effectively to sell the CL-282 to the White House and finally edged out the competition. Eisenhower signed off on the plane, eventually to be called the U-2 ("U" for the ambiguous "utility") but insisted it be managed by the CIA; that is, by civilians. He made the decision, Killian would later write, so "it would not become entangled in the bureaucracy of the Defense Department or troubled by rivalries among the services."

The high flyer's life expectancy was put at two years or less, during which time it was supposed to collect a windfall of intelligence from deep inside the USSR. John Foster Dulles later quoted Ike as saying: "Well, boys, I believe the country needs this information, and I'm going to approve it. But I'll tell you one thing. Some day, one of these machines is going to be caught, and we're going to have a storm." That was prescient.

CIA director Allen Dulles gave the U-2 operation to Richard W. Bissell, Jr., a tall, courtly, Yale-educated economist. Bissell's Air Force counterpart in the project, which was code-named Idealist, was Brig. Gen. Osmund J. "Ozzie" Ritland, vice-commander of the Ballistic Missile Division. They got along harmoniously. The mood would change when reconnaissance moved to space.

They also worked exceptionally well with Kelly Johnson and others at the Skunk Works. Johnson had a penchant for cutting through the bureaucratic thicket and getting things done. In the Skunk Works, he created a small, goal-oriented organization that encouraged ingenuity, not endless memos and bureaucratic obstacles. He insisted memos be short and to the point. He also directed his engineers to work near where prototype planes were hand-made, on the shop floor, so they and the "metal benders" could solve design problems quickly in conversation, not by sending endless fusillades of memorandums from one floor to another. Johnson's institutional ethic boiled down to: "Be quick, be quiet, be on time." Or, as Ben R. Rich, who succeeded Johnson, put it, the secret of the organization's success was mixing extreme secrecy with high efficiency. He called that being "black and skunky."

Bissell came from a place, Washington, which thrived on pretension and power. But he had none of it. He never pretended he grasped aeronautical engineering or tried to second-guess Johnson. Instead, he gave Johnson whatever money he needed out of the agency's "black" budget without micromanaging how it was spent. The only rule was: get it done. Johnson, a Swedish-American from a poor family in upper Michigan, repaid the trust with honesty, ingenuity, and speed. Neither had any use for what they saw as pervasive bureaucratic torpor, even in the White House. Both reacted to having to wait weeks or months while Eisenhower pondered a mission or a program by sarcastically referring to him as "Speedy Gonzales."

The first U-2, called "Article 341," was delivered to a secret air base at Groom Lake, Nevada, on July 25, 1955; less than eight months later it was given final approval. Its heart was a camera whose lens was designed by Baker, the Harvard physicist, which could spot a basketball from 70,000 feet. The U-2 would work best at that altitude, what the engineers call its "design point." Baker's lens amounted to a 240 percent improvement over existing lenses. And even it would be refined. The project itself was now called Aquatone.

The new high flyer was designed to work in a realm that was scarcely imaginable to the men who prowled at far lower, better-known altitudes. The U-2's environment was both intensely hostile and superlatively beautiful. Where the human body was concerned, 70,000 feet and higher—more than thirteen miles up—amounted to the edge of space. A pressure failure at that altitude would boil blood almost instantly, for example, and repeated exposure to radiation could cause cellular damage. Ordinary flight suits were therefore out of the question. Instead, space suits had to be invented that would fully enclose their wearers and inflate immediately in the event of rapid decompression—sudden pressure failure—in the cockpit. The suits amounted to self-contained environments within the cockpit's larger environment. And the top of the canopy was given a white shield that reduced solar glare and offered some protection against radiation.

The aesthetic reward of being above 70,000 feet was easily worth the risk to men who loved to fly, and who therefore tended to measure their significance in terms of altitude. It was near the rarified place where Wernher von Braun and the other prophets of space travel promised human beings were headed. Thirteen miles was above the ostensible atmosphere. Daylight therefore gave way to a darkened sky. The curvature of the Earth could be seen. Mottled clouds were not the towering edifices that lower-flying men skimmed and penetrated, but mere blankets that covered the distant patchwork of a remote landscape far below. Whatever its considerable merits as an intelligence collector, the U-2 was therefore also the first real harbinger of spaceflight.

The first operational U-2 mission was flown from Wiesbaden on June 20, 1956, and photographed targets in East Germany, Poland, and Czechoslovakia. It was followed by two more penetrations on July 2 that "revisited" (as the technical intelligence collectors delicately put it) those countries and added Bulgaria, Hungary, Rumania, and Yugoslavia.

Then, on the Fourth of July, the CIA went for the big one. A U-2 climbed steeply out of Wiesbaden and flew a course that took it over East Germany, Poland, Estonia, Latvia, Belorussia, and on to Leningrad, where it photographed a large submarine construction facility. It also photographed several air bases to inventory the worrisome M-4 Bisons. The route took it southeast of the Kola region Hal Austin had covered fourteen months earlier in the RB-47E. Unlike Austin's flight, however, no MiG laid a glove on the U-2. The next day another sailed over five Eastern European countries and the Moscow area, its camera taking hundreds of photographs the intelligence collectors had until then only been able to dream about. The aircraft returned with pictures of the plant where the Bisons were built, Ramenskoye Air Base, where they were tested, a missile plant at Kaliningrad, and a rocket engine factory. It was marvelous, riveting intelligence. The damned curtain was finally being parted.

When Allen Dulles returned to CIA headquarters from his Independence Day holiday on Thursday, July 5, he asked Bissell whether there had been any U-2 flights over the Soviet Union. Both Moscow and Leningrad had been photographed, Bissell answered. "Oh, my Lord," Dulles said, "do you think that was wise the first time?" "Allen," the sagacious U-2 program director answered, "the first is the safest."

Despite some cloud cover over Moscow, the pictures were generally good. But there was more in them than factories, air bases, a shipyard, and other nuggets of intelligence. Photointerpreters scrutinizing hundreds of the photographs also picked out tiny MiG-15s and MiG-17s far below the U-2 trying desperately to get close enough for a shot: straining to climb, flipping over, and falling back down. The CIA had assured Eisenhower that the Russians would not see the U-2s. That was obviously wrong. On July 10, a note was delivered to the U.S. embassy in Moscow protesting the overflights.

The year before, in 1955, Eisenhower had proposed at a summit meeting in Geneva that East and West adopt an Open Skies program in which reconnaissance planes from each side would be given free access to the other. He believed an open exchange of intelligence information would stabilize relations between the two antagonists because it would reduce the possibility of nasty surprises.

To show Khrushchev how dependable good aerial photographs could be, Ike handed him a yellow brochure, "Aerial Reconnaissance Serving Peace," which vividly showed the quality of U.S. aerial reconnaissance (taken from an RB-47E's relatively low altitude, not from the U-2's far loftier reaches). Khrushchev took the gift home and showed it to his son, Sergei. "The photographs were indeed impressive," the younger Khrushchev recalled years later. The first photograph showed a large section of a city. Then, dramatically, succeeding pictures zoomed closer. "In the next you could distinguish houses, and in the next, cars. Finally, in the last you could make out the murky figure of a man reclining on a lounge chair in the courtyard of his home reading a newspaper."

Nikita Khrushchev was impressed. And he was deeply suspicious. Eisenhower, he concluded, had hatched a diabolically ingenious plan to collect detailed photographs of every target in the country *with the permission of the Soviet government*. It was breathtaking in its audacity. Eisenhower was suggesting American planes be granted permission to criss-cross the entire country, taking detailed photographs and collecting other information that would go directly to LeMay's bomber crews so they could obliterate the USSR. The argument that the Russians would be able to take pictures over the United States was not persuasive for Khrushchev. The pictures, after all, were only as good as the long-range bombers and ballistic missiles using them. And contrary to what he boasted to the world, he knew full well his opponent had both a quantitative and a qualitative advantage.

It is fair to suppose that Khrushchev equated the Open Skies proposal with the nonaggression pact that had been signed with the Third Reich in 1939. One led to an unspeakable calamity and the other would almost undoubtedly lead to a far worse one. He had therefore rejected Eisenhower's honest offer out of hand. In one of the cold war's multiple ironies, Nikita Khrushchev thereby in effect started the U-2 program.

The Soviet Union was penetrated twenty-three times between that first flight on the Fourth of July, 1956, and April 9, 1960, each time with Eisenhower's last-minute, grudging approval. Haunted by the prospect of a U-2 going down on Soviet territory, Ike signed off on each mission reluctantly and with foreboding.

And in doing so he had real empathy for Khrushchev. "Nothing would make him [Eisenhower] request authority to declare war more quickly than violation of our air space by Soviet aircraft," his son, John, quoted him as saying at a National Security Council meeting in February 1959.

Khrushchev himself was infuriated by the brazen overflights because he knew the photographs went into SAC's target catalogue, marking his country for certain destruction in the event of all-out war. But there was more to it than that. The American planes violated his homeland's sovereignty, impinged on its airspace, with absolute impunity. They came in without permission and went where they pleased and he was powerless to do anything to stop them. The intrusions were so deeply humiliating that they filled him with rage. Protests were made to Washington, Sergei would remember, but they were done reluctantly. "He felt the Americans must be chortling over our impotence and that diplomatic protest would only add to their pleasure." There was at least some satisfaction in knowing the Americans understood that, far from being invisible, their penetrations were detected, but he was powerless to stop them.

Khrushchev therefore called together his top fighter and missile designers—Mikoyan, Tupolev, Pavel Sukhoi, and Pyotr Grushin among them—and warned them that one of the high-flying American planes could drop an atomic bomb. Tupolev corrected him on that score. He explained that the intruders were flying on the edge of what was possible: through air so thin that aircraft weight was measured to the last gram. That being so, Tupolev assured Khrushchev, there was no possibility one of the planes could carry any kind of bomb, let alone a tremendously heavy nuclear one. Nikita Khrushchev was not mollified. He ordered his designers to come up with a way of shooting down the intruders, whether they carried bombs or not.

Whatever Ike's qualms, the U-2 operation was an unmitigated success. During the forty-five months of operations over the Soviet Union, three flights were flown from Alaska and Japan, six from Wiesbaden, and fourteen from Peshawar, Pakistan, a strategic backwash that jutted into the underbelly of Eurasia where the two great Communist monoliths came together. The flights covered 1,300,000 square miles—15 percent of the Soviet Union—and returned with strips of film which, laid end to end, would have been 250 miles long. The *Target Data Inventory* and *Bombing Encyclopedia* were stuffed with the U-2s' take. So were 5,425 separate analytical reports supplemented with photographs.

National Intelligence Estimates, or NIEs, of Soviet long-range bomber and ballistic missile strength knocked down once and for all the alleged "bomber gap" and "missile gap" that were said to exist between the two superpowers. In 1959, the intelligence community produced an NIE that used U-2 material and other sources, including agents, to show the Kremlin was forsaking long-range bombers to leap ahead in ballistic missiles. It predicted the Russians would have only 120 heavy bombers by mid-1964 (even that number was exaggerated, according to a dissenting Army intelligence official who put it at 75). The NIE also maintained that, contrary to Khrushchev's boasting that a single factory turned out 250 ICBMs a year, there were only 35 on launchers, with from 350 to 450 more predicted for mid-1963. While the prospect of the Soviet Union having as many as 450 ICBMs on launchers in four years was hardly cause for rejoicing, the intelligence estimate did show there was no gap.

After the overflights abruptly ended, Secretary of Defense Thomas S. Gates, Jr., would lavish praise on the operation. "From these flights we got information on airfields, aircraft, missiles, missile testing and training, special weapons storage, submarine production, atomic production and aircraft deployment . . . all types of vital information. . . ." And U-2s worked elsewhere, as well, including China, Suez, and Cuba at the time of the missile crisis.

Nationalist China was given its own U-2s. Together with reconnaissance satellites in the Corona program that started orbiting the Earth in 1960, and intensive communication monitoring by the NSA on land and in the air, the planes closely monitored the Red Chinese ballistic missile and nuclear weapons program, including the Lop Nor test area. Four of the planes were shot down over mainland China and in September 1962 Peking offered

$280,000 in gold to any Nationalist U-2 pilot who defected with a plane. None did.

The Kennedy and Johnson administrations were so alarmed at the prospect of China's developing atomic bombs that they seriously considered bombing the facilities, assassinating important scientists, instituting a blockade, backing an invasion by the Nationalists, and supplying nuclear weapons to India, China's rival in South Asia. Ultimately, all of the options were rejected in favor of diplomatic action. The first Chinese atomic test, also carefully monitored, took place on October 14, 1964.

COMMUNIST CHINA WAS not the only nation where force was considered to thwart a nuclear weapons threat. Cuba was another. And as was the case with China, reconnaissance played an overwhelming role in spotting the danger and monitoring it.

From the late summer of 1962, through the dangerous October days of the missile crisis, through the withdrawal of the medium-range ballistic missiles and afterward, Cuba was reconnoitered systematically and relentlessly by Air Force and Navy squadrons.

The brunt of the Air Force low-level tactical requirement went to the 363d Tactical Reconnaissance Wing, based at Shaw Air Force Base at Sumter, South Carolina, which flew RF-101 Voodoos and larger RB-66 and EB-66 photoreconnaissance and ELINT aircraft, respectively. The 363d moved to MacDill Air Force Base near Tampa, Florida, during the crisis. So did the Fifty-fifth Strategic Reconnaissance Wing, which sent five RB-47s from Forbes. The Fifty-fifth was made responsible for photographing all ships heading toward Cuba and ferreting both surveillance and surface-to-air missile radars. It also supported U-2 operations by noting weather conditions and reporting them to SAC headquarters, which relayed them to Laughlin Air Force Base at Del Rio, Texas, where the Air Force–piloted CIA U-2s were based.

U-2s actually began flying monthly missions over Cuba in a program called Nimbus soon after the Bay of Pigs invasion failed in April 1961. The flights were stepped up when Soviet activity on the island was reported to increase in the spring of 1962. The discovery of at least eight V-750 missile sites in western Cuba by a SAC U-2 on August 29 provided the first clear indication that medium-range ballistic missiles were on the way there. Between then and October 22, when the missile crisis entered its dangerous, confrontational stage, the island was repeatedly photographed by U-2s. A U-2 flying over the San Cristobal area on October 14 returned with the first unambiguous evidence that SS-4 MRBMs were being set up there.

Thirteen days later, Air Force Maj. Rudolf Anderson, Jr., was killed over northern Cuba when his U-2 was hit by a V-750 as he hunted for more MRBMs. Anderson was the second U-2 pilot shot out of the sky by one of the missiles.

Navy aerial reconnaissance operations during the missile crisis fell to VP-56, based at Norfolk, Virginia, which was deployed to the Guantánamo Naval Base in Cuba to track ships coming into the area. VF-41 was moved from Virginia to Key West to patrol the Florida Keys. And Light Photographic Squadron Sixty-two, flying single-engine F8U-1P Crusader jets, was given the dangerous assignment of scouring Cuba itself for hidden missile sites at low level.

Anderson was the only pilot shot down by enemy fire in the tense encounter. But as all the world knew, the downing of his U-2 had been preceded two and a half years earlier by another carrying Francis Gary Powers in one of the most infamous incidents of the cold war.

WHILE ANOTHER U-2 flew a conspicuous route along the Soviet-Iranian border as a diversion, the twenty-third U-2 to fly over the Soviet Union left Peshawar in the pre-dawn darkness on April 9, 1960, and headed for Saryshagan, where it took the first photographs of a Hen House and Hen Roost, two new radars. It then sailed on to the huge nuclear test site at Semipalatinsk and then to Tyuratam, where it photographed a new two-pad, road-serviced launch area that suggested to analysts at the National Photographic Interpretation Center in Washington that a new missile was in the works.

But Mission 4155, or Operation Square Deal, as it was also called, returned to Peshawar with ominous tidings. Its electronic intelligence package, which included a fuzz buster, had picked up signals from Soviet tracking radar exceptionally early in the flight: 150 miles inside Soviet territory. Less than a month earlier, on March 14, Col. William Burke of the Air Technical Intelligence Center had warned in a report to Bissell that "the SAM (Guideline) has a high probability of successful intercept at 70,000 feet *providing that detection is made in sufficient time to alert the site*" (italics added). Khrushchev did not protest the latest intrusion, which the White House erroneously took to mean that he tacitly accepted the situation. "This was virtually inviting us to repeat the sortie," George Kistiakowsky, Eisenhower's science adviser, remarked.

Francis Gary Powers was therefore sent on the twenty-fourth and last overflight on the morning of May 1, 1960. Operation Grand Slam, as it was prophetically called, was planned to fill an intelligence collector's ultimate wish list. It would start at the missile test site at Tyuratam and continue on to Chelyabinsk-40, the plutonium production facility at Kyshtym, and the nearby nuclear research installation at Sverdlovsk. It was then to head northwest to Kirov and Plesetsk, where ICBM launch sites were being built, and on to the naval installations at Severodvinsk and Murmansk. Then Powers was supposed to land at a remote air base at Bodø (pronounced "Buddha") in Norway with his valuable cache.

He was supposed to but he never did. The same early warning radar the ferrets had previously found spotted Powers while he was still fifteen miles inside Afghanistan and heading northwest. The U-2 carried more than cameras. It carried an irony that was not wasted on Khrushchev. As the annual parade to celebrate Soviet military prowess was getting under way in Red Square, former Soviet intelligence officer Aleksandr Orlov would recall years later, "a not-yet-identified foreign aircraft was flying over the heart of the country and Soviet air defenses appeared unable to shoot it down." The enraged Khrushchev had berated Marshal Sergei S. Biryuzov, the commander in chief of the Air Defense

Forces, several times for the apparent inability of his antiaircraft system to bring down one of the American planes. "If I could become a missile," Biryuzov had lamented, "I myself would fly and down this damned intruder." The premier still was not mollified.

That May Day morning, Biryuzov sat at a large table facing a standing map of the Soviet Union in the Air Defense center not far from the Kremlin. A sergeant sitting behind the map plotted Powers's progress as he passed over Tyuratam and headed northwest. Several senior officers milled around Biryuzov and watched the intruder inch forward. Antiaircraft missile batteries at Sverdlovsk equipped with V-750 missiles were warned that the plane was headed their way. MiG-19s were scrambled.

And since Sukhoi's Su-9 fighter was especially designed for high-altitude intercepts, Marshal Yevgeny Savitsky, the Air Defense Aviation Commander, ordered them up too. The problem, at least at first, was that no pilots could be found because it was a holiday. Then someone spotted Capt. Igor Mentyukov at a bus stop in Perm, a small city 250 miles northwest of Sverdlovsk. He was rushed to the local air defense headquarters, told that he was the only hope of stopping the approaching American spy plane once and for all, and ordered to get his Su-9 into the air immediately. Mentyukov protested to Marshal Savitsky that he was not ready to jump into a fighter and take off and that, more to the point, his interceptor was unarmed. That last part ought to have decided the matter, since it took some time to load cannon rounds and missiles onto an interceptor. Savitsky quickly relayed the news to Moscow. Just as quickly, he was ordered to tell Mentyukov to fly in his civvies and ram the intruder if that's what it took to bring it down. It was a death sentence.

"Take care of my wife and mother," the fighter pilot told his superiors. His wife was pregnant.

"Don't worry," someone told Igor Mentyukov. "We'll take care of everything." He was not reassured.

But providence intervened. Or maybe it was the realization that men who didn't even know him were willing to squander his life as whimsically as if he were a bug. Mentyukov slammed his Su-9 into afterburner and shot up to near the U-2's altitude. He was somewhere behind Powers when he came out of his climb at roughly 70,000 feet.* Indicated airspeed was 1,200 miles an hour. The ground controllers who were guiding him had Powers on radar. But Mentyukov reported there was so much interference on the Su-9's radarscope that he couldn't find his quarry. "The target is ahead!" the controllers implored. "Look! Look!" He looked, but he insisted he could not see, so he shot past the much slower U-2. Then Mentyukov told the controllers he was low on fuel. One of them, exasperated, finally told the pilot to shut off his thirsty afterburner and land. The expectant father was happy to do as he was told.

Powers, unaware that Mentyukov had passed him, now came within range of a V-750 battery that tried to shoot three missiles at him. Only one made it into the air. But it was enough. At 8:53 a.m. Moscow time, the men in the missile battery saw a fiery puff in the sky far above them and, seconds later, heard a faint explosion. The V-750 exploded just behind the U-2, sending shrapnel into its tail. The metal fragments and the blast effect from the explosion sent the plane violently out of control. Its long wings tore off and fluttered to earth like falling leaves while the fuselage itself tumbled.

Powers was pitched forward into the instrument panel and knew that both of his legs would be torn off if he tried to eject. He therefore blew the canopy off so he could climb out of the cockpit. But as soon as he unlocked his seat belt, g forces pulled him out, and he went into a free fall until his parachute popped open. Powers became the only American to be shot down while collecting intelligence over the Soviet Union during the cold war.

But he was not the only pilot who was shot down that day.

---

*The U-2's altitude has been the subject of debate. A White House report of July 7, 1960, said that it was "possible but unlikely" that the plane was hit at cruising altitude and that some malfunction "probably" forced Powers to drop to roughly 60,000 feet. ("Future of the Agency's U-2 Capability," p. 5.) Col. Aleksandr Orlov, who was in the Soviet Air Defense Forces when Powers was shot down, put his altitude at above 60,000 feet. (Orlov, "The U-2 Program: A Russian Officer Remembers," p. 10.) Powers himself said after his release from prison that he had convinced his captors he had been flying at 68,000 feet and that it was the U-2's maximum altitude, but that he had really been higher than that. (Pocock, *Dragon Lady*, p. 50.) The CIA's own history of the U-2 program, which is the most credible and which squares with Powers's account, puts the altitude at 70,500 feet. (Pedlow and Welzenbach, *The CIA and the U-2 Program, 1954–1974*, p. 176.)

Since the excited Russians at the missile site couldn't be sure they had hit the American, they reported that the engagement was continuing. So as Powers floated down, a pair of MiG-19s was sent up to join the fray. When one of the pilots saw he was low on fuel, he pushed his stick forward and quickly dove out of the area. That left Senior Lt. Sergei Safronov, whose fighter now appeared as a solitary dot on the ground radar. The dot was taken to be the U-2, so another V-750 was fired. It blew Safronov's MiG-19 out of the sky. He ejected safely and there is no record of his thoughts on having been shot down by his own side. But the missile battery's score that day was therefore even at one and one.

The night shift in the Operations Center at CIA headquarters in McLean, Virginia, knew within two hours that there was trouble near Sverdlovsk. How it knew provides insight into the infinitely devious, constantly functioning, multidimensional world of technical intelligence collection. The CIA realized there was a problem because the Soviet radars that tracked the U-2s were themselves monitored, and so were Soviet communication channels.

Powerful antennas in the high mountains in eastern Iran constantly pulled in all manner of signals from the missile test facility at Tyuratam, the Sverdlovsk region, and elsewhere in the vast area in a program code-named Tacksman. At 3:30 a.m. E.D.T. that May 1, the center received an urgent message saying the radar that had been tracking Powers as he flew southwest of Sverdlovsk had suddenly gone dead two hours earlier. There could be only one plausible reason for turning off the radar that was tracking the intruder: tracking it was no longer necessary because it was no longer in the air.

When word that Grand Slam had gone awry reached the White House, a cover story in the durable tradition of the *Graf Zeppelin*'s foray over the British Isles in 1939 was frantically hatched:

Following is cover plan to be implemented immediately. U-2 aircraft was on weather mission originating in Adana, Turkey. Purpose was study of clear air turbulence. During flight in Southeast Turkey, pilot reported he had oxygen difficulties. The last word heard at 0700Z [Zulu] over emergency fre-

quency. U-2 aircraft did not land Adana as planned and it
can only be assumed it is down. A search effort is under way
in Lake Van area.

That was turned into a news release under the NASA letterhead
on May 5 saying, "One of NASA's U-2 research airplanes" on a
mission over Turkey to study "gust-meteorological conditions
found at high altitude" had disappeared. NASA owned ten of the
planes, the release continued, which were originally built by
Lockheed to serve as a "flying test bed." Their maximum altitude
was given as 55,000 feet, or roughly three miles less than their
real capability. Khrushchev immediately ordered that no mention
be made of the shootdown. He shrewdly decided to let the news
unfold a little at a time so the Americans would take the bait and
lie, as they always did, about their spy missions. He savored the
coming payback for the years of humiliation.

Khrushchev held his fire until May 5 to tell a meeting of the
Supreme Soviet in the Kremlin's Great Hall that a U.S. "spy
plane" had been downed near Sverdlovsk. He did not mention the
fate of its pilot. "Our intention here was to confuse the government circles of the United States," he would later explain. "As
long as the Americans thought the pilot was dead, they would
keep putting out the story that perhaps the plane had accidentally
strayed off course and been shot down in the mountains on the
Soviet side of the border." As he figured, the Americans took the
bait. That same day the Department of State and NASA cranked
out the phony statement about the plane disappearing on a routine weather mission.

The "storm" Ike had feared when he approved the U-2 program struck two days later, on May 7, when a smirking Nikita
Khrushchev sprung the trap. Clutching a briefcase, he strode into
another meeting of the Supreme Soviet and did a show-and-tell.
He began by giving a detailed account of the incident as explained
by the Americans. Then he methodically, exquisitely demolished it
with unabashed relish.

He proclaimed that the missing "weather" plane had been shot
down deep inside Soviet territory and that the pilot was alive and

in custody. "The pilot is safe and sound," Khrushchev told his cheering, applauding audience. "The pilot's name is Francis G. Powers. He is thirty years old. According to his testimony, he is a first lieutenant of the United States Air Force in which he served up to 1956, when he joined the Central Intelligence Agency." The jubilant premier then read excerpts from Powers's interrogation, traced the U-2's route, and described the equipment it had carried. Finally, he displayed developed film from the Type B camera that clearly showed air bases, nuclear storage sites, oil depots, and factories. "The whole world," Khrushchev added triumphantly, "knows that Allen Dulles is no great authority on meteorology." Wags in Washington snickered that "CIA" stood for "Caught in the Act."

That same day, the 7th, Eisenhower approved a recommendation from his top foreign policy advisers to end missions as provocative as the U-2 Soviet overflights. There were fifty-one U-2 missions between June 20, 1956, and May 1, 1960, and they included flights over Communist China, Mongolia, Tibet, Laos, North Vietnam, and Burma, as well as Eastern Europe and the Soviet Union. Many of them, certainly over mainland China by Nationalist pilots, continued. On the 11th, in fact, Eisenhower told reporters that he took full responsibility for the Powers flight but left open the possibility there would be others.

Contrary to a widely held belief, Khrushchev did not plan to use the incident to scuttle a summit meeting planned for Paris later that month. He said at a reception at the Czech embassy on May 9 that he was prepared to put the intrusion behind him and search for peace and friendship with the United States. All he expected from President Eisenhower, he went on, was an apology and a promise that there would be no more violations of his country's territory. Ike had indicated as much, though with some waffling.

What was not generally known, however, was that Khrushchev was far from being as monolithic as he appeared. He had hard-line enemies in his own camp: Communist purists who took any accommodation of the West, and certainly arms control, as an unforgivable strategic blunder and a desecration of Marxism-

Leninism. Chief among his opponents was Vyacheslav Molotov, a reverential Stalinist and an ally of the Chinese Communist and Albanian zealots, who combined to denounce and undermine Khrushchev for "appeasing the imperialists." Two and a half years later, when Khrushchev withdrew Soviet ballistic missiles from Cuba under pressure from President Kennedy, he would again be vehemently attacked, particularly by China, for betraying the socialist cause. He would in part respond by writing a long letter to Fidel Castro in which he pointed out that China had done nothing to help Cuba and that its attacks on the United States came from "a paper tiger, dung." So Khrushchev constantly worried about the jackals in his own camp and had to give the appearance of being tough to keep them at bay.

Then the Department of State issued yet another release not only admitting that Ike had personally approved the fateful mission, but adding that the United States reserved the right to do it again and keep doing it until the Soviet Union opened its borders for inspection. That is, it insisted it could send reconnaissance aircraft over the Soviet Union anytime it decided that the Kremlin was being too secretive. And there was no apology. Seeing this, and knowing that his enemies would take any accommodation now as proof that he was dangerously soft on their mortal enemies, Khrushchev went into a rage. He had no choice but to solidify his political position by vehemently denouncing the Americans and scuttling the summit. It was in response to a speech by a Philippine delegate to the United Nations that autumn—an "American lackey," as he put it—that the still-posturing premier famously pulled off his shoe and banged it on his desk in protest. That was the image—of a gruff and ill-mannered peasant, not a shrewd politician skillfully maneuvering between enemies at home and abroad—that played on television and in the newspapers around the world. If Americans needed proof that their enemies were barbarians with nukes, the shoe-pounding episode did it.

Powers had in the meantime been carted off to Moscow's infamous Lubyanka political prison, where he languished in a small cell awaiting trial for espionage. He was the only American airman in the massive KGB-run fortress. But that was about to change.

AT TEN O'CLOCK on the morning of July 1—two months to the day after Powers was shot down—an RB-47H belonging to the 343d Strategic Reconnaissance Squadron of the Fifty-fifth Strategic Reconnaissance Wing roared off the runway at RAF Brize-Norton and headed almost due north and then northeast along the familiar track that paralleled Norway. The route took it past Bodø, which had been Powers's destination, and then swung eastward over the top of Norway and on to the Barents Sea. The 343d's insignia, which none of the six men on the plane wore, showed a raven (or crow) riding a lightning bolt. This particular "lightning bolt" was taking three ravens to an area north of the Kola Peninsula, where they were to ferret radar at the usual naval and military air facilities—Murmansk, Severomorsk, and Archangel—plus Novaya Zemlya, where there were air bases and a nuclear weapons test facility. The crews called it Banana Island because it looked like one.

The ten-and-a-half-hour mission had been flown so many times it had a name: Boston Casper. And with two important exceptions, this one was the same as the others. It was the first strategic reconnaissance mission flown since Powers went down. And it would not return.

The pilot and aircraft commander was Maj. Willard G. Palm. The copilot sitting behind him was Capt. Freeman B. Olmstead, known to everybody as Bruce. Palm and Olmstead worked under the long bubble canopy and therefore had the view. Up front, in the semidarkness of the nose, or "mole hole," Capt. John R. McKone sat hemmed in by his radarscope and the other tools of his trade: left and right navigator's instrument panels, two periscope sextants, a radar recording camera control panel, a radar control unit, a radar transmitter control, a table for aeronautical charts, a true reading transmitter, and other hardware.

As always, the three ravens sat squeezed in behind and below the flight crew in the Stratojet's modified bomb bay. With their parachutes strapped to their backs, they had to climb into the plane through a hatch in its forward wheel well and then crawl on their hands and knees along a narrow aisle just below and to the left of Palm and Olmstead. The passageway was notorious for catching parachute straps and cords; everybody had a story about some large or chubby, cursing raven whose chute opened when it got snagged by something in the crawlway. It was yet another, subtle drawback to ferreting in airplanes that were designed for other purposes. The men doing the ferreting on 53-4281 that day were Maj. Eugene E. Posa, Capt. Dean B. Phillips, and Capt. Oscar L. Goforth.

Unlike Palm and Olmstead, whose ejection seats would fire them up and out of the RB-47H in an emergency, Posa, Phillips, and Goforth would be propelled straight down by exploding 40-millimeter cannon shells, after large blades under their seats had cut through the honeycomb glass floor beneath them. Bruce M. Bailey, a retired lieutenant colonel and longtime raven, would explain years later that RB-47H crews had been told when their planes were delivered that the ejection systems had been thoroughly tested. "It had indeed been thoroughly tested," Bailey would assert sardonically, "but failed in every case. Every dummy blown out of the plane with this system had been decapitated." In fact, the system had been dummy-rated, according to Olmstead, but it had never been man-rated. And since firing the three of them straight down while the plane was still on the runway or was just taking off would kill them instantly, they had to stay huddled in the aisle for takeoff and landing. They crawled from there to the ravens' compartment while the Stratojet was still below 10,000 feet. Then their cramped, windowless dungeon was pressurized, and they settled down for an invariably long mission. On approach to land, the process was reversed, and they again squatted in the narrow crawlway. Ravens in RB-50Gs developed hearing problems. When they graduated to RB-47Hs they grew hemorrhoids and probably blood clots.

Ordinarily, Palm would have flown the RB-47H as close as possible to the radar it was ferreting without violating Soviet airspace. But not that day. That day the Russians were to be given a wide berth because the diplomatic catastrophe that had happened near Sverdlovsk exactly eight weeks earlier still hung heavily in the air. Eisenhower was in no mood for another embarrassing reconnaissance fiasco and everyone down the line understood that. Major Palm was therefore given strict orders to stay fifty or more miles off the Soviet coast. And Palm would have known, as everybody in the business knew, that the aircrew that violated Russian territory against orders would be stationed on Shemya until they fossilized.

Palm flew up the Norwegian coast almost wingtip-to-wingtip with his all-jet KC-135 tanker so both planes appeared as a relatively unthreatening single blip on radar. When the ferret had been topped off, at the northern edge of Norway, the KC-135 dove hard down to the deck and turned back to England.

The RB-47H flew on, alone, down the length of the Kola Peninsula while Posa, Phillips, and Goforth worked the knobs on their receivers like safecrackers as they searched for radar hits, oblivious to what was happening outside. They were flying parallel to Murmansk at 30,000 feet when Palm and Olmstead noticed a single large fishing boat in the distance. They also noticed an ominous contrail at their altitude and to the right, some twenty-five miles between them and the coast. Then it disappeared.

McKone took a radar fix. It showed that 53-4281 was sixty-four miles off the Kola Peninsula, between the Holy Nose and Kanin Nose capes that form the mouth of the White Sea. He told Palm to make a ninety-degree turn to the north, which would point them away from the naval bases and toward Banana Island. That's when the MiG-19 appeared just off the right wing.

"Where the hell did that guy come from?" McKone heard someone ask.

The MiG swung in behind and just below 53-4281 as Palm banked to the left. Olmstead swiveled his seat so he faced backward, abruptly turning from copilot to tail gunner. Capt. Freeman Bruce Olmstead and Capt. Vasily Ambrosievitch Polyakov were now looking at each other across a distance of perhaps 1,000 yards. With the RB-47H clearly lined up in the gunsight on his windshield, Polyakov squeezed his thumb on the trigger button. The fighter shook as the two cannons in its wing roots and the one in its nose opened fire. Olmstead saw white flashes on the

MiG-19. He also saw that the Russian had crossed the "firing line," which brought him in range of Olmstead's two guns, so he fired back. The cannons sprayed bullets up and down at the MiG, ineffectively "hosing" it until they ran out of ammunition.

Polyakov did better. He hit the RB-47H's two inboard engines on the left wing, causing loud explosions. A second burst raked the nose, punching holes the size of a grapefruit near where McKone sat. Both of the engines that were hit jerked so violently that the pod they were in twisted ninety degrees to the airstream. It was like sticking the flat side of a paddle in the water while a canoe is moving forward. Like the canoe, 53-4281 lurched abruptly to the left, and even with Palm and Olmstead kicking the right rudder pedals for all they were worth, it started into an uncontrollable spin. The engines were on fire and, looking behind him, McKone saw that the aisle was burning, too. Palm hit the claxon. Its long continuous ring told everyone to get out.

Explosive charges blew off the canopy. Palm and Olmstead shot straight up in their ejection seats. McKone, following procedure, pulled up the arm supports of his seat, yanked a D-ring, and was shot through a hatchway under him. Posa, Phillips, and Goforth blasted through 53-4281's shattered glass belly.

Olmstead passed out almost immediately. He woke up a few moments later, after his parachute had automatically popped open at 14,000 feet, and pulled the cord that opened his inflatable "rubber ducky" dinghy. That's when he saw somebody falling toward the sea without a parachute. He thought he counted four other open chutes and that seemed to account for everyone else. McKone also saw chutes on his way down. And he saw the body of an airmen floating lifeless on the sea without boots on. Bill Palm had preferred cut-down engineers' boots to the regulation kind that laced halfway up the calf. McKone guessed that they had been torn off when his aircraft commander ejected.

Whatever regulations said, no one had climbed into the plane wearing a rubberized survival suit because a man could lose ten pounds of sweat in one during a long mission. And it took a contortionist to get one on in the cramped confines of an RB-47. So when Olmstead hit the water, which was one degree above freezing, he was in a nylon summer-weight flight suit, T-shirt, and cotton socks under his boots. The briefing officer at Brize-Norton had given them eighteen minutes in that water with those flight suits. To make matters worse, Olmstead had smashed at least one vertebra, was numb from the waist down, and was almost unbearably cold. Pulling himself into the dinghy on six- to eight-foot swells was agonizing. When he was in it, he started to drift in and out of consciousness. At one point during the six and a half hours before he was picked up, he seriously considered killing himself.

"I looked around and couldn't see anything, and it was getting cold, and I was feeling sorry for myself, so I took my survival rifle and loaded it and put the barrel in my mouth," Olmstead would recount many years later as he thought about the .22-caliber Hornet that was standard issue in survival kits. "I figured, well, with this I'll take the easy way out." Then he thought again. "Boy, if they find you," he told himself, "Gail is really going to be pissed off at you." He and Gail had an infant daughter named Karen back in Topeka. And although he didn't know it as he floated on the Barents Sea that miserable afternoon, another girl was on the way. He tossed the Hornet overboard.

McKone, who was hallucinating five hours after he hit the water, had a religious experience after praying to God to take care of his wife and three children. "All of a sudden, in broad daylight, here's this very bright light that was only about five feet off the end of my dinghy," he would vividly remember.

> A tremendous light. I couldn't look at it. It was so bright I couldn't focus on it. It was brighter than the sun. I could look at the sun and shade my eyes a little bit, but I couldn't shade my eyes from this, it was so bright. Nobody talked to me or anything. It was about human size, about five or six feet high; just a bright light. And at that particular time, I suddenly felt much warmer physically, I knew that I'd be rescued, and that everything was going to be all right. It was the most wonderful thing that's ever happened to me.

Olmstead thinks that the Russian fishing trawler that eventually pulled him and McKone out of the frigid water was the same one they had seen at 30,000 feet. That would figure importantly for the other members of the crew. He remembered being taken to the boiler room, stripped of his flight suit, wrapped in blankets, and fed hot tea and honey. McKone remembered that half the crew were jovial women (though "not drop-dead beauties"), a few of whom ripped off his flight suit and underwear and confiscated the knife he kept in his boot. Then they fed him hot tea and greasy fish soup. The tea was wonderful.

The Americans were soon put on a border patrol boat and separated. Olmstead saw a pile of orange-and-white-striped parachutes in a corner of the cabin he was in and surmised that they covered the remains of Bill Palm. Nor did he hold out hope for Posa, Phillips, and Goforth. Olmstead was convinced that Polyakov or his wingman had raked the ravens' compartment with cannon fire as the RB-47H rolled to the left while changing course. If he was right, the explosive cannon shells had blasted into the small area where the three ravens sat and created carnage. He supposed they were therefore probably severely wounded when they punched out. That would have been bad enough. But to make matters worse, the fishing trawler was the only ship within many miles, the sea was cold and rough and sprinkled with "lesser icebergs," and the wounded ravens were not wearing survival suits. He therefore had almost no doubt that they had died in the bitter cold water.

On October 14, another Russian trawler would raise part of the plane's wing and tail and an ejection seat holding the skeleton of an American airman who KGB chief Aleksandr Shelepin told Khrushchev was "POZ Evgenij Ehrnest," whose identification card said he had been born in 1922. It was Gene Posa. Shelepin also informed Khrushchev that the wreckage was recovered sixty to seventy miles out to sea. That said something about where the plane was relative to Soviet airspace.

Gene Posa's disappearance took a terrible toll on his family. His older brother, Philip, carefully kept the news from their elderly parents, Joseph and Isabella, who were immigrant Italians living in Santa Monica, California. He was afraid it would kill them. Even though his parents spoke no English, Philip, who lived with them, carefully screened phone calls and visitors so they wouldn't learn the truth. He even forged his brother's signature on letters that supposedly came from England and sent them a Christmas present and note, which he said was written by Gene, saying how much he missed them and his daughters, Vicki and Cathy. But it was no use. One day the old man went to a neighborhood Italian grocery store without Philip. That's when someone expressed sympathy over Gene's disappearance. As Philip had feared, his parents soon grew ill and died. Then Philip, who was overcome with both grief over his lost brother and guilt because his parents had discovered the truth, went to a shooting gallery on the Santa Monica Pier and committed suicide with one of the guns. Ironically, Gene's daughters were hanging out under the pier at that moment and heard the shot that killed their uncle.

Olmstead and McKone were turned over to the KGB in Murmansk, flown to Moscow in a dark green military transport, and then stuffed into cages in the back of a truck and driven to their first jail. The cages were sized for dogs. That would have been bad enough if Olmstead had felt all right. But he was far from all right. He correctly guessed that a vertebra had been broken when he ejected. Now, squeezed into the dog cage, he was in agony. They were soon delivered to a prison for criminals and immediately separated. McKone was told that Olmstead was being taken to a hospital, but that was a lie. He was merely driven around while McKone was taken inside the building and isolated in a small cell. Then Olmstead, grimacing in pain and limping, was also put in a cell alone. Absolute isolation was the foundation of the technique that would be used to try to break them. A few days later, both officers were transferred separately to the dour Lubyanka Prison in the center of Moscow. Except for two occasions, they would remain separated there for more than six months.

U.S. airmen who were captured in the Far East were treated like troublesome but inconsequential pawns who collected scraps of intelligence the way vagrants in markets steal apples. Perhaps because of their number, they were interrogated, brutalized, and devoured. Not Olmstead and McKone. These two were prize political plums picked out of the air by Polyakov (who was publicly awarded the Order of the Red Banner for his heroic exploit). Olmstead and McKone were living proof—for all the world to see—that the dangerously provocative imperialist spymasters who had sent Powers on a mission that blatantly violated another nation's territory were at it again. Olmstead and McKone were important because they showed that the Powers flight was not an aberration but rather part of a systematic campaign to undermine the USSR. And they showed that Eisenhower had lied when he indicated (whatever the Department of State said) that overflights were over.

It was therefore decided that the two new arrivals would stand trial with Powers on espionage charges the following month. But first they would have to admit their crime. That required carefully controlled conditions and expert interrogation, not strong-armed stuff. Each would have to be subtly, relentlessly worn down physically and emotionally. They would be kept separated and isolated and made to believe that they were absolutely on their own, that their country had forsaken them and so had their families, and that their only hope for salvation lay in confessing that they had deliberately overflown Soviet territory on orders from Eisenhower. The penalty for espionage, Olmstead and McKone were told repeatedly, was execution by a bullet in the head. On the other hand, it didn't have to come to that. A confession and repentance could get them off with only a ten-year prison sentence. Socialism, after all, was humanitarian.

The cells were ten feet by six feet with ten-foot-high ceilings and were painted dark green. Each had a window with opaque glass near the ceiling; a constant, subtle reminder that they were caged like birds and that other birds were free. Each had a steel cot with a thin mattress, a porcelain commode, and an opening in the hardwood door through which their food—mostly heavy black bread and a cup of water—was passed in. There was also a judas hole, a "nasty little round window," as Olmstead would put it, through which they were watched day and night as a constant reminder that they had no privacy: they were, as the saying had it, open books. And open books gave up their secrets. When Olmstead's back had healed enough so he could move around, he started rubbing the side of his nose with his finger and then rubbing the oil from his skin onto the glass. "They couldn't see all that clearly, so they'd open the door and shake their finger at me, and polish it up. As soon as they closed the door, I'd do it again.

And if I didn't have oil on my nose," Olmstead added, laughing, "I'd find other things to rub on it. You have to do that to keep from going nuts in solitary, for crying out loud."

Each cell had a 300-watt bulb that dangled from the ceiling and was never turned off. When the prisoners pulled their blankets over their heads for darkness, a guard would come in and take the blanket away. The prisoners wore black denim shirts and pants without belts, a kind of "fatigue suit," as Olmstead put it, and leather slippers without laces. Their captors did not want suicides.

Later, after they were freed, some people who were told about their imprisonment would indicate to McKone that he was lucky there had been no rough stuff; that they weren't strapped to chairs and beaten senseless, as in movies about the Gestapo. That was true enough, as he was the first to admit. But the notion that he and Olmstead had merely been detained and not tortured would raise John McKone's ire. "I'll tell you what you do," the native Kansan would say. "Go in the largest closet in your house. Take all the clothes out of that closet. Put a 300-watt bulb in the ceiling, turn the light on in that closet, get yourself a chair, and sit in there for an hour. And if that's not enough, sit in there for two hours. See how that feels. Then try it for 208 days."

No torture, as Bruce Olmstead put it, but "head games" galore. They would be given a meal, for example, and then another meal half an hour later. But it would take twelve hours for the next food to appear, "so your body clock got all screwed up," he said.

There were a couple of interrogations a week, always individual, in a room that was painted dark green halfway up the walls and white to the ceiling. The interpreters, sympathetic-looking individuals, and the KGB interrogators played good cop–bad cop and the topics were wide-ranging. Both men were led to believe that their captors already had a great deal of information about them, their mission, and the Fifty-fifth Strategic Reconnaissance Wing. When Olmstead was told exactly when his RB-47H left Forbes Air Force Base and exactly when it arrived at Brize-Norton, he concluded that agents at both bases routinely photographed departing and arriving planes' tail numbers and sent them east.

When the Kremlin simultaneously handed a note protesting

the RB-47H's intrusion to the U.S. chargé d'affaires in Moscow and announced the shootdown to the news media on July 11, it was made known that Olmstead and McKone were in custody and that Palm's body had been recovered. This was an evident attempt to show that the two surviving airmen were Powers's successors. It was a good human interest story, especially given the number of airmen who had been lost on similar missions and never heard from again, so reporters and photographers headed for Topeka looking for relatives. They found Gail Olmstead pregnant and reported that fact. The stories ran with pictures of her "showing." This was not news to the father, since they had tried to get her to conceive before he left, and also because she had hinted as much in letters to Lubyanka.

But the pregnancy was useful news to Olmstead's interrogator, who showed the airman a newspaper photograph of his bulging wife and then asked him, in apparent sympathy, how he felt about his wife's taking a lover while he was spying on the people's paradise from a base in far-off England.

"Do you ever beat your wife when she cheats on you?" the KGB man asked as if he were trying to bond with his powerless, pitiful, cuckolded adversary.

"Only if I catch her," Olmstead answered with a straight face.

Bruce Olmstead, a graduate of Kenyon College, was a literate opera buff with a taste for French cuisine and good wine—the "better things in life," as they were called in those days. Robb Hoover would classify him as a "liberal arts" type rather than a "techno-nerd." He and McKone were formally imprisoned on writs of preventive measures, "which," Olmstead would explain wryly, "is the equivalent of a court in Georgia arresting you for parking with intent to speed. They think you're going to commit espionage, so they put you in jail to protect you from yourself."

Meanwhile, the political equivalent of a food fight was starting far beyond the thick walls that held Olmstead, McKone, and, elsewhere on their floor, Powers. The Russians got off the first salvo on July 11 in a demarche that not only placed the RB-47H just within their twelve-mile limit, which was not true, but reminded the world that only two months earlier the U-2 "spying mission" and the "proclamation of such provocative acts as a matter of the national policy" of the United States had wrecked the summit. The next day, in a one-two punch, Khrushchev told reporters in Moscow that his government had delayed news of the shootdown for eleven days to give the United States enough time to make conflicting statements about the flight just as it had after the U-2 was shot down. Eisenhower must have groaned.

During a furious clash at the United Nations two weeks later, Soviet first deputy foreign minister Vasily V. Kuznetsov lambasted Henry Cabot Lodge, the U.S. delegate, for lying about the RB-47H's mission and position just as he had lied about the U-2's.

Washington knew the United States was vulnerable on the U-2 issue and would get flagellated on it unless it went on the offensive. The Department of State therefore went after the Russians for their own wide-ranging technical espionage. Within forty-eight hours of that first Soviet broadside, the Navy fired back with the news that a Soviet trawler that had cruised through a Polaris submarine missile-firing test area off Long Island in late April was in reality an "electronic spy ship." The Russians had routinely monitored U.S. naval operations for years with no outcry made in public.

Rear Adm. Charles G. Kirkpatrick, the Navy's chief of information, carefully emphasized several times that the "snooper" was not molested because it was in international waters. "We are a legal people and we abide by international law," the admiral said with studied sanctimoniousness. No reporter at the hastily called news conference missed the connection between the *Vega*, as the antenna-laden 600-ton Soviet ship was called, and the hapless American jet. Lodge not only again referred to the vessel at length on the floor of the U.N. thirteen days later, but added that Soviet planes routinely flew close to Alaska and American outposts in the Pacific. He was right again. There were indeed Bears in the air.

And on the very day that the Soviet Union was scheduled to bring the RB-47H incident to the floor of the U.N., a third secretary in the Soviet embassy in Washington named Pyotr Y. Yezhov was ordered expelled for paying a photographer more than $1,000 to take aerial pictures of Navy installations and other intelligence targets. The *New York Times* reporter who covered the story found the connection between developments in the Security Council and Yezhov's being made persona non grata "more than coincidence."

But the strategists in Washington won a temporal victory. Following long-established procedure, the editors who laid out the front page of *The Times* for July 23 put the story about Yezhov right next to the lead story, which had the Russians asking the Security Council to demand that the U.S. Air Force stop committing "new aggressive actions" against their country. Along the bottom of the page ran a four-column-wide picture of the six wives and other relatives grimly watching the debate and wearing headphones that provided simultaneous translation.

After a hat had been passed around the Fifty-fifth Strategic Reconnaissance Wing, the wives were flown in from Forbes and housed at Mitchell Air Force Base for the three days they attended the session. All six were high-profile weapons in the American public relations arsenal and they were used unsparingly. They were portrayed as the innocent and bereaved victims of Soviet thuggery.

"We felt like we were on parade," Patricia Phillips remembered many years later. "We went to the U.N. as a whole. We were just there to be recognized," she said. They were ferried back and forth from the Long Island air base to the U.N. with no more than two of them in a car at a time and had lunch with Lodge and his wife in their suite at the Waldorf-Astoria on Park Avenue. "These little hicks from Kansas," Pat Phillips added, laughing. "We were so scared."

Three large, heavy Russian women sat behind Kuznetsov and glowered at them every day. Several times, Mrs. Lodge, acting like a house mother, personally escorted all six to the ladies' room as a group and stood guard outside the door. Nor was the PR offensive confined to the U.N. "For two years, they told us, go here, do this, do that. . . . Every two or three months there was something we attended. . . . I must have had fifty news people sitting on my front lawn" in Sacramento.

Olmstead and McKone, who were incommunicado, knew nothing of all this, of course, nor of how entangled their case was with the U-2 imbroglio. As Olmstead was being escorted to the toilet one day, he caught his first and only glimpse of Powers, whom he recognized from photographs, standing behind his own guard. But both men were kept separated.

What he did know was that Roman Rudenko, the chief prosecutor in the Powers case, desperately wanted him and McKone to plead guilty so he could convict all three at the same time. Careers were made of such stuff, even in the USSR in 1960, where a privileged power elite quietly thrived.

Rudenko somehow had gotten it into his head that they would agree to admit they had deliberately violated Soviet airspace on Eisenhower's orders. So sometime before Powers's show trial started on Wednesday, August 17, he called them into his office separately and asked them whether they were guilty as charged. When Olmstead stated emphatically that he was not guilty of flying over Soviet territory, Rudenko lost his temper, turned red, and flew into a rage. As Olmstead would put it years later, the chief prosecutor "went ballistic." But, the airman added, "that was better than saying, 'Yes sir, Yes sir, three bags full' and ending up in a gulag someplace."

On August 19, after a three-day trial, Francis Gary Powers was handed a ten-year sentence for committing espionage against the USSR.* It was a historic week for U.S. intelligence—historic, supremely ironic, and much better than anyone on the outside had reason to know. The day before, on the 18th, while more than 2,000 people in the glittering Hall of Trade Unions watched a staged pageant that was symbolically ringing down the final curtain on U-2 missions over their country, the first successful American photoreconnaissance satellite—Powers's robotic replacement—was snapping pictures over their heads. The machine was called Discoverer 14. Before its payload floated down from orbit with 3,000 feet of exposed film and was snagged by an Air Force transport plane on the very day Powers was sentenced, it had covered 1,650,000 square miles of the Soviet Union in twenty-seven hours. That was more photographic coverage than all twenty-three successful Soviet U-2 flights combined. The future had very quietly arrived.

---

*Two years later he would be exchanged for William Fischer, a KGB spy who operated under the name Col. Rudolph Ivanovich Abel.

Meanwhile, days in Lubyanka stretched into weeks and then months. Olmstead had at first thought he'd be out of the place quickly. But the summer ended, Thanksgiving came and went, and Christmas approached with the two of them still locked up. At least, he was now convinced, they weren't going to put a bullet in his head.

With the sentencing of Powers, the interrogations ended and indoctrination began. "After the Powers trial," Olmstead concluded, "they didn't know what to do with us." So they held discussions on the glory of revolution ("Surely, having had your own revolution, you must understand the benefits of revolution?") and were given books—never hard-core Marxist theory—that glorified revolution. The list included works by Howard Fast, the author of a memoir, *Being Red*, and dozens of books whose theme was the justness of overthrowing tyrants. One, *Spartacus*, celebrated a revolt of gladiators in ancient Rome and became a film starring Kirk Douglas. Fast's "progressive" politics landed him a place on the Hollywood blacklist in the 1950s. The prisoners were also given Dickens ("Why do you want to spy for a society that oppresses children?" Olmstead's indoctrinator wanted to know). It was like getting pummeled with marshmallows:

"Have you ever read Soviet literature?"

"Well, I've read *War and Peace*."

"That's not Soviet. That's Russian."

Life in the great political prison in the middle of Moscow became tedious. Olmstead saved enough paperbacked tinfoil from the packages of foul-smelling cigarettes he was rationed so he could make a pack of playing cards, each about an inch by two inches, which he slipped to McKone for a Christmas present so he could play solitaire in solitary. He tied them with the pull-away cellophane strips that went around the tops of the packs, which he arranged in a bow.

Knowing their mail would be pored over by other eyes, he and Gail wrote banal letters to each other, carefully avoiding anything substantive enough to help the KGB. But the Russians weren't the only ones who scrutinized their correspondence. The Air Force asked for a look at his letters so chemicals could be used to bring out hidden messages, perhaps written with lemon juice to make them invisible. No lemon juice messages. But the chemicals stained the paper.

Olmstead drew a Yule log, three candles, and holly leaves on his Christmas letter, written on November 17: "I will be with you in spirit, then (as always), Gail, and I hope that Karen, in realizing a little bit more of what is going on, will, in part, make up for my not being present." He told her in another letter that he was "thrilled silly" to learn that "K-babe" was talking to his picture, meaning she remembered her daddy, however dimly. Then his exasperation came through. "I've completely abandoned my attempt to 'get used' to this situation, and instead, have desperately preoccupied myself with our reunion—but since this is still an almost abstract conception, the result is only slightly less tedious, and ever so much more frustrating. So I have to content myself with the 'maybe next week' treatment." Those words were written on January 8, 1961, by which time the quality of his and McKone's meals had markedly improved. His time frame for release was off. But only by a week.

At about four o'clock on the morning of Sunday, January 22, keys rattled on the other side of Olmstead's door. In walked Aleksandr N. Shelepin and two generals. The KGB chief told Olmstead that he had to get a good night's sleep because he was going to have "a big day" later on. Mindful that there were people around who would have made a big day out of his execution or shipment to Siberia, Olmstead, never abandoning his sense of humor, asked his captor: "*Good* big or *bad* big?" Shelepin was noncommittal.

But Olmstead's spirits began to soar hours later when a barber appeared, followed by ham and eggs, buttered toast, and coffee. Then they brought in a suit of sorts, an overcoat, and a hat. This, Bruce Olmstead reasoned, was not a send-off to a gulag. Shelepin finally told them that Khrushchev had absolved them of *personal* responsibility for crimes against the state and that they would be taken to the U.S. embassy and from there to a plane that would take them home that very day. As the senior member of the RB-47H's crew, Shelepin added, did Olmstead have anything to say to the benevolent people of the Soviet Union?

"Yeah," answered a straight-faced Capt. Freeman B. Olmstead.

"Let's not miss that plane." Even Aleksandr Shelepin and the others laughed.

The release was not whimsical. It had been negotiated immediately after John F. Kennedy was elected president the previous November. Walt W. Rostow, a senior Kennedy aide and eventual national security adviser, had gone to Moscow to work out a peace initiative with Khrushchev. After preliminary wrangling, both sides agreed that each would benefit from Khrushchev making an inauguration present of both airmen to JFK. The Soviet premier had gotten as much propaganda out of them as he was going to get. Returning them made him look magnanimous. And it made John Kennedy appear to command Khrushchev's respect, which was the way his own strategists wanted his administration to begin. Everybody won.

Kennedy met Olmstead and McKone at Andrews Air Force Base in Maryland and drove with them, Gail Olmstead, and Constance McKone to the White House for his and Jackie's first official event there. Gail would remember Jackie as being radiant and gracious, but nervous. That was definitely not a problem shared by Captains Olmstead and McKone, who went on to hold a news conference back at Forbes. They were also featured in a spread in *Life* magazine. As usual, there was no official recognition of what, precisely, they had done to warrant the ordeal they had been through. But no one missed the fact that, whatever it was, they were among the very few to be shot down on such a mission and make it home alive.

In the summer of 1960, when Olmstead, McKone, and the others were shot down, the per diem allowance for airmen stationed overseas was $6 a day. Although regular paychecks were issued to their families throughout their imprisonment, Olmstead was mystified to see that the first paycheck he received after his release was, as he put it, "light by $90." When he explained to the paymaster at Forbes Air Force Base that he had gone to Brize-Norton on a thirty-day tour of duty, and was therefore entitled to $180, he was told that the amount had been cut in half because he had spent only fifteen days at the base.

Olmstead was amused by the irony of the situation. "You won't believe this," he told his wing commander, Col. William D. Kyle, at lunch one day, "but. . . ." Kyle was not amused. He was angry. He was so angry that he went back and said, "If you won't give him six bucks a day for Brize, give him 211 days at the Moscow Station allowance." That was $31 a day. The request went right up to the comptroller of the Air Force and the response was negative.

The reason the extra pay was denied, as related by Bruce Olmstead, is in the folklore of the Fifty-fifth Strategic Reconnaissance Wing and never fails to draw appreciative laughter from its alumni and other veterans. The comptroller reasoned: "You weren't ordered to Moscow, and you had your quarters and meals provided."

FOR LORENZO AND Vivian Phillips, the parents of Dean Phillips, unofficial recognition of their son's sacrifice came from 1st Lt. Joseph B. Maddalena, who had been Dean's roommate in aviation cadet school for almost a year. As it happened, Maddalena was on one of the planes that searched in vain for survivors of the downed RB-47H. He wrote to the Phillipses ten days after the shootdown:

> I know that you must have been disturbed when Phil [Dean] made his decision to stay in service as indeed my mother was so deeply upset. The main reason for my writing to you is to try to set your mind at ease as to the "why" of things. It would have been easy for Phil to have gotten out of service and become one of those other careerists with so much more respect in people's eyes, such as a doctor or lawyer or engineer. That would have been the easy road. These professions are viewed as being the height of respectability, but without officers in the Air Force like Phil, none of these other people could live in a society as free and democratic as ours. Phil and thousands more like him do their jobs each day so that millions of others may live in peace and comfort.
>
> Please don't ever think that his life was wasted or in vain. His name will never be recorded as a great hero among the annals of history, but I feel certain that somewhere there is a

place wherein is recorded the names of the thousands of men who died for their ideals. I lived with Phil long enough to know that his reasons for remaining in service were inspired not by monetary considerations or for a life of ease but rather for a purpose of upholding our way of life and helping to keep us free. . . .

Sincerely yours
Joseph B. Maddalena
1/LT U.S.A.F.

WONDERLAND

THE ONLY ONES who were surprised when Francis Gary Powers was shot down were those who shot him down.

Eisenhower was neither an aeronautical engineer nor an expert on Soviet air defenses. But it didn't take one of the ubiquitous think tanks or the CIA's Directorate of Intelligence—organizations that were supposed to divine so-called intentions and capabilities from raw data—to understand that the U-2 was basically a jet-propelled glider with wonderful but glaringly finite capabilities. He knew it flew very slowly and had an altitude advantage that would sooner or later evaporate as Soviet fighter-interceptors and missiles kept stretching higher. Ike had known since his days at West Point that the offensive-defensive cycle is as old as warfare and is immutable. That's why when he approved it he predicted that one day the plane would be "caught."

Kelly Johnson, who *was* an aeronautical engineer and who had conceived the U-2 at Lockheed's Skunk Works, knew better than Ike that the high flyer would become increasingly vulnerable. "Almost as soon as the U-2 was in operation," Johnson would write, "we began to plan its successor."

Richard Bissell also understood that the U-2's capability was finite, at least against advanced Soviet defenses. He knew by 1958 that the opposition was pouring billions of rubles into the development of a missile that could take out U-2s, not only to protect the Soviet Union's secrets but to salvage its honor. So the idea was to stay ahead—far ahead—of the Russians by advancing to more sophisticated, higher-performing systems. They would include the use of satellites. But satellite development, in the wake of the lingering shock over *Sputnik 1* and its successors, was in its infancy in 1958 and was highly speculative. What was clearly needed was a superhigh-performing airplane that could bridge the gap between the U-2 and satellite reconnaissance from space.

Like the U-2 itself, the follow-on aircraft had three fundamental goals: improve coverage, reduce risk to the crews, and avoid political trouble on missions (political trouble at home could never be avoided). All three would not be completely achieved until the satellites started operating. But the plane that followed the U-2 would be an extraordinary leap in that direction.

From an engineering standpoint, one requirement for the new reconnaissance plane was an absolute given: altitude. A plane carrying cameras to do strategic reconnaissance had to fly very high, both for the view and for protection. The U-2 couldn't fly much higher without a lot more speed. But even a small increase in speed would tear off its long, graceful, fragile wings. So, Kelly Johnson mused, a radically new design was necessary. "We set up our own requirements. There were none officially yet—just the need. We knew we needed more altitude and, especially, more speed." He decided that if the new reconnaissance plane was going to stay far ahead of its opponents, it would have to get above 90,000 feet, fly at three or more times the speed of sound, and have a range of 4,000 miles. "The higher and faster we fly the harder it will be to spot us, much less stop us," he told his engineers.

Ben Rich, who was foremost among them, was flabbergasted when Johnson described the proposed flight envelope. "I didn't know about Richard Bissell of the CIA, but Ben Rich of the Skunk Works reacted to Kelly's idea with jaw-dropping disbelief," Rich himself remembered. "He was proposing to build an airplane that would fly not only four times faster than the U-2 but five miles higher," Johnson's effusive and animated successor added, still astounded at his boss' brilliant audacity.

The A-12 (for Archangel design number 12), designed and built for the CIA, would be faster than a speeding bullet and able to leap tall missile shields in a single bound. It was given the code name Oxcart, Johnson explained a quarter of a century later, barely suppressing a smirk in his trophy-filled study in Encino, California, "because it was so slow."

It was, in fact, the fastest, highest-flying operational aircraft in the world and set records that still stand. Although its optimal speed was Mach 3.2—1,825 nautical miles an hour—it could get up to 3.5 and higher if the air it flew through was cold enough. Unlike other very fast planes—the rocket-propelled X-15 research aircraft, for example—Oxcart was designed to cruise at faster than three times the speed of sound, not for a couple of minutes, but for hours. And unlike the U-2, which was built with off-the-shelf technology, nearly everything that went into Oxcart had to be invented from scratch, including the tools that made it and even the paint used for the Air Force insignia. Air friction at three times the speed of sound made Oxcart's skin so hot that a single flight cooked the red, white, and blue "Stars and Bars" until they were scorched brown.

Rich, who was renowned for speaking his mind, bridled at the notion of painting the insignia at all. After the order to do so came from the Air Force, he challenged it in his own inimitable way.

"You dumb son-of-a-bitch," he told the hapless officer who delivered the directive, "you know how hot that airplane is [at Mach 3 plus]? It's six hundred degrees. You know what six hundred degrees is? It's the temperature under your broiler. Take a piece of metal, paint it, and stick it under your broiler." Heat became Oxcart's engineers' implacable enemy every step of the way. Long before the first A-12 flew, they calculated that without radical air-conditioning, the cockpit would become hot enough to bake a cake.

Paint would be the least of the problems. Oxcart's working environment—its operational altitude—would be so high that the word *air*craft bordered on being a misnomer. The engineers had to make trade-offs, as they always did, with that most overused of all technological terms, cutting edge, being their goal in the intellectual as well as physical sense. Oxcart would have to function for hours in an environment so dangerous and unforgiving it would have been all but unimaginable to Stan O'Kelley, Warren Sanderson, Frank Tejeda, and the others who flew on *Little Red Ass*. Oxcart would fly nearly nine times faster and more than three times higher than the RB-50G. And the staggering part was that Oxcart first took to the air in December 1964, only eleven years after *Little Red Ass* went down. No one could have predicted it at the time, but that extraordinary technological leap presaged the outcome of the cold war. There was no way the Soviet Union could match either the plane itself or the managerial genius that created it. And that competitive disadvantage haunted high technology in general, including the USSR's justly admired space program, which staged impressive feats despite daunting political opposition, an inherently weak industrial infrastructure, and severely limited resources.

THE NEW HIGH-SPEED, high-altitude environment—the "envelope"—changed everything. Cotton flight suits went the way of knickers and the Panama hat where the U-2, let alone Oxcart, was concerned. At altitude—above 70,000 feet for the U-2 and even higher for Oxcart—a sudden loss of pressure would quickly boil the blood in an unprotected body.

So the days of simply deciding not to wear protective clothing in favor of more comfortable cotton flight suits, as Willard Palm and his crew had done before they flew their fateful mission on July 1, 1960, in the RB-47H, were over for high-flying airmen. Four-layer pressure suits and airtight helmets had to be designed to protect their wearers from sudden decompression, air leaks, extremes of heat and cold, and other physiological dangers. The suits had to provide a protective environment within the cockpit's own environment, and they were therefore the precursors of the outfits that would shortly get Mercury and Gemini astronauts to Earth orbit, and then Apollo crews to the Moon. They and their large "goldfish bowl" helmets were in fact virtual spacesuits and were the heart of the U-2's and Oxcart's aptly named life-support system. It was a system that, together with the machines in which it operated, was designed to protect American reconnaissance crews from the extreme environment that protected them from the enemy.

Special hydraulic fluid was created that would function at terrifically high temperature, and so was a special fuel that had a flash point so high a lighted cigarette tossed into a pail of it would go out. Highly inflammable fuel inside the fuselage and wings of an airplane that was hotter than 500 degrees Fahrenheit would turn it into an incendiary bomb. Pure rubber tires filled with air would have exploded and caught fire even when retracted in the wheel wells. So B. F. Goodrich came up with tires whose rubber was mixed with aluminum powder to make them fire-retardant. And they were filled with nitrogen, not air, so they wouldn't burn in the heat. The wheel wells into which the landing gear retracted were themselves shielded and surrounded by tanks of very cold fuel. The tanks became what the engineers called heat sinks: they absorbed heat in the wheel wells and elsewhere the way a cold compress absorbs heat from a fevered forehead. Then the hot fuel, which had absorbed much of the plane's body heat, was pumped into the engines, which made them more efficient. The glass on Oxcart's underside, through which its all-important cameras peered at targets, had to be distortion-free, even though the temperature inside the camera bay was 150 degrees Fahrenheit and the temperature on the other side of the glass was 550 degrees at cruising speed. The glass in the windshield would become so hot that pilots could not keep their gloved hands on it for more than a couple of seconds.

And the wings would grow so hot they'd melt plastic or rubber fuel cells. So there weren't any cells. Instead, the empty wings themselves held the fuel that wasn't in the plane's five fuselage tanks. Since the heat at cruising speed would make Oxcart's skin expand (its fuselage grew ten inches longer and then contracted when it came down), the plates that collectively formed its skin had to be set far enough apart to allow for expansion. They became nice and tight at high speed, as planned. But on the ground, when they were relatively cool, they shrank enough so the fuel slowly leaked out. An A-12 parked in a hangar or on an apron with fuel in its wings therefore had more drip pans under it than there were in large service stations.

Knowing that the difference between aerodynamics and hydro-dynamics was basically a matter of density—the air in front of the plane would not only become terrifically hot, but would thicken as speed built up—the designers shaped Oxcart's fuselage like the hull of a high-speed boat and blended it into delta wings. (Five centuries earlier, Leonardo da Vinci had made the connection between moving through air and water when he observed that birds and fish "fly" through different fluids in the same basic way.) The effect was increased by extending the hull's forward edges outward so it would ride on the thick air like a flat stone skimming on water.

The tapered extensions were called chines. Leaving no space unused, the engineers turned them into nine payload bays stuffed with electronic countermeasures equipment, infrared sensors, an electromagnetic reconnaissance system that ferreted radar, high-resolution, pointable cameras on both sides, and other hardware. And like the U-2 (and many 35-millimeter cameras), Oxcart was designed to use interchangeable noses that held different kinds of cameras and other sensors.

They also provided Oxcart with a spate of warning devices and electronic jammers collectively called the Defensive systems, or DEF (pronounced "deaf"). The CIA's A-12, which held only a pilot, was short-lived. It was replaced by the SR (for Strategic Reconnaissance) -71A, which was assigned to SAC and which carried a second crewman behind the pilot. He was called the Reconnaissance Systems Officer, or RSO, and he worked not only the cameras and other intelligence collectors but the DEF from a console on his left side.

One of the SR-71A's clever defensive tools was a "deception jammer." It was an ingenious device that absorbed and memorized an enemy radar signal as it hit the reconnaissance plane, then sent back a radar signal similar to the SR-71A's but stronger, and projected it away from the plane. A radar operator tracking an SR-71A in the air or on the ground would therefore see a ghost blip. A surface-to-air missile that could intercept an SR-71A at 90,000 feet or higher—and the plane's combination of surprise,

Neptune crews like this one, based in Japan, searched for enemy submarines and photographed surface ships. The members of the flight crew were (from left) Lt. Carlos C. Campbell, Lt. (jg) David W. Adams, Lt. (jg) Peter E. Requa, and Lt. Charles F. Clark. The enlisted men were technical specialists

Lt. Carlos C. Campbell was the navigator of a Navy P2V-5, and then an intelligence officer, in VP-22 from 1960 to 1962. His Neptune was jumped by Soviet fighters several times. He went on to become an assistant secretary of commerce for economic development in the Reagan administration

RC-135s remain the workhorses of airborne intelligence collection. This "hog-nosed" RC-135M flew Combat Apple missions over the Gulf of Tonkin during the war in Vietnam. It monitored North Vietnamese radio communication, radar beams, and other signals. Similar operations took place during the war in the Persian Gulf and afterward

A Rivet Joint RC-135V at Offutt Air Force Base. Its black "hog-nose" holds special radar and the "cheek" in front of the wing holds small antennas and receivers that automatically locate radar, radio, and other signals

The Air Force SR-71A (above) and its CIA A-12 counterpart were true techno-logical breakthroughs. Flying at more than three times the speed of sound, an SR-71A could photograph 100,000 square miles in just over an hour from above 80,000 feet

In April 1954, RF-86F Sabrejets of the Fifteenth Tactical Fighter Squadron photographed the Spassk-Dal'Niy East Air Base north of Vladivostok from 42,000 feet. The first photograph shows the base as the RF-86F pilots saw it. The enlargements revealed Tu-4 bombers

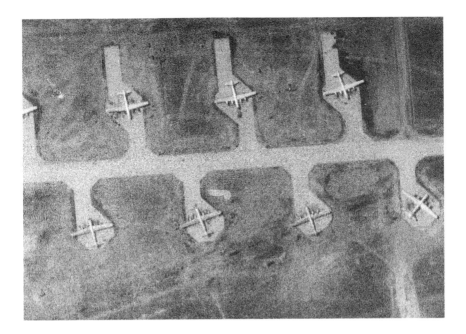

The U-2 was a revolutionary reconnaissance aircraft whose long wings and light structure got it above 70,000 feet. The silver-finish early model is similar to the one Francis Gary Powers was flying when he was shot down. Its successors, the midnight-black U-2R and U-2S, are thirteen feet longer than the original version, have 40 percent more wing area, are almost twice as heavy, and carry state-of-the-art sensors

A preliminary U-2 flight was made over Eastern Europe on June 20, 1956, and two more on July 2, before the Soviet Union itself was overflown on the Fourth of July. This recently declassified map traces the routes of the first three penetrations

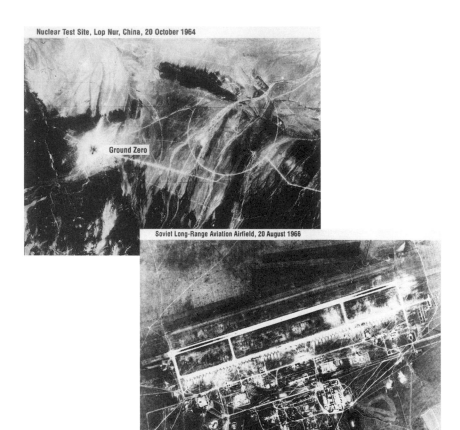

Nuclear Test Site, Lop Nur, China, 20 October 1964

Ground Zero

Soviet Long-Range Aviation Airfield, 20 August 1966

Sary Ozek IRBM Complex, USSR, 17 September 1971

On June 22, 1960—less than seven years after Capt. Stanley O'Kelley's RB-50G was downed—a radar ferret satellite was rocketed into Earth's orbit. It was followed two months later by the first operational Corona imaging reconnaissance satellite. These photographs are typical Corona imagery

speed, altitude, and jamming made that virtually impossible—
would therefore be targeted on thin air (*very* thin air), not on the
plane. The DEF could be worked manually or be set on automatic
to jam any threat it picked up. It was constantly updated to counter
advances in enemy radar, which was yet another reason for continuous ferreting, some of which the SR-71As did themselves.

Like its U-2 forebear, the SR-71 carried no weapons, since they
would have been heavy, bulky, and useless. Its protection came
from its DEF, its extraordinary speed and altitude, and from what
the people at the Skunk Works called a "low-observable" design.
(They scrupulously avoided the word "stealth," although Oxcart
pioneered stealth technology.) The plane's blended body, many
curves, and twin fins slanting inward reduced its radar image. So
did radar-absorbing plastic panels made of silicone and asbes-
tos. The toughest challenge in making Oxcart low-observable was
shaping its edges so they not only absorbed radar signals but redi-
rected them around the plane until they dissipated. That was
done by shaping the plastic into a series of wedge-shaped steps
with exquisite nuance so they sent radar pulses sweeping over the
plane like water rushing around a rock.

The only low-observable design element that could be said to
work against the Blackbird, as the SR-71 was called by everybody
except those who flew it, was its color: black. Like later versions
of the venerable U-2, SR-71s were painted flat black. Ostensibly,
this was to make them invisible to the naked eye at high altitude.
But Ben Rich maintained that pastels, not black, were the best
low-observable colors since the sky itself is pastel. Black was
picked, he muttered in his office in Burbank one day, "because
real men don't fly pink jets." It was vintage Rich.

But as Kelly Johnson maintained from the outset, the SR-71A's
ultimate defense was its combination of blazing speed and a
cruising altitude that caressed space. Viktor I. Belenko, who defected to Japan in a MiG-25 in 1976 (it was disassembled and
scrupulously photographed before it was returned to its owners),
told of the frustration of chasing SR-71s as they streaked along
the Siberian coast and of never being able to get off a missile
shot. He couldn't reach within two miles of an SR-71's altitude.
And not only wasn't his MiG fast enough to catch one, even his

missiles weren't fast enough. And a frontal shot would be futile because his missiles' computers couldn't cope with a combined closing speed of Mach 5. That was not surprising. The specialists who took his MiG-25 apart were astounded to see that its electronics system ran on vacuum tubes, like an old television set, not on circuitry. Typically, though, the Russians got the most out of what they had.

The SR-71's speed came from a pair of Pratt & Whitney afterburning turbojets called JT11D-20s by the company and J-58s by the Pentagon. One of the twenty-foot-long, 6,500-pound corncobs was mounted in each wing and developed 32,500 pounds of thrust. The J-58 was a masterpiece of engineering and precise machining in its own right. When it reached high speed, the turbojet turned into a more powerful ramjet that produced 80 percent of its thrust.

The key to the J-58's performance was a cone, called a "spike," that was in the engine's inlet and that regulated the speed of air coming into the engine by moving back and forth. The spike protruded all the way out when the plane was on the ground or flying at low speed. But as Oxcart's speed increased to high Mach numbers, the spikes moved back into the inlet as much as twenty-six inches to regulate the shock wave that hit the compressors.

When one of the spikes didn't move back fast enough, the rush of supersonic air overwhelmed the compressors, which reacted the way a person would who swallows too much food or water: they gagged and coughed it back out. This was the dreaded "unstart," and it haunted A-12 and then SR-71 pilots for years. Unstarts happened suddenly and without warning. There was a thunderous bang and the plane jerked so violently that pilots' and RSOs' helmeted heads smashed against the canopy. Experiencing an unstart has been compared to running into a brick wall. At least one pilot's head was slammed against the cockpit sill so hard his helmet cracked and he was momentarily knocked unconscious.

Lockheed test pilots who had unstarts were calm and clinical on the radio until they came down, according to Albert D. (Bud) Wheelon, who ran the Oxcart program for the CIA from 1960 to 1963, when he was the agency's deputy director for science and technology. "And then," he said, "they'd start weeping." The real danger was that an unstart at high speed could create an imbalance in engine thrust that would make the plane yaw sharply to the left or right, causing a loss of control and a catastrophic disintegration. A computerized flight and inlet control system eventually solved the problem by moving the spikes to where they were supposed to be automatically and almost instantly.

SR-71As started flying operational missions in SAC's Ninth Strategic Reconnaissance Wing in 1966 in a program called Senior Crown. The unit was and remains headquartered at Beale Air Force Base in California, just north of Sacramento, from where its Blackbirds, like its U-2s, ranged over much of the world. It sent SR-71As over Nicaragua in 1982, when the Marxist Sandinista government ran afoul of the Monroe Doctrine by building a military base with help from the Soviet Union and Cuba. Two years later, other SR-71As flew over the Latin American nation looking for evidence—never found—that MiG-21s were being delivered. To make the point to both Moscow and Managua that Nicaragua was being carefully watched, the SR-71As repeatedly flew faster than the speed of sound, creating sonic booms that rattled windows and nerves on the ground. They often did it over Havana at high noon as well.

The Ninth SRW covered the northern periphery of the Soviet Union, Eastern Europe, and the Middle East with two planes on rotation at RAF Mildenhall in England. Two others were based at Kadena Air Base on Okinawa and flew missions throughout the Far East, including over Vietnam, North Korea, and along the Siberian coast. When the Okinawans saw the long, sleek, black reconnaissance plane for the first time, they named it "Habu" after a local pit viper. The name stuck. The elite group of men who flew SR-71As and were its reconnaissance systems officers called it Habu, or the sled, or simply the SR, but never the Blackbird.

Lt. Col. Jerry Glasser, an SR pilot, described it as an exceptionally "cerebral" airplane. The view from the front cockpit at altitude was breathtaking, he said, and gave him a sense of what it was like to be in orbit. But the curvature of the Earth, the darkness of the sky at midday, spectacular sunrises and sunsets, and other natural splendors were rarely enjoyed because the instruments two feet in front of him had to be monitored constantly. "Every time you look out of the window," he explained, "something bad happens." Navigating without the plane's astro-tracker could be particularly challenging. "When the astro-tracker burps," he added, "you're doing thirty-three miles a minute. And every minute you don't know where you are, you're thirty-three miles *farther* from where you don't know where you are. You're basically thinking about 400 miles ahead of the airplane—twelve to thirteen minutes ahead—and while you don't have to be fast, you have to be right the first time."

SR-71s and their ever-present tankers—their performance made them exceptionally thirsty—prowled most of the world until they were retired in 1990. They collected intelligence on virtually every militarily important crisis or potential crisis that affected the United States or its allies, including the Israeli-Arab Six-Day War in 1967. So did their U-2 sisters.

During their twenty-four years of operational reconnaissance missions, sleds flew 3,551 sorties that lasted a total of just over 11,000 hours. They ran up 11,675 hours at Mach 3 or higher. In the process, they became a textbook example of how to use very high technology to increase efficiency and save lives. They proved, as did the U-2s, that designing high-performance reconnaissance planes from scratch—using fresh design concepts to keep airmen above harm's way—was infinitely better than modifying fighters, bombers, and transports. Not one of the twenty-nine SR-71As delivered to the Air Force was ever lost to the enemy, though more than 1,000 missiles were fired at them, and MiG-25s, such as the one flown by Belenko, sometimes tried to intercept them. Several of the high-strung planes were destroyed in accidents, though.*

TODAY, A SPANKINGLY refurbished SR-71A is on display in a glass-enclosed part of the SAC Museum not far from Offutt Air Force Base, where Roger Ihle takes visitors on tours. It is mounted on pedestals and positioned at a jaunty angle, as if it's banking down and to the left, so people can see inside its cockpit. A block of

*Thirty-two SR-71s were produced. Three were trainers.

polished marble in front of the SR explains that it is "Dedicated to those valiant strategic airborne reconnaissance crewmembers who gave their lives during the cold war, and to their families, whose sacrifice continues."

Ihle is the guy who carried a Hallicrafters receiver by overnight Pullman from Boston to Wright-Patterson Field in 1943, bolted it into a B-17, and then rattled off to Algeria with Matthew Slavin II to ferret German radar at appallingly low altitude in the middle of the night.

The black high flyer behind him did the same thing to the Russians from appallingly high altitude day and night. Most visitors to the museum have no way of knowing it, and Roger Ihle would never tell them, but he and the sled are tightly bonded. After all, for many years they were in the same line of work.

SO IS THE TORTOISE. The parable of the tortoise and the hare describes the relationship between the SR-71 and the much slower line of reconnaissance planes variously called KC-135s and RC-135s. When Boeing planned the first American civil jet transport, eventually to be called the Model 707, it did so believing there would also be a vast market for the four-engine airplane in the military. It was a shrewd decision. Airlines around the world bought the 600-mile-an-hour aircraft to whisk passengers in record time and in a startlingly smooth and vibration-free environment.

The 707's development coincided with Curtis LeMay's tenure as head of SAC and therefore with his determination to make the bomber force capable of reaching any place on Earth. That meant air-to-air refueling. LeMay quickly grasped the notion that a jet-propelled tanker version of the 707 would make a perfect marriage with his jet B-47s and B-52s. Both bombers were hobbled by dependence on the KC-97, a tanker whose straight wings and piston engines forced bomber pilots to throttle back almost to a stall in order to gas up. The 707 was therefore modified to hold large fuel tanks in its fuselage and a "flying boom" that telescoped out from under its tail and which fitted into the fuel receptacles of the bombers, the SR-71s, and fighters the way a nozzle does at a filling station. This filling station was called the KC-135 Stratotanker, and it cruised at 530 miles an hour. By 1962, 636 Stratotankers had been ordered for deployment throughout the United States and overseas and were being turned out at a rate of six a month.

Meanwhile, a military transport version called the C-135 was being produced to carry people and cargo. And it was that rendition of the ubiquitous lifter that led to its further refinement for reconnaissance. The new snooper in its many forms either kept its KC-135 identification or was called an RC-135 or a WC-135 (for that old snooping standby, weather observation).

Even at the outset, in 1961, no one thought the RC-135s and their stablemates could penetrate Communist airspace and tangle with fighters. The Russians had demonstrated their defensive capability by shooting down Powers, mangling scores of ferrets and other planes on peripheral missions, and successfully attacking still others on shallow penetration missions into Eastern Europe. Furthermore, reconnaissance satellites were coming on line. Sending the transports over Soviet territory would therefore have been as unnecessary as it was dangerous.

What the '135s had going for them, however, made them exceptionally good at flying peripheral missions in the ongoing Peaceful Airborne Reconnaissance Program, which was using RB-47s.* KC-135s and RC-135s were large enough to hold many more receivers, amplifiers, recorders, and other electronic equipment and crewmen than were the severely cramped RB-47s. Furthermore, their much higher fuel capacity meant they could stay in the air longer without air-to-air refueling. Not insignificantly, they were also spacious enough to hold a real galley and allow ravens and the flight crew to walk around. Finally, since they were transports, not bombers, they were less provocative than RB-47s and therefore were less likely to be shot at by Soviet and Chinese fighter pilots. Their job during more than three decades of cold war and afterward was to ferret radar, intercept communications

---

*It became Peacetime Reconnaissance and Certain Sensitive Operations (PRCSO) in 1990.

and telemetry, and occasionally take long-distance photographs from international airspace or over friendly territory.

The entire operation was run by the Fifty-fifth Strategic Reconnaissance Wing (renamed the Fifty-fifth Reconnaissance Wing with the demise of the Strategic Air Command after the cold war) at Offutt. Planes from there range all over the world as requirements come up, typically staging out of Shemya, Eielson, Mildenhall, Rhein-Main, Yokota, Kadena, Hellenikon in Greece, Riyadh in Saudi Arabia, and elsewhere. Robb Hoover noted that there are days when not one RC-135 is on the Offutt flight line.

Missions run the gamut from routine collection of radar, communication, and other signals in an ELINT program named Rivet Joint to highly specialized intercepts in a "technical" program known as Combat Sent. Within the framework of those two generic programs, there exist more than two dozen subsidiary operations, some of them long-term, some one-shot, which have been given so many different mission cover names that friend and foe alike have been bewildered by them for years.

Beginning in 1961, for example, the naming of individual KC-135 and RC-135 planes and missions was made deliberately devious because of the pervasive penchant for secrecy. Unit insignia such as the Fifty-fifth's distinctive camera peering down at the whole planet and the motto *Videmus omnia* ("We see all") are never worn on the planes. As was the case with the Navy Mercators operating out of Japan in the 1950s, tail numbers on KC-135s and RC-135s were sometimes changed to make following their whereabouts and identifying their missions more difficult. "Consequently," one former RC-135 pilot has written in a book on the subject, "the names by which these missions are known, the airplane operational names, and the names of the airplane modification programs are a constant source of confusion, particularly as these names change and programs evolve." Robert S. Hopkins III deserves a medal just for navigating the labyrinth.

In essence, companies such as Ling, Temco Vought, and later Raytheon's E-Systems in Greenville, Texas, have customized standard C-135s in very specific ways to do highly specialized intelligence collecting. The work started on RB-29s in 1953 and included modifying C-130s in the Sun Valley program that began in 1957. The C-130A shot down over Soviet Armenia on September 2, 1958, with all crewmen lost, was a Greenville-customized aircraft.

Virtually all the modifications on the C-135s are done under the Big Safari special reconnaissance program. The aircraft lined up on the Offutt flight line on any given day are the equivalent of highly customized cars. Some are only slightly different from the others, while some have been altered so radically they almost look like a different species of airplane. Most have protruding noses that make them look like the Pinocchios of aviation. These "thimble nose" radomes, which are called "hog noses" by most RC-135 air and ground crews, hold special navigation radars used to help prevent the kind of navigational errors that led to some shootdowns during the cold war. The radars are continuously monitored by videocassette recorders to show the plane's precise course throughout its mission, and therefore where its targets are. Air and ground crews staging out of bases around the world have "hog-marked" several of them: Kadena is Hog Heaven; Mildenhall is Hoghenge; Hellenikon is Hogcropolis; and Eielson is the Hog Pole.

Many RC-135s also have long "cheeks" mounted on either side of the forward fuselage that hold small antennas and receivers which automatically locate radar, radio, and other electronic signals. These planes and others also carry antenna "farms" on their backs or bellies, sliding doors behind which are cameras of one sort or another, including infrared for picking up the heat from rocket engines, assorted windows of varying sizes, and bulges that conceal other radars. Some of the modified workhorses, called EC-135Ns, were used to track spacecraft reentering the atmosphere during the Apollo Moon program. They were therefore given very special nose jobs: downward-pointing radomes so bulbous they made the planes look like they had goiter.

The C-135 special modification program got off to a spectacular start in October 1961, following an announcement by Nikita Khrushchev that his country was going to demonstrate Marxist-Leninist scientific prowess by exploding a hundred-megaton H-bomb. But, as usual, there was more to the statement than mere boasting about the largest man-made pyrotechnic display in history.

A hundred-megatonner would be the most powerful weapon ever tested and would develop a fireball roughly the size of Maryland. Khrushchev's message was that whatever the West's superiority in bombers, missiles, and nuclear weapons, the consequences of an attack on the Soviet Union would be a counterattack that brought unimaginable death and destruction; that turned the United States into a furnace. The announcement caught the attention not only of the intelligence and military communities, but of the chemists and physicists at the Los Alamos National Laboratory and other weapons design centers who had a professional interest in learning how such a monster bomb worked. Everyone agreed that the test would therefore have to be recorded and studied.

There would have been no doubt whatever in the Kremlin that the United States was going to monitor the test by every scientific means possible, both seismically in Norway and elsewhere and in the air. And that would have been exactly what Khrushchev and his generals wanted, because it would prove that he was not bluffing or boasting idly. The launch of the first Sputnik in October 1957 had been particularly sweet because it proved that, far from being the backward bumpkins they thought the West believed them to be, Russian scientists and engineers were first-rate. And now the explosion of this behemoth of a bomb, this harbinger of hell, would underscore the point that Soviet science and the command economy supporting it were supreme.

The Air Force contracted with General Dynamics to quickly modify a KC-135A to monitor the test as part of Big Safari. The project's code name was Speed Light. The planes—there would soon be three of them—were fitted with suites of sensors specifically designed to record electromagnetic radiation from a thermonuclear blast in both the radio and visible frequencies. They also would carry cameras to photograph the "event."

Following communication intercepts explaining exactly where and when the big test would take place (and that were undoubtedly made easy to collect since the Russians didn't want their antagonists to miss the demonstration), the Speed Light KC-135A with its elaborate measuring equipment was sent to loiter around the test site on Novaya Zemlya on October 30, 1961.

Sure enough, there was an immense fireball and a towering mushroom cloud of unprecedented size as countless tons of radioactive earth erupted and were lifted into the atmosphere. The reconnaissance plane recorded the explosion with its various instruments and brought the precious data home. But that's not all it brought home. The KC-135A was so close to the explosion that it returned with skin scorched brown. Analysis showed that the nuclear blast had been fifty-eight megatons, not the one hundred megatons Khrushchev had predicted. It was a good thing, too, since the KC-135A had been too close to the explosion to survive a hundred-megaton fireball. The blast, or shock wave, would have blown away the quarter-of-a-million-pound aircraft as though it had been a toy.

The KC-135 program really got under way in 1961, not only with Speed Light, but with a technical collection program called Office Boy that used upgraded versions of the same communication intercept equipment as had been carried by the C-130A lost over Armenia. By the end of 1962, three Office Boy KC-135As were sent to Eielson to work in a signals intelligence program directed against targets in eastern Siberia. From then on, all Big Safari planes and specialized operations would be given special names. To make the system as incomprehensible as possible to outsiders, the project names were in turn incorporated in abstract operational names that had no bearing on the missions. Office Boy, for example, worked in an operation named Cotton Candy.

Unlike U-2s and SR-71s, which pretty much did the same thing all of their operational lives, C-135s were considered "platforms" that could be modified and remodified indefinitely as new requirements developed. There is confusion because very often a plane's designation changed every time it was modified, and so did its name and the name of its operation. By 1963, for example, all three KC-135As in the Speed Light program were changed yet again so they were better adapted to do that job worldwide. They were rechristened Rivet Stand.

The pantheon of C-135 derivatives, constantly adapted and readapted throughout the cold war and afterward as changing situations required, includes a bewildering assortment of planes designated RC-135C, RC-135E, RC-135M, KC-135R, KC-135T, RC-135U, RC-135V, RC-135W, and many others. One RC-135M was converted from a C-135B, for instance, and then was itself turned into an RC-135W. Each time, its equipment and mission changed. And the planes and their unique missions were themselves named Wanda Belle, Yogi Bear, Rivet Gym, Rivet Brass, Rivet Amber, Rivet Cord, Rivet Ball, Rivet Quick, Rivet Dandy, Rivet Joint, Cobra Jaws, Cobra Ball, Cobra Eye, Combat Apple, Combat Pink, and Combat Sent, among others.

RC-135Ms flying Combat Apple missions, to take one well-known example, were mainstay signals-intelligence collectors during the war in Vietnam. As many as two missions a day, each lasting up to nineteen hours, were flown from Okinawa to the Gulf of Tonkin starting in September 1967. The planes constantly monitored radio traffic, radar emissions, and other signals coming out of North Vietnam as they flew long circular sweeps over the gulf. A year later, Combat Apple was extended to cover Laos and the Ho Chi Minh Trail, where the planes orbited for hours listening for telltale signs of North Vietnamese troop movements. Others picked up MiGs taxiing and taking off and sent warnings to Air Force and Navy fighter squadrons in the region. The RC-135Ms were themselves escorted by Air Force or Navy fighters riding shotgun to protect them from MiGs.

Cobra Ball, to take another important Big Safari mission, was and remains a ballistic missile monitoring operation using RC-135S aircraft modified to record long-range missile tests in several ways. Soviet ballistic missile tests ran an immense intelligence gauntlet that began before launch and ended when the warheads slammed into or near their targets on the Kamchatka Peninsula. Communication announcing a launch was going to happen was typically picked up by NSA listening stations in Norway, Iran, and elsewhere. The intercepts were then relayed down the line to alert a number of intelligence "assets" on the ground, at sea, and in the air that monitored the missiles and then their individual, separated warheads in space as they arced high over Siberia and bore down on Kamchatka.

The intensely hot plumes of burning gas from the missiles' exhaust as they lifted off their pads at Tyuratam, Kapustin Yar, or Plesetsk were spotted immediately by Defense Support Program satellites that carried twelve-foot-long infrared cameras. Telemetry from the missiles themselves, which reported on-flight progress and how the systems were functioning—acceleration, stage separation, fuel consumption, vibration, and turbopump operation—was intercepted at a number of ground sites, including those in Iran and Pakistan, and in space by Rhyolite satellites that carried their own colossal antennas.

The planes in the Cobra family waited for the warheads at the end of the line. Meanwhile, a huge radar on Shemya called Cobra Dane closely tracked the warheads as they streaked toward their targets on Kamchatka. So did an antenna-festooned ship that operated as Cobra Judy. It would be parked off Kamchatka, along with its Soviet counterparts, which also monitored the tests. They were like outfielders waiting for a long fly ball. High above Cobra Judy, the RC-135S Cobra Ball flew a racetrack pattern off the Kamchatka coast with several sensors trained on the fast-approaching targets.

Cobra Ball crews on Shemya lived near their planes and rotated on alert status because there often would be little warning of an impending launch. When it came, they raced to their plane, got into the air, and headed for Kamchatka. The planes themselves were packed with sophisticated cameras and other sensors, a collection system collectively called Jolly Polly, which originally included a ballistic framing camera system and a medium-resolution camera system that photographed everything coming back into the atmosphere. They were eventually replaced by a real-time optical system that transmits the imagery to ground stations as it comes in and by an advanced telemetry system that automates the collection process.

The missile analysis operation is notoriously arcane and painstaking. The colors that flash around a reentry vehicle as it is heated by the atmosphere during its plunge back to Earth can tell analysts what it is made of and whether it has hardened titanium warheads for deep penetration of targets. The vehicle's flight path offers clues to its speed and maneuverability, while its speed of rotation indicates its stability and accuracy.

The end of the cold war in no way ended missile tests, and therefore did not end Cobra Ball. In 1997, the program was scrutinizing, among other weapons, tests of the Russian SS-X-27, which some experts said was the best ICBM in the world. Nor does the program confine itself to Russia. Any serious missile program, including relatively short-range Scuds such as those used by Iraq during the Gulf War, draws Cobra Ball aircraft. The list of countries includes China, North Korea, India, Israel, and South Africa.

No Cobra Ball aircraft has ever been shot down, but two of them crashed on Shemya in 1969 and 1981 because of bad weather. Shemya is renowned for dreadful flying conditions much of the year, which can include sixty-five-mile-an-hour winds and fog at the same time. Six men were killed in the first crash and six more in the second. These got very little public attention, and neither did Cobra Ball in general until September 1, 1983, when Korean Air Lines Flight 007 was shot down as it crossed over Sakhalin Island. In fact, a Cobra Ball operation was in progress that night, watching for an SS-25 missile that was launched from Plesetsk. The airliner had nothing to do with the Cobra Ball operation.

Combat Sent, another of the core programs in Big Safari, began using RC-135Us to collect specific technical electronic intelligence in 1971. Used against radar, for example, their highly sensitive receivers absorb signals with such precision and depth that jammers can be programmed to counteract them. Rivet Joint, which started the following year, uses RC-135Vs to collect more general, or operational, intelligence that fixes the various types of radar and their locations without going into great detail. Rivet Joint aircraft also intercept communication around the world and are therefore subsidized by the National Security Agency. That delights the Air Force because it spreads out the cost of the missions.

ALMOST FROM THE time the EC- and RC-135s began operations in the early 1960s, they flew in very close proximity to Soviet fighters. The opponents often photographed each other at distances so close they couldn't get the whole plane into the picture. When a MiG, a Yak, or a Sukhoi came in at a distance that could be measured in feet, it was said to be "tucked in." Sometimes fighter pilots and reconnaissance crews waved; sometimes they exchanged more pointed greetings. Once in a while, RC-135 crewmen held *Playboy* centerfolds to the window, drawing the appreciative fighter pilots in to breathtakingly close quarters. And sometimes a cocky Russian would pull in close behind one of the Rivet Joint or other aircraft to show its crew he had them covered; that he could blow them away with the flick of a finger.

There were two ways to respond to that kind of harassment. One was to ignore it, which happened most of the time. But once in a while pilots eased back on the throttles ever so slightly until their plane, and therefore the fighter that was trailing it, hit the fighter's stall speed. The Russians sometimes became so engrossed in studying the large American reconnaissance aircraft just ahead of them that they didn't notice the trouble until they fell into a dangerous high-altitude stall.

And one story claimed that fuel dump tubes were sometimes opened on the four-engine jets, dousing the trailing fighters with fuel. The metaphor of the unarmed reconnaissance plane urinating on its heavily armed pursuer smacked of machismo. It was a great story. But it was late-night officers' club malarkey spun by someone with an identity problem. Spraying fuel on a fighter, and therefore endangering it, could easily have gotten its pilot so enraged that he'd have opened fire. Missions against the Russians were dangerous enough without needlessly provoking them into destroying a plane and killing its crew for the sake of a self-satisfying prank.

HOWEVER MANY AIRMEN waved hands, extended middle fingers, or displayed centerfolds throughout the 1960s, bullets still flew and men continued to be killed in the twilight war.

On April 28, 1965, an RB-47H from the Fifty-fifth Strategic Reconnaissance Wing flying out of Yokota in the sixth hour of a seven-and-a-half-hour ferret mission was attacked without warning by North Korean MiG-17s over international waters as it flew toward Wonson. First, one of the ravens picked up a weak airborne intercept radar signal that could have meant a MiG was nearby. Then there was a message from somewhere that "bogies" were in the area. But neither Lt. Col. Hobart D. Mattison, the aircraft commander, nor 1st Lt. Henry E. Dubuy, the copilot, saw anything threatening. Suddenly, the Stratojet was hit by cannon fire from two MiGs that were above and in the five o'clock position, just off to the right. Mattison put the plane into a dive while Dubuy swung his seat around and asked for permission to shoot back. "Shoot the bastard down," Mattison shouted before asking Capt. Robert J. Rogers, the navigator, for a heading "to get the hell out of here."

"By this time," 1st Lt. George V. Back, the raven 2, would recall, "all hell had broken loose. The pilot had his hands full of rapidly deteriorating airplane, the copilot was trying to shoot the bastards visually, the navigator was trying to give the pilot a heading, the raven 1 was dumping chaff, and the second MiG-17 was moving in for his gunnery practice." Mattison did have his hands full.

Each of the MiGs made two hit-and-run firing passes that severely damaged the hydraulic system and the number three engine and caused other damage. Turbine blades from the engine broke off while spinning at high speed and not only damaged the number two engine next to them, but sliced into the fuselage. Number three was shaking violently and number four was so badly shot up that it had to be shut down altogether. Number five also spit some turbine blades but it somehow continued to work. If that wasn't bad enough, the rear main fuel tank was hit by cannon fire, ruptured, and was burning and leaking fuel, the rear wheel well bulkhead buckled because of the heat from the fire, there were shrapnel holes on both sides of the fuselage, the tail was badly damaged, ammunition canisters took a direct hit, and one of Dubuy's guns was knocked off its mount, making it impossible to use. Aside from that the Stratojet was in fine shape.

Dubuy used his other gun to get off more than 300 rounds visually—the MiGs were so close and low that the fire control radar couldn't get a lock on them—and actually nailed one of them. It nosed up slightly and then fell away, fatally hit, most likely with its controls shot up. The other MiG broke for home.

George Back would report that both fighters tried, unsuccessfully, to fire into the RB-47H's belly, where the ravens were. Unlike the ravens on Bill Palm's RB-47H, which was shot down off the Kola Peninsula on July 1, 1960, the three on Mattison's aircraft lived to tell about the attack. The plane, 43290, limped back to Yokota bleeding fuel vapor, rattling badly, and on emergency power. The story of getting it down could have been scripted in Hollywood. The landing gear hydraulic system was so badly shot up that Capt. Robert C. Winters, the raven 1, had to use the emergency system to crank it down. And when an air traffic controller told Mattison to pick up the proper glide slope and adjust his rate of descent, after being told by Mattison that he had to get the crippled plane down any way he could, the pilot lost his composure and "growled" that if he needed any further instructions from the Yokota tower, he would ask. The RB-47H finally hit the runway, bounced so high it nearly struck a fire suppression helicopter flying above it, and finally screeched to a stop after narrowly missing fire trucks and ambulances. All six of its crew walked away. It had been 43290's first and last operational mission. The plane was a write-off.

Eight months later, on December 14, an RB-57F from Big Safari's 7407th Support Squadron went down under mysterious circumstances. The stretch-winged recce aircraft was based in West Germany but was staging out of Incirlik in Turkey that day for work over the Black Sea. Ten days after the plane disappeared, Vasily Kuznetsov, the Soviet deputy foreign minister, called U.S. ambassador Foy Kohler into his office in Moscow and delivered a sternly worded sermon on the evils of American aerial espionage. Kuznetsov's lecture smacked of the sort of veiled, Byzantine reference for which the men in the Kremlin were notorious. He specifically mentioned the flight of the lost RB-57F as an example of unacceptable behavior, but would provide not one additional scrap of information even after Kohler asked for it. U.S., Soviet, and Turkish ships found part of the plane's wreckage floating where it went down. But neither its pilot not its reconnaissance systems officer was ever heard of again.

The North Koreans had a reputation for being particularly aggressive in ranging far out to sea to attack both reconnaissance planes and ships. On January 23, 1968, they sent patrol boats into international waters and surrounded the Navy electronic intelligence ship *Pueblo*, carrying a crew of eighty-three. When its skipper, Cmdr. Lloyd Bucher, tried to break out of the trap, the North Koreans opened fire with machine guns, killing a twenty-one-year-old seaman. The other eighty-two crewmen were thrown in prison in Pyongyang. They were released eleven months later after hard negotiations.

The North Koreans struck again on April 15, 1969. The target this time was an EC-121M Warning Star, the Navy's version of Lockheed's distinctive, three-finned, propeller-driven Super Constellation airliner. The civilian version was an exceptionally clean-lined, graceful airplane. Its intelligence-collecting and early warning cousin carried a high radome that protruded on top of its curved spine like a dorsal fin and a huge bulging dome on its belly that made it look pregnant. It also carried a crew of thirty-one, most of whom worked at rows of consoles on either side of the cabin.

This particular EC-121M was attached to the VQ-1 reconnaissance squadron at Atsugi and was on a routine signals intelligence mission, which included communication intercepts, well out over international waters off the coast of the Musu Peninsula south of Chongjin. The unarmed aircraft was supposed to fly a 120-mile-long racetrack pattern for several hours, soaking up signals coming from North Korea, then land at Osan Air Base in South Korea. The project was called Beggar Shadow and had been flown for two years by Air Force and Navy Warning Stars without incident. There had been more than 190 similar flights off the east coast of North Korea in the first three months of 1969 alone.

Six hours after takeoff, the lumbering aircraft, which was being followed on Air Force radar in Japan and South Korea, transmitted a routine radio-teletype position and activity report. Forty-seven minutes later it disappeared off the radarscopes ninety miles southeast of Chongjin. While the big plane was being tracked by the two Air Force radar stations, the Air Force Security Service, which worked for the NSA, was intercepting North Ko-

rean radar that was also tracking the Navy plane. Minutes before
the blip went off the radar screens, two other blips—North Korean air force MiGs—were spotted heading for it and communication intercepts of North Korean voice and Morse code signals
clearly indicated that an attack was about to start. The Air Force
Security Service station in Osan warned Lt. Cmdr. James H.
Overstreet, the aircraft commander, to get out of there. But it was
too late. The MiGs caught up with the plane as Overstreet was
turning toward South Korea. The defenseless aircraft vanished a
minute later. Two bodies and some wreckage were all that was recovered. The other twenty-nine men disappeared.

The loss of the EC-121M was an especially sobering experience for the Navy because of the number of men lost, the fact
that the plane itself was as helpless as an airliner, and because it
really was far from land when it was shot down. Its loss was a wa-
tershed event that shook the technical intelligence community.
Transcripts of enemy fighter pilots talking to each other and to
their controllers as they closed in and then attacked, which were
produced after the RB-47H shootdown off the Kola Peninsula on
July 1, 1960, for example, showed the NSA's prowess at communication intercepts, but they were too late to save the lives of the
men under attack. The Pentagon decided after the loss of the
thirty-one airmen to make an all-out effort to increase the warning time to crews on peripheral reconnaissance missions that an
attack was imminent. Intercepts and radar signals showing that
fighters were scrambling and being vectored to a reconnaissance
aircraft—that an attack was starting—had to be used at the earli-
est possible moment to warn the crew to break and run.

And there was another repercussion. The shootdown forced
mission planners to think particularly hard about whether a given
operation was really worth the loss of a crew. The tendency to
send ferrets on missions that were of dubious value, or that were
marginal, abruptly changed after the EC-121M was lost. It was a
monumental event in airborne reconnaissance.

THE CREW OF the last American reconnaissance plane to come under fire by Soviet MiGs was far luckier. They were flying in a

KC-135R in a program called Briar Patch, which preceded the highly specialized Combat Sent technical missions. On that day, November 17, 1970, the Americans were trailing a hundred-foot-long antenna with a signal emitter over international waters off Vaygach Island in the hope it would get the Russians to turn on a special defense radar code-named Part Time. It was like trolling for a bite from the back of a fishing boat. Vaygach, just south of Novaya Zemlya and near the big fighter base at Amderma, was squarely in the path of an American polar bombing attack. Furthermore, the Russians were testing new missiles in the area, so they were particularly sensitive to intrusion.

The KC-135R flew toward the radar from a distance of thirty miles and then turned back toward the open sea. As it did, a pair of MiG-17s appeared and slipped into formation with it. "The MiGs were in so tight on that leg you could not see their entire airframes," Max R. Moore, a navigator, would vividly recall thirty years later to the day. Just after the reconnaissance plane turned, both MiGs fired warning shots. Ignoring them, but wary of a collision, James W. Jones, the aircraft commander, and his copilot used hand signals to tell the MiG pilots that he was going to turn back toward Vaygach for a second pass at the radar.

The pilot of the lead MiG radioed his controller at Belusa Guba to report that the American reconnaissance plane was turning inbound once again and asked for instructions. The KC-135R was monitoring the conversation very closely; that's why it carried Russian-speaking linguists. "The tension was palpable while we waited," Moore added. "The Russian controller's first reply was in the best of our beloved SAC's tradition: 'Stand by.' It may have only been minutes thereafter," the veteran navigator went on, "but it seemed like an eternity until the word came back to 'escort the target.' Then," Max Moore added with a whimsical flourish, "they shot us down and we all died!" In fact, the fighters held their fire and finally peeled off and disappeared. The Briar Patch KC-135R made it home without a scratch.

Certainly the radar was a priority target for the U.S. intelligence collector. But something else was going on. The KC-135R flew the entire mission over international waters. In flying a second track at the Vaygach radar, even after being warned off with cannon fire, Jones was making a statement: he was asserting his plane's right to be there. While the Department of State fretted continuously about the political repercussions of violating Soviet and other nations' sovereign frontiers, and possibly causing yet another international incident, it also adamantly insisted that U.S. aircraft, like U.S. ships, be guaranteed the right of free passage for whatever reason outside the territorial limits set by international law. Many ferret and other reconnaissance flights in the Peacetime Airborne Reconnaissance Program therefore flew not only to collect intelligence, but to maintain their legal right to be where they were. The lawyers at Foggy Bottom had no doubt that if the Russians succeeded in keeping U.S. aircraft beyond thirty miles, a de facto precedent would be set and eventually extended to fifty miles, and then to seventy-five, and then to who-knew-where.*

And in that regard, one aspect of international law haunted the peripheral shootdowns. There is a very old precedent that attacking another country's ship in international waters is an act of war. But that doctrine was never applied to the shooting down of reconnaissance planes, nor, apparently, was it even raised in public. Going to war because a ship was attacked, let alone an airplane, would be absurd on the face of it (unless the "plaintiff" wanted to get into the war and needed an excuse, as happened in the Tonkin Gulf in 1964, when U.S. destroyers were allegedly attacked by North Vietnamese patrol boats). But legality aside, there was a tacit understanding that the nature of collecting intelligence, certainly of ferreting, was inherently provocative, and that made it political. Lawyers therefore routinely assembled shootdown cases for presentation at the U.N. or the World Court, but they did so knowing that international law was subservient to higher political considerations.

One of those lawyers, Samuel Klaus, specialized in the controversy over peripheral reconnaissance. He amassed an enormous

---

*In 1999 the United States unilaterally extended its own domain to twenty-four nautical miles where the enforcement of narcotics, fishing, and pollution laws were concerned. Coast Guard and other federal agencies were given the right to board foreign ships within that range. ("U.S. Doubles Offshore Zone Under Its Law," *The New York Times*, September 3, 1999.)

file on virtually every aspect of U.S. operations, together with applicable international laws, for use in prosecuting claims against the Soviet Union after shootdowns. Most of the records are still stored in boxes at the National Archive in College Park, Maryland. Others are secreted elsewhere and remain classified to this day. Klaus was an unheralded prodigy who graduated Phi Beta Kappa from the City College of New York in 1924 and, three years later, from Columbia Law School. He went on to become a brigadier general in the Army while serving in postwar Germany as a legal consultant and then began specializing in the shootdowns and related incidents as a special counsel at the Department of State in Washington. The fruits of much of Klaus's work went to support his country's position at the United Nations and in diplomatic exchanges with the Soviet Union and Communist China. He died of a heart attack outside his home in Washington in the summer of 1963 at the age of fifty-eight.

THE EC-121M ATTACKED in 1969 was the last strategic reconnaissance plane to be shot down during the cold war. By the early 1970s, both superpowers were settling into a political modus vivendi. For one thing, by then the Soviet Union had enough nuclear weapons, as well as a reconstituted army and navy, to ease the old paranoia about being destroyed without a reprisal. While allowing for the fact that some deranged, Strangelovian individual could actually attack the Soviet Union, successive Soviet leaders and their advisers knew that no rational person would order an attack, given the certainty of a devastating counterattack. In that circumstance, the Russians gradually became less brittle about the sanctity of their Siberian boundary.

In addition, satellite reconnaissance was then more than a decade old, with each side collecting avalanches of intelligence from the protected precinct of space. While aerial reconnaissance remained important, and certainly for ferreting, most of the action had shifted to low earth orbit, at least where prying secrets out of the USSR and Communist China were concerned.

Finally, by the time the Briar Patch mission was flown in the autumn of 1970, President Richard M. Nixon had started strategic arms limitation talks with the Kremlin and a period of détente between the superpowers had begun. Two years later, he made an unprecedented visit to the People's Republic of China. Neither the Russians nor the Chinese were going to risk changing that climate by shooting down an American reconnaissance plane. The Russians, in particular, were becoming noticeably calm. Then, in 1980, Ronald W. Reagan was elected president.

IF THERE WAS ever going to be a major clash because of U.S. flights along the Soviet border, perhaps leading to all-out war, it came in the third year of Ronald Reagan's presidency, when a war of words escalated to what is now called the 1983 Soviet war scare. Its basis was a growing belief in the Kremlin that Reagan was an unsophisticated mental lightweight and right-wing ideologue whose irrational aberrations could have led him to do something as insane as starting a third world war.

The so-called post-détente second cold war began in March 1983, though it had been building since the Reagan presidency started a little more than two years earlier. That month, Reagan announced that he wanted a ballistic missile defense system, which even he acknowledged was not only destabilizing, but would violate the 1972 Anti-Ballistic Missile Treaty that was the linchpin of the Strategic Arms Limitation Treaty, or SALT. It was soon lampooned as "Star Wars" by the news media. The Pentagon responded by calling it the Strategic Defense Initiative, or SDI, which was loftier-sounding.

Meanwhile, Reagan denounced the Soviet Union as the "focus of evil in the world" and as an "evil empire." Yuri Andropov, a KGB alumnus and Soviet general secretary, responded by calling Reagan insane and a liar. "Then," as a CIA history of the war scare episode wryly noted, "things got nasty."

Andropov may or may not have known that Reagan was fascinated by the biblical prophecy of Armageddon, the final world-ending battle between the forces of good and evil, but as early as May 1981 he told a closed meeting of KGB officers that the United States was preparing for a surprise nuclear attack. He was so convinced he was right that he took the occasion to announce a new intelligence collection effort, code-named Ryan, to monitor indications the United States was preparing to launch a major war.

It was preparing for no such thing, although Curtis LeMay's dictum about being prepared to strike first was by then accepted in the Kremlin (as SAC's patron saint no doubt would have wished). But within months of the start of Reagan's first term, Andropov, Brezhnev, the Politburo, and the General Staff looked beyond their country's vast frontier and saw clear indications to the contrary.

The United States was in fact embarked on a wide-ranging secret psychological warfare program called psyops, for psychological operations, that Reagan authorized in March 1981, two months after taking office. In essence, it was intended to keep the Reds off balance, jumpy, and guessing about U.S. intentions. It was therefore the antithesis of superpower stability.

The operations consisted mostly of air and naval probes, some of them hair-raising, along the Soviet periphery. Although servicemen and -women in the many thousands were involved in the feints (the Russians correctly called them provocations), the big picture was known only to a small number of higher-ups on the White House staff, in the Pentagon, and, of course, in the Kremlin. Fred Ikle, the undersecretary of defense at the time, called the operation "very sensitive. Nothing was written down about it, so there would be no paper trail."

Gen. John T. Chain, Jr., who took over command of SAC in 1986, recalled years later that Air Force fighters and bombers roared straight at the Soviet Union from all sides. "Sometimes we would send bombers over the North Pole and their radars would click on. Other times [nuclear-capable] fighter-bombers would probe their Asian or European periphery." There would be several flights a week during "peak" periods, he added, and they would come irregularly "to make the effect all the more unsettling." Then they would suddenly stop. A few weeks later, they would start again, frazzling jittery Russians who unquestionably believed that when the Americans became convinced that they, the Russians, were beginning to take the phony attacks for granted and relax their defenses, the real one would come.

"It really got to them," said Dr. William Schneider, an undersecretary of state for military assistance and technology, who saw top-secret "after action" reports. The feints were made to order for ferrets, which took part in them. The Russians "didn't know what it all meant," Schneider explained. "A squadron would fly straight at Soviet airspace, and other radars would light up and units would go on alert. Then at the last minute, the squadron would peel off and return home." It was a technique the reconnaissance crews had used for years. This time, however, the Russians undoubtedly believed Reagan might have been trying to provoke them into an attack that justified all-out war. They were therefore prudent enough to hold their fire. So no reconnaissance crewman had his name added to the long shootdown list.

THE DANGEROUS WAR scare of 1983, and the events leading up to it, were watched and listened to by robots that had been in orbit for several years. Ironically, the day after the KC-135R became the last reconnaissance plane to face enemy fire—November 18, 1970—a U.S. reconnaissance satellite blasted off from Vandenberg Air Force Base near Santa Barbara, California, and streaked south, climbing into an orbit that would take it safely over the same territory that had consumed so many Americans, dead and missing in action, in the twenty years since the Navy Privateer was shot down over the Baltic. And that satellite, which was part of a top-secret program called Corona, was far from the first to sail over very dangerous places well out of reach of the fighters and missiles. A succession of them had been doing it for a decade.

The reconnaissance revolution that accelerated in the 1970s and then well into the 1980s sent back photographs and signals intelligence which, collectively, described an enemy caught in the throes of relentless stagnation and disintegration. No intelligence analyst could study the satellite imagery and conclude that seventy years of communism had produced an economic and political system whose inefficiency and inequities were causing it to implode. But hints abounded. As the 1980s began, the "spies in the sky" showed the once-vaunted Red Army locked in a war in Afghanistan with guerrillas who were bleeding it as the U.S. military had been bled in Vietnam. The army that had vanquished Napoleon and Hitler was being drained by well-organized irregulars who hit and ran, then hit again.

Four years later, the ubiquitous satellites sent down very detailed imagery of the results of a series of massive explosions at the Northern Fleet's ammunition depot at Severomorsk (which, like nearby Murmansk, had been a frequent target for ferrets working out of Great Britain). Then, a year later, the infamous reactor at Chernobyl, in the Ukraine, blew its top after an ill-conceived experiment went awry and its core melted down. Radioactive air pervaded the area and contaminated a swath of territory that extended to parts of Germany and Sweden. Chernobyl quickly became a metaphor for the danger of nuclear energy, runaway technology, and institutional incompetence. It was a symbol worthy of Dostoevsky; a sign of a society in growing disarray. So was an aging air force, repeated accidents on nuclear submarines, and a costly space program that returned nothing anyone could use. Old babushkas standing in line for hours to buy bread and sausage were not thinking about Mars. Decay was infecting the system subtly but massively.

THE DISINTEGRATION OF the Soviet Union, the decade of intermittent warfare in Yugoslavia, and the war in the Persian Gulf in 1991 following Iraq's invasion of Kuwait, coincided to transform Rivet Joint, Combat Sent, Cobra Ball, other Big Safari operations, and Ninth Reconnaissance Wing U-2 operations. They had been almost exclusively cold war–oriented; now they focused on regional conflicts as well as on Russia, the remaining Communist giant, China, and smaller threats in Asia and the Middle East.

The days of fine-tuning receivers the way tumblers are worked on a safe are over. Cobra Ball, Combat Sent, Rivet Joint, and other such operations became fully automated when digital computing took hold in the 1980s. They are programmed to search the various wavelengths, lock onto preselected or new signals, and not only record them, but transmit them to ground stations in real time—as they are picked up.

It's axiomatic in the news business that disasters make headlines, while routine activities don't. This also applies to air combat operations. Planes shot down in war are news. Those not shot down, and particularly those that fly alone in the clandestine programs, go about their work unnoticed, unrecognized, and unacknowledged by the public.

Allied air combat losses both during the Gulf War in 1991 and in the air war against Kosovo and Belgrade eight years later were negligible. Only two fighters were lost over Yugoslavia, an F-117A Nighthawk stealth fighter and an F-16A Fighting Falcon, both of which seem to have been downed by lucky-shot "golden BBs." The fact that other fighter-bombers pummeled Iraqi and Serbian air bases and other military installations, destroyed bridges and communication complexes, and generally ranged freely over enemy territory without loss, did not make headlines. But it happened because Fifty-fifth Strategic Reconnaissance Wing Rivet Joint and Combat Sent ferrets quietly got the measure of the opposition's radar so it could be jammed—its brains scrambled—by the attackers. Every time Saddam Hussein's air defense radars locked onto American and other coalition aircraft during the Gulf War and for years afterward, they were almost always jammed, attacked, and demolished. The attackers made the headlines as usual. The recce crews who ferreted the radar for them and the NSA operators who monitored communication and the whereabouts of Iraqi defensive units did so in total obscurity, also as usual.

The Cold War and Beyond, a 163-page abbreviated history of the U.S. Air Force, published in 1997 on the service's fiftieth birthday, was filled with arcane facts, including humanitarian operations, record-breaking flights, and personal achievements. It noted, for example, that in 1990 Marcelite Jordan Harris became the first black woman to reach brigadier general; that same year, Gen. Claire L. Chennault of World War II Flying Tiger fame was honored by having his portrait put on a forty-cent postal stamp. It reported hundreds of facts, important and trivial: although F-117A fighter-bombers amounted to less than 2.5 percent of all coalition aircraft in Desert Storm, they attacked more than 31 percent of strategic targets in Iraq on the first day of the war. It also noted that on January 17, 1991, B-52Gs flew the longest bombing mission in history when they went from Barksdale Air Force Base in Louisiana to Iraq, fired thirty-five cruise missiles, and returned to Barksdale unscathed. Yet, as usual, there was no mention of the fact that Iraqi radar was either knocked out of action or jammed because it had been ferreted during Desert Shield. Nowhere in the compendium of information was there a single reference to an operational reconnaissance mission of any kind, let alone to ferreting radar, tapping communication traffic, and collecting piles of imagery from planes and satellites. As usual, the shadow warriors were studiously kept out of the public domain; in effect, they were once again airbrushed out of the picture.

DECADES BEFORE THE wars in Iraq and Yugoslavia, the technical intelligence collectors had created robots that would increase the "take" by a very wide margin while lowering or ending altogether the risk to humans. The idea, which went back to the camera-carrying balloons in the late 1940s, was to turn the collection process over to machines.

Knowing that Soviet overflights were dangerous, particularly after what happened to Powers, Kelly Johnson's bountiful imagination conceived of a drone—an unmanned aircraft—that could be carried, piggyback, on a specially modified A-12. If the thing had a 1,250-nautical-mile range, could reach Mach 3 or faster, and could cruise at 90,000 feet, he reasoned, it could be sent over any denied territory (certainly including China) with virtual impunity. It would have so tiny a radar cross section that it would be nearly invisible and, in any case, would be unstoppable because of its high performance.

The plan was to mount a manta-shaped, ramjet-powered drone called a D-21 on the rear back of the A-12, which was whimsically rechristened the M (for Mother) -12. The M-12 would take off carrying the D (for Daughter) -21 and a second crewman, called a launch control officer, sitting behind the pilot in a compartment that would eventually be used by reconnaissance systems officers in SR-71s. The M-12 was supposed to launch the D-21 at triple sonic speed to get its own ramjet started, and then turn back for home. The drone would penetrate enemy airspace steered by its programmed inertial navigation system, take pictures at timed intervals, and then speed away. When it was back in friendly airspace, the waterproof camera unit containing the film would be jettisoned by parachute. The D-21 itself would descend to an altitude at which a barometric timer would set off an explosive charge that blew it to pieces. The camera and film would be snagged by a C-130 as they floated down and taken to an air base where the film would be processed. As usual, the operation, which was called Tagboard, was a lot harder to accomplish than to invent.

It took more than a year of practice, starting in late December 1964, just to get the M-12 and the D-21 conditioned to fly together. After a half dozen launch failures, "Mother and Daughter" finally broke the filial bond at 72,000 feet over the Nevada desert on July 3, 1966. The Lockheed test pilot pulled the M-12 up ever so slightly, then nosed it just as slightly down. As he did so, a blast of compressed air in the pylon that connected them pushed the D-21 up. It fired clear and was on its way. This was followed by another successful test.

Then disaster struck on July 31. The third test took place 300 miles off the California coast with the first D-21 that was fully loaded with fuel and at a slightly faster speed than the other two. With Mother streaking along at a little more than Mach 3.2, Ray Torrick, the launch control officer, hit the button that separated the Daughter. At that worst of all possible moments, the D-21's ramjet had an unstart. It shot back down and slammed into the M-12's pylon. Like coming down hard on one end of a seesaw, that sent the other end of the M-12 pitching upward. In an instant, the plane's chines and the rest of its flatish underside caught the airstream. The effect of the wide surface running into air while it was moving at more than three times the speed of sound was exactly the same as a kite being pulled by a car going sixty miles an hour. It broke up. The front of the fuselage, with Torrick and test pilot William Park strapped in and being hit by incredible gravitational force, was ripped off the wings and tumbled through the sky. Both punched out. Park was picked up by a helicopter. But Torrick, who was trapped under his parachute, drowned before he could be pulled out of the water.

That was the last attempt at launching a D-21 from an M-12. A handful of modified D-21s flew over the Lop Nor nuclear test facility in China after being launched by B-52s in a highly secret operation called Senior Bowl. The Chinese did pick up at least one of the D-21s on radar, but mistook it for an SR-71 and, following Russian practice with the U-2s, sent a demarche to Washington. When President Nixon visited China early in 1972, he promised his angry hosts that the "SR-71" flights over their country would be stopped. And they were. The problem-ridden program was ended and the remaining Daughters were shipped to the Air Force's boneyard at Davis-Monthan Air Force Base in Arizona, where they remain stored.

The D-21 was undoubtedly the most complex remotely piloted vehicle, or unmanned aerial vehicle, or drone, to be designed to collect intelligence. But it was no means the only one. The United States and several other nations figured out early that drones used for tactical reconnaissance—in direct support of ground operations as opposed to collecting strategic intelligence for the bigger picture—were cheaper and safer than manned aircraft for many kinds of missions. Teledyne Ryan, the biggest U.S. producer of remotely piloted reconnaissance aircraft, suggested turning U-2s into unmanned collectors in a program it called Red Wagon after Powers was shot down. Funds went to the SR-71 instead. Two years later it came up with its Model 147, first called Firebee, which was developed primarily as a photoreconnaissance collector in the Big Safari program. More than 2,500 Firebee missions were flown over Vietnam alone, all of them carried and released by C-130s, with most used to collect intelligence. Others were used to jam North Vietnamese radar. Still others were used over other Communist countries, including China, and by Israel during the Yom Kippur War for reconnaissance and other jobs. (One reportedly decoyed thirty-two SA-2 missiles and made it safely home.)

Lockheed came up with a battlefield surveillance drone named Aquila in 1972 that has a large twelve-foot wingspan and uses a pusher-type propeller engine to carry video and infrared cameras within thirty-one miles of where it is launched. Yet another Army drone named Predator, this one patterned after a successful Israeli design, the Tadiran Mastiff, has even better performance. And there have been, and are, scores of others.

The old Red Wagon idea of using U-2-sized drones was resurrected at the turn of the century in a program called Global Hawk. The idea was to use the large unmanned aircraft for high-altitude, long-endurance missions in direct support of battlefield commanders. They would take digital pictures of the battlefield and the enemy's rear positions and send them to U.S. units in near-real time—virtually as they occurred. Unlike Firebees, which are fast, and Raptors, which are relatively small, Global Hawk was designed to loiter high over an area for hours with a large array of sensors, sending back a continuous stream of intelligence.

SATELLITES ORBITING EARTH were understood as early as the 1940s to be the logical extension of the high-flying strategic reconnaissance planes' domain. Space was considered to be the ultimate reconnaissance perch because it has two decisive advantages over operations in the atmosphere. At six times the altitude the highest-flying aircraft could reach, satellites increased the breadth of worldwide coverage by an enormous margin. The Soviet Union, Communist China, and other countries—allies such as France and Israel included—could now be "penetrated" with impunity. A satellite could photograph more targets in the USSR on a single pass than had all the U-2 flights combined.

The other advantage lay in the fact that, like unmanned aerial vehicles, no lives were put at risk. No one would grieve when one of the high-flying robots came to a fiery end while plunging back into the atmosphere or blew to smithereens on a launchpad, scattering its smashed glass eye and mirrors, electronic components, tubular innards, and shards of burning, twisted metal in all directions. The satellites were not only more efficient intelligence collectors, they were politically and emotionally liberating because they flew without the most vulnerable component in the collection loop: humans. No more Americans were going to lose their lives or be thrown in prison, no more Air Force and Navy planes were going to be shot up for collecting strategic intelligence over denied territory.

And with robots doing that chore, the potential political embarrassment that haunted the Truman and Eisenhower administrations with every penetration flight evaporated. The air over a nation might be sovereign, but the void above the air was not. It was an international domain like the high seas.

In fact, while poor Eisenhower faced the country's wrath when Sputnik 1 became the first satellite to reach space, the news made his top foreign policy advisers almost jubilant. They knew that the Soviet Union had no real technological advantage over the United States. But Sputnik 1 and its two successors set a precedent that Sam Klaus and other international lawyers at State loved. If Soviet satellites had the right to fly over the United States, then U.S. satellites had as much right to fly over the Soviet Union. But unlike the Sputniks, they would carry cameras.

The desperate need to know what was going on behind the Iron Curtain had, if anything, increased in the frenzied decade between 1947 and 1958, when the C-118 courier and then the eavesdropping C-130A were shot down over Soviet Armenia. That is why the nation's first satellite programs, collectively called WS-117L (Weapons System 117 Lockheed), were specifically designed to collect intelligence. One, called Samos, was supposed to take photographs in orbit, electronically read out the images, and then transmit them to Earth in near-real time. It was an important goal, and one that would eventually be realized, but it ran into technical problems early on.

Meanwhile, the program called Corona was thrown into the breach. It was approved by the Eisenhower White House in mid-April 1958 for development by the CIA and the Pentagon's Advanced Research Projects Agency, or ARPA. The program got its name from a Smith-Corona typewriter that happened to be in the room when the engineering concept was finalized.

Science, the amorphous cover for the Peacetime Airborne Reconnaissance Program's "electromagnetic detection" flights and other forays, was invoked again and extended to the new realm of space. Corona therefore used satellites called Discoverers that flew under science's respected mantle. They were designed to be built into all-purpose Agena upper stages that would be carried to space on top of modified Thor intermediate-range ballistic missiles. Agena would carry the Discoverer payload in its nose. Thor, the first stage, would get the Agena high enough so its own rocket could kick in and make it to an orbit around Earth that was near-polar—almost over the two poles. Then the Thor would separate from the Agena and fall away. The intelligence people wanted a near-polar orbit because almost every place on Earth, including all of the Eurasian landmass, would pass beneath a satellite on that route and could therefore be photographed.

Discoverer's camera system, which was named the KH-1, for Keyhole Number One, would take the photographs. That done, the Agena's gold-plated nose cone, which contained the film, would be shot out of orbit—"de-orbited," in the new space vernacular—and parachute down to an area northwest of Hawaii, where it would be snagged in midair by Air Force transport planes trailing trapezes. It wasn't easy. But it also wasn't unprecedented. Genetrix cameras were caught that way after their balloons floated across the USSR; the D-21 drone's cameras and film were caught that way; and Air Force transports assigned to the Corona program practiced capturing simulated nose cones that were dropped from very-high-altitude balloons and parachuted to earth.

Discoverer 1, the first Corona launch, went up from Vandenberg Air Force Base in California on February 28, 1959, and was a success in that it made it to orbit, though without a capsule. The next eleven Discoverer launches, starting on April 13, were punishing failures for one reason or another. Richard M. Bissell, Jr., who ran the CIA's U-2 operation, also ran Corona. As with the U-2 program, he gave the contractor—this time the Lockheed Missile Systems Division, not the Skunk Works—a free hand to get the job done with a minimum of second-guessing. But Corona, like Oxcart, was vastly more complicated than the U-2 program and was therefore prone to the mechanical equivalent of heart attacks. There was no satellite program book to follow. Lockheed, its subcontractors, the CIA, and the Air Force (which launched and was supposed to recover the things) had to write the book. And as they did so, the failures continued.

Some Discoverers never made it to orbit. Others went into the wrong orbit, or had subsystem malfunctions, or recovery failures, or booster problems. Discoverer 10's Thor blew up seconds after launch, creating a pyrotechnic display that could be seen for miles and showering the launchpad and the surrounding area with flaming debris. Eisenhower began asking Allen Dulles, his director of Central Intelligence, for explanations, and Dulles asked Bissell.

Bissell called it "a most heartbreaking business. If an airplane goes on a test flight and something malfunctions, and it gets back, the pilot can tell you about the malfunction, and you can look it over and find out. But in the case of a recce satellite, you fire the damned thing off and you've got some telemetry, and you never get it back. There is no pilot, of course, and you've got no hardware. You never see it again. In the case of Corona, it went on and on."

The first break came when Discoverer 13 splashed into the Pacific on August 11, 1960, and was recovered. Discoverer 14 became the first successful reconnaissance satellite and the first spacecraft recovered directly from space when it floated down on August 18 and was snagged by a C-119 Flying Boxcar of the 6594th Test Wing. The plane's crew was quietly decorated as soon as they landed at Honolulu with the capsule. The film was rushed to Washington and shown to Eisenhower, who was amazed not only by the quality of the images but by the breadth of the coverage. Photointerpreters who pored over clear pictures of 1,650,000 square nautical miles of the Soviet Union said they were "flabbergasted" and called the take nothing short of "stupendous." And, again, no lives had been put at risk.

The Corona program used a series of satellites progressively called KH-1–KH-4B to sweep the Soviet Union, Communist China, the Warsaw Pact nations, and elsewhere through the last launch on May 25, 1972. More than one hundred of the satellites turned up bomber and ballistic missile bases, nuclear weapons and production facilities, submarine construction factories, and many hundreds of other military operations in their twelve years of service. As with aerial reconnaissance, the principal emphasis was on finding and describing (in order of importance) long-range land- and submarine-launched ballistic missiles, long-range bombers, and nuclear facilities.

The Corona satellites were succeeded by progressively refined spacecraft in the KH series that could take pictures in which objects as small as five or six inches could be identified. And starting in December 1976 with the KH-11, the imagery was sent down digitally in near-real time.

THE SAME PROCESS took place in electronic intelligence, where satellites that could monitor all kinds of electronic signals, including communication, were quickly invented and refined. The most revolutionary was conceived by the CIA's Directorate for Science and Technology in 1965 as an integrated satellite that could be parked 22,300 miles out, where it would remain facing the Soviet Union and China while its huge antenna soaked up telemetry from missile tests and as many as 11,000 microwave telephone calls simultaneously. Rhyolite satellites, which like many reconnaissance spacecraft were built by TRW, started going up in June 1970. They and the other high-flying intelligence collectors were bought and operated by the National Reconnaissance Office, an organization so secret its letterhead logo (a satellite circling Earth) was classified. The NRO went public in 1995 but still guards the secrets of its intelligence-collecting spacecraft.

FERRETING MOVED TO space as well, or at least radar-sniffing satellites did. For purists, the term "ferret" belongs exclusively to manned aircraft that in effect do what the furry critters on the plains do: actively flush out vermin by pursuing them. Satellites don't do that. They are totally passive and simply record whatever comes their way. But they are generally called ferrets anyway.

Whatever they are called, it didn't take long for the Department of Defense to produce spacecraft that located and measured Soviet and other nations' air defense radars. Eisenhower approved the first of them in 1959. It was named GRAB, for Galactic Radiation and Background, and was operated by the Naval Research Laboratory. The heavily classified radar sniffer, which was relatively small and looked a little like the metal helmet on old-time deep-sea divers' outfits, went up with a publicly announced Solar Radiation satellite for the first time on June 22, 1960.

GRAB was soon joined by other radar searchers. During the 1961–62 period, a second type was designed to go up with the larger Agena-Discoverer photoreconnaissance spacecraft in near-polar orbits. The relationship between the radar and PHOTINT satellites was intimate. They were made by Lockheed Missiles and Space Company in Sunnyvale, California, and were designed to be compatible with the Agena spacecraft Lockheed made to carry Discoverers. The little ferrets were so compatible with the Agena upper stages, in fact, that they rode piggyback near their bottom, with the Discoverers on the front end. The top-secret Air Force program was known as 7300. Its successive satellites were code-named after a different kind of heavenly body: Raquel and Farrah. But because they hitchhiked on the Agenas, they were also called Aft Rack Packages, or simply Aft Rack Packs.

"Electronics wasn't very snazzy in those days," one highly knowledgeable intelligence veteran explained. "But from the peripheral flights, they knew what to look for, and so they could build preset tuners: receivers that would react when they were painted, when they were in the field of view of a ground radar." The orbiting ferrets could pick out the radar pulses even from altitudes of several hundred miles, because, unlike a radar signal that bounces off a plane and then returns to the receiver after a round-trip, the trip the signal made to the little spacecraft was one-way. So the satellite, he explained, was getting the pulse's "main bang as it came up from the ground. One-way tickets are a lot cheaper in that game."

The radars' location could not be pinpointed in those days, but they were within sight of the orbiting spacecraft, so knowing where the satellite was at all times and calibrating that information with the radar hit got it down to "the right county." Those first ferret satellites could spot the radars because, in effect, they were told to report back when they picked up the signal they were looking for.

Their successors, currently in use, can scan the entire microwave spectrum and locate every radar in an area, sorting them out by their signals' distinct frequency. In other words, what the Aft Rack Packers could see as a solitary radar emitting one signal, the new ones can see as perhaps three different radars in a cluster sending slightly different signals, or even Token types working on multiple frequencies. And the satellites' size and capability have increased steadily in forty years. They are now like searchlights that scour the night, exposing radars as they go and illuminating all of the important details. The radars' vital signs are recorded and then "dumped" by the satellites, which send down enough of the radars' working parameters so they can be jammed as well as pinpointed.

Navy radar ferreting was and remains a so-called geo-locational program. While the Air Force looks for "quality" radar intelligence from fixed land sites, which it would have to jam in a bomber attack, the Navy uses its ferret satellites to locate the radars of specific kinds of foreign warships and measure their signals. For the Navy, as the saying goes, there is good news and bad news. The good news is that all ships, including the warships that are its primary quarry, keep their radar on all the time when they are at sea. Theoretically, that makes finding them easier. But the bad news is that since all ships move around when they're not in port, finding them is more difficult than collecting against fixed land radars.

"The Navy figured, quite properly, that all you've got to do is listen to these things all the time and you know where the ships are," the veteran intelligence officer said. The key is "all the time." The Air Force program was based on the proposition that the land-based radars it collected against didn't move. It therefore used single, long-lived satellites that stayed up for years and relentlessly soaked up signals on repeated orbital passes.

The Navy, on the other hand, had a time problem because its targets sailed the high seas; they were always moving and therefore had to be followed, not just located. "Part of the thing which drove the sense of the Navy program," another veteran intelligence officer explained, "was to cut down the amount of time between visits."

So at the outset, the Naval Research Laboratory, which designed and built the first Navy ferrets, had to invent a system that would dramatically shrink the time it took for the satellites to collect data from constantly moving targets. The NRL's answer was to use from two to four clusters of satellites flying in staggered formations. In other words, there would be a small armada of them that continuously combed the high seas for targets. A cluster of spacecraft would triangulate the vessels to establish their precise locations. This was similar to an entirely different Air Force anti–ballistic missile radar ferret called Jump Seat. The latter used three satellites flying in a very high elliptical orbit to fix an ABM (not aircraft) radar's precise position by measuring the tiny time difference between the instant a signal hits each satellite.

The Navy program was originally called Poppy and was funded by the National Reconnaissance Office. The satellites were relatively small, weighed roughly 165 pounds, and were orbited by pencil-shaped Scout solid-fueled rockets developed by NASA. Over the Navy's strenuous objections, the NRO ordered that later models be built by a commercial contractor, not by the Naval Research Laboratory. The satellites downlink data are transmitted to five or six receiving stations around the world because of the need for speed. Air Force ferrets have been manufactured by TRW from the start and downlink their data at the Satellite Control Facility at Sunnyvale, California, an hour's drive south of San Francisco.

As good as the satellites are, they have their limitations, as do all robots. Their orbits are predictable, which allows their quarry to turn off radar before they pass overhead. It is the same basic response that can happen when an imaging satellite is due to appear: the opposition stops doing whatever it is doing and "covers up" until the prying eye passes beyond the horizon. Reconnaissance satellite orbits can and have been calculated by schoolboys in England and can be pulled down on a personal computer by anyone with orbital prediction software. Furthermore, the NRO now announces launches on its website and orbital parameters are registered with the United Nations.

Manned aircraft, on the other hand, are unpredictable. They fly their missions as ordered and can therefore appear at any place any time. Furthermore, planes can stay on the scene constantly, flying back and forth all day or night collecting data. And if need be, one can be replaced by another for close, extended coverage. "The rationale for manned aircraft has always been their ability to go and linger where you have a crisis," a former intelligence official observed, whereas satellites are literally a passing phenomenon. There is also a direct interchange between the people in the reconnaissance aircraft and those who need their data on enemy radar or other targets.

John Bergen, the retired Air Force intelligence specialist, has pointed out that aircraft "are designed from the beginning to be an integral part of the commander's warfighting capability. Consequently, they are integrated completely into his command and control structure." In a serious combat situation, Bergen added, reconnaissance planes can "chop," or change operational control, to the military commander on the scene, who then decides what they collect. That will apply to Global Hawk as well as to the U-2s and RC-135s.

Finally, there is the human dimension. People can make sense out of what they're collecting and communicate it immediately to the combat forces that need it. They can also "fuse" several kinds of intelligence and relay it for use. And since satellites are passive, they can't get search and fire control radars to operate reactively. In other words, they can't really provoke the opposition into getting turned on. It takes a live ferret to do that.

YET CONTINUED MANNED electronic intelligence collection would always be risky, as the world learned in April 2001 when it got its first graphic look at airborne electronic intelligence collection in action. The Soviet Union may have relaxed its air defense posture by then, but China did not. Like North Korea, China remained hard-edged on the matter. Even reconnaissance flights well out over international waters were taken to be unacceptably intrusive.

It was that attitude which led to the most sensational aerial reconnaissance incident since Bruce Olmstead and John McKone were jailed in Lubyanka after their RB-47H was shot down by MiGs on July 1, 1960. As in the attack on their Stratojet, prisoners were taken. But unlike that episode, the aircraft itself was captured, making it the first U.S. reconnaissance plane to fall into an opponent's hands intact. It also shoved George W. Bush into the first crisis of his presidency.

A little after 9 o'clock on the morning of April 1, 2001, a Navy EP-3E Aries II reconnaissance plane was struck by a Communist Chinese F-8 fighter and had to make an emergency landing at Lingshui air base on China's Hainan Island, due east of Vietnam in the South China Sea.

With the collapse of the Soviet Union and its diminished military power, the United States began sending reconnaissance aircraft on vastly increased forays against the People's Republic of China in the mid-1990s. China's growing economic strength was making it substantially more powerful militarily. Beijing's increasing power emboldened it to sell arms and other equipment to Iran and elsewhere, to continue threatening Taiwan, and to try forming what the United States took to be an ominous alliance with the Russian Federation, Iran, and North Korea.

When China looked east, however, it saw matters very differently. The Chinese continued to resent what they saw as a groundless European and American attitude of superiority and a history of exploitation that went back to the Opium War in the mid-nineteenth century, which led to the Boxer Rebellion. By the time of the EP-3E incident itself, Beijing felt enmity because of America's emergence as the planet's sole superpower and what it took to be concomitant arrogance. There were still vivid memories of a NATO air attack that had left three Chinese dead at their embassy in Belgrade two years earlier. And the Bush administration's rekindling ballistic missile defense, planning to provide Taiwan with advanced Aegis radar on new destroyers, and the defection to the United States of a high-level army colonel, only added to the anger.

China responded to the almost constant peripheral reconnaissance flights off its shores, as had the Soviets decades earlier, by sending up fighters to shadow, intercept, and intimidate the prowlers. Several times in the months before the incident, the fighters had come so close to the Navy patrol planes that the United States registered formal complaints. In one maneuver, called "thumping" by U.S. aircrews, an opposing jet fighter would streak under the reconnaissance plane from behind, then abruptly pull almost straight up in front of it. "It not only creates the shock of seeing another aircraft appear right in front of you, it also forces you to fly through the thumping aircraft's jet wash, spilling your coffee," explained Bill Ernst, a veteran of the Fifty-fifth Strategic Reconnaissance Wing, who has both thumped and been thumped.

The EP-3E, which was seventy miles off Chinese territorial waters when it was jumped, was a variant of the four-turboprop Lockheed P-3 Orion, which itself evolved from the venerable P2V Neptune. Its home base was the Whidbey Island Naval Air Station, north of Seattle, but it was deployed at Kadena Air Base on Okinawa, the roost for the Fifty-fifth Reconnaissance Wing's various RC-135s and at one time the Ninth Strategic Reconnaissance Wing's SR-71s. It was one of twelve EP-3s belonging to Fleet Reconnaissance Squadron One, or VQ-1, and it carried a crew of twenty-four, including three women. The plane, PR-32, was conducting its customary mission: routinely ferreting radar, intercepting communication traffic, rigging Chinese naval vessels—inspecting them—and looking for submarines to track. It was well into a typical ten-hour flight, flying at 22,500 feet at a plodding 207 miles an hour, when disaster struck.

The two Chinese fighters that approached PR-32 were relatively ancient Shenyang F-8s, which were radar-equipped interceptor versions of the jet-propelled Soviet MiG-21. The pilot of one of the F-8s, Wang Wei, became dangerously exuberant, as he had on previous intercepts, when the temptation to show off by trying to intimidate the Americans overcame prudence. He made three passes at the Aries, which as usual was flying straight and level on autopilot as the technicians in the cabin collected and recorded electronic signals. On each pass, the young Chinese pilot slowed his fighter almost to stalling speed and pulled in so close to PR-32—three to five feet—that a member of its crew could plainly see him salute on the first pass and say something on the second with his oxygen mask off.

In the last maneuver of his life, that third pass, Wang Wei clipped the number one engine's propeller—the left outboard prop—splintering it. But the propeller bit into the F-8 like an electric saw, slicing it in two. The fighter's nose swung violently to the right and slammed into the EP-3E's nose, shattering its radar dome. Parts of the dome flew back and disabled the right inside propeller, severely damaged a flap, and pierced the pressurized cabin. The patrol plane's pitot tubes were also knocked off, eliminating air-speed and altitude data in the cockpit. And the bracket for its high-frequency radio antenna flew back and wrapped around the tail.

There was a deafening roar inside the Aries as it snap-rolled so hard to the left that it nearly turned over and plunged 7,500 feet toward the sea.

"This guy just killed us," Lt. Shane J. Osborn thought as he looked up and saw water. The twenty-six-year-old commander and senior pilot fought to get the crippled plane under control while warning bells and claxons rang and the instrument panel lit up like a Christmas tree. With the nose, sensitive pitot tube, and other sensors gone, Osborn had little idea of his speed and altitude, while the rush of air against the EP-3E's flat nose caused violent buffeting. The number one propeller could not be feathered, so it faced full into the airstream, windmilling and creating heavy drag to the left. Osborn had to fight that, too, as well as the flight controls themselves because of the debris wrapped around the tail. The men and women in the cabin behind him, as well as those on the flight deck, also thought they were going to die.

Osborn finally managed to stabilize the Aries at about 7,500 feet. He called for a bailout, but as the crew put on their parachutes, he changed his mind and began thinking about ditching. Finally, with no response coming from PR-32's rudder and flaps, and knowing he couldn't reach Kadena, which was four and a half hours away, he began thinking of a closer landing site. With the plane finally stabilized, Lt. Patrick C. Honeck confirmed with a navigation chart what he already knew: Lingshui military air base, on the southern edge of Hainan Island, had the closest runway. Osborn ordered the destruction of the electronic equipment, a contingency that had been practiced many times. The enlisted men and women in the cabin began wielding axes and sledgehammers to smash the receivers, analyzers, and computers, and to destroy every sensitive document and piece of software they could. They were not wholly successful. Some manuals on tactics and operations were salvaged by the Chinese and so, too, were data that could be taken off even smashed hard drives. Short of blowing up the plane, there was simply no way to completely eliminate the loss of valuable information.

Meanwhile, Shane Osborn radioed the standard Mayday distress call and asked for permission to land on Hainan several times, he later reported, but got no answer. The noise coming through the holes in the plane's fuselage could have been the problem; it was so loud crew members had to shout to be heard.

In a piece of flying that other pilots familiar with the Aries and Orion called almost unbelievable, Osborn "muscled" his mangled aircraft to Hainan. All twenty-four naval aviators were soon safe on Lingshui's lone runway as PR-32, their battered derelict, rolled to a stop. As much could not be said of Wang Wei, who ejected out of his burning jet and was never seen again.

During the EP-3E's first fifteen minutes on the runway, as Chinese troops surrounded it, the crew frantically went through a checklist of more items to be destroyed. Then they opened the hatch and surrendered. An interpreter told the Americans not to move. Osborn told the interpreter he wanted to phone the U.S. ambassador and was assured it had already been done. And it had. He then climbed down a ladder, followed by the other twenty-three. All of the crew, including eight cryptologic technicians, were then offered water and cigarettes and taken by van to the Chinese navy's Nanhang No. 1 Guesthouse, a relatively posh building just off a raucous street lined with brothels, beer halls, and discos. An international imbroglio the likes of which hadn't been seen since North Korea grabbed the *Pueblo* in 1968 was under way.

The first salvo was fired by a spokesman for China's foreign ministry, who insisted on television the next day that "the U.S.

side has total responsibility for this event." That argument quickly evolved into a charge that the Aries suddenly veered and struck the Chinese jet, which was absurd. "It was the U.S. side that caused this incident, and China is the victim," the spokesman added the next day. "The United States should take full responsibility, make an apology to the Chinese government and people, and give us an explanation of its actions." The missing pilot's wife was then sent into the fray. Within a week of the incident, she got a letter off to Bush, made public by the official Xinhua news agency, accusing him and his administration of being "too cowardly" to apologize. "Our six-year-old son has kept asking me when his father will come home. I pray and call out time and again, hope in tears that there will be a miracle." A Chinese newspaper reported that the woman, Ruan Guoqin, was so overcome by grief she had to be hospitalized.

The Bush administration, aware that China held the cards, played its part with consummate care while the world's press reported the rhetorical exchanges like some sporting event. Readers and television viewers who tuned in to the "spy plane" story got their first look under the black curtain that had protected electronic intelligence for decades. They also had an ongoing lesson in the nuances of language and the infinite subtleties of diplomacy. While demanding the immediate release of the plane and its crew, the president delicately expressed regret that Wang Wei had been lost. Secretary of State Colin L. Powell did the same and added that he was "sorry" the collision occurred.

But an apology was out of the question. Taking responsibility for the collision and apologizing for it would have set a dangerous precedent and put more crews at risk by in effect validating attacks on them. China, North Korea, or any nation that shot down one of the reconnaissance planes would defend its action by pointing out that the United States had previously apologized for the same sort of incident, meaning the Americans acknowledged they were wrong. In addition, an apology would have demoralized the men and women who flew the missions. It also would have set off a political firestorm on the far right at home, which was already grumbling about economic retaliation, keeping the 2008 Olympics out of China, and worse. They called the Americans on

Hainan Island "hostages." One senior admiral in the Pacific suggested publicly that the aircraft carrier *Kittyhawk* be sent to the area. He was quietly told to shut up.

While Beijing continued to bluster about an apology, Bush grabbed the "humanitarian" high ground. He answered Ruan Guoqin's letter with one of his own that expressed regret over the loss of her husband and looked to the future for improved relations between their two nations. Then both sides dug in as they searched for a way out of the impasse that would save face.

Meanwhile, running accounts in the news media in the United States described the prisoners as "spies" whose "spy plane" had been forced down. The stories correctly reported that EP-3Es could not only intercept enemy voice communication, but could copy a person's speech pattern and electronically put other words in his or her mouth and retransmit them, creating the kind of havoc the British caused the Germans in World War II using a far less sophisticated technique. Press reports also noted that another of the plane's missions was to "eavesdrop" on Chinese radar. Consistently left out of the stories, however, was the reason for collecting the intelligence: so the radar could be jammed and targets obliterated if there was a war. The Chinese knew it, of course, because they flew their own reconnaissance missions against Japan, India, and Russia. But unlike the clearly marked U.S. military planes—PR-32 wore the Stars and Bars and had "U.S. Navy" painted on it—the Chinese really did fly spy planes. One of them, a Soviet-made Tu-154M, carried a powerful American-made synthetic aperture radar and electronic intercept equipment inside a fuselage that was painted in China United Airlines markings. The airline is owned by the Chinese air force.

Nanhang No. 1 Guesthouse wasn't the Waldorf-Astoria. But it wasn't Lubyanka, either. It was a very lightly guarded, clean inn populated by mosquitoes and other bugs, some of them electronic. Shane Osborn was given his own room (as befitted the commander of the aircraft, in the view of his captors), the three women shared a triple, and the remaining twenty were paired in ten other rooms on two floors. They were interrogated for up to five hours at a time, usually in the middle of the night, during which they were videotaped.

But there was no rough stuff. PR-32's crew was allowed to watch television and read the English-language *China Daily*, e-mail from friends and relatives, and paperback novels brought to them by visiting U.S. diplomats. They also played cards, did crossword puzzles, and had meals together. Some told Brig. Gen. Neal Sealock, the U.S. defense attaché who came from Beijing to see them, that the food was excellent. Others complained about indigestion. None cared for the fish heads they were served. The Chinese understood that when their prisoners were released, as they surely would be, the propaganda advantage would lie in having treated them humanely.

The break came eleven days after the collision, when China formally accepted a meticulously worded letter from Bush saying the United States was "very sorry" that Wang Wei had been lost and that the EP-3E had made an emergency landing on Chinese soil. He did not apologize for the incident, but the Chinese satisfied themselves that they had won an important concession, and ordered the American reconnaissance crew released.

By then, a Continental Airlines passenger jet had been ordered to Guam with a repatriation team consisting of fourteen specialists, including physicians and psychologists, all dressed in casual civilian clothes. The 155-seat jet was fitted with two stretchers bolted over seats, plus oxygen tanks and intravenous bottles and other emergency medical equipment.

The big jet left Guam at 2:15 on the morning of April 12 and landed at a civilian facility, the Haikou airport, at 6:07 a.m., just as the sun was coming up. The flight crew saw many Chinese soldiers but no weapons. One Chinese, an English-speaking representative of Air China, told the crew members to fill out arrival and departure documents and turn over their passports. While they waited for a sign of the twenty-four passengers they were there to pick up, a U.S. Army general stormed in a rage up the stairs that had been rolled to the plane's doorway and demanded to speak to the captain. He said the entire operation was in jeopardy because whoever had filled out the general declaration, a standard document for international flights, had listed the airliner's destination as Haikou, China R.O.C. The initials stood for Republic of China, or Taiwan. The error angered the already sensitive Chinese, so the captain crossed out R.O.C. and wrote P.R.O.C., for People's Republic of China. The Chinese were mollified.

Two buses finally pulled up. All twenty-four Americans saluted, bolted up the stairs, and settled into the back of the plane. The crew's passports were returned, the door was shut, and the jet took off for Anderson Air Force Base on Guam. When word came over the public address system that the sailors were back over international airspace, there was loud cheering. Osborn later put on headphones on the flight deck and accepted congratulations from the U.S. ambassador to China, Adm. Joseph W. Prueher, who told Osborn he was speaking for the president in commending him. Meanwhile, the repatriated Americans were shown a film, *Men of Honor*, and were given a first-class meal that did not include fish heads.

They flew from Guam to Pearl Harbor, where they were debriefed before heading back to Whidbey Island Naval Air Station and a national heroes' welcome for Easter. They were told while still in Hawaii that they could describe the collision and their captivity to the news media, but the nature of their mission, let alone their equipment and how they destroyed it, were out of bounds as usual.

The crew of PR-32 left its battered, picked-over, and forlorn "spy plane" sitting where it had rolled to a stop, a temporary monument to the danger that attends the shadow war.

On May 7—five weeks after the incident—reconnaissance flights in the area were resumed when an Air Force Rivet Joint RC-135 flying out of Kadena picked up where PR-32 had left off. Certainly the mission was flown to collect intelligence. But, far more important, it was staged to demonstrate to China that the United States had no intention of being intimidated into ending such operations or flying them at great distances from their targets. The consequence of not resuming the flights would have been to set a dangerous precedent, not only encouraging China and other nations to attack again, but seriously undermining U.S. national security. That could not be allowed to happen. The Chinese knew it and gave the RC-135 a wide berth.

 **TO RAISE THE DEAD**

FOR NEARLY HALF a century—the duration of the longest foreign conflict in American history—airmen risked their lives, lost them, and were brutalized in virtual obscurity to get the measure of their nation's enemies.

Their relentless war in the shadows had consequences that were profoundly more significant than any gang war fought by fighters in the sky or the bombing campaigns in Korea and Vietnam. The consequences were inversely proportional to the obscurity. They were truly strategic and as fundamentally important as war and peace.

But the airmen lived with an apparent paradox. Unlike other soldiers who are lionized in victory and martyred in defeat, reconnaissance crews that flew their missions during the cold war were officially ignored when they succeeded and were a political embarrassment when they were shot down.

The collection of information—intelligence—by aerial reconnaissance gave the United States two obvious advantages. And in doing so it provided a less obvious, but decisive, third advantage as well.

On the face of it, the airmen who ferreted radar, intercepted communication, photographed military and industrial facilities, and mapped territory helped to target the enemy. The "product" of that massive effort translated directly into providing bomber crews and then the missileers with the means to strike the enemy. That was not only true, it was obvious. The reconnaissance crews were the vital instrument without which the bomber crews could not function. And the consequences of the bomber crews', Air Force and Navy, not being able to function—not being able to strike their targets—would have been calamitous for deterrence. But they would have indeed struck their targets.

Less obvious but no less important was the fact that the Soviet Union, its proxies, and a particularly belligerent Communist China knew it. They understood nuclear weapons made their vast frontiers dangerously irrelevant, and that where reconnaissance planes could penetrate, bombers could as well. The intelligence collectors who constantly prowled along every edge of the Communist frontier and occasionally went on deep forays over it were unknown to their countrymen. But they were exceedingly well known to their quarry. Their presence left no doubt in the Kremlin and elsewhere that every component of their nation was precisely targeted, was in the metaphorical crosshairs, and that a third world war would therefore effectively mean extinction. This was the doctrine of deterrence. And it worked. LeMay—and by no means only LeMay—took it as gospel that the surest way to invite war was to be unprepared to wage it.

At the same time, precise targeting lessened reliance on monster bombs or, for that matter, on any nuclear weapons. For all practical purposes, and "practical" is the operative word, both sides knew that nuclear weapons couldn't be used. There were circumstances in which a single air base or naval facility marked for destruction could be demolished with traditional "iron bombs" instead of nuclear ones that would devastate an entire region. Knowing exactly where the flea was meant it was no longer necessary to kill the dog to get rid of it; the "dog" being Iraq or Serbia, as well as the former Soviet Union. Accurate target information provided by the recce crews gave war planners a flexibility they did not have when it was nukes or nothing.

Peripheral flights and penetrations also made an enormous

contribution to the overall intelligence pool, replacing conjecture with hard information about military strength, industrial capacity, transportation systems, and what the warriors call the enemy's order of battle. Much of the information went into the National Intelligence Estimates, which were (and remain) prepared by the armed forces intelligence divisions, including the National Security Agency and the CIA. NIEs focus on the so-called intentions and capabilities of other countries and are vital to the National Security Council, the Department of State, and Congress, which use the information to make foreign policy. Aerial reconnaissance ended the "bomber gap," for example, and that, in turn, canceled the production of hundreds of fighter-interceptors no longer needed to protect the continental United States against a phantom threat. It also ended the "missile gap."

Finally, the missions had the intangible but supremely important effect of demonstrating to successive Soviet leaders that however closed they tried to make their country, their most important secrets—those relating directly to the protection of their society—could not be kept. The secrets could be exposed by superior technology and resolve.

This is big stuff. It takes nothing away from the men and women who fly fighters, bombers, and transports to say that reconnaissance is fundamental to the overall, long-term strategic health and safety of the United States. Yet the paradox is that by the nature of how the process works, the very people who have been on the front line protecting national security have been obscured in its name. They have always understood the reason for being kept in the deep shadow and have readily accepted it.

At the same time, the intelligence collectors have bridled at being called spies. They point out that unlike real spies, who pose as loyal citizens while operating as secret agents, they have done their work and continue to do it in clearly marked military airplanes and are almost always a known presence near or over foreign territory. Others—certainly including the Russians and the Chinese, but also many Western intelligence experts—define espionage as collecting protected information by any means. And contrary to what some outsiders have suggested, those who have survived the dangers of their profession believe they have had am-ple recognition from within their own services. The initiated have always honored themselves, and been honored, quietly.

THE DEAD AND MISSING, and their survivors, are a far different matter. William L. White wrote a book about the shootdown of Willard Palm's RB-47H. It was published two years later and titled *The Little Toy Dog* after a small Snoopy doll mascot that hung in Palm's cockpit. If White had written about all the cold war reconnaissance losses, and included the effects on the families and the response of a government cloaked under the amorphous mantle of national security, he might have chosen a title from another of his books: *They Were Expendable*.

Everything related to cold war aerial reconnaissance missions, certainly including their effect on the families of the men who flew them, happened under the all-inclusive blanket of national security. But the ambiguity of that term and its potential for misuse was foretold by Charles Lutwidge Dodgson, who wrote *Through the Looking-Glass* under the name Lewis Carroll:

> "When *I* use a word," Humpty Dumpty said, in rather a scornful tone, "it means just what I choose it to mean— neither more nor less."
> "The question is," said Alice, "whether you *can* make words mean so many different things."
> "The question is," said Humpty Dumpty, "which is to be master—that's all."

During the entire course of the cold war, national security dictated that reconnaissance missions against other nations, certainly including the Communist bloc, be conducted in absolute secrecy. This made sense on the operational level. Sending aircrews on overt peripheral flights, let alone on penetrations, would have cost so many more lives than were lost in secret that they would have amounted to suicide missions. It was not a matter of tactics: the Soviets and Red Chinese almost always knew when and where they were being reconnoitered and could have attacked any time they wanted. It was a matter of politics: flying

the missions openly—in effect brazenly bragging about them—
would have embarrassed the Communists to the point of provoking many more attacks. That, in turn, would have meant either
ending the operations, which was unthinkable, or protecting all of
them with fighter escorts, which would have been both horren-
dously expensive and likely to touch off air battles that would
have been highly destabilizing (a well-worn euphemism for increasing the likelihood of war).

But the fixation on national security extended beyond the limits
of operational requirements and into the lives of the families of
the men who flew the missions and, after at least ten major shootdowns, never returned. From the beginning of the Peacetime Airborne Reconnaissance Program through June 1992 the families
of the missing lived in a murky netherworld of ignorance and supposition, of ghostly loved ones who vanished without a trace and
who therefore could not be laid to rest, and with a federal bureaucracy that remained stubbornly elusive.

Confused and grieving wives, brothers, sisters, and children
were becalmed by a vast, impersonal, bipartisan Humpty Dumpty
political system that was as stubbornly and pervasively vaporous
as the ghosts themselves. To inquire about the fate of the missing
was to engage in a dialogue with an ethereal, vacuous jack-o'-
lantern called "the Government." The Government responded to
the searchers, to those who needed to bring closure to their loss,
with: "We will require additional time to . . . We are making every
effort to . . . We have again requested . . . You are assured that you
will be immediately notified when . . . An examination of our files
indicates . . . Unfortunately . . ."

Unfortunately . . . family members were left to spend years trying to unravel the Gordian knot of official, reflexive, national
security double-talk. The supposed requirements of national security caused profound individual insecurity and abiding frustration and bitterness.

"We've been lied to over the years for such a long time," Charlotte Busch Mitnik complained in 1994. Her brother, Maj. Samuel N. Busch, was the commander of the RB-29 that was shot
down off Vladivostok on June 13, 1952. Another brother was
killed in World War II. "It's not what they say, it's what they do.

Citizens need to know that the government will get the men home, alive or dead, whether twenty years later or forty years later. These men didn't have a Purple Heart, an Air Medal—nothing, absolutely nothing. I want these men to be honored as they should have been."

They finally were honored, though characteristically, with sharply mixed efforts and results. Some survivors requested and received written recognition from the government of their loved one's loss. Susan Hand Hansen, whose father, James F. Hand, vanished on Jesse Beasley's Neptune on the night of January 4, 1954, requested a Cold War Recognition Certificate in October 1999. It arrived just before Christmas 2000. It was a buff-colored piece of paper with an eagle on top and these words of appreciation, followed by a reproduced signature of the secretary of defense:

CERTIFICATE OF RECOGNITION
JAMES F. HAND

In recognition of your service during the period of the cold war (2 September 1945–26 December 1991) in promoting peace and stability for this Nation, the people of this Nation are forever grateful.

Susan Hansen was deeply underwhelmed. "The certificate looks like something I could have whipped out on my own computer, sort of like the gift certificate for ballet lessons I created for my granddaughter," she lamented. "It is a preprinted form with my father's name the only original addition. It doesn't mention his specific date of service, his service number, rank, anything other than what is above. I can't imagine why that took over a year to produce. And it is certainly hollow testimony for the sacrifice my father made. I found it insulting, at the very least."

ON OCTOBER 21, 1995, the remaining loved ones of Samuel Busch and his crew did quite a bit better. All twelve of the missing airmen were awarded posthumous Purple Hearts and Distinguished Flying Crosses in a ceremony attended by 450 people, including about 150 family members and several hundred from Air Force intelligence, at National Security Agency headquarters at Fort Meade, Maryland.

A published report of the event the following month noted that all twelve airmen were presumed dead. They no doubt were. By then. But most of them were not killed in the shootdown. Busch and at least nine of the others were pulled out of the water by Russians and imprisoned as spies, according to a highly credible "memoir" by an unnamed Russian engineer who traveled to gulags in Siberia at the time of the shootdown and long afterward and then went into internal exile before migrating to the West. The memoir was released in February 2000.

The anonymous Russian got his information from several people, including members of his engineering institute, so it was thirdhand. But it was reliable information because it named names: "Bush" and "Moore." The last would have been M. Sgt. David L. Moore, a crewman on the RB-29. Busch, Moore, and eight others in the crew were taken to Khabarovsk, on the Manchurian border, for interrogation. The place was the hub of an infamous detention and holding center for U.N. prisoners of war from Korea and for some of the airmen like Busch and Moore who were shot down on unrelated missions. It was there, according to one of the engineer's associates, that Sam Busch and David Moore were "finished off"—probably beaten to death—by their interrogators.

"Yes, at first ten people were alive," the engineer was told. "Yes, first they were brought to Khabarovsk. But then, of course, they were sent off to Svobodnyi [ironically, a name meaning 'Freedom']. They were supposed to have been met by people from the Ministry of Defense. They were not met, though. You see, there was some screw-up in Moscow. . . . What happened to them after that, I do not know. And I would advise you not to know as well!" It was straight out of Solzhenitsyn's *The Gulag Archipelago*.

"The guys from within 'worked over' the Americans so badly that only eight were taken [to Svobodnyi]. And those had nowhere to go after all that. And so what? Do [you] know what sort of arrogance they had? They were Americans! You understand!!!"

"They probably drowned them," I offered as a supposition.

"Well, well! And how did you find that out?"

It was a supervisor who directed "hydromechanical" construction who told the engineer about "Bush and Moore, who will forever remain in the soil of the Khabarovsk Region. And however blasphemous this thought may appear to the uninitiated, let people take my word. By their horrible fate they were spared the vastness of the gulag's underworld, a prison isolation cell with the proud name 'Svobodnyi.' " Charlotte Busch Mitnik's suspicions were finally confirmed. However awful her brother's fate had been, she at last learned the truth.

BY THE TIME word finally came about the fate of Sam Busch and most of his crew, the families of other flyers who had been lost on the peripheral missions had been going through a period of renewed hope that they, too, were close to finding their own closure. The resurrection began as the unintended result of one of those small asides, passing gestures, which frustrated people grasp and cling to when they are otherwise in an emotional void.

The occasion was a visit to the United States by Russian President Boris Yeltsin in mid-June 1992. It was roughly two years after the spectre that had haunted America finally collapsed under its own ponderous weight. The dismantling of state communism was engineered by President Mikhail S. Gorbachev, a heroic realist who understood that the USSR had run its historical course and was decaying under a hopelessly flawed political system. (He would be reviled in his own country for years as the culprit who demolished the modicum of stability and security ordinary Russians were allowed as the price for living in a political and spiritual purgatory.)

At any rate, barely ten months before his visit to the United States, Yeltsin had defied an attempted coup by Communists who wanted to reverse the course taken by Gorbachev. Yeltsin came to his country's old nemesis, the surviving superpower, to confer with President George H. W. Bush in a first-ever Russian-American summit to negotiate "a new partnership" that entailed a major nuclear weapons reduction agreement and very generous economic aid.

Yeltsin, trying to sweeten the pot and no doubt undermine his hard-line Communist opponents, admitted to a television correspondent on the plane to the United States that North Vietnam had sent some American prisoners captured during the war there to the Soviet Union, where they were used as forced laborers. He said his information came from a first impression he had gotten after archives were opened, and added, almost as an afterthought, that some of the GIs might still be alive. It was sensational news, particularly to an organized coalition of family members who had never doubted that their missing loved ones had been captured and imprisoned. The group announced immediately it would challenge the Department of Defense to declassify documents that had a bearing on the issue.

But there was more. Yeltsin broadened the scope of the prisoner issue and got down to specifics in a letter to a Senate committee. He electrified the congressmen and other family members by acknowledging for the first time that 23,000 American troops were taken from German prison camps at the end of World War II and that some had not been released. He also said 262 flyers shot down over North Korea during that war had been captured and at least 59 of them had been interrogated by Russians. Last, but by no means least, Yeltsin added that nine American planes had been shot down "over" Soviet territory in the 1950s, and that in 1953 at least twelve crew members were in Soviet prisons or hospitals.

The silver-haired politician went on to announce at a joint meeting with Bush at the White House: "The most important thing is that we know the numerical picture. We know how many people there were on the territory, how many were left, what camps the POWs were held in, the citizens of the United States; which war they were from, whether it was World War II or the Korean War or any other incident. So that part of the picture is clear. We know who died; where they are buried. We know that also."

Bush praised Yeltsin for his courage and announced that Malcolm Toon, a former ambassador to the USSR who already headed a U.S.-Russia Joint Commission on POW/MIA Affairs, would be dispatched to Moscow immediately to dig into the archives. Toon's Russian counterpart on the Joint Commission was Dmitri A. Volkogonov, a retired three-star general and a historian.

Two days later, the spirit of cooperation was further enhanced when the White House proclaimed it would urge the International Monetary Fund to lower the bar for economic reform as a condition to signing an aid agreement with Russia. That was as good as the situation was going to get.

The American side of the Joint Commission in turn divided into working groups to find prisoners of war and those missing in action (MIAs) from World War II, from the Korean War, from Vietnam and elsewhere in Southeast Asia, and from "Cold War Losses." The last was to deal specifically with aircraft lost near or over Soviet territory between 1950 and 1965. That, of course, meant the Air Force and Navy planes that were shot down in the Peacetime Airborne Reconnaissance Program.

The working groups were in turn supported by two Republican legislators, two Democrats, and representatives from the Departments of State and Defense, the National Archive, and the specially created Defense POW/Missing Personnel Office (DPMO). The DPMO was overseen by a deputy assistant secretary of defense in the Pentagon who was made directly responsible for locating the missing servicemen and keeping their families fully informed.

The Joint Commission itself seemed to get off to an enthusiastic start. An organization called Task Force Russia had already been set up by the Army to provide the commission with an institutional support system that could analyze the situation, help the commission's Moscow office, and act as a liaison with the families. It would make a sincere effort to collect information on the missing airmen and keep their families informed and comforted.

Bruce Sanderson, who was born on July 29, 1953—the day his father, Warren J. Sanderson, was shot down on O'Kelley's RB-50G—spent decades trying to find out what happened to his father. He and others, including Mary Dunham Nichols, thought Task Force Russia did a first-rate job, at least in the beginning. "Those guys made a legitimate effort; a really great effort," Sanderson said. But after two years, Task Force Russia was absorbed. The situation then began slowly, almost imperceptibly, to erode.

The organization that absorbed Task Force Russia was the DPMO, the POW/MIA office. News media coverage of its regular, pro forma briefings for families was prohibited on the ground that their privacy had to be respected. That was balderdash. It was family members who went to the media over the years (and cooperated enthusiastically with this author), while the DPMO carefully avoided scrutiny by journalists and even insisted on censoring references to the missing men the family members themselves wanted to give to journalists.

The Joint Commission's and DPMO's record for locating the remains of any cold war shootdown casualties, let alone those who had been captured, was on the whole abysmal. It wasn't because the people who worked in the office were incompetent. Rather, the failure to find the captured men reflected the desiderata, as political wish lists are called, of both the United States and the Russian Federation.

In reality, Yeltsin's apparent revelation was a sham, smoke and mirrors, a public relations stunt of breathtaking proportion. His information was almost undoubtedly correct. But neither side wanted the Joint Commission or the DPMO to turn up anything, because there were higher political considerations.

Peter C. Johnson, a Russian-speaking former military intelligence officer who was involved in tracking the missing ferret crews, said soon after Yeltsin's statement that "the chances are pretty good" that at least six of O'Kelley's crew were captured, but politics was keeping the lid on the situation. The United States in fact had openly said they were captured at the time of the shootdown. But then the charge conveniently evaporated, never to be mentioned again, at least officially.

"Eisenhower didn't confront them because they were our enemies," Johnson said, referring to the Russians. "And we don't confront them because they are our friends." He meant that turning up the missing airmen would spoil the new relationship. The search for them, which could not be called off after a Russian leader finally gave their loved ones cause for hope, therefore degenerated into a textbook case of cynical, institutional hypocrisy.

The United States and the Russian Federation did not want the unseemly and embarrassing cold war "losses"—and the reason for them—to impair their newly established bonds. With both nations eager to shed the deep mutual suspicions that confounded their relations during the cold war, resurrecting the spirit of those times and the lost airmen would have amounted to an awkward and unnecessary setback.

The imperative to collect strategic intelligence near and sometimes over the Soviet Union, and the Soviet Union's equally vital stake in preventing it, both rested squarely on the prospect of fighting a nuclear war. Having avoided that catastrophe and having established a promising, if tenuous, relationship, neither side wanted to be pulled back by the ghosts of cold war past. There was no conspiracy between them. But there was a clear, tacit understanding that resurrecting bitter episodes from that dangerous, and in many respects vicious, time would be counterproductive.

The existentialism was reinforced by hard politics. The last thing the Kremlin needed was for atrocities against American prisoners to be exposed and publicized when it was trying desperately to foster goodwill (not to mention billions of dollars in international loans and investments). Similarly, neither the Bush nor the Clinton administrations saw any good to come from publicizing missions that were flown to prepare the way for the incineration of what was now democracy's newest experiment (not to mention the owner of thousands of nukes, a potential market, and Red China's foil). Giving the fragile new democracy's internal opposition, and particularly the hard-line nationalists on the far right and the unreconstructed Communists on the left, ammunition by reminding them of how their mortal enemy had used its muscle was considered a serious political blunder.

So now there was a higher requirement than honoring the dead and bringing peace to their loved ones. The two sides in the Joint Commission gave every appearance of mutual cooperation and in fact turned up a mountain of information. But almost all of it was superfluous. Measured by weight, it appeared impressive. Measured by substance, it was paltry. Cooperation between the two sides mostly had to do with making certain that real cooperation was held to a minimum, certainly where the cold war losses were concerned.

The families therefore continued to be caught in a hopeless quagmire. Making the shootdown cases public during the cold war would not only have embarrassed the Department of Defense and its constituent intelligence agencies, but successive presidents from Eisenhower on, who would have been accused of being weaklings for abandoning brave American flyers to the mercy of the brutal, detested Communists. American prisoners really were treated savagely. But bringing that fact to public attention would have been a serious political mistake in the estimation of successive administrations. The revelations would have amounted to a tacit admission that the United States aggressively stole military secrets from the Soviet Union—"spied," as most outsiders called it—and then was unable or unwilling to rescue the men who got caught doing it.

For their part, the Russians had equally compelling reasons to lay the whole nasty business to rest. First, and most obviously, the men in the Kremlin understood there was everything to lose and nothing to gain by showing that their predecessors' henchmen in the KGB and military intelligence ran gulags, brutalized prisoners, and discounted human life. They therefore decided at the beginning, as a matter of policy, to conceal information about the gulags and those who suffered and died in them. Less obviously, they undoubtedly sensed that the overwhelming success of Western aerial reconnaissance operations, and certainly the overflights, showed beyond doubt that their country had been frighteningly vulnerable to bomber attack. That was not exactly the image the Kremlin wanted to project to the West, nor to its own citizens, even after the cold war: the government never could have protected you from annihilation; don't trust the government. So the Russians, too, treated the situation with malevolent neglect.

Gen. Bernard Loeffke, who headed Task Force Russia, and Col. Stuart Herrington, his deputy, were both career soldiers but political neophytes. They were too new at the game, and not on a high enough political perch, to grasp the political implications that more realistic insiders thought would follow the discovery that American prisoners had been treated savagely and murdered

in gulags. Since they didn't understand the big picture, they inno-
cently took their mandate at face value, and tried to get real answers for the families.

Ambassador Toon, on the other hand, was an ardent realist and
he therefore knew that to succeed was to fail. He understood the
score from the start and so did successive directors of the DPMO.
Careerists inside the Beltway don't need pieces of paper for political direction. They pick up signals from the Executive Branch
and Congress the way hunting dogs pick up the trail of pheasants
and raccoons: by sniffing the air, listening carefully, and watching
for faint movement.

Margaret (Jean) O'Kelley, whose husband died near John
Roche in the water off Vladivostok at the end of July 1953, was at
a meeting with Toon and Volkogonov forty years later and came
away with a mental snapshot that made her suspicious at the very
start. "Toon kept looking at his watch," she said. "Like, 'We're due
at that cocktail party.' "

Bruce Sanderson got the same message, but more explicitly. He
was in Moscow in mid-September 1992 when Toon and his delegation arrived to begin conferring with Volkogonov and the other
Russians. The Joint Commission's U.S. co-chairman had no
sooner gotten off the plane, Sanderson would later recall with exasperation, when he said: "My gut feeling is that we're going to
find absolutely nothing." It was like a coach telling his players before a game that his gut feeling was they were going to get killed.

Gregory P. Skavinski became seriously obsessive about finding
out what happened to his uncle, M. Sgt. William B. Homer, who
was on Busch's RB-29. Homer was at Pearl Harbor when the
Japanese attacked and he was shot down twice in World War II.
Skavinski, too, saw a clear difference between Task Force Russia
and the DPMO. "When TFR was in business," he said in his
home in Virginia one morning in July 1999, "you could pick up
the phone and talk to somebody. Just pick up the phone: 'What's
going on with my case?' And you'd get answers. Now, you can't do
that. You can't talk to the people down there. You have to go
through channels. *The families are their customers.*"

Greg Skavinski, like Bess Tejeda Bergmann, Bruce Sanderson,
and some others, was one of the first and most active members in

the national network of families that coalesced immediately after Yeltsin dropped his bombshell. From his perspective, the DPMO was "defensive" and there was friction with the families "since day one."

"The bottom line is, I'm not impressed with the way they've treated the family members," he said. "There are a lot of good people down there," he explained of the DPMO. "But there are some people down there that, for whatever reason . . . I think they look at the family members as being adversaries. It shouldn't be an adversarial relationship. They should do everything possible to answer our questions."

When he testified on the missing airmen before a Senate committee, Skavinski heard the same message Jean O'Kelley and Bruce Sanderson got from Malcolm Toon, except it was from the senators themselves. He was saddened to see that Sen. Robert Smith, a New Hampshire Republican, was the only member of the committee on the dais. "That was sort of a disgrace," the soft-spoken but tenacious Virginian said. So he made his own contribution to setting the record straight. "I stood up and read their names. I read the guys' names, starting with Sam Busch. I read their hometowns. I said the reason I'm doing this is because their names aren't in any history books, and their names aren't on any monuments.

"Can you imagine the love there?" Skavinski said of the other searchers, of men and women who lost husbands, brothers, and fathers. "I'm frustrated. You hear, well, maybe they're going to do a salvage operation. Okay. Three or four of the planes were shot down near Vladivostok and the Sea of Japan. And then you don't hear anything about that. 'Well, it's too expensive, or the Russians won't let us in there, or—' C'mon. If they want to do it, then let's do it. We'll pay for it. Think of this. If they can find the *Titanic*, certainly they can look for these planes if they're there. Those are the things you wonder about. If this is the highest national priority—to find those guys—then let's do it. If we can spend billions of dollars in Bosnia and Kosovo, which to me is just an absolute national disgrace . . . We can't take care of the veterans back here, yet they're spending this kind of money . . . You wonder where the priorities are."

Sanderson was also scornful of the DPMO. "They dragged their feet. If they don't have a family member pushing, pushing, pushing every day, week, and month, they'd do absolutely nothing."

FOR HIS PART, Dmitri Volkogonov saw the big picture as well as Toon, his American counterpart. Perhaps he saw it even better. The Joint Commission was really a test bed, a trial balloon, for cultivating other relationships. As the politically savvy Russian general would say privately, the commission was merely a "tuning fork" to demonstrate his country's goodwill. In fact, at a meeting with Toon and the families of missing servicemen in the two Asian wars and the cold war that was held in the Pentagon on March 1, 1994, Volkogonov stunningly rewrote history, in the process directly contradicting his boss.

Asked by Sanderson whether he could identify the twelve Americans mentioned by Yeltsin, Volkogonov stunned the family members by blithely explaining that "President Yeltsin was referring to those who in the past or currently were in the Soviet Union *on a voluntary basis* [italics added]. That list was first thirty-nine names long; now it is about fifteen. . . . They involved certain groups of individuals who were compelled to become Soviet citizens (some had a Slavic background who were in the Soviet Union on the eve of World War II, had their passports revoked, and were made to be Soviet citizens after serving in prison camps)."

The twelve Americans Yeltsin had specifically said were military airmen who had been shot down and captured in 1953, then, turned into holdovers from before the war, not airmen, and in any case hadn't really wanted to leave the Soviet Union. The backpedaling had begun.

Yet like Bernard Loeffke, Stuart Herrington, and a few other Americans, some Russians were slow to catch on to the pervasive, deeply embedded deceit. One of them was Col. Gavril Ivanovich Korotkov, an English-speaking military interrogator who from mid-1950 to mid-1954 was in an intelligence unit responsible for analyzing and reporting on the morale and psychological state of

U.S. servicemen in the Korean War. He questioned a number of American POWs, some of whom had been captured in North Korea and sent to Soviet prison camps. When he was himself questioned in Moscow in 1992 by General Loeffke, Colonel Herrington, and others, Korotkov stated unequivocally that crewmen from *Little Red Ass*, Stan O'Kelley's RB-50G, had indeed been pulled out of the water and taken to Vladivostok and then to Khabarovsk for questioning. He was not allowed to question the prisoners himself, he explained, but he knew they were there.

"I remember this incident very well," he said. "As a matter of fact, the war had just ended in Korea. . . . I remember this episode very well because we thought then that they would take us to talk with these flyers, the Americans. Because we knew that many of them, after they had landed, were picked up. They were rescued. One of them died but the majority of them survived." Korotkov said he vividly recalled being kept away from the Americans by the civilian KGB. "They told us that we would not be able to meet them. Some reason or another. I don't know. When we tried, as specialists, to get information: 'It is forbidden to talk with them?' 'Where are they?' Then they said that we were forbidden to meet them." Korotkov added that the prisoners were quickly taken out of Khabarovsk. The reason he and his army colleagues were not allowed to interrogate the American airmen soon became grimly clear.

"As a matter of fact, they already were not considered prisoners of war; that's where the problem was. They were already considered to be spies. And that's why we didn't have access to them. As to the fact that so many of them were picked up, and that many of them were alive, it turns out that there is no doubt about that."

There was certainly no doubt in Korotkov's mind that 1st Lt. Warren J. Sanderson, the "big raven" on O'Kelley's aircraft, had been taken alive. He told Bruce as much when the North Dakotan was in Moscow with Toon in September 1992. Gavril Korotkov was convinced that Sanderson was not treated as a POW. Instead, he was convicted of espionage—the Korean War having been over for two days when he was shot down—and died serving a twenty-five-year prison sentence. Korotkov noted that the American's immediate tormenters were from the KGB's notoriously ruthless counterintelligence arm, Smersh. As readers of Ian Fleming know, the term means "Death to Spies."

Korotkov's story was supported by Georgi Yakovlevich Kravchenko, who was a sergeant in an antiaircraft gun battery on Russkiy Island on the morning of July 29, 1953, and who claimed to have watched the attack on O'Kelley's plane. In May 1993 he told a reporter from the *Izvestiya* news agency that the Superfortress— "the exact same type that dropped the bombs on Hiroshima and Nagasaki," his commanders said—was bearing down on Vladivostok when two MiGs intercepted it at a distance of roughly fifteen miles. Kravchenko continued:

> Well, as soon as our fighters started drawing close to this aircraft, he [the RB-29] opened fire. One of the fighters started smoking, flew past the aircraft, turned around, and headed off back in the direction of Vladivostok. But the second fighter at this time also flew past the intruder, turned around, came up behind him, and opened fire at the tail of this bomber. The engagement didn't take long, but it was decisive. The bomber caught fire, and he was flying along, straight at our battery. As soon as it caught fire, we started seeing parachutes. We counted, there, all of us, we counted seven men.

He added that the intruder crashed four miles from where he stood, that there was no order to rescue the men who bailed out that he knew of, and that the visibility on the water was poor (corroborated by John Roche). He said he saw the Americans hit the water and had no idea what happened to them after that. The fact that he heard no rescue order might well mean the patrol boats were, indeed, already in position to pick up the airmen.

While Georgi Kravchenko felt no personal animosity toward the Americans, he was positively delighted they had been shot down. His reason was personal, not political, and it sheds light on the extent of U.S. ferret operations against the home port of his country's Pacific fleet. The former antiaircraft gunner explained that the alert claxon sounding general quarters went off as many as eighteen times a day and made life almost unbearable for the gun crews. The American planes would typically fly to within eighteen miles to get the radar turned on, he said, and then turn and fly away. Since the antiaircraft guns had a range of only twelve miles, and therefore couldn't hope to hit the ferrets, he and the other gunners were frustrated as well as exhausted and edgy. If even a significant fraction of the alerts alleged by Kravchenko happened, and the evidence suggests they did, it indicates the intensity of ferret operations.

BY MARCH 1993—roughly six months after telling Loeffke and Herrington that most of O'Kelley's crew had been taken to Khararovsk for interrogation as spies—Gavril Korotkov abruptly claimed he had been badly misquoted and, in any case, he had only repeated rumors. He flatly repudiated what he had said in the interviews. Now the backpedaling was really under way. Korotkov very likely was quietly told that he had harmed his country by making the revelations and, in any case, that such talk could bring nothing but trouble to him and his family. Trouble, the old military intelligence officer would surely have known, might mean anything from losing his pension, to having his apartment vandalized, to falling in front of a bus. Korotkov's retired cronies, the military and KGB interrogators, probably were afraid of legal action by the Americans' families, and, seeing no reason to invite trouble of any kind, no doubt issued the warning. But the order to shut Korotkov up and get him to renounce his statements came from a higher authority.

It came from the top. Six years later, a deeply angry Bruce Sanderson recalled the events of March 1993. "After Korotkov had made his first statements, there was talk of nothing else [among the families]: 'We have taken so many Americans . . .' [and] his group wanted to interrogate them. Then it was denied. The Russians, at the next plenary session [of the Joint Commission], asked Toon, . . . their exact words were: 'Will you help abrogate this man's [Korotkov's] statement?' It means to help nullify by official action. *They asked our side to help crush Korotkov's statement*," a still incredulous Bruce Sanderson said. "And that's in the notes. That's in the minutes. That's part of the damned record," he added. "And," he continued, his voice still edged in disbelief, *"Toon said, 'Yes, we will help you with this.'"*

Cooperation had been achieved. Both sides implicitly agreed to cooperate in sabotaging the project by expunging from the record the testimony of an authoritative witness who insisted a SAC reconnaissance crew had been captured, charged with espionage, and swallowed alive by the enemy. Gavril Korotkov had good reason to know his system's capacity for ferocious retribution. He therefore quietly disappeared into the safety of obscurity.

VLADIMIR TROTSENKO, WHO claimed to have seen four American airmen in Military Hospital 404 in Novosysoyevka in November 1951 following the shootdown of a Neptune on the 6th of that month, was handled differently. As far as is known, he was neither threatened nor made to disappear. But instead of using him to provide solid leads that could have traced the Navy prisoners back to the Far East (which the American side should have insisted upon), the Russian government carefully discredited Trotsenko in the traditional way.

Volkogonov's minions claimed that Trotsenko's record showed he had been in Military Hospital 404 between March and May 1951, not in November. So he had been released before the Americans allegedly arrived and therefore could not have seen them even if they had been there. More to the point, if the man could not even be trusted to remember when he was in the hospital, the Russians told the Americans with what amounted to a shrug, he certainly could not be trusted to remember who the other patients were. No one on the American side objected. No one asked to see the record. Case closed.

THE DPMO GENERATED a lot of paper and continues to do so. There is endless work, including trips to Moscow for meetings, and the publication of pamphlets, testimony, and reports of all sorts, that a casual observer could take for progress. But there is a difference between activity and progress. The activity has camouflaged an inhibition to succeed. And the inhibition—the failure to make an all-out effort to find the MIAs—has increased with time as part of a deliberate, consistent pattern of deception.

There have been complaints over the years, for example, that poor record keeping by the Russians vastly complicated the process of tracking down the prisoners. To the contrary, the KGB, its precursor agencies, and their border guards kept careful records. A representative from the border guards archives was appointed to Volkogonov's staff when the Joint Commission was formed, yet the archives themselves have remained almost completely out of bounds. So have the KGB archives in Moscow and elsewhere. When the U.S. side asked to see the KGB's records, it was told that the records would be opened when the CIA's records were opened. Since the CIA wouldn't dream of doing that, and since there was a feeling that a close examination of the KGB archives would create more problems than it would solve, both sides tacitly agreed to accept the standoff.

There also has been a persistent failure to pursue leads aggressively. Reports of sightings of American prisoners of war by Eastern Europeans and Japanese have usually been reflexively dismissed as "unsubstantiated." As a result, the quality of information collected by the DPMO has been uniformly poor, with thousands of tiny bits of unrelated information adding up to nothing.

Paul Cole, who was doing painstaking research on the POW/MIA issue for the Rand Corporation even before Yeltsin dropped "the turd in the punchbowl," as he put it, claimed to have been thwarted by the "court eunuchs" in the Department of Defense, meaning the Joint Commission and DPMO. "The Russian general staff offered to allow my team to photocopy everything in exchange for a photocopying machine," he said. It would have been, in Cole's words, an "opportunity unprecedented in history." But he was turned down. "I was a 'dupe.' 'They' just wanted to get a xerox machine, which I was too naive to understand," the still angry scholar said years later. "You can travel the world and never find a monument built to commemorate a commission," said Paul Cole. "Commissions are designed to bury things, not to find them."

Patricia Service would probably agree. Her father-in-law, 1st

Lt. Samuel D. Service, was also on Sam Busch's RB-29. She came out of her loss as deeply troubled as Charlotte Mitnik, Bruce Sanderson, Greg Skavinski, and scores of others. Trying to get information out of the Department of Defense, she said, was "one of the most frustrating experiences of my life." She recalled writing a stream of letters that produced answers professing total ignorance. "*We're* viewed as the enemy," she added. "I don't know why we are, but we are. I think they have information that would be quite embarrassing," said Pat Service. "I think they're doing damage control."

"I PLEDGE TO the families of unaccounted-for Americans and to the Americans placed in harm's way to uphold the nation's commitment," Gen. Robert L. Jones, the DPMO's panjandrum in 1999, wrote in its report that year. "We shall unceasingly seek to account for those who are missing, ensure proper resources and training for our recovery forces, and do our utmost to bring every American home."

That is the "party line," one knowledgeable Department of Defense official explained ruefully, and it allegedly has the highest national priority. "If this is the highest national priority," he added, "I'd be curious to know what zeal we devote to the lowest."

EVERYONE WHO FLIES bombers knows about collateral damage. The Air Force defines it as "the damage to surrounding resources, either military or non-military, as a result of actions or strikes specifically against enemy forces or military facilities." The survivors of the men who were lost on reconnaissance missions during the cold war know about a different kind of collateral damage.

Although none of them thought about it just that way, they were the resources who suffered the damage, who went through the pain and confusion and disorientation that arrived with the chaplains and the dreaded telegrams.

Mary Dunham was married just twenty-eight months when she suffered collateral damage. She was wed to 2d Lt. John R. Dunham in the chapel at Annapolis on June 4, 1950, the day he graduated, and walked with him under the traditional crossed swords. Their daughter, Suzanne, was born at the Walter Reed Army Hospital in Bethesda on August 29, 1952. By then, John—nicknamed Chute—was a first lieutenant in the Ninety-first Strategic Reconnaissance Squadron at Yokota and navigating *Sunbonnet King*, the RB-29 that was shot down off Hokkaido on October 7, 1952. It was Dunham's body that was pulled out of the water by Sgt. Vasily Saiko of the Soviet Maritime Border Guards and taken for burial on nearby Yuri Island. And it was Dunham's Annapolis class ring that Saiko pocketed and would keep for years.

Mary, of course, knew nothing of that at the time of the incident. The first hint of trouble came from television, which reported a B-29 had been shot down over the Sea of Japan. She was ironing at her mother-in-law's house when the report came on. "I wonder whether Chute knows anyone on that plane?" Mary thought. Then the telegrams came: one to her and one to Dunham's widowed mother, Anna. Anna Thompson Dunham, who lived in Easton, Maryland, "absolutely went to pieces," her daughter-in-law would remember later.

So did Mary. The telegram announcing her husband was missing sent her into a state of shock so severe she would eventually call it trauma. It was the start of a wracking emotional odyssey which, to some degree, was widely shared by the loved ones of most of the missing airmen. Missing. Absent. Vanished. Unaccounted for. Not here. But not necessarily there. Nowhere. There was no way she could move through a life that was formed like a question mark.

"Not knowing is the cruelest thing," she explained. "When a man is killed, and the body comes home, you bury him, and you see it—the funeral—and everybody comes. The whole bit. You know it's done. In this case, I'd wake up in the morning: 'Is he coming home? No. He's missing. Maybe he's dead. Maybe he's being tortured in a Soviet prison.' It was just an up-and-down nightmare. It was just like a yo-yo; up and down and nobody to talk to about it."

Three years later, as usual, John Dunham was officially certified by his employer to have been killed in an "Aircraft accident (military)." It didn't help very much. Nor did living in Easton,

Maryland, their hometown. Where her husband's family was concerned, "I was just a bad reminder of his death." Nor did a counselor who told her she had slipped through all the cracks and her life amounted to "a comedy of errors."

In 1959, still desperately traumatized and alone, the grieving widow with the seven-year-old daughter turned to the Episcopal church for help. That took her even closer to hell.

"This minister pressured me into being a parish assistant. It's so hard to talk about," she said one morning in her sunny kitchen in north Baltimore forty years later. "He did not have good intentions. What this man did—and his wife knew about it—any young widow, or young woman, who came there for counseling. . . . He would propose sex to her. And some women did have sexual relations with him. Not with me. It didn't work. He pressured me. I lost all my confidence when my husband's plane was shot down. I had no confidence at all in myself," she explained, rapping the kitchen table. "I was very vulnerable but it just didn't happen." At the end of the summer, the thwarted Lothario told her he didn't need her services as a parish assistant and fired her. "I was so angry," Mary added, "I wanted to kill him."

Instead, she went to another Episcopal church for counseling, and finally found a minister who was genuinely sympathetic. She told him about the propositioner and he prayed for her. That Christmas of 1959 Mary Dunham had a religious experience, just as John McKone would have the following year after his RB-47H was shot down over the Barents Sea. Sitting in church, she thought she saw John very clearly, and he seemed to tell her he was with God. "Mary," she believed she heard him say, "we're all right. We want you to go and have a good life."

"It freed me. I knew that he had died. To me, this was proof. I thought, Well, I don't have to worry anymore. He's with God." And years later there was healing of another kind. She had the deep satisfaction of hearing that the first minister, the predator, had been removed from his parish. "He messed around with some socialite down there and they got him out of there. The church is *so* corrupt," Mary Dunham Nichols said (she remarried in 1965). "Yet I go faithfully. God has never failed me."

Suzanne Dunham, who was six weeks old when her father was

shot down, went to Wellesley College, became a lawyer, and married a man she met at Harvard. By her mother's account, and in common with the sons and daughters of other airmen who flew cold war reconnaissance and never returned, Suzanne carried her own abiding anger for having been born into a painful situation that was not her doing. She grew up without a father, Mary said, and with a mother who didn't talk about him. It left a void that was not filled by her stepfather. To that day in June 1999, Mary and Suzanne had never talked about the consequences of Mary's remarrying.

Mary Dunham Nichols's journey through the labyrinth was not yet finished. In 1992, soon after the U.S.-Russia Joint Commission on POW/MIA Affairs was formed, it turned up in a Moscow archive in a telegram to Air Force General Vasily Stalin reporting the recovery of John Dunham's body. When Roy Dunham, one of his two surviving brothers, found out about the telegram, he went to the press with the news and wound up on CNN.

One evening in the late autumn of 1993, Vasily Saiko and his wife, Lyuba, were watching television in Rostov when they saw a clip featuring Roy Dunham appealing for information about his brother John. Vasily and Lyuba instantly remembered the ring he had pulled off the dead American's finger on that cold day in October 1952 near Yuri Island.

The next day, the wary Lyuba called the number given on the news segment and reported only that her husband had information about an American aviator who had been shot down near the Kurile Islands in 1952. She lived in a country that had suddenly come on hard times and where such a heavy gold ring could cost a life.

With the ring sewn into a pouch in his right pants pocket, Vasily assured Lyuba that he would in no circumstance turn it over to a Russian. He took the twenty-two-hour overnight train to Moscow. Then he went straight to the Joint Commission office, where he told the story of pulling Dunham out of the water and, after fumbling to open the pouch, showed commission members on both sides the prized class ring. The next day he handed it directly to Malcolm Toon, who brought it to the U.S. embassy.

Early on the morning of December 8, 1993, Kaye Whitley, a

Pentagon official at the embassy, called Mary with the news. Whitley was another early member of the Joint Commission who won praise from the families. The woman on the other end of the line in Maryland was too stunned to say anything for several moments. Then she started to cry. When she got off the phone with Whitley, Mary called Suzanne in Michigan and relayed the news.

"It has taken forty-one years," she told her daughter. "What does it mean?"

"It means it's finally over," Suzanne told her mother.

But it wasn't over. Saiko also reported he knew where the American was buried on Yuri Island. Using documents and a map found in the Border Guards archives in the Far East, three Russian and four American representatives of Task Force Russia went to Yuri Island in May 1994 and spent ten days searching unsuccessfully for John Dunham's grave. They were finally told by the Russians to pack up and leave. Another group returned three months later, and after two more weeks of digging, found what they were looking for on September 2. John Dunham's skeleton—with most of his skull and part of a leg missing—was sent to Moscow for examination by Russian forensic specialists. It went from there to the Department of Defense's Central Identification Laboratory in Hawaii for positive identification.

Years later, Mary Dunham Nichols praised Task Force Russia and, in particular, Col. Herrington. "In the very beginning, it was wonderful," she said. "The original crew really cared about the families. They really wanted to get answers." She also commended General Loeffke for his sensitivity to family needs. But after TFR was subsumed by DPMO, she added, matters worsened. "And then things changed after that," the wise and straight-talking Marylander added. "Now," she said of the organization that absorbed it, "it's just a charade. It's a shameful thing. No question about it."

With Vasily and Lyuba Saiko looking on, as well as Mary Dunham Nichols and her husband Donald, Suzanne Dunham Fong, her husband Bobby, their two young sons, other relatives, and members of the Naval Academy's class of 1950, Capt. John Robertson Dunham was taken to Arlington National Cemetery on a horse-drawn caisson on August 1, 1995, and finally laid to rest.

Mary, then nearly seventy years old and still the clear-headed iconoclast, accepted a folded Stars and Stripes from an Air Force colonel, while Suzanne, clutching five-year-old Colin, finally let herself cry. "The first time I'm ever going to be physically with my dad is when I see his coffin," she had remarked before the ceremony.

Four years later the redoubtable Mary Dunham Nichols, the famous class ring hanging on a gold chain around her neck (it was the subject of an article in Reader's Digest and several newspaper accounts), offered some pointed observations about the system through which she had passed, virtually unnoticed and unaided, for years. She deplored the fact that veterans' groups don't help and comfort the widows and orphans of servicemen who are lost fighting for their country. It's not a matter of money—benefits— but of humanity. Nor is it a matter of the federal government starting some new program. She is resolutely convinced that the effort has to come from the private sector, and specifically, the veterans' organizations.

And, Mary explained, there is a model. It is called Legacy, and it was started in Australia in 1923 by veterans who returned from World War I thankful they had survived and eager to help the widows and orphans of those who hadn't. The men started groups all over the country that sought and found families in need of help. Many of them took on the roles of surrogate fathers to children, in the process forging a support system without government assistance. "They had an organization that provided all services: emotional, social, legal, financial, medical, whatever the need was," Mary said, "and there has never been a hint of scandal since 1923." It's a practical, trained group, not a collection of ignorant do-gooders, she added, and it raises the money it needs on its own.

"From my experience, from the time my husband was shot down in 1952 and in the years immediately following—I had a baby six weeks old—I heard nothing from the American Legion or the VFW [Veterans of Foreign Wars] from that time to this. They never helped; never offered any kind of assistance. They do not see the widows and orphans as their responsibility." All the veterans do is complain, she added with modulated anger. "Mention

American Legion to anybody and they'll say, 'They're a bunch of boozers.' That's the answer I always get. They've got wonderful PR, but it's not for the widows and orphans."

The closest thing the United States has to a support group such as Legacy is TAPS, the Tragedy Assistance Program for Survivors, a privately run group to which Mary Dunham Nichols belongs. The organization holds a meeting every year around Memorial Day that requires a registration fee and includes keynote speakers, peer support groups, a banquet, and workshops on topics such as how to handle grief, military entitlements, relaxation and stress reduction, and the use of humor.

One workshop, called Hello From Heaven, is built on a dubious "new field of research" called After-Death Communication, in which people are allegedly contacted by dead loved ones. The research, which is available in a paperback that sells for $5.99 at the meetings, is said to be based on more than 3,300 firsthand accounts. Another paperback purporting to show that "there *is* life after death, for you and everyone you've ever known" is also available to any widow who is willing to suspend reason to be comforted. TAPS also has a Web site and a volunteer telephone support system called SurvivorLINK. The idea is to show the hundred-or-so widows and others who attend the meeting, and many others who don't, that they are not alone in their grief.

"I walked in and I have never felt greater relief in my life," Mary Dunham Nichols explained at the 1999 meeting. "And you walk in, and be with people. You don't have to explain anything. It was like a terrific load taken off me." The idea, one of the group's organizers explained succinctly, is to "honor our loved ones and honor ourselves."

FOR JEAN O'KELLEY, too, there was initially loneliness and confusion; a sense of isolation and helplessness and of trying to grapple with a faceless bureaucracy. The heart of the problem in 1953, when her husband's RB-50G went down, was the lack of communication among the widows. The pervasive secrecy that had run through their lives when their husbands were flying reconnaissance missions carried over after they disappeared. On some psychic level, the institutionalized segregation of secrets—"sensitive compartmented information," or SCI, as intelligence people call it—spilled over into the larger community. However subliminally, the old "need to know" culture in which a man was made privy only to the secrets he needed to know to do his job, and not one secret more, necessarily spilled over on the wives. Ironically, they needed to know a great deal, but they, too, were effectively compartmented by the military culture. And equally ironic, the walls were finally demolished, or at least cracked, by an explosive remark by a visiting Russian president.

"In the beginning . . . I was just fighting it by myself because I didn't know what happened to the other crew members' wives," Jean O'Kelley said of her long effort at trying to find out what really happened to her husband and his plane. "So I was just writing letters all the time, by myself, and I'd always get the same answer: refer you to the Air Force. The Air Force would say they're doing everything in their power to help me, but at this point, they didn't know. And this was *after* they knew I had a body. . . . They would always say, 'We're investigating. . . . We'll let you know.' "

The lack of tangible information, the frustration of not being able to come to grips with the real nature of the tragedy, often made Jean O'Kelley irritable. It affected her daughter, Denise. "Every time I got upset, she'd break out and she'd get a fever, and I'd have to take her to the doctor. It was just unbelievable."

So was her lonely battle to get Social Security payments for Denise. The Social Security Administration withheld the checks, Jean O'Kelley explained, "because they said I wasn't living with my husband when she was born! I said, 'How could I? *He was TDY!*' " The fact that Stan O'Kelley was on temporary duty in the Far East flying an RB-50G did not seem to be an adequate excuse for being absent.

It would have been no consolation, but Stan O'Kelley's widow shared that experience with countless other widows, the foremost being Alexander Hamilton's. In their groundbreaking book about the treatment of American combat veterans from Valley Forge to Vietnam, *The Wages of War*, Richard Severo and Lewis Milford recounted how Elizabeth Hamilton petitioned Congress for financial assistance in 1810, six years after her husband was killed in the famous duel with Aaron Burr.

The mother of seven children asked for five years' unclaimed back pay, but was told "the prayer of the petition ought not to be granted" because the statute of limitations had expired. Mrs. Hamilton didn't make her case on her husband's having helped draft the Constitution, write *The Federalist Papers* with James Madison and John Jay, and in several other ways invent the United States. She made it on his having been a veteran: a retired lieutenant colonel in New York's First Artillery Company who had fought valiantly at Yorktown, the last campaign of the Revolutionary War. Still in need of help, she overcame humiliation and tried again in 1816, and Congress finally relented. So did the Social Security Administration in the case of Jean O'Kelley.

The sense of helplessness extended to home repair, and that caused its own delicate but insidious problem. After Jean O'Kelley returned to Napa, her hometown, she found she was "a novelty" that neighbors couldn't quite fathom: an attractive young widow with three children. When major household repairs had to be done, she explained, old Air Force buddies of her husband would help out. "People would fly in with their tool kits and do whatever I needed done. I wasn't going to ask them to stay at a motel—I was friends with their wives—so they stayed at my house. And that," she added, laughing, "was kind of frowned upon" by the neighbors. She calmed the wives in the neighborhood with a subtle but effective bit of diplomacy. She had a swimming pool built and invited the women, their husbands, and children to use it.

ROXANN PHILLIPS, WHOSE father was one of the three ravens who disappeared on Willard Palm's RB-47H over the Barents Sea on July 1, 1960, was fifteen months old when the attack happened. She had no father from then on, but she had an exceptionally strong mother who helped her adjust to the situation.

"The only time I ever remember being angry or disappointed—and it wasn't the fact that I didn't have a father—was when people felt sorry for me because I didn't have a father," Roxann said emphatically. The pity came mostly from her classmates in grade and high school in Sacramento. "Well, so big deal. My mother was a very strong woman. She did everything she had to do. She did it all for me. And we had a tremendous support group with family and friends," she said at a Fifty-fifth Strategic Reconnaissance Wing reunion in Reno in October 1999. Being with veterans who knew her dad, she explained, being around people she had known on and off for years, and who had done what he had, brought her closer to him. She had a palpable feeling that the veterans of the Fifty-fifth were an extended family and that through them her father's spirit was alive.

Yeltsin's revelation brought her closer to her father, too, and gave her insight into her mother's lingering pain. "Once détente started and Russia started to unravel, our government got a little bit more forthcoming with this information," Roxy Phillips continued. "We would get these packages of stuff in the mail from the Air Force. It was all declassified documents and pictures and helmets. It just kept coming and coming. I'd come home and she'd be crying."

THE KEYNOTE ADDRESS at the Fifty-fifth's reunion that year was given by retired Maj. Gen. Charles D. Metcalf, director of the U.S. Air Force Museum at Wright-Patterson Air Force Base outside Dayton. "The whole mission of the peripheral reconnaissance—the RB-29s, the RB-50s, RB-45s, RB-47s—was accomplished only by a handful of organizations, and you carried the whole load of the cold war on your back," he said to the silent people in the banquet room, men and women who knew they were slowly fading into history. "The Baltic, Russia, Siberia, each side of the Iron Curtain, White Sea, Korea, Cuba, all became your operational areas. Make no mistake: these were very dangerous missions, and I don't need to tell you that. It was not a bloodless war. But you rose to the occasion. You went. You knew the risks. And you felt that freedom was worth dying for. I don't think that anybody really appreciated the depth of your accomplishments. You couldn't tell anybody. The veil was drawn around all of your actions. Only now it's coming out, what a magnificent story it is."

ON FEBRUARY 22 AND 23, 2001, the story was told openly at last. More than two hundred grandfathers, some of them infirm and nearly all grown gray, came together in Tighe Auditorium at the Defense Intelligence Agency headquarters at Bolling Air Force Base in Washington, D.C. The occasion was a symposium, Early Cold War Overflights, which for the first time publicly recognized what the veterans of the reconnaissance war did and let them speak for themselves. There were some grandmothers attending, too.

Gen. Andrew J. Goodpaster, who had been Eisenhower's military alter ego during his presidency, put the situation in perspective when he recalled that Ike had likened the overflights to an act of war and knew they were hard for the Russians to stomach. It was only desperation, Goodpaster continued, that drove the dangerous missions: penetrations which, by mutual agreement among Red China, the Soviet Union, and the United States, were never publicized for fear that embarrassing the Communists would provoke even more bloodshed.

There were panels on the big picture, on Asian overflights, European overflights, overflights of the Soviet Arctic, and imagery interpretation. There was Col. Stacy Naftel, finally talking about flying over the Chinese nuclear weapons test facility, and of suddenly dropping out of the clouds to roar right over the ships at Vladivostok as startled Soviet sailors scrambled to get to their guns.

There was Lt. Col. Lloyd Fields, still trim in a dark blue suit, though now with severely impaired sight, describing the daring Home Run overflights back in 1956, when Siberia was repeatedly penetrated by the RB-47s. And, he remembered quite vividly, some of the Stratojets "drew flies"—attracted Soviet fighters. Col. Burton Barrett and Gen. Earl O'Loughlin, who also flew the Home Run penetrations, remembered the flies as well.

Lt. Col. Roy Kaden was there, too. Kaden had been around so

long that he actually went back to the Martin B-10, which became operational in the Army Air Corps in 1934 and could reach an impressive 197 miles an hour. By the time he retired in 1960, Kaden had overflown Franz Josef Land in an RB-50 and had then moved on to RB-47Hs.

Cmdr. Richard Koch, the Navy's lone representative ("It was once eight hundred to one; this time it's only two hundred to one," he quipped), described a joint Navy–Air Force operation in 1952 in which his "one-of-a-kind" P2V-3W Neptune ferret teamed up with a camera-carrying RB-50 to fly up the length of far eastern Siberia looking for Tu-4s and plotting radar sites in absolute radio silence. Being shot down was considered so likely that an ancient B-17 carrying a large lifeboat under its belly tagged along.

Fighter pilots Col. Laverne Griffin, Col. Robert Morrison, and Col. Samuel Dickens were among a contingent of Fifteenth Tactical Fighter Squadron alumni who were on hand. RF-86Fs from the Fifteenth streaked 42,000 feet over cloud-dappled Spassk-Dal'Niy East Air Base north of Vladivostok in April 1954 and returned with clear shots of forty or more Tu-4s lined up adjacent to the facility's only runway. Sam Dickens, a compact West Point graduate (one of the SAC pilots quipped that the main requirement for a fighter pilot is that he be short), sported a yellow cap and the squadron's yellow checkerboard silk scarf. Later, they all had their pictures taken together as a parting souvenir. So did the veterans from other units.

On the second day, in a very moving gesture, a man in the audience who identified himself only as a former bomber pilot stood up to express his appreciation to the men who had risked their lives to find the targets that convinced the opposition that it would be annihilated in another war.

Later, when the presentations were over and the group pictures had been taken, a plenary session—a last gathering—was held at a hotel in nearby Crystal City, Virginia. Every man in the room was presented with a medallion, a final medal, that honored what he had done: "In Recognition of Those Who Served; Early Cold War Overflights 1950–1956."

"This grand gathering has afforded us the opportunity to

pay homage to those whose sense of duty never faltered," Robb Hoover, the master of ceremonies, told them. "You, the overflight veterans, sallied forth to shine light on the unknown; to remove that doubt so that critical national security decisions could be made on the basis of fact, not conjecture. Your missions not only brought back the imagery and electronic intelligence about an aggressive enemy's burgeoning offensive power, but your aircraft stimulated his air defense system to reaction. That's how we knew how advanced and proficient they were.

"There are those who say that technology—those eyes way up in the sky—has passed you by," Hoover added. "But today's on-scene commanders continue to clamor for the services of a responsive airborne recce fleet. Fear not. Your tradition is secure. Your reputation shines brightly. Let your names be inscribed in the book of memorable deeds."

The living and the dead finally were in from the cold.

 In Memoriam

PB4Y-2 APRIL 8, 1950

Lt. John H. Fette
Lt. (jg) Howard W. Seechaf
Lt. (jg) Robert D. Reynolds
Ens. Tommy L. Burgess
AD1c. Joe H. Danens Jr.

AD1c. Jack W. Thomas
AT1c. Frank L. Beckman
CT3c. Edward J. Purcell
AT3c. Joseph N. Rinnier Jr.
AL3c. Joseph J. Bourassa

P2V-3W NOVEMBER 6, 1951

Lt. (jg) Judd C. Hodgson
Lt. (jg) Samuel Rosenfeld
Ens. Donald A. Smith
AO1c. Reuben S. Baggett
AD1c. Paul R. Foster

AT1c. Erwin D. Raglin
AL2c. Paul G. Juric
AT2c. William S. Meyer
AL2c. Ralph A. Wigert
AD3c. Jack D. Lively

RB-29 JUNE 13, 1952

Maj. Samuel N. Busch
Capt. James A. Sculley
Capt. Samuel D. Service
1st Lt. Robert J. McDonnell

S. Sgt. William A. Blizzard
S. Sgt. Miguel W. Monserrat
S. Sgt. Eddie R. Berg
S. Sgt. Leon F. Bonura

M. Sgt. William R. Homer
M. Sgt. David L. Moore

S. Sgt. Rosco G. Becker
A1c. Danny H. Pillsbury

RB-29 OCTOBER 7, 1952

Capt. Eugene M. English
Capt. John R. Dunham
1st Lt. Paul E. Brock
S. Sgt. Samuel A. Colgan

T. Sgt. John A. Hirsch
A1c. Thomas G. Shipp
A2c. Fred G. Kendrick
A2c. Frank E. Neail

P2V-5 JANUARY 18, 1953

Ens. Dwight C. Angell
AT3c. Paul A. Morley
AD3c. Lloyd Smith

AL3c. Ronald A. Beahm
PH1c. William F. McClure
AT3c. Clifford Byars

RB-50G JULY 29, 1953

Capt. Stanley K. O'Kelley
Capt. John C. Ward
Maj. Francisco J. Tejeda
Capt. Edmund J. Czyz
Capt. Lloyd C. Wiggins
Capt. James G. Keith
Capt. Warren J. Sanderson
Capt. Robert E. Stalnaker

Capt. Frank E. Beyer
M. Sgt. Francis L. Brown
S. Sgt. Donald W. Gabree
A1c. Roland E. Goulet
A2c. James E. Woods
A2c. Charles J. Russell
S. Sgt. Donald G. Hill
A2c. Earl W. Radlein

P2V-5 JANUARY 4, 1954

Lt. Jesse Beasley
Lt. Fredrick T. Prael
Ens. Stanley B. Mulford
Ens. Paul D. Morelli
AL2c. Allen R. Claussen

AL3c. David B. Berger
AT2c. Loyd B. Rensink
ADC Robert G. Archbold
AD2c. James F. Hand
AO3c. Gordon Spicklemier

P2V-5 SEPTEMBER 4, 1954

Ens. Rodger H. Reid

RB-47E APRIL 17, 1955

Capt. Robert N. Brooks
Capt. Richard E. Watkins

Maj. Lacie C. Neighbors

P4M-1Q AUGUST 22, 1956

Lt. Cmdr. Milton Hutchinson
Lt. (jg) James B. Deane
Lt. (jg) Francis A. Flood Jr.
Lt. Cmdr. James W. Ponsford
AT2c. Donald W. Barber
AO2c. Warren E. Caron
AT3c. Jack A. Curtis
AT1c. William F. Haskins

AO3c. William M. Humbert
AD1c. Harold E. Lounsbury
AT3c. Albert P. Mattin
AT3c. Donald E. Sprinkle
AT2c. Leonard Strykowsky
AD3c. Lloyd L. Young
AT2c. Carl E. Messinger
AF2c. Wallace W. Powell

RB-50G SEPTEMBER 10, 1956

Maj. Lorin C. Disbrow
Capt. Rodger A. Fees
Capt. William J. McLaughlin
Capt. Pat P. Taylor
1st Lt. Peter J. Rahaniotes
2d Lt. Richard T. Kobayashi
T. Sgt. Palmer D. Arrowood
T. Sgt. Bobby R. Davis

S. Sgt. Raymond D. Johnson
S. Sgt. Paul W. Swinehart
S. Sgt. Theodorus J. Trias
A1c. John E. Beisty
A1c. William H. Ellis
A1c. Wayne J. Fair
A1c. Harry S. Maxwell Jr.
A1c. Leo J. Sloan

RC-130 SEPTEMBER 2, 1958

Capt. Paul E. Duncan
1st Lt. John E. Simpson
Capt. Rudy J. Swiestra
1st Lt. Ricardo M. Villareal
Capt. Edward J. Jeruss
S. Sgt. Laroy Price
T. Sgt. Arthur L. Mello
M. Sgt. George P. Petrochilos
A1c. Robert J. Oshinskie

A2c. James E. Ferguson Jr.
A2c. Joel H. Fields
A2c. Gerald C. Maggiacomo
A2c. Harold T. Kamps
A2c. Robert H. Moore
A2c. Archie T. Bourg
A2c. Clement O. Mankins
A2c. Gerald H. Medeiros

RB-47H JULY 1, 1960

Maj. Willard G. Palm
Maj. Eugene E. Posa

Capt. Oscar L. Goforth
Capt. Dean B. Phillips

U-2 OCTOBER 27, 1962

Maj. Rudolf Anderson

RB-57 DECEMBER 14, 1965

Maj. Lester L. Lackey

1st Lt. Robert A. Yates

EC-121M APRIL 15, 1969

Lt. Cmdr. James H. Overstreet
Lt. John Dzema
Lt. Dennis B. Gleason
Lt. Peter P. Perrottet
Lt. John H. Singer
Lt. Robert F. Taylor
Lt. (jg) Robert J. Sykora
Lt. (jg) Norman E. Wilkerson
ADRC Marshall H. McNamara
AEC Laverne A. Greiner
CTC Richard E. Smith
ADR1c. Ballard F. Connors Jr.
AT1c. Stephen C. Chartier
AT1c. Bernie J. Colgin
ATR2c. Timothy H. McNeil
Lt. (jg) Joseph R. Ribar

AT1c. James L. Roach
CT1c. John H. Potts
ADR2c. Louis F. Balderman
ATN2c. Richard H. Kincaid
ATR2c. Dennis J. Horrigan
CTC Frederick A. Randall
CT2c. Stephen J. Tesmer
S. Sgt. Hugh M. Lynch
ATN3c. Gene K. Graham
ATN3c. David M. Willis
CT3c. Gary R. Ducharme
CT3c. John A. Miller Jr.
CT3c. Philip D. Sundby
AMSAN Richard Prindle
AT1c. Richard E. Sweeney

Notes

1. DEATH OF A FERRET

4 O'Kelley at the party: Keeffe interview.

4 Parr and the I1-12: Futrell, *The United States Air Force in Korea*, pp. 684–85; Wagner, *The North American Sabre*, p. 76.

5 Soviet position on the I1-12: memorandum from Bohlen to Dulles, no. 141, July 31, 1953; Soviet Note No. 24/OSA, July 31, 1953, Klaus Files; Soviet Note of July 30, *Department of State Bulletin*, August 17, 1953, p. 207; "Soviet Airplane Incidents of July 27 and July 29, 1953," Department of State Press Release, No. 90, p. 1.

5 Operations briefing: Roche deposition of May 14, 1954, pp. 3–4.

6 Keeffe's briefing: Keeffe interview.

7 Position reports: Keeffe interview.

9 Tokens on the Black Sea: Price, *The History of US Electronic Warfare*, Vol. 2, p. 84.

10 The pilot's expression: Burrows, "Beyond the Iron Curtain," p. 31.

11 The milk trick: O'Kelley interview.

12 *Little Red Ass*: Bentley interview; honorific O': Sanderson interview.

13 "ravens steal things": Gardner interview.

14 Marks and the ice: Price, *The History of US Electronic Warfare*, Vol. 2, p. 85.

14 "poorest paid spies": Bentley interview.

14 APR-9 and other equipment: *Superfortress*. Standard Aircraft Characteristics (RB-50G), p. 7; Price, *The History of US Electronic Warfare*, *passim*.

15 Mission reports: Price, *The History of US Electronic Warfare*, Vol. 2, p. 174.

16 Brown's recitation: *Utility Flight Manual*, RB-50G, pp. 2–15.

16 Hill and Radlein: Bentley interview.

17 The Russian DP: Sanderson interview.

17 Sports: Keeffe interview.
18 Engine start-up: *Utility Flight Manual, RB-50G*, pp. 2–21.
20 B-50 ear and vibration: Parrish interview.
21 Russian version of the penetration: text of Soviet note transmitted by Bohlen, July 30, 1953.
21 "Fighters do not fight": Saint-Exupéry, *Flight to Arras*, p. 61.
22 Yablonovski and Rybakov: Decoration Order of October 27, 1953; interviews with both by Colonel Osipov.
22 Description of the attack: Roche deposition of May 14, 1954, pp. 13–18; debriefing by Weyland, pp. 2–3.
23 A hole the size of a grapefruit: Roche interview.
23 "The fighter has become": Saint-Exupéry, *Flight to Arras*, p. 78.
24 Keith's condition: Roche deposition, p. 16.
25 The chute and suit on fire: Roche interview.
25 Seventy-five-foot separation: Weyland debriefing, p. 4.
26 Sharks: Roche interview.
26 SB-29 survivor report: Thirty-seventh Air Rescue Squadron report, 3 August 1953, pp. 1 and 2.
28 Delayed rescue: Keeffe interview.
28 Roche during emergency practice: Roche interview.
28 Death of O'Kelley: Roche interview and deposition, p. 29.
29 Koch told Roche: Sanderson interview.
29 Roche's rescue: Roche interview and deposition, pp. 31–34.
30 "Just keep your mouth shut": Roche interview.
30 Roche and a State Department leak: video interview at Old Crows meeting, August 1994 (Robb Hoover collection); Roche interview.
31 Cover story: Latta, "Cover Story for Forced Landing in the Far Eastern USSR," Klaus Files.
32 Bohlen's note: "U.S. Protest of Shooting Down of American Plane by Soviet MiG Aircraft," Department of State Press Release, No. 408.
32 Gromyko's protest note: "21 Killed, Charges Moscow," *Nashville Tennessean*, August 1, 1953.
33 Bess Tejeda getting the news: Bergmann interview.
34 "I like to think": Bergmann interview.
34 "We never could have a fight": O'Kelley interview.
35 "that some people just didn't": O'Kelley interview.
35 son's reaction: O'Kelley interview.
35 "the families of the dead": Jones, "The Cold War," last page.
35 Jean's hatred of Bentley: O'Kelley interview.
36 Radar view of the attack: "Security Information: Air Force Security Service Roundup," No. 149, p. 2.
36 Tracking the SB-29s: "U.S. RB-50 Aircraft Downed in Peter the Great Bay Area, 29 July 1953," p. 2, DPMO.
36 Gourley's statement: Edwin P. Gourley's deposition, pp. 1, 5, and 7.
37 Wagner's account of the rescue: Wagner interview.
37 Parrish's opinion: Parrish interview.
38 Doyle's memo: Doyle, letter, "To get CIA to release info," p. 2.
38 Movement of Soviet heavy ships: Security Information, Far Eastern Naval Information Summary, p. 5.
38 Kravchenko: Kravchenko interview.

38 NSC meeting and Ike's response: "Discussion at the 157th Meeting of the National Security Council," pp. 7 and 8.
39 State Department's billing for damages: "Presentation of Claim Against Soviet Government For Destruction of B-50 Off Cape Povorotny in 1953," No. 566, p. 1, Klaus Files.
40 "I am now convinced": unaired *Prime Time Live* tape, July 1995; Keeffe interview.

2. A SPECTRE HAUNTING AMERICA

41 "A spectre is haunting": Marx and Engels, *The Communist Manifesto*, p. 2.
43 Membership of the CPUSA: Isserman, *Which Side Were You On?*, pp. 18–21.
43 "Independent thinking": Philbrick, *I Led Three Lives*, p. 73.
44 Krivitsky: Henderson memorandum, Benson and Warner, eds., *Venona*, pp. 5–10.
44 Krivitsky's death: Benson and Warner, *Venona*, pp. 87–92.
44 "The people demand": Philbrick, *I Led Three Lives*, p. 47.
44 Kennan to Henderson: Kennan, *Memoirs, 1925–1950*, p. 133.
45 Truman's view: Truman, *Memoirs*, Vol. 1, p. 229.
45 Churchill's warning and the captured U-boat: Conquest, *Reflections on a Ravaged Century*, pp. 150–51.
45 Tupolev's reverse engineering: Hardesty, "Made in the U.S.S.R.," p. 68.
47 Hoover's letter to Hopkins: Benson and Warner, *Venona*, p. 49.
48 Enormous: Benson and Warner, *Venona*, p. xix.
48 "If it explodes": Sharnik, *Inside the Cold War*, p. 9.
48 "a new weapon": Sharnik, *Inside the Cold War*, p. 12.
48 Quarter of a million casualties: Truman letter to Prof. James L. Cate, *The Final Months of the War with Japan*, p. 516.
49 USSR cherished and defended: Kennan, "The Sources of Soviet Conduct," p. 573.
50 Gouzenko's defection: Andrew and Mitrokhin, *The Sword and the Shield*, pp. 137–38.
50 Gouzenko, Bentley, and Chambers: Benson and Warner, *Venona*, pp. xix–xx.
50 Attack on Chambers: Conquest, *Reflections on a Ravaged Century*, p. 130.
50 Doubling Bentley: Benson and Warner, *Venona*, p. xx.
50 Kennan's telegram: Kennan, *Memoirs*, p. 557.
50 Truman and the EAM danger: Truman, *Memoirs*, Vol. 2, p. 98.
51 Massive espionage: Benson and Warner, *Venona*, p. xxi.
51 Notorious spies: Benson and Warner, *Venona*, pp. xx–xxvii.
52 "I'm not talking politics": Grayson and Andrews, *The Woman on Pier 13*, p. 51.
53 "long-term, patient": Keenan, "The Sources of Soviet Conduct," p. 575.
53 Office of Policy Coordination: Grose, *Operation Rollback*, passim.
53 Creation of the NSC and CIA: Truman, *Memoirs*, Vol. 2, p. 52.
54 "In the summer of 1947": Park, "Welcome to Planet Earth," p. 23.
56 Three commands and SAC's responsibility: Moody, *Building a Strategic Air Force*, pp. 63, 65–66.
57 Spaatz Report: Moody, *Building a Strategic Air Force*, pp. 56–58.
58 LeMay and the atomic bomb: Moody, *Building a Strategic Air Force*, p. 55.
58 "Maximum effort" against New York: Coffey, *Iron Eagle*, p. 271.
59 LeMay on cross-training and confusion: Coffey, *Iron Eagle*, p. 274.

59 "All responsible airmen": Coffey, *Iron Eagle*, p. 273.

60 "Such a suggestion": LeMay and Smith, *America Is in Danger*, p. 63.

60 Standardization: Moody, *Building a Strategic Air Force*, p. 255.

61 New bomber force: Moody, *Building a Strategic Air Force*, p. 256.

61 "If you lost": Price, *The History of US Electronic Warfare*, Vol. II, pp. 68–69.

61 Urschler's predicament: Urschler interview.

63 First aerial refueling: Smith, *Seventy-five Years of Inflight Refueling*, p. 1.

63 "Invisible" foundation: Smith, *Seventy-five Years of Inflight Refueling*, p. 75.

63 Hokkaido to Chicago: Rhodes, *Dark Sun*, p. 23.

63 *Lucky Lady II*: Moody, *Building a Strategic Air Force*, pp. 254–55.

64 "Every hour of every day": Gustafson, "They Fly the Iron-Curtain Patrol."

64 LeMay's quotes: Brugioni, *Eyeball to Eyeball*, p. 265.

66 Casey Jones: "Report: Casey Jones 306th Bomb Group."

67 Pincher report: Farquhar, "A Need to Know" (dissertation), pp. 47–49 and 53.

67 Tu-4 attack: Farquhar, "The Untold Story of Airborne Reconnaissance," video.

68 Masquerading Tu-4s: Hopkins, "Diplomatic Dimensions of Cold War Reconnaissance," video.

69 PARPRO: Hall, "The Truth About Overflights," pp. 25–27.

69 Armstrong's and Twining's memos: Armstrong, "Photographic Coverage of Northeastern Siberia," pp. 1 and 2. Twining's response is appended.

69 Capability of the hundred-inch camera: telephone conversation with Merton E. Davies, May 27, 2000.

71 Nuking the North Koreans: "CPC" to General Edwards, "Action to Prevent a Dunkirk in Korea."

72 Truman and the penetrations: Hall, "The Truth About Overflights," p. 28.

72 Truman's meeting with the British and the joint program: Truman, *Memoirs*, Vol. 2, pp. 410–11; Hall, "The Truth About Overflights," pp. 28–29.

74 Attack on the *Liberty*: Carlos Campbell e-mail, January 11, 2001.

75 *Liberty* and *Pueblo*: Bamford, *The Puzzle Palace*, pp. 222–24, 233–35.

75 Red subs on the West Coast: Campbell interview.

75 NURO: Sontag and Drew, *Blind Man's Bluff*, pp. 82–83.

3. FIRST BLOOD

78 Radar defense of England: Churchill, *The Gathering Storm*, pp. 154–55.

78 The saga of the *Graf Zeppelin*: Wood and Dempster, *The Narrow Margin*, pp. 17–20; Johnson, *The Secret War*, pp. 63–64.

80 Different wavelengths: Johnson, *The Secret War*, p. 64.

81 Meaconing: Churchill, *Their Finest Hour*, p. 383.

82 Operation Corona: Taylor and Mondey, *Spies in the Sky*, pp. 45–46.

82 Emil: Taylor and Mondey, *Spies in the Sky*, pp. 47–48.

82 Churchill on the Wizard War: Churchill, *Their Finest Hour*, p. 381.

83 Ihle's story: Ihle interview.

87 Goddard at Cornell: Goddard, *Overview*, p. 8.

87 German photographs of the front: Stanley, *World War II Photo Intelligence*, p. 26.

89 Cotton and Rowehl: Stanley, *World War II Photo Intelligence*, pp. 40 and 43.

89 Color, strip, and flash photography: Goddard, *Overview*, pp. 240–45.

89 Trimetrogon: Burrows, *Deep Black*, p. 38; Stanley, *World War II Photo Intelligence*, pp. 270–71.

90 Spotting V-2s: Babington-Smith, *Air Spy*, p. 209.

90 D day: Stanley, *World War II Photo Intelligence*, p. 61.

91 Auschwitz-Birkenau concentration camp: Brugioni and Poirier, "The Holocaust Revisited," *passim*.

91 Three high-altitude recce planes: Stanley, *World War II Photo Intelligence*, p. 35.

93 Casey Jones: "Report: Casey Jones 306th Bomb Group."

93 Port Arthur intrusion: George, "Case Studies of Actual and Alleged Overflights, 1930–1953," pp. 27–30.

93 Dairen intrusion: George, "Case Studies of Actual and Alleged Overflights, 1930–1953," pp. 31–34.

93 Big Diomede intrusion: George, "Case Studies of Actual and Alleged Overflights, 1930–1953," p. 35.

94 Attack on the DC-4: George, "Case Studies of Actual and Alleged Overflights, 1930–1953," pp. 151–52.

95 Swedish-Russian relations: George, "Case Studies of Actual and Alleged Overflights, 1930–1935," pp. 124, 171.

96 Modifying the B-29F and rescuing survivors: White, *World in Peril*, pp. 12–13, 15.

96 The Forty-sixth's mandate: White, *World in Peril*, p. 11.

97 Spies in Fairbanks: White, *World in Peril*, p. 29.

98 Location of Siberian air bases: Lashmar, *Spy Flights of the Cold War*, pp. 28–29.

98 Wack's recollection: Lashmar, *Spy Flights of the Cold War*, p. 29.

98 Medals: Lashmar, *Spy Flights of the Cold War*, pp. 29–30.

99 Ferreting Greenland: Farquhar, "A Need to Know" (dissertation), pp. 60–61.

99 White and LeMay: White interview.

99 LeMay at the Forty-sixth: White, *World in Peril*, pp. 63–64.

100 *Kee Bird*'s name: White, *World in Peril*, pp. 89–90.

100 B-29–Tu-4 mixup: White, *World in Peril*, p. 37.

100 Cabell's order: Cabell, "ECM Ferret Program—Alaskan Air Command," pp. 1, 3.

101 History of the Ninety-first Squadron: Ferrer, "91st Squadron 'Demon Chaser's' 81 Year History," p. 1.

102 History of the Fifty-fifth Squadron: Bailey, "*We See All*," p. 1.

102 Norstad's orders: Norstad, "USAF Electronic Reconnaissance Program," pp. 1, 2.

102 Meyer's recollection: Burrows, "Beyond the Iron Curtain," p. 31 (letter to the author).

103 Cover story order: Latta, "Cover Story for Forced Landing in the Far Eastern USSR," Klaus Files.

103 Locked in a locker: Urschler interview.

103 "messed with your mind": Hoover interview.

104 Diplomatic couriers: Price, *The History of US Electronic Warfare*, Vol. 2, p. 45.

104 PB4Y-2 ferreting radar: Bradley, "Special Electronic Airborne Search Operations," p. 1.

105 Shrapnel holes in life raft: "Bullet Holes Are Reported Found in Second Raft Picked Up in Baltic," *The New York Times*, April 23, 1950.

105 Rafts and dye markers: Whitener letter to Karig, p. 1.

105 Open, empty compartments: "Ship Picks Up Raft in Baltic of Type Used by Privateer," *The New York Times*, April 17, 1950.

106 Orders to shoot down American spy plane: George, "Case Studies of Actual and Alleged Overflights, 1930–1953—Supplement," p. 12.

106 The Swedish connection: Farquhar, "A Need to Know," p. 92.
106 The Soviet note: "Text of Protest by Soviet to U.S.," *The New York Times*, April 12, 1950.
107 The U.S. note: "Text of U.S. Statement on Baltic Plane Incident," *The New York Times*, April 19, 1950.
107 *Newsweek* report: "Hornet's Nest That Cost Us a Plane," *Newsweek*, April 24, 1950, p. 28.
107 Childs, Pearson, and Lippmann: Farquhar, "A Need to Know," pp. 144–46.
108 The Joint Chiefs memo (Bradley): Bradley, "Special Electronic Airborne Search Operations," *passim*.
109 Noble's story: Navy Baltic Case, September 11, 1956, pp. 2–3, Klaus Files.
109 Gunerinssen: "American Fliers in Vorkuta," Klaus Files.
109 U.S. protest note: "U.S. Says Soviet Holds Americans of 2 Lost Planes," *The New York Times*, July 17, 1956.

4. MORE BLOOD

111 Truman on Korea: Truman, *Memoirs*, Vol. 2, p. 337.
113 *Bombing Encyclopedia* and target folders: Farquhar, "A Need to Know," p. 89; Bergen interview.
114 TDI's existence: *Target Data Inventory*, Vol. II, p. v.
114 The six categories of target significance: *Target Data Inventory*, Vol. II, pp. viii–xi.
115 Predicting bomb damage: *Target Data Inventory*, Vol. II, p. 423.
116 The Vladivostok radar: *Target Data Inventory*, Vol. II, p. 435.
116 RF-84 and RF-86: Wagner, *The North American Sabre*, pp. 58–59.
116 RF-86s over Soviet territory: Hall, "The Truth About Overflights," p. 33.
117 RF-86s over Manchuria and Saylor: "Secret Pilots Can Finally Tell Their Tales," Gannett News Service, October 15, 2000.
118 Effect of B-45 damage: Farquhar, "A Need to Know," p. 177.
118 RB-36 passageways in wings: Welch, *RB-36 Days at Rapid City*, p. 45.
119 "every kind of camera": Ihle interview.
119 Scanning camera and golf balls: Goddard, *Overview*, pp 379–80.
120 Mapping of Portugal by Peacemakers: Welch, *RB-36 Days at Rapid City*, p. 152.
120 Flight over Poland: Welch, *RB-36 Days at Rapid City*, pp. 154–55.
121 Ihle and the RB-36: Ihle interview.
122 Vasily Stalin's picture: Lashmar, *Spy Flights of the Cold War*, p. 53.
123 The RB-45C shootdown: "Persistent women get answers on MIA fathers," *The Washington Times* (AP), December 2, 1994.
123 McDonough's fate: "Persistent women get answers on MIA fathers."
124 Lovell's fate: Cole memorandum of June 15, 2000, to the author; Lashmar, *Spy Flights of the Cold War*, pp. 52–53; U.S.-Russia Joint Commission POW/MIA (USRJC), Korean War Working Group Session, minutes, April 12, 1995, pp. 2–4.
126 The aborted Chukotski mission: Hall, "The Truth About Overflights," p. 28.
127 The mission to Harbin: Naftel interview, Oral History Program, pp. 9–11.
128 The Neptune shootdown: George, "Case Studies of Actual and Alleged Overflights, 1930–1953," pp. 131–37.
128 "Under no circumstances": Hoover interview.
129 Walsh's letter: Walsh to Maj. Gen. John A. Samford.

130 Trotsenko: "Decades Later, Tales of Americans in Soviet Jails," *The New York Times*, July 19, 1996.

130 Rosenfeld the prisoner: Herrington, "Case Studies," p. 3.

130 Jack Lively: Dickinson interview.

131 Meyers on clouds: letter to the author.

132 Crampton and Barksdale/Lockbourne: Hall, "The Truth About Overflights," p. 29; Jackson, *High Cold War*, p. 50.

132 Austin's recollection: Lashmar, *Spy Flights of the Cold War*, p. 66.

133 Three Tornado penetrations on map: Hall, "The Truth About Overflights," p. 29; Lashmar, *Spy Flights of the Cold War*, p. 69.

134 Anstee's reaction: Lashmar, *Spy Flights of the Cold War*, p. 70.

134 The three Tornado penetrations: Hall, "The Truth About Overflights," p 29; Lashmar, *Spy Flights of the Cold War*, pp. 62–75.

135 Beria and the commission: Lashmar, *Spy Flights of the Cold War*, p. 71.

135 Sergei Khrushchev's recollection: Hall and Leghorn, interview with Sergei Khrushchev, pp. 2–3.

136 Directive of May 28, 1952: Shower, Mission Directive DO 322, *passim*.

137 Bergen on collection: Bergen interview.

138 P2V-3W and RB-50 penetrations: Hall, "The Truth About Overflights," pp. 30–31.

139 Kuznetsov's report: Kuznetsov letter to Comrade V. I. Stalin.

139 Robitaille's recollection: "Downed RB-29," undated three-page recollection.

140 Combs's recollection: undated letter to Steele.

140 Koski's recollection: Koski letter to Steele, January 26, 1956.

140 Radio Moscow broadcast: Steele letter to Klaus.

141 June 15 announcement: "Far East Superfort Down in Japan Sea," *The New York Times*, June 15, 1952.

141 Reports of U.S. prisoners: "Secrets of the Cold War," *U.S. News & World Report*, March 15, 1993.

142 Corso and Eisenhower: Lowther, "Shadow of a Doubt," p. 22.

142 Erskine: Lowther, "Shadow of a Doubt," p. 24.

142 *The New York Times* and the note: Lowther, "Shadow of a Doubt," p. 24.

142 Philadelphia story: "Flier's Mother Prays For His Safe Return," *Philadelphia Daily News*, July 17, 1956.

143 The attack on *Sunbonnet King*: CG FEAF/COFS USAF, 080850/Z Oct. 1952, pp. 1–2.

144 Yosamatsu's story: Goto Yosamatsu, statement dated January 21, 1953.

144 Saiko's story: Sidoruk, "The Ring of Fate," *passim*.

146 Casualty report: DUNHAM Casualty Report.

5. WIZARD WAR

147 A-bombs and B-36s: Truman, *Memoirs*, Vol. 2, pp. 304–05.

148 Pearl Harbor: Bissell interview.

149 Eisenhower on annihilation: "Discussion at the 257th Meeting of the National Security Council, Thursday, August 4, 1955," pp. 9, 11.

149 Military intelligence program Wringer: Lashmar, *Spy Flights of the Cold War*, p. 30; Farquhar, "A Need to Know," p. 55.

150 Amory on work at Kapustin Yar: Lashmar, *Spy Flights of the Cold War*, p. 77.

151 Amory and Welzenbach confirmation: Lashmar, *Spy Flights of the Cold War*, pp. 77, 81; Goddard: Goddard, *Overview*, pp. 388–89.

151 Shulga: Lashmar, *Spy Flights of the Cold War*, p. 82.
152 "never again": Lashmar, *Spy Flights of the Cold War*, p. 77. See also Van der Aart, *Aerial Espionage*, p. 19.
152 RB-57As to Shaw: Swanborough, *United States Military Aircraft Since 1909*, p. 341.
152 "dog": Goddard, *Overview*, p. 389.
153 Incident in the Formosa Strait: Grossnick, *United States Naval Aviation, 1910–1995*, p. 774.
155 Versions of the B-47: Swanborough, *United States Military Aircraft Since 1909*, pp. 104–05.
156 Preparations for Project 52 AFR-18: Hillman and Hall, "Overflight," pp. 30–32.
156 The flap incident: Hillman and Hall, "Overflight," p. 34.
157 The plan: Hillman and Hall, "Overflight," p. 36.
159 Mission results: Hillman and Hall, "Overflight," pp. 37–38; Hall, "The Truth About Overflights," p. 32.
159 LeMay versus FEAF: Farquhar, "A Need to Know," p. 178.
160 Fisher to Montgomery: Farquhar, "A Need to Know," p. 176.
160 RB-50–MiG fight: "U.S. Demands Soviet Punish Flier for Attack Off Siberia," *The New York Times*, March 19, 1953; "Soviet Attack on U.S. Plane in North Pacific Ocean," *Department of State Bulletin*, April 20, 1953, p. 577.
160 T. Sgt. Prim's account: Bailey, "We See All," p. 44 and 45.
163 The investigative report: Smith, "Investigation of the ditching of the P2V-5 aircraft BuNo. 127752 on 4 January 1954," p. 5.
163 Resink's smashed head: air rescue squadron at Seoul Air Field, Mission 3-39-2.
163 The flight and loss of Three Cape Cod: "A Cold War Cover-Up: A Son's Story," Beasley's website (http://3capecod.com).
165 "additional time": Lugar, letters to Beasley.
165 "no credible evidence": Jones letter to Ed Bryant.
166 Wayne and the GCI radar: Wayne, "Siberian Coast Incident," p. 1.
167 Wayne's defensive maneuver: Neptune attack of September 4, 1954, Department of State Press Release, No. 534, p. 4.
167 Attack and rescue: Wayne, "Siberian Coast Incident," pp. 2–3.
168 Verbatim from the protest note: Neptune attack of September 4, 1954, Department of State Press Release, No. 534, p. 4.
168 The U.N. exchange: "U.S. Seeks Action By World Court On Downed Plane," *The New York Times*, September 11, 1954.
169 Holdridge recollection: e-mail to the author, October 11, 2000.
170 RB-69As: Pace, *Lockheed Skunk Works*, p. 277; Mutza, *Lockheed P2V Neptune*, pp. 109–16.
172 The standard medical report: Medical Report of AF Aircraft Accident, February 26, 1952.
172 Parker account of RB-50G crash at Offutt: Parker interview.
173 Fighter escorts: Aerospace Studies Institute, *Some Significant Air Incidents Involving the United States and Communist Nations 1945–1964*, p. 4; Jackson, *High Cold War*, p. 90.
173 Escorts through the Yalu corridor by Sabrejets: Naftel oral history, p. 8.
173 Cathay Pacific attack by Chinese: "Airliner, 17 Aboard, Down Off Red China," *The New York Times*, July 23, 1954.
174 Rescue planes: "Airliner, 17 Aboard, Down Off Red China," *The New York Times*, July 23, 1954.

174 China's protest note: "U.S. and Peiping Protests on Air Clashes Off China," *The New York Times*, July 28, 1954.

175 Air France attack: George, "Case Studies of Actual and Alleged Overflights, 1930–1953," pp. 151–52.

175 KAL 007: Hersh, *The Target Is Destroyed*, pp. 227–39.

175 Wagner and Dien Bien Phu: Wagner interview.

176 Parrish and the penetration: Parrish interview.

176 Reporting on the Seventh Fleet: Wagner interview.

177 Croix de Guerre: Wagner interview.

177 French atomic test: Pocock, *Dragon Lady*, p. 109.

179 "over Moscow": Austin, "A Cold War Overflight of the USSR," p. 15.

183 "intelligence weenies": Austin, "A Cold War Overflight of the USSR," p. 15.

184 LeMay on fighter pilots: Austin interview.

185 The Helsinki newspaper report: Austin, "A Cold War Overflight of the USSR," p. 17.

186 Mission narrative and quotes: Austin interview.

6. THE RAVEN'S SONG

188 Background of the 7499th and 7405th aircraft: Current status of aerial reconnaissance programs briefing, untitled, undated document, p. 2; Mitchell, "U.S. Air Force Peacetime Airborne Reconnaissance During the Cold War, 1946–1990," p. 8.

190 Operations and fake planes of the 7405th: Mitchell, "U.S. Air Force Peacetime Airborne Reconnaissance During the Cold War, 1946–1990," pp. 23 and 25.

191 Gardner's route: Gardner interview.

193 Had its own agents: Gardner interview.

194 Hoover's reflection: Hoover interview.

197 Ferreting Ostrov Vize: Hoover interview.

200 Campbell's reflection: Campbell interview.

201 First RB-47 shootdown; Herrington, "Case Studies," Case Study 6.

203 Maziarz's recollection: Maziarz, "The Reds Shot Us Down," p. 14.

204 Maziarz and Shields: Sonnek interview.

205 Sonnek's burned hands: Sonnek interview.

206 Dulles on the Neptune: "Bering Sea Plane Incident," *Department of State Bulletin*, p. 53.

206 Monetary damages from Kremlin: "Soviet Payment of Damages For U.S. Navy Neptune Plane," Department of State Press Release, No. 148.

207 Genetrix launch, failure, and end: Richelson, *American Espionage and the Soviet Target*, pp. 130–38; Moody, Neufeld, and Hall, "The Emergency of the Strategic Air Command," pp. 63–64.

208 Project Home Run: Hall, "The Truth About Overflights," pp. 36–37.

209 "incredible demonstrations": Hall, "The Truth About Overflights," p. 38.

210 Mercator details: Lake and Dorr, "Martin P4M Mercator: Cold War Elint-Gathering Operations," *Wings of Fame*, pp. 138–49.

210 Hutchinson's message: "Report of a U.S. Navy Aircraft Attacked by Hostile Aircraft," Navy memorandum of August 22, 1956; Dorr and Burgess, "Ferreting Mercators," p. 221.

211 Finding wreckage and more bodies: Mercator incident, untitled Department of State Press Release, No. 464; Dorr and Burgess, "Ferreting Mercators," p. 221;

"Statement of Facts Concerning Loss of P4M-1Q Mercator Patrol Plane on Night of 22 August 1956," p. 4.

211 The British letter and Chang's answer: "Text of a letter sent by British Chargé d'Affaires, Peiping, to Chinese Communist Vice Minister for Foreign Affairs, Chang Han-fu, dated August 25, 1956," Department of State Press Release, No. 465.

212 Eisenhower on the Mercator: "Memorandum of Conference With the President," August 30, 1956, p. 2.

213 Theory of death on impact: "Statement of Facts Concerning Loss of P4M-1Q Mercator Patrol Plane on Night of 22 August 1956," p. 4.

213 Japanese account of survivors: "Memorandum for the File, Mercator Case."

213 Chiu's deductions: "Information on Surviving Crew Members of the Downed US Naval Aircraft" (IR 1900–57), p. 2.

214 Emma and the "weather" mission: "U.S. Plane Is Lost Tracing Typhoon," *The New York Times*, September 11, 1956.

214 Discounting a shootdown: Goldrich, "Cold War Shoot-Down Incidents Involving U.S. Military Aircraft Resulting in U.S. Casualties," p. 10.

216 Fake wing tanks: Ferrer interview; Price, *The History of US Electronic Warfare*, Vol. 2, pp. 165–66.

217 Duncan, Villareal, and the missions: Swanson deposition, p. 6.

217 The beacon at Van: Steakley, "C-130 Incident of 2 September 58," Klaus Files.

217 The Yerevan station: Assistant Chief of Staff, Intelligence, USAF, "C-130 Incident of 2 September 1958," p. 3, Klaus Files.

218 MiG pilots' conversation: Cole, *POW/MIA Issues*, Vol. 2, p. 64.

219 Photographs of the crash site: DPMO.

219 The C-118 shootdown: Cole, *POW/MIA Issues*, Vol. 2, pp. 60–61.

219 The navigator's error: Assistant Chief of Staff, Intelligence, USAF, "C-130 Incident of 2 September 1958," p. 3, Klaus Files.

219 Gardner and meaconing: Gardner interview.

219 Fields letter to Eisenhower: Moses Fields letter to Eisenhower.

220 The Russian rebuke: Soviet aide-mémoire (C-130A) of May 25, 1959.

220 Khrushchev letter to Eisenhower: Khrushchev letter to Eisenhower, October 10, 1959, Klaus Files.

220 Two-part series: "The Target Is Detected" and "A Swift Attack," *Sovetskaya Aviatsiya*, translated in the *Department of State Bulletin*, February 23, 1959, pp. 268–69, Klaus Files.

221 CIA "unevaluated" information report: "Crash of US Military Aircraft in Armenia, September 1958," Information Report, Central Intelligence Agency, November 7, 1958.

221 Destroyed bodies: Memorandum on Georgian contacts, p. 1.

7. A PRISON CALLED LUBYANKA

227 Parrish on mutual pushing: Parrish interview.

227 La-250: Gordon, "Lavochkin La-250 Anaconda," pp. 150–57.

228 Hoover and the AA-5: Hoover interview.

229 Ferreting the *Kittyhawk* and moving Bears: "Pentagon Says Russian Bombers Are Expected Off Alaskan Coast," *The New York Times*, December 1, 2000.

229 Soviet long-range reconnaissance: "Soviet electronic warfare aircraft," Parts 1 and 2; "Naval electronic reconnaissance aircraft," Parts 1 and 2, *Jane's Defence Weekly*, pp. 18–19, 64–65, 726–28, 778–79.

231 "Invisible" dirigible: Pedlow and Welzenbach, *The CIA and the U-2 Program, 1954–1974*, pp. 18–19.

231 Beacon Hill recommendation: Pedlow and Welzenbach, *The CIA and the U-2 Program, 1954–1974*, pp. 18–19.

232 LeMay on the CL-282: Pedlow and Welzenbach, *The CIA and the U-2 Program, 1954–1974*, p. 12.

233 Killian on Eisenhower: Killian, *Sputnik, Scientists, and Eisenhower*, p. 82.

233 The "storm" prediction: Killian, *Sputnik, Scientists, and Eisenhower*, p. 84.

234 "Speedy Gonzales": Rich and Janos, *Skunk Works*, p. 195.

235 First U-2 flights: "U-2 Overflights of Soviet Bloc," CIA memorandum for Brig. Gen. Andrew J. Goodpaster.

235 First flights over the USSR: Pedlow and Welzenbach, *The CIA and the U-2 Program, 1954–1974*, pp. 104–05.

236 Photographs of tiny MiGs: Pedlow and Welzenbach, *The CIA and the U-2 Program, 1954–1974*, p. 108.

236 Protest note: Pedlow and Welzenbach, *The CIA and the U-2 Program, 1954–1974*, p. 109.

236 Open Skies brochure: Khrushchev, "The Day We Shot Down the U-2," p. 38.

237 Eisenhower's empathy: John S. D. Eisenhower, "Memorandum for Record," p. 1.

238 Khrushchev's humiliation and the designers: Khrushchev, "The Day We Shot Down the U-2," p. 38.

238 Number of U-2 operations: Dulles, "Statistics Relating to the U-2 Program."

239 The 1959 NIE: Steury, *Intentions and Capabilities: Estimates on Soviet Strategic Forces, 1950–1983*, p. 75.

239 Gates and the U-2: Dulles, *The Craft of Intelligence*, pp. 67–68.

239 Reward for a defection: "Chinese U-2s Seek Nuclear, IRBM Data," p. 29.

239 Stopping the Chinese nuclear program: "60's Administrations Considered Bombing Nuclear Sites in China," *The New York Times*, January 13, 2001.

240 Reconnaissance over Cuba: Brugioni, *Eyeball to Eyeball*, pp. 162, 179, 291.

240 U-2s and the Cuban missile crisis: Pedlow and Welzenbach, *The CIA and the U-2 Program, 1954–1974*, pp. 199–209.

241 Mission 4155: Pedlow and Welzenbach, *The CIA and the U-2 Program, 1954–1974*, p. 168.

242 Burke's warning: Pedlow and Welzenbach, *The CIA and the U-2 Program, 1954–1974*, p. 168.

242 Kistiakowsky's remark: Beschloss, *May Day*, p. 242.

242 Powers's itinerary: Pedlow and Welzenbach, *The CIA and the U-2 Program, 1954–1974*, p. 176.

242 Biryuzov's lament: Orlov, "The U-2 Program: A Russian Officer Remembers," p. 11.

243 Powers mission and the intercept order to Mentyukov: Powers, "A Few Words in Defense of Francis Gary Powers," p. 42; Khrushchev, "The Day We Shot Down the U-2," pp. 40–43: Pedlow and Welzenbach, *The CIA and the U-2 Program, 1954–1974*, p. 177.

245 Safronov's shootdown: Khrushchev: "The Day We Shot Down the U-2," p. 44.

245 Tacksman: Richelson, *American Espionage and the Soviet Target*, pp. 90–91.

245 Monitoring Soviet radar: Pedlow and Welzenbach, *The CIA and the U-2 Program, 1954–1974*, pp. 177–78.

245 White House cover story: untitled and undated single-page memorandum (Eisenhower Library).

246 NASA news release on Powers: NASA, News Release No. 60-193, May 5, 1960.
246 Khrushchev's intention: Pedlow and Welzenbach, *The CIA and the U-2 Program, 1954–1974*, p. 179.
246 Khrushchev's show-and-tell: Khrushchev, "The Day We Shot Down the U-2," p. 47; Wise and Ross, *The U-2 Affair*, pp. 95–98.
247 U-2 flights in Asia and Eastern Europe: "U-2 Overflights of Soviet Bloc," CIA memorandum for Brig. Gen. Andrew J. Goodpaster.
247 Eisenhower assumes responsibility: Pedlow and Welzenbach, *The CIA and the U-2 Program, 1954–1974*, p. 180.
248 "appeasing the imperialists": Whitney, *Khrushchev Speaks*, p. 376.
248 Khrushchev's letter to Castro: "In Letter, Khrushchev Tells of Mockery Over Cuba Crisis," *The New York Times*, January 22, 1992.
248 Khrushchev at the U.N. summit: Khrushchev, "The Day We Shot Down the U-2," pp. 47–48.
250 RB-47H ejection system: Bailey, "We See All," p. 226.
251 RB-47H's position at the time of attack: McKone interview.
251 Olmstead and the MiG: Olmstead interview.
252 McKone on Palm: McKone interview.
253 Olmstead's thoughts of suicide: Olmstead interview.
253 McKone's religious experience: McKone interview.
254 Shelepin to Khrushchev: Memorandum of October 17, 1960. (U.S.-Soviet joint commission.)
254 Gene Posa's disappearance: "Family Hopes to Find Body of Spy Shot Down by Soviets," *Los Angeles Times*, May 15, 2001.
255 Life in Lubyanka: McKone and Olmstead interviews.
258 Olmstead and McKone formally imprisoned on preventive writs: Olmstead interview.
258 Soviet protest: "USSR Protests Aggression by U.S. Plane," TASS, July 11, 1960, Klaus Files.
259 Khrushchev's statement: "Khrushchev Charges U.S. Provokes Serious Conflict," *The New York Times*, July 13, 1960.
259 Kuznetsov's statement: "Excerpts from Addresses to Security Council on Soviet Downing of RB-47," *The New York Times*, July 27, 1960.
259 Kirkpatrick's comments on Soviet trawler: "Soviet Trawler Called Spy Ship," *The New York Times*, July 14, 1960.
259 Lodge's comments on Soviet planes: "Excerpts from Addresses to Security Council on Soviet Downing of RB-47," *The New York Times*, July 27, 1960.
259 Yezhov expelled: "Diplomat Ordered Out Hired a Photographer to Take Aerial Views," *The New York Times*, July 23, 1960.
260 Using the wives: Phillips interview.
261 Rudenko's interview with Olmstead: Olmstead interview.
261 Discoverer 14: McDonald, "CORONA: Success for Space Reconnaissance, A Look into the Cold War, and a Revolution for Intelligence," p. 691.
262 Olmstead's letters: Olmstead collection.
265 Maddalena's letter: Patricia Phillips collection.

8. WONDERLAND

267 Kelly Johnson on U-2's successor: Johnson, *Kelly*, p. 134.
268 More altitude and speed: Johnson, *Kelly*, pp. 134–35.

268 Rich on Rich: Rich and Janos, *Skunk Works*, p. 193.

269 Oxcart being slow: Johnson interview.

269 Mach 3.5 and higher: Rich interview.

270 Oxcart design details: Lockheed Advanced Development Company and GALCIT, "Course Ae107: Case Studies in Engineering: The SR-71 Blackbird," *passim*.

272 DEF systems and the RSO: Graham, *SR-71 Revealed*, p. 75.

272 Deception jamming: Crickmore, *Lockheed SR-71: Blackbird*, p. 108.

273 Rich's comment on color of SR-71: Rich interview.

274 Unstarts: Burrows, "The Oxcart Cometh," pp. 70–71.

275 SR-71s and Nicaragua: "U.S. Offers Photos of Bases to Prove Nicaragua Threat," *The New York Times*, March 10, 1982; "Sonic Booms Shake Cities In Nicaragua For the Fourth Day," *The New York Times*, November 12, 1984.

275 Glasser on the SR: Glasser interview.

279 Robert S. Hopkins on the naming of planes and missions: Hopkins, *Boeing KC-135 Stratotanker*, p. 135.

280 Hog nose and cheeks: Hopkins, *Boeing KC-135 Stratotanker*, p. 137; Streetly, "US airborne ELINT systems." Part 3: "The Boeing RC-135 family," p. 460.

281 Speed Light: Hopkins, *Boeing KC-135 Stratotanker*, p. 139.

282 Speed Light rechristened Rivet Stand: Hopkins, *Boeing KC-135 Stratotanker*, p. 139.

283 Combat Apple missions: Hopkins, *Boeing KC-135 Stratotanker*, pp. 146–47.

283 Cobra Ball missions: Hopkins, *Boeing KC-135 Stratotanker*, p. 148.

285 The new Cobra Ball missions: "Cobra Ball Revamped For Battlefield Missions," pp. 48–50.

285 Plesetsk SS-25 test: Hersh, *The Target Is Destroyed*, p. 42.

286 Handling harrassment from Soviet fighters: Hopkins, *Boeing KC-135 Stratotanker*, p. 150.

286 The flight of 43290 on April 28, 1965: Back, "North Korean Attack on RB-47, AC# 43290," *passim*.

288 Missing RB 57: Herrington, "Case Studies," Case Study 10.

289 EC-121M incident of April 1969: "Peripheral Reconnaissance Incidents and Losses."

290 The last shots at a U.S. recce plane: Hoover interview; Max Moore e-mail of November 17, 2000.

292 Klaus: "Samuel Klaus, 58, U.S. Legal Adviser," *The New York Times*, August 3, 1963.

294 "things got nasty": Fischer, "A Cold War Conundrum: The 1983 Soviet War Scare," p. 1.

294 Surprise attack: Fischer, "A Cold War Conundrum," p. 5.

295 Ikle, Chain, and Schneider on psychological warfare programs: Fischer, "A Cold War Conundrum," pp. 6–7.

298 Air Force history and omissions: Shaw and Warnock, *The Cold War and Beyond*, pp. 130, 131.

299 The M-12 and D-21: Crickmore, *Lockheed SR-71 Blackbird*, pp. 38, 41; Rich and Janos, *Skunk Works*, pp. 22–23.

301 Remotely piloted vehicles: Gunston, *Spy Planes and Electronic Warfare Aircraft*, pp. 150, 156–57.

305 Eisenhower asks for explanations: McDonald, "CORONA," p. 79.

305 Bissell on Corona: Bissell interview.

305 Quality and breadth of film coverage provided by Discoverer 14: McDonald, "CORONA," p. 82.

305 Corona program: McDonald, "CORONA," *passim*.

305 Satellite order of importance: Ruffner, ed., *CORONA: America's First Satellite Program*, p. 49.

306 Rhyolite satellites: Ball, *Pine Gap*, pp. 12–20; Burrows, "The Coldest Warriors," pp. 75–76.

307 GRAB: Hall, "The NRO at Forty," p. 2.

307 Raquel and Farrah: Hersh, *The Target Is Destroyed*, p. 38.

310 Bergen's observations: e-mail to the author, September 7, 2000.

311 The most sensational incident: "U.S. Plane in China After It Collides With Chinese Jet," *The New York Times*, April 2, 2001.

312 Bill Ernst and "thumping": e-mail of April 6, 2001, from Ernst to the author.

312 Wang Wei's exuberance: "Chinese Pilot Reveled in Risk, U.S. Aides Say," *The New York Times*, April 6, 2001.

313 "This guy just killed us": "Navy Pilot Thought His Plane Was Doomed After Collision," *The New York Times*, April 15, 2001.

314 They were not wholly successful: "Some Papers on Downed Spy Plane Were Not Destroyed," *The New York Times*, May 16, 2001.

314 Wei's ejection out of burning jet: "A Warm, If Quick, Heroes' Welcome, Then on to Long Hours With Debriefing Teams," *The New York Times*, April 13, 2001.

314 "A checklist of items to be destroyed": "U.S. Says Spy Crew Wiped Out Secrets In Frantic Landing," *The New York Times*, April 14, 2001.

315 Should take full responsibility: "China Faults U.S. in Incident; Suggests Release of Crew Hinges on Official Apology," *The New York Times*, April 4, 2001.

315 She had to be hospitalized: "Bush Sends Letter to Pilot's Wife," AP, April 8, 2001.

315 Expressed regret over the loss: "Bush Sends Letter to Pilot's Wife," AP, April 8, 2001.

316 Chinese spy planes: Charles R. Smith, "China's Illegal Spy Plane—Armed With Advanced Radar by R.S.," newsmax.com, April 16, 2001.

316 Interrogated for up to five hours: "Navy Crew's Ordeal of Terror and Tedium," *The New York Times*, April 16, 2001.

317 Routine at Nanhang No. 1 Guesthouse: "Detainees Develop a Routine," *The Washington Post*, April 10, 2001.

317 A Continental Airlines passenger jet: Capt. Guy Greider, "An Inside Look at the China Rescue Mission, April 12, 2001," Internet, April 18, 2001.

318 Picked up where PR-32 had left off: "Eyes Back in the Sky," *Air Force Times*, May 21, 2001.

9. TO RAISE THE DEAD

323 Mitnik on lying: Burrows, "Beyond the Iron Curtain," p. 35.

324 Susan Hansen and the certificate of recognition: e-mail to Charles Beasley, January 5, 2001.

324 Ceremony honoring Busch's crew: "Recognition—at last," *Air Force Times*, November 13, 1995.

325 The Russian engineer's tale: "Memoirs" (excerpts), pp. 4, 5. Also see: "Russian Émigré's Memoir Tells of Americans in Gulag in '50s," *Omaha World Herald* (AP), February 27, 2000.

327 Vietnam prisoners: "Gulag Held M.I.A.'s, Yeltsin Suggests," *The New York Times*, June 16, 1992.

327 Specifics on prisoners: "President Praises Yeltsin on M.I.A.'s," *The New York Times*, June 17, 1992.

327 Yeltsin's statement: "The President's News Conference With President Boris Yeltsin" (transcript), June 17, 1992, pp. 8–9.

328 Sanderson's comments on Task Force Russia: Sanderson interview.

329 Johnson's assertion: Burrows, "Beyond the Iron Curtain," p. 35.

332 O'Kelley's comments on her meeting with Toon and Volkogonov: O'Kelley interview.

332 "find absolutely nothing": Sanderson conversation on November 20, 2000.

333 "where the priorities are": Skavinski interview.

334 "pushing, pushing, pushing": Sanderson interview.

334 Volkogonov on the twelve Americans: Minutes of the Meeting Between General Volkogonov and Ambassador Toon With Families of Missing Americans from the Korean/Cold/Vietnam Wars, p. 5.

335 Korotkov's interview: Selected Interviews, Cold War Incident, July 29, 1953, pp. 4, 5, 6.

336 Kravchenko interview: Selected Interviews, Cold War Incident, July 29, 1953, pp. 1–3.

337 Sanderson on Toon's response to the Joint Commission: Sanderson interview.

339 Paul Cole's observations: e-mail to the author.

340 Service on the enemy and damage control: Service interview.

340 Jones's pledge: "POW/MIA Accounting," 1999, p. 2.

341 Mary Dunham Nichols's story: Nichols interview.

343 Saiko and the ring: Nichols interview.

344 "a shameful thing": Nichols interview.

345 Mary Nichols on Legacy and her experience with the American Legion and the VFW: Nichols interview.

348 Elizabeth Hamilton's petition: Severo and Milford, *The Wages of War*, p. 101.

348 Jean O'Kelley's story: O'Kelley interview.

348 Roxann Phillips's story: Phillips interview.

Sources

BOOKS

Andrew, Christopher, and Vasili Mitrokhin. *The Sword and the Shield*. New York: Basic Books, 1999.

Babington-Smith, Constance. *Air Spy*. New York: Harper & Brothers, 1957.

Bailey, Bruce M., ed. *"We See All."* Fifty-fifth ELINT Association, 1982.

Ball, Desmond. *Pine Gap*. Sydney: Allen & Unwin, 1988.

Bamford, James. *The Puzzle Palace*. Boston: Houghton Mifflin, 1982.

Barron, John. *MiG Pilot: Lt. Viktor Belenko's Final Escape*. New York: Reader's Digest Press, 1979.

Benson, Robert Louis, and Michael Warner, eds. *Venona: Soviet Espionage and the American Response, 1939–1957*. Washington: National Security Agency and Central Intelligence Agency, 1996.

Beschloss, Michael R. *May Day*. New York: Harper & Row, 1986.

Brugioni, Dino A. *Eyeball to Eyeball*. New York: Random House, 1990.

Burrows, William E. *Deep Black: Space Espionage and National Security*, New York: Random House, 1986.

Cate, James L. *The Final Months of the War with Japan*. n.p., n.d.

Churchill, Winston. *The Gathering Storm*. Boston: Houghton Mifflin, 1948.

———. *Their Finest Hour*. Boston: Houghton Mifflin, 1949.

Coffey, Thomas M. *Iron Eagle*. New York: Crown, 1986.

Conquest, Robert. *Reflections on a Ravaged Century*. New York: Norton, 2000.

Crickmore, Paul F. *Lockheed SR-71 Blackbird*. London: Osprey, 1986.

Dulles, Allen. *The Craft of Intelligence*. New York: Harper & Row, 1963.

Futrell, Robert F. *The United States Air Force in Korea, 1950–1953*. Washington: U.S. Air Force Office of Air Force History, 1983.

Goddard, George W. *Overview*. Garden City, N.Y.: Doubleday, 1969.

Graham, Richard H. *SR-71 Revealed*. Osceola, Wis.: Motorbooks International, 1996.

Grayson, Charles, and Robert Hardy Andrews. *The Woman on Pier 13 (I Married a Communist)*. New York: Frederick Ungar, 1949.

Grose, Peter. *Operation Rollback*. Boston: Houghton Mifflin, 2000.

Grossnick, Roy A. *United States Naval Aviation, 1910–1995*. Washington: Naval Historical Center, 1997.

Gunston, Bill. *Spy Planes and Electronic Warfare Aircraft*. New York: Salamander, 1983.

Hersh, Seymour M. *The Target Is Destroyed*. New York: Random House, 1986.

Hopkins, Robert S., III. *Boeing KC-135 Stratotanker*. Leicester, England: Midland Publishing (Aerofax), 1997.

Jackson, Robert. *High Cold War*. Nr. Yeovil, Somerset, England: Patrick Stephens, 1998.

Johnson, Brian. *The Secret War*. London: Methuen, 1978.

Johnson, Clarence L. "Kelly," with Maggie Smith. *Kelly: More Than My Share of It All*. Washington: Smithsonian Institution Press, 1985.

Kennan, George F. *Memoirs, 1925–1950*. Boston: Atlantic Monthly Press, 1967.

———. *Russia and the West Under Lenin and Stalin*. Boston: Little, Brown, 1960.

Killian, James R., Jr. *Sputnik, Scientists, and Eisenhower*. Cambridge, Mass.: MIT Press, 1977.

Lashmar, Paul. *Spy Flights of the Cold War*. Phoenix Mill, England: Sutton Publishing, 1996.

LeMay, Gen. Curtis E., with Maj. Gen. Dale O. Smith. *America Is in Danger*. New York: Funk & Wagnalls, 1968.

Marx, Karl, and Friedrich Engels. *The Communist Manifesto*. New York: Modern Reader Paperbacks, 1964.

Moody, Walton S. *Building a Strategic Air Force*. Washington: Air Force History and Museum Program, 1995.

Mutza, Wayne. *Lockheed P2V Neptune*. Atglen, Pa.: Schiffer, 1996.

Nalty, Bernard C., ed. *Winged Shield, Winged Sword: A History of the United States Air Force* (two vols.). Washington: Air Force History and Museums Program, 1997.

Pace, Steve. *Lockheed Skunk Works*. Osceola, Wis.: Motorbooks International, 1992.

Philbrick, Herbert A. *I Led Three Lives*. New York: Grosset & Dunlap, 1952.

Pocock, Chris. *Dragon Lady: The History of the U-2 Spyplane*. Osceola, Wis.: Motorbooks International, 1998.

Price, Alfred. *The History of US Electronic Warfare* (two vols.). Association of Old Crows, 1989.

Rhodes, Richard. *Dark Sun: The Making of the Hydrogen Bomb*. New York: Touchstone Books, 1995.

Rich, Ben R., and Leo Janos. *Skunk Works*. Boston: Little, Brown, 1994.

Richelson, Jeffrey. *American Espionage and the Soviet Target*. New York: Morrow, 1987.

Saint-Exupéry, Antoine de. *Flight to Arras*. New York: Reynal & Hitchcock, 1942.

Severo, Richard, and Lewis Milford. *The Wages of War*. New York: Simon and Schuster, 1989.

Sharnik, John. *Inside the Cold War: An Oral History*. New York: Arbor House, 1987.

Shaw, Frederick J., Jr., and Timothy Warnock. *The Cold War and Beyond: Chronology of the United States Air Force, 1947–1997*. Washington: Air Force History and Museum Program, 1997.

Sontag, Sherry, and Christopher Drew. *Blind Man's Bluff*. New York: Public Affairs, 1998.

Stanley, Col. Roy M., II. *World War II Photo Intelligence*. New York: Scribner's, 1981.

Swanborough, F. G. *United States Military Aircraft Since 1909*. New York: Putnam, 1963.

Taylor, John W. R., and David Mondey. *Spies in the Sky*. New York: Scribner's, 1972.

Truman, Harry S. *Memoirs*, Vol. 1. Garden City, N.Y.: Doubleday, 1955.

———. *Memoirs*, Vol. 2. Garden City, N.Y.: Doubleday, 1956.

Van der Aart, Dick. *Aerial Espionage*. New York: Arco/Prentice Hall, 1986.

Wagner, Ray. *The North American Sabre*. Garden City, N.Y.: Macdonald Aircraft Monographs (Doubleday), 1963.

Welch, John F., ed. *RB-36 Days at Rapid City*. Rapid City, S. Dak.: Silver Wings Aviation, 1994.

White, Ken. *World in Peril*. Elkhart, Ind.: Ken White, 1994.

White, William L. *The Little Toy Dog*. New York: Dutton, 1962.

Whitney, Thomas P., ed. *Krushchev Speaks*. Ann Arbor: University of Michigan Press, 1963.

Wise, David, and Thomas B. Ross. *The U-2 Affair*. New York: Random House, 1962.

Wood, Derek, and Derek Dempster. *The Narrow Margin*. New York: McGraw-Hill, 1961.

ARTICLES

Austin, Col. Harold. "A Cold War Overflight of the USSR." *Daedalus Flyer*, spring 1995.

Brugioni, D., and R. Poirier. "The Holocaust Revisited." *Studies in Intelligence*, winter 1978.

Burrows, William E. "Beyond the Iron Curtain." *Air & Space/Smithsonian*, September 1994.

———. "The Coldest Warriors." *Air & Space/Smithsonian*, December 1999/January 2000.

———. "The Oxcart Cometh." *Air & Space/Smithsonian*, March 1999.

"Chinese U-2s Seek Nuclear, IRBM Data." *Aviation Week & Space Technology*, September 17, 1962.

"Cobra Ball Revamped For Battlefield Missions." *Aviation Week & Space Technology*, August 4, 1997.

Dorr, Robert F., and Richard R. Burgess. "Ferreting Mercators." *Air International*, October 1993.

Gordon, Yefim. "Lavochkin La-250 Anaconda." *Wings of Fame*, Vol. 19. London: Aerospace, 2000.

Gustafson, Phil. "They Fly the Iron-Curtain Patrol." *Saturday Evening Post*, October 24, 1953.

Hall, R. Cargill. "The Truth About Overflights." *Military History Quarterly*, spring 1997.

Hardesty, Von. "Made in the U.S.S.R." *Air & Space/Smithsonian*, March 2001.

Hillman, Donald E., with R. Cargill Hall. "Overflight." *Air Power History*, spring 1996.

Kennan, George F. ("X"). "The Sources of Soviet Conduct." *Foreign Affairs*, July 1947.

Khrushchev, Sergei. "The Day We Shot Down the U-2." *American Heritage*, September 2000.

Lake, Jon, and Robert F. Dorr. "Martin P4M Mercator: Cold War Elint-Gathering Operations." *Wings of Fame*, Vol. 19. London: Aerospace, 2000.

Lowther, William. "Shadow of a Doubt." *Destination Discovery*, July 1993.

Maziarz, Thaddeus. "The Reds Shot Us Down." *Life*, July 11, 1955.

McDonald, Robert A. "CORONA: Success for Space Reconnaissance, A Look into the Cold War, and a Revolution for Intelligence." *PE&RS*, June 1995.

Miles, Rufus E., Jr. "Hiroshima: The Strange Myth of Half a Million American Lives Saved." *International Security*, fall 1985.

"Naval electronic reconnaissance aircraft [Soviet]," Parts 1 and 2. *Jane's Defence Weekly*, May 12 and 19, 1984.

Orlov, Alexander. "The U-2 Program: A Russian Officer Remembers." *Studies in Intelligence*, winter 1998–99.

Park, Robert L. "Welcome to Planet Earth." *The Sciences*, May/June 2000.

Powers, Francis Gary, Jr. "A Few Words in Defense of Francis Gary Powers." *American Heritage*, September 2000.

Roche, John E. "Incident in the Sea of Japan." *Reader's Digest*, September 1957.

Sidoruk, Arkadiy. "The Ring of Fate." *Echo of the Planet* (Russian), October 25–31, 1995.

"Soviet electronic warfare aircraft," Parts 1 and 2. *Jane's Defence Weekly*, July 14 and 21, 1984.

Streetly, Martin. "US airborne ELINT systems." Part 3: "The Boeing RC-135 family." *Jane's Defence Weekly*, March 16, 1985.

SPECIAL REPORTS AND OTHER SCHOLARSHIP

Aerospace Studies Institute. *Some Significant Air Incidents Involving the United States and Communist Nations 1945–1964*. USAF Historical Division Research Report, Maxwell Air Force Base, undated.

Back, George. "North Korean Attack on RB-47, AC# 43290, 28 April, 1965." Fifty-fifth Strategic Reconnaissance Wing website (55srwa.org/55).

Farquhar, John T. "A Need to Know: The Role of Air Force Reconnaissance in War Planning, 1945–1953." Doctoral dissertation, Ohio State University, 1991.

Ferrer, Frederick J. "91st Squadron 'Demon Chaser's' 81 Year History." Undated.

Fischer, Ben. B. "A Cold War Conundrum: The 1983 Soviet War Scare." Washington: Center for the Study of Intelligence, September 1997.

George, A. L. "Case Studies of Actual and Alleged Overflights, 1930–1953." RM-1349. Santa Monica: Rand Corporation, August 15, 1955.

———. "Case Studies of Actual and Alleged Overflights, 1930–1953—Supplement." RM-1349(S). Santa Monica: Rand Corporation, August 15, 1955.

Hall, R. Cargill. "The NRO at Forty." Chantilly, VA: NRO History Office, 2000.

Hall, R. Cargill, and Richard S. Leghorn. Interview with Sergei Khrushchev at Brown University, July 5, 1995.

Jones, Mindi. "The Cold War." Term paper, 1998.

Lockheed Advanced Development Company and the Graduate Aeronautical Laboratories, California Institute of Technology. "Couse Ae107: Case Studies in Engineering: The SR-71 Blackbird." spring term, 1991. Hans Hornung collection.

MacEachin, Douglas J. The Final Months of the War With Japan: Signals Intelligence, U.S. Invasion Planning, and the A-Bomb Decision. Washington: Center for the Study of Intelligence (CIA), December 1998.

Mitchell, Vance O. "U.S. Air Force Peacetime Airborne Reconnaissance During the Cold War, 1946–1990." Paper delivered at a CIA conference in Berlin, September 1999.

Moody, Walton S., Jacob Neufeld, and R. Cargill Hall. "The Emergency of the Strategic Air Command." In Nalty, Winged Shield, Winged Sword, Vol. 2.

Pedlow, Gregory W., and Donald E. Welzenbach. The CIA and the U-2 Program, 1954–1974. Washington: Center for the Study of Intelligence (CIA), 1998.

Ruffner, Kevin C., ed. CORONA: America's First Satellite Program. Washington: Center for the Study of Intelligence (CIA), 1995.

Smith, Richard K. Seventy-five Years of Inflight Refueling. Washington: Air Force History and Museum Program, 1998.

Steury, Donald P., ed. Intentions and Capabilities: Estimates on Soviet Strategic Forces, 1950–1983. Washington: Center for the Study of Intelligence (CIA), 1996.

NEWS RELEASES

Mercator incident. Untitled Department of State Press Release, No. 464, August 31, 1956,. National Archive.

NASA News Release, No. 60-193, May 5, 1960 (Powers shootdown).

Neptune attack of September 4, 1954. Department of State Press Release, No. 534. National Archive.

"Soviet Payment of Damages For U.S. Navy Neptune Plane." Department of State Press Release, No. 148, March 19, 1956. National Archive.

"Text of a letter sent by British Chargé d'Affaires, Peiping, to Chinese Communist Vice Minister for Foreign Affairs, Change Han-fu, dated August 25, 1956." Department of State Press Release, No. 465, September 1, 1956. National Archive.

"U.S. Protest of Shooting Down of American Plane by Soviet MiG Aircraft." Department of State Press Release, No. 408, July 31, 1953. National Archive.

OFFICIAL DOCUMENTS

"Action to Prevent a Dunkirk in Korea." Memorandum from "CPC" to Lt. Gen. Idwal H. Edwards, July 12, 1950.

Air Rescue Squadron at Seoul Air Field, Mission 3-39-2, undated. Beasley collection.

"Bering Sea Plane Incident." *Department of State Bulletin*, July 11, 1955.

Bradley, Gen. Omar N., "Special Electronic Airborne Search Operations." July 22, 1950. Harry S. Truman Library.

Cabell, Maj. Gen. C. P. "ECM Ferret Program—Alaskan Air Command." July 26, 1948.

CG FEAF/COFS USAF Wash. D.C., 080850/Z Oct. 1952 (*Sunbonnet King*). National Archive.

"Crash of US Military Aircraft in Armenia, September 1958." Information Report, Central Intelligence Agency, November 7, 1958. CIA.

Current status of aerial reconnaissance programs briefing, untitled, undated. Eisenhower Library.

Decoration Order for Yablonovski and Rybakov from N. Bulganin, October 27, 1953. James Beyer collection.

"Discussion at the 157th Meeting of the National Security Council, Thursday, July 30, 1953." Eisenhower Library.

"Discussion at the 257th Meeting of the National Security Council, Thursday, August 4, 1955." Eisenhower Library.

Dulles, Allen W. "Statistics Relating to the U-2 Program." Memorandum to Brig. Gen. Andrew J. Goodpaster, August 19, 1960. Eisenhower Library.

Dunham, John Robertson. Casualty Report (Non-Battle), November 30, 1955, signed by Maj. G. R. Hamilton. Mary Dunham Nichols collection.

Eisenhower, John S. D. "Memorandum for Record" (NSC meeting), February 12, 1959. Eisenhower Library.

Far Eastern Naval Information Summary, 26 July–1 August 1953. Security Information, NSA. DPMO.

"Future of the Agency's U-2 Capability," July 7, 1960. Eisenhower Library.

Goodpaster, Col. A. J. "Memorandum of Conference With the President," August 30, 1956. Eisenhower Library.

Herrington, Col. Stuart. "Case Studies: Ten Unresolved Cold War Shootdowns (April 1950–December 1965)." Task Force Russia, 1993. DPMO.

Interview with Georgi Y. Kravchenko, May 21, 1993. James Beyer collection.

Interview with Rybakov by Colonel Osipov, October 27, 1993. Beyer collection.

Interview with Yablonovsky by Colonel Osipov, undated. Beyer collection.

Jones, Robert L. Letter to Rep. Ed Bryant, U.S. House of Representatives, Dec. 15, 1999.

Kuznetsov, N. Letter to Comrade V. I. Stalin, 14 June 1952, No. 1899ss. Task Force Russia 185-21.

Lugar, Cmdr. M. D. Letters of April 14 and May 7, 1999, to Charles M. Beasley. Charles Beasley collection.

Medical Report of AF Aircraft Accident, RB-50G, 26 Feb. 52. Robb Hoover collection.

"Memoirs" of the Russian émigré (excerpts). Washington: U.S.-Russia Joint Commission on POW/MIAs, undated.

Memorandum on Georgian contacts. Department of State, March 12, 1960. Eisenhower Library.

Minutes of the Meeting Between General Volkogonov and Ambassador Toon With Families of Missing Americans from the Korean/Cold/Vietnam Wars. Tuesday, March 1, 1994.

Norstad, Lt. Gen. Lauris. "USAF Electronic Reconnaissance Program." July 21, 1949.

"Report: Casey Jones 306th Bomb Group." Archives Branch, Aerospace Studies Institute, Maxwell Air Force Base.

"Report of a U.S. Navy Aircraft Attacked by Hostile Aircraft." Chief of Naval Operations memorandum, August 22, 1956. Eisenhower Library.

Security Information, Air Force Security Service Roundup, No. 149, July 1953. DPMO.

Selected Interviews, Cold War Incident, July 29, 1953, Appendix III (interviews with Mr. Kravchenko and Mr. Korotkov).

Shower, Col. Albert J. Mission Directive DO 322, to Commanding Officer, 91st Strategic Reconnaissance Squadron, Medium, 28 May 1952. Simpson Historical Research Center, Maxwell Air Force Base.

Smith, Lt. Cmdr. James L. "Investigation of the ditching of P2V-5 aircraft BuNo. 127752 on 4 January 1954." February 1, 1954. Beasley collection.

Soviet aide-mémoire (C-130A) received on May 25, 1959. Eisenhower Library.

Soviet note protesting overflight on July 29, 1953 as transmitted by Ambassador Bohlen on July 30, 1953, No. 136. Beyer collection.

"Statement of Facts Concerning Loss of P4M-1Q Mercator Patrol Plane on Night of 22 August 1956." JAG:10.1:cmr, undated. National Archive.

Target Data Inventory, Vol. 2, Categorical Listing. Washington: Air Force Intelligence Center, February 1960. National Archive.

Task Force Russia Report to the U.S. Delegation, U.S.-Russia Joint Commission on POW/MIAs, June 18, 1993. DPMO.

U.S.-Russia Joint Commission on POW/MIAs (USRJC), Korean War Working Group Session, April 12, 1995.

"U-2 Overflights of Soviet Bloc." Memorandum for Brig. Gen. Andrew J. Goodpaster, Central Intelligence Agency, August 18, 1960. Eisenhower Library.

Wayne, Cmdr. John B. "Siberian Coast Incident, 4 September 1954." Statement, September 23, 1954. National Archive.

Whitener, J. E. Letter to Capt. Walter Karig, June 21, 1950.

KLAUS FILES (NATIONAL ARCHIVE)

Assistant Chief of Staff, Intelligence, USAF. "C-130 Incident of 2 September 1958" (reply to questions from Hugh S. Cumming, Department of State, April 2, 1959).

Department of State News Release No. 422.

Diplomatic claim by the U.S. government against the Soviet Union for the B-50 shootdown of July 29, 1953. Washington: Department of State, undated.

Foreign Service Dispatch. "Soviet Note of December 31, 1954, Concerning Shooting Down of American B-50 Off Siberian Coast July 29, 1953." U.S. embassy in Moscow, January 2, 1955.

"Information on Surviving Crew Members of the Downed US Naval Aircraft." IR 1900-57, March 25, 1957 (Capt. Henry D. Chiu).

Khrushchev, Nikita. Letter to Eisenhower, October 10, 1959.

Latta, 1st Lt. Farley A. "Cover Story for Forced Landing in the Far Eastern USSR," August 24, 1949.

Mercator Case (memorandum by Klaus), September 25, 1956.

Navy Baltic Case (memorandum by Klaus), September 11, 1956.

Navy Baltic Case (memorandum by Klaus), October 2, 1956.

"Presentation of Claim Against Soviet Government For Destruction of B-50 Off Cape Povorotny in 1953." No. 566. Washington: Department of State, October 9, 1954.

Redline Personal For White From Weyland, V 0521, 184-1H-53.

"Soviet Airplane Incidents of July 27 and July 29, 1953." No. 90. Washington: Department of State, February 24, 1954.

Steakley, Col. Ralph D. "C-130 Incident of 2 September 58." June 24, 1959.

Steele, Lt. Col. Richard A. Letter to Samuel Klaus regarding the Radio Moscow broadcast, October 3, 1955.

"The Target Is Detected" and "A Swift Attack." *Sovetskaya Aviatsiya (Soviet Aviation)*, September 19 and 20, 1958. (Translated in *Department of State Bulletin*, February 23, 1959.)

"U.S. Note on Shooting Down of American Plane by Soviet MiG Aircraft,"(n.d.).

VIDEOS

Farquhar, John. "A Cold War Perspective of the Times." *Cold War in Flames* conference. Omaha: Strategic Air Command Museum, Sept. 12, 1998.

———. "The Untold Story of Airborne Reconnaissance." *Cold War in Flames* series. Omaha: Strategic Air Command Museum, 1999.

Hopkins, Robert. "Diplomatic Dimensions of Cold War Reconnaissance." *Cold War in Flames* conference. Omaha: Strategic Air Command Museum, Sept. 12, 1998.

McKone, John, and Bruce Olmstead. "RB-47 Shootdown in the Barents Sea." *Cold War in Flames* conference. Omaha: Strategic Air Command Museum, Sept. 12, 1998.

Olmstead, Bruce. Interview, Old Crows Reunion, June 1993. Hoover collection.

Roche, John. Interview, Old Crows Reunion, August 1994. Hoover collection.

AUTHOR INTERVIEWS

Austin, Harold R.	January 16, 2000
Behler, Maj. Robert	June 11, 1984
Bentley, Albert S., Jr.	April 9, 2000
Bergen, John	August 28, 1999
Bergmann, Bess	October 1, 1999
Beyer, James and Barbara	October 2, 1999
Bissell, Richard M., Jr.	May 23, 1984
Campbell, Carlos C.	July 14, 1999
Dickinson, Patricia Lively	January 20, 1994
Ferrer, Frederick J.	May 25, 1999

Gardner, Donald   October 3, 1999
Glasser, Lt. Col. Jerry   June 11, 1984
Hoover, Robert   August 29, 1999
Ihle, Roger   August 23, 1999
Johnson, Clarence L.   January 26, 1983
Keeffe, James H.   April 20, 2000
Kistiakowsky, George B.   August 12, 1981
Koch, Richard   May 8, 2000
McKone, John R.   January 10, 2000
Nichols, Mary Dunham   June 9, 1999
O'Kelley, Margaret   October 1, 1999
Olmstead, Freeman B.   May 27, 1999
Parker, Edward W.   July 1, 1999
Parrish, Jack   July 12, 1999
Phillips, Patricia and Roxann   October 3, 1999
Rich, Ben R.   June 19, 1984
Roche, John E.   October 3, 1999
Roure, Joseph D.   July 20, 1999
Sanderson, Bruce   April 30, 2000
Service, Patricia   January 25, 1993
Skavinski, Gregory P.   July 16, 1999
Sonnek, Donald E.   August 24, 1999
Urschler, Regis F. A.   August 25, 1999
Vergin, Carl   September 30, 1999
Wagner, John   August 23, 1999
White, Maynard   December 1, 2000

OTHER INTERVIEW

Naftel, Col. Stacy D., by R. Cargill Hall, Oral History Program, National Reconnaissance Office, December 27, 1997.

DEPOSITIONS, DEBRIEFINGS, AND LETTERS

Doyle, James M. Letter to CIA, "To get CIA to release info," fall 1996.
Fields, Moses. Letter to Eisenhower, May 10, 1960. Eisenhower Library.
Gourley, Edwin P. Deposition, December 2, 1953. Klaus Files.
Roche, John E. Deposition, Washington, DC, May 14, 1954. Klaus Files.
Interview with Gen. Otto Weyland, Tokyo, July 31, 1954.
Swanson, Maj. Paul H. V. Deposition, Rhine-Main Air Base, undated.
Yosamatsu, Goto. Statement dated January 21, 1953. Mary Dunham Nichols collection.

TECHNICAL PUBLICATIONS

RB-50G Superfortress. Standard Aircraft Characteristics, T.O. 1B-50®G-1. Washington: U.S. Air Fortress, October 16, 1953.
Utility Flight Manual, RB-50G & RB-50G-II Series Aircraft Flight. Washington: U.S. Aircraft, February 15, 1957.

Acknowledgments

The cooperation I had researching and writing this book came from men and women—veterans, wives, widows, and offspring—who passionately wanted their collective, long-suppressed story finally told in its human dimension. No request for an interview or personal documents, including original letters, memorandums, reports, photographs, and albums, was ever turned down.

The ubiquitous Robb Hoover is this book's godfather. He was there from the beginning, alerting me to relevant events, generously supplying sources and volumes of reading material, arranging meetings. He drove with me three and a half hours each way (in one day) from Bellevue, Nebraska, to the Eisenhower Library in Abilene, Kansas, where he helped with the research, and remained involved to the conclusion. He also read the manuscript for technical problems and, by no means least of all, grilled a corn-fed Nebraska T-bone steak at home with his wife, Shirley, for a hungry, itinerant writer.

Ditto John Bergen, who also plied me with information, put airborne reconnaissance in a historical perspective, drove Robb and me to Abilene where he, too, did rapid reading for important material, read the manuscript, caught other mistakes, and provided a thoughtful critique. The third member of the trinity is Gen. Reg Urschler, the Mustang-flying "Gunfighter" who also cheered me on and pored over the manuscript. These three "faithful native companions" read every chapter but the last. Historical interpretation and surviving mistakes, as they say, are mine alone.

Albert D. Wheelon, a former deputy director of the CIA for science and technology and an old friend, generously contributed his perspective to this story and encouraged me from the start to write it.

R. Cargill Hall, a widely respected Air Force historian and another friend, now attached to the National Reconnaissance Office, supplied material I didn't know I needed, wrote a groundbreaking journal article that was a lodestone for my own research, saw to it that I attended the Early Cold War Overflights symposium that he put together, and otherwise was present for this project every step of the way, as usual. So was Carlos C. Campbell, who shared his own perspective from long experience in Naval intelligence, and who was another generous and thoughtful resource from beginning to end. Dave Winkler of the Naval Historical Foundation generously donated his time, documents, and the fruits of his own research.

Fred Ferrer, Air Force sergeant *cum* professor and historian emeritus of the Ninety-first Strategic Reconnaissance Squadron, donated a great deal of time to provide background information on reconnaissance operations and guided me through his enduring project: the National Vigilance Park Aerial Reconnaissance Memorial at the National Security Agency at Fort Meade, Maryland. Bill Ernst, another Fifty-fifth Strategic Reconnaissance Wing alumnus and true believer, very graciously took lots of time to shepherd me around Offutt and add significant amounts of detail to the story. Kevin C. Ruffner, an old and dependable source at the CIA's Center for the Study of Intelligence, contributed a wealth of information, not the least of which concerned the great Soviet war scare of 1983.

Al Lloyd of the Boeing Company, another reconnaissance alumnus, provided valuable background material and photographs of the early aircraft and remained a ready and enthusiastic resource even during the earthquake in Seattle in February 2001. Edward Mark of the Air Force History Office at Bolling Air Force Base contributed a pile of specialized histories that were valuable for their overviews. David Haight at the Eisenhower Library was immensely helpful in digging up valuable letters and memorandums on very short notice. Paul Cole, a former Rand researcher and an exceedingly smart guy, provided reality checks during my excursion through the hall of mirrors in Crystal City.

Brig. Gen. Kevin P. Chilton, the former commander of the Ninth Reconnaissance Wing at Beale Air Force Base and a veteran astronaut, will forever have my gratitude for arranging the dance with the Dragon Lady.

So will Col. Eric Stroberg, the wing's vice commander, and Maj. Brad Berry, who is one great "deuce driver." Capt. Michael D. Strickler, who masterminded the logistics of my visit to Beale, and 1st Lt. Stacy Mooney, my faithful native guide, also have my deepest gratitude.

I am also indebted to many individuals who devoted generous amounts of time and thought to the project: Phil and Bess Bergmann, Pat and Roxann Phillips, Mary Dunham Nichols, Greg Skavinski, Jean O'Kelley, Hal Austin, Stan Bentley, John McKone, Gail and Bruce Olmstead, Ed Parker, Jack Parrish, John Wagner, Joseph Roure, Bruce Sanderson, Carl Vergin, Steven Fields, Don Gardner, John Roche, and Don Sonnek, who drove all the way from Minneapolis to Omaha to share his recollections.

Sarah Whitworth, my assistant at NYU, yet again fronted for me and carried burdens that were rightfully mine while I tried to be the keeper of the story.

And, as usual, Joelle scrutinized the manuscript, made thoughtful suggestions, added a fresh perspective, and otherwise cared for the resident hermit crab. As I have said more than once, this is why authors acknowledge their wives, and why acknowledgments do not suffice.

Index

Permissions Acknowledgments

Grateful acknowledgment is made to the following for permission to reprint photographs and other images in this book: Albert S. Bentley for the photographs of M. Sgt. Francis Brown and A2c. James Woods, Capt. Stan O'Kelley, and Capt. John E. Roche of the RB-50G and its crew; Margaret O'Kelley for the photograph of Margaret and Stan O'Kelley, and for the telegram; Robb Hoover for the photographs of Mary Dunham Nichols, and of the Fifty-fifth Strategic Reconnaissance Wing RB-47H; Shirley Hoover for the photograph of Robb Hoover and Brig. Gen. Regis Urschler; the Russian Federation and the DOD POW/MIA Office for the Soviet gun camera film footage; William E. Burrows for the image of the *Target Data Inventory*, and for the photograph of the Rivet Joint RC-135V; the Boeing Company for the photographs of the RB-50G, the RB-47H, the KC-97G refueling a RB-47E, the tanker refueling a SAC RF-84F, and the RC-135M; Sigmund Alexander for the photograph of the MiG-19; the U.S. Air Force for the photographs of the Spassk-Dal'Niy East Air Base; Carlos C. Campbell for the photographs of the Neptune crew and himself; Lockheed Corporation for the photograph of the Air Force SR-71A; Lockheed-Martin Skunk Works for photographs of the U-2 and the U-2S, and for the image of the recently declassified map; the Central Intelligence Agency for the images from the Corona imaging reconnaissance satellite; and AP/Wide World Press for the photographs of Mary Nichols being given the flag by Col. Robert Hill, and of Chinese pilot Wang Wei.

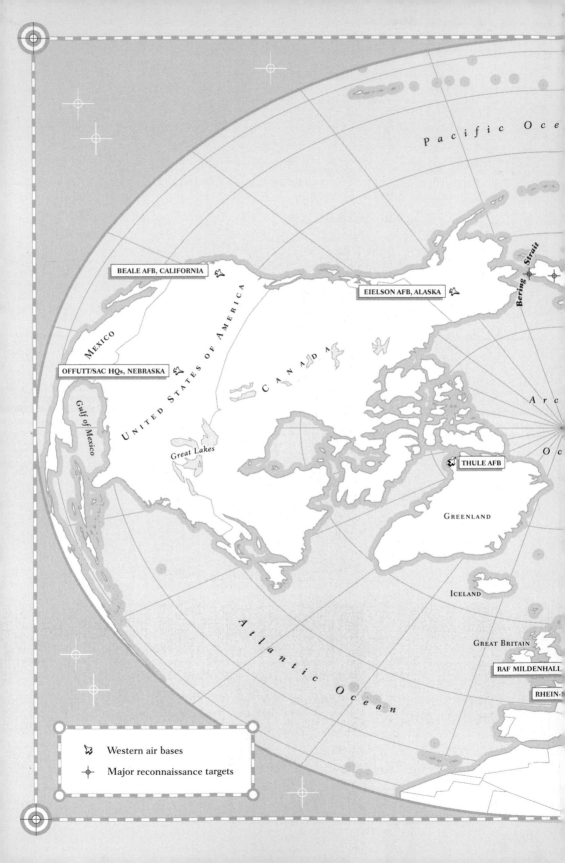